D1566418

Thinking
Through
Confucius

SUNY Series in Systematic Philosophy
Robert Cummings Neville, Editor

Thinking
Through
Confucius

David L. Hall

Roger T. Ames

STATE UNIVERSITY OF NEW YORK PRESS

Published by
State University of New York Press, Albany
© 1987 State University of New York

For information, address State University of
New York Press, State University Plaza,
Albany, N.Y., 12246

**Library of Congress Cataloging-in-
Publication Data**

Hall, David L.
    Thinking Through Confucius.

    (SUNY series in systematic philosophy)
    Bibliography: p.
    Includes index.
    1. Confucius. I. Ames, Roger T., 1947–
II. Title. III. Series.
B128.C8H35   1987   181'.09512   87–6454
ISBN 0-88706-376-4
ISBN 0-88706-377-2 (pbk.)

10 9 8 7 6 5 4 3 2 1

For Bonnie
who also authored this work

Walking in a company of three,
I will surely find a teacher.

ANALECTS, 7/22

Confucius said,

"At fifteen my heart-and-mind were set upon learning;

at thirty I took my stance;

at forty I was no longer of two minds;

at fifty I realized the ming *of t'ien;*

at sixty my ear was attuned;

*and at seventy I could give my heart-and-mind free rein
without overstepping the mark."*

—ANALECTS, 2/4

Contents

I

"At fifteen my heart-and-mind were set upon learning. . . ."

II

". . . at thirty I took my stance. . . ."

Foreword

THE BOOK that David L. Hall and Roger T. Ames have written here, an analysis of Confucius' *Analects*, is both the consummation of a century-old scholarly effort and the beginning of a new stage of philosophic understanding among Chinese and Western thinkers. The great projects, begun in the nineteenth century, of translating classical Chinese writings into English and other European languages searched among the Western philosophies for categories adequate to Chinese culture. Increasing sophistication has revealed the subtle but pervasive otherness between these cultures that distorts the effectiveness of even the best translations. Hall and Ames turn the tables on the search for matching Western categories. The Western categories are inadequate even for Western culture, and like many others Hall and Ames call for a deconstruction of their own languages' representation of the Western tradition, or the Anglo-European tradition as they call it. Unlike the negative deconstructionists who leave their destructive work where it falls, however, they recommend a reconstructive effort based at least partly on the need to reorder the available Western linguistic and conceptual resources so as to be able to translate, and thereby appropriate, the classical Chinese mind. There are no adequate Western categories to translate Confucius, the case in point here, but Western culture should be reconstructed with new categories precisely so as to be able to resonate with and give expression to the riches of Chinese culture. Ames and Hall hope with this volume to inaugurate a project of scholarly and cultural interchange that raises "translation" to a new level, that of the creative reconstruction of each culture so as to be able sensitively to appreciate the other.

This is a brilliant book, filled with ideas that by their very sweep and novelty call into question common assumptions about Chinese and Western cultures. By this very fact, the book will be controversial. The author's guiding thread is that ancient Chinese culture must be understood in immanental terms where Western culture has emphasized transcendence, leading to innumerable, almost inevitable misunderstandings between them. Of course the contrast between immanence and transcendence is a generalization with exceptions; the controversial question will be whether the contrast does indeed catch the main drift of the cultural differences. The subtlety with which Hall and Ames give flesh to the distinction in the later chapters is extraordinary.

Another area of controversy will be the distinction between aesthetic and rational order. Although both China and the West recognize both, the authors say, many of the roles in personal and social life that rational order plays in Western culture are played by aesthetic order in Confucian thought. The development of this idea provides the authors an opportunity for extraordinarily fresh and insightful interpretations of the Confucian "gentleman" or "author- itative person" and of the sage. One of their conclusions is that the Confucian heroes are "aesthetic," and not moral at all in the Western sense of being bound by an externally normative rational order.

The cumulative result of their reconstruction of the Confucian world is a set of new readings for what have become technical terms in Confucian scholarship. These will be controversial for Confucian scholars, but I believe will for the most part win the day because the Confucian community is now drawn in to a creative interchange with Western philosophy for the sake of its own development.

Although *Thinking Through Confucius* is in the genre of a scholarly philological and philosophical commentary, it is in substance a work in cross-cultural systematic philosophy. This is but one of the many types of systematic philosophy. None of them, however, should ignore the experiential world focused so adroitly in this volume.

The authors will inaugurate a new series to be published by the State University of New York Press entitled *Chinese Philosophy and Culture.* It is launched on the premise that, while we presently have some of the Chinese corpus available in English, we do not have many sophisticated conceptual analyses of the translations. What is needed and will be published in this series are philosophical essays as companion commentary for existing translations. Of course, beyond the specifically philosophical, the series should bring to print fine research from any discipline that illuminates Chinese culture in an important way.

Robert Cummings Neville

Preface

SINCE THE AUTHORS of this work have themselves been authored by their teachers, colleagues, students, and scholarly informants, *Thinking Through Confucius* is obviously the result of a collaborative effort much broader than that suggested by the names that appear on the title page and cover. We are, therefore, both obliged and pleased to celebrate that wider collaboration here.

Clifford Ames was present at the very beginning of our writing and was kind enough to provide the first word. The authors accept sole responsibility for any deficiencies in the remainder of the text.

After the lineaments of our interpretation of Confucius had been developed we were bold enough to take it on the road, spending considerable time in the Orient, exchanging ideas with scholars at the Chinese University of Hong Kong, National Taiwan University, Tunghai University, the Shanghai Academy of Social Sciences and Fudan University. Both for their expertise and their encouragement we are thankful to the faculties, students and staff of these institutions. In particular we are grateful to Professors D.C. Lau, Yang Yu-wei, K'o Ch'ing-ming and Lin Yi-cheng whose insights and stimulating criticisms helped to shape the argument of these pages. Jiang Yiwei is responsible for translating our text into Chinese for publication with Shanghai Peoples' Press.

Henry Rosemont, Jr., postponed the completion of his book on Confucian ethics by the number of hours it took to read our manuscript and to suggest many valuable philosophic and editorial emendations. Conversations with Professor Rosemont and with Herb Fingarette on specific aspects of our interpretation were most helpful. George Allan, a confessed reader for SUNY Press, made criticisms which led us to revise one of our chapters—we hope Professor Allan will agree for the better. Eliot Deutsch, Robert C. Neville and Tu Wei-ming, by their own distinctive contributions to comparative philosophy, have each served as important models for our reflections on Confucius.

Several graduate and undergraduate philosophy classes at the University of Texas at El Paso, the University of Hawaii and National

Taiwan University, and two National Endowment for the Humanities summer seminars in comparative philosophy held in Hawaii, offered us challenging, if often bemused, audiences for our ideas concerning Confucius.

The distinguished calligraphy in this book was provided by Wu Kuang-ming. We are happy to welcome this unreconstructed Taoist to our collaborative circle. Stephen Goldberg shared his considerable knowledge of Chinese art in helping locate materials for the cover. Flo Dick prepared the successive drafts of the manuscript with an efficiency and finesse that has placed us in perpetual awe of her skills. Malcolm Willison, a copyeditor for SUNY Press, scrutinized every jot and tittle of our text with a keen and ruthless eye—for which we offer humbled (stet) thanks.

We shall not forget Josie Lucker who added some sanity to the latter stages of this enterprise by insisting upon using the desk as an ironing board.

Finally, each of the authors would like to thank the other for his unexcelled patience and forebearance.

D.L.H.
R.T.A.

Nakusp, British Columbia

Wade-Giles/Pinyin Conversion Table*

A	a	ch'iao	qiao
ai	ai	chieh	jie
an	an	ch'ieh	qie
ang	ang	chien	jian
ao	ao	ch'ien	qian
		chih	zhi
CHA	zha	ch'ih	chi
ch'a	cha	chin	jin
chai	zhai	ch'in	qin
ch'ai	chai	ching	jing
chan	zhan	ch'ing	qing
ch'an	chan	chiu	jiu
chang	zhang	ch'iu	qiu
ch'ang	chang	chiung	jiong
chao	zhao	ch'iung	qiong
ch'ao	chao	cho	zhuo
che	zhe	ch'o	chuo
ch'e	che	chou	zhou
chei	zhei	ch'ou	chou
chen	zhen	chu	zhu
ch'en	chen	ch'u	chu
cheng	zheng	chua	zhua
ch'eng	cheng	ch'ua	chua
chi	ji	chuai	zhuai
ch'i	qi	ch'uai	chuai
chia	jia	chuan	zhuan
ch'ia	qia	ch'uan	chuan
chiang	jiang	chuang	zhuang
ch'iang	qiang	ch'uang	chuang
chiao	jiao	chui	zhui

* Excerpted from Leng Shao Chuan, *Criminal Justice in Post-Mao China* (Albany: State University of New York Press, 1985).

ch'ui	chui	hsi	xi
chun	zhun	hsia	xia
ch'un	chun	hsiang	xiang
chung	zhong	hsiao	xiao
ch'ung	chong	hsieh	xie
chü	ju	hsien	xian
ch'ü	qu	hsin	xin
chüan	juan	hsing	xing
ch'üan	quan	hsiu	xiu
chüeh	jue	hsiung	xiong
ch'üeh	que	hsü	xu
chün	jun	hsüan	xuan
ch'ün	qun	hsüeh	xue
		hsün	xun
E, O	e	hu	hu
en	en	hua	hua
eng	eng	huai	huai
erh	er	huan	huan
		huang	huang
FA	fa	hui	hui
fan	fan	hun	hun
fang	fang	hung	hong
fei	fei	huo	huo
fen	fen		
feng	feng	I, YI	yi
fo	fo		
fou	fou	JAN	ran
fu	fu	jang	rang
		jao	rao
HA	ha	je	re
hai	hai	jen	ren
han	han	jeng	reng
hang	hang	jih	ri
hao	hao	jo	ruo
hei	hei	jou	rou
hen	hen	ju	ru
heng	heng	juan	ruan
ho	he	jui	rui
hou	hou	jun	run

jung	rong	kuo	guo
		k'uo	kuo
KA	ga		
k'a	ka	LA	la
kai	gai	lai	lai
k'ai	kai	lan	lan
kan	gan	lang	lang
k'an	kan	lao	lao
kang	gang	le	le
k'ang	kang	lei	lei
kao	gao	leng	leng
k'ao	kao	li	li
ke, ko	ge	lia	lia
k'e, k'o	ke	liang	liang
kei	gei	liao	liao
ken	gen	lieh	lie
k'en	ken	lien	lian
keng	geng	lin	lin
k'eng	keng	ling	ling
ko, ke	ge	liu	liu
k'o, k'e	ke	lo	luo
kou	gou	lou	lou
k'ou	kou	lu	lu
ku	gu	luan	luan
k'u	ku	lun, lün	lun
kua	gua	lung	long
k'ua	kua	lü	lü
kuai	guai	lüan	luan
k'uai	kuai	lüeh	lue
kuan	guan		
k'uan	kuan	MA	ma
kuang	guang	mai	mai
k'uang	kuang	man	man
kuei	gui	mang	mang
k'uei	kui	mao	mao
kun	gun	mei	mei
k'un	kun	men	men
kung	gong	meng	meng
k'ung	kong	mi	mi

miao	miao	p'a	pa
mieh	mie	pai	bai
mien	mian	p'ai	pai
min	min	pan	ban
ming	ming	p'an	pan
miu	miu	pang	bang
mo	mo	p'ang	pang
mou	mou	pao	bao
mu	mu	p'ao	pao
		pei	bei
NA	na	p'ei	pei
nai	nai	pen	ben
nan	nan	p'en	pen
nang	nang	peng	beng
nao	nao	p'eng	peng
nei	nei	pi	bi
nen	nen	p'i	pi
neng	neng	piao	biao
ni	ni	p'iao	piao
niang	niang	pieh	bie
niao	niao	p'ieh	pie
nieh	nie	pien	bian
nien	nian	p'ien	pian
nin	nin	pin	bin
ning	ning	p'in	pin
niu	niu	ping	bing
no	no	p'ing	ping
nou	nou	po	bo
nu	nu	p'o	po
nuan	nuan	pou	bou
nun	nun	p'ou	pou
nung	nong	pu	bu
nü	nu	p'u	pu
nüeh	nue		
		SA	sa
O, E	e	sai	sai
ou	ou	san	san
		sang	sang
PA	ba	sao	sao

se	se	t'ang	tang
sen	sen	tao	tau
seng	seng	te	de
sha	sha	t'e	te
shai	shai	tei	dei
shan	shan	teng	deng
shang	shang	t'eng	teng
shao	shao	ti	di
she	she	t'i	ti
shei	shei	tiao	diao
shen	shen	t'iao	tiao
sheng	sheng	tieh	die
shih	shi	t'ieh	tie
shou	shou	tien	dian
shu	shu	t'ien	tian
shua	shua	ting	ding
shuai	shuai	t'ing	ting
shuan	shuan	tiu	diu
shuang	shuang	to	duo
shui	shui	t'o	tuo
shun	shun	tou	dou
shuo	shuo	t'ou	tou
so	suo	tsa	za
suo	suo	ts'a	ca
ssu, szu	si	tsai	zai
su	su	ts'ai	cai
suan	suan	tsan	zan
sui	sui	ts'an	can
sun	sun	tsang	zang
sung	song	ts'ang	cang
szu, ssu	si	tsao	zao
		ts'ao	cao
TA	da	tse	ze
t'a	ta	ts'e	ce
tai	dai	tsei	zei
t'ai	tai	tsen	zen
tan	dan	ts'en	cen
t'an	tan	tseng	zeng
tang	dang	ts'eng	ceng

tso	zuo	yang	yang
ts'o	cuo	yao	yao
tsou	zou	yeh	ye
ts'ou	cou	yen	yan
tsu	zu	yi, i	yi
ts'u	cu	yin	yin
tsuan	zuan	ying	ying
ts'uan	cuan	yu	you
tsui	zui	yung	yong
ts'ui	cui	yü	yu
tsun	zun	yüan	yuan
ts'un	cun	yüeh	yue
tsung	zong	yün	yun
ts'ung	cong		
tu	du		
t'u	tu		
tuan	duan		
t'uan	tuan		
tui	dui		
t'ui	tui		
tun	dun		
t'un	tun		
tung	dong		
t'ung	tong		
tzu	zi		
ts'u	ci		
WA	wa		
wai	wai		
wan	wan		
wang	wang		
wei	wei		
wen	wen		
weng	weng		
wo	wo		
wu	wu		
YA	ya		
yai	yai		

Apologia

THE WORK which follows involves "translation" in two very important, and ultimately inseparable, senses. We shall, of course, be translating a number of Chinese terms into English, whenever that is essential to the task at hand. Secondly, both in the act of translating Chinese characters as well as in the exegetical and speculative portions of the book, we shall be involved in translating concepts from one cultural context into another. Essential to both acts of translation is some recognition of the hermeneutical principles employed in the articulation of terms and concepts. Before words such as *chih* 知, *ssu* 思, *te* 德, *yi* 義, *hsüeh* 學, and so forth, can be responsibly provided English equivalents, they must first be put into appropriate Chinese. The character of Chinese Confucianism being what it is, many of the terms and concepts crucial to this tradition accrued decidedly different connotations from their original meanings with the passage of centuries. Thus our project will require us, first, to translate a given term, idea, insight, or argument back into an idiom that at least approximates the meaning of Confucius himself. Then it will be necessary to find English language equivalents suitable to translate this restored meaning.

The point is so important that we must risk redundancy in order to be absolutely clear. The language of a basic dictionary contains the common usage of words. If one seeks the meanings of terms, that is, words with stipulated meanings, more specialized dictionaries must be employed. The philosophical lexicon we will be employing in our translations is that constructed from our understandings of the Chinese and Anglo-European philosophical traditions. Unlike many other sorts of specialized vocabularies, a philosophical lexicon requires conceptual coherence as a primary criterion of translation. That is to say, the definition provided a term must enable it to serve as a meaningful element in some coherent vision. Thus, in addition to the specific skills of the professional sinologue associated with his or her mastery of the Chinese language and literature, it is essential that philosophical skills grounded in an understanding of the contrasting cultural traditions be continually brought to bear upon the comparative doctrines which are to be articulated.

Collaboration of the sort which has produced this work is increasingly essential if comparative philosophy is to make effective progress. For we have presently reached a stage at which further translation of Chinese philosophic texts must proceed in a self-consciously philosophic manner. In the earlier stages of the translations of classical Chinese texts, a great deal of work was done by sinologists who too often approached the original texts with a rather naive, often theologically inspired, agenda. These interpreters, the best of whom relied to some considerable degree upon Chinese scholars for assistance with the language, provided Western readers with many of the basic texts. In the process they established a set of translations for key philosophical concepts that have constituted a conceptual formula for further translation. While efforts by more recent translators have been reflected in an improved grammatical understanding of the texts, the analysis and reconstruction of philosophical terminology has simply not kept pace.

This same problem is apparent in the careers of most contemporary interpreters of Chinese philosophy, led by scholars such as W. T. Chan, D. C. Lau, and Wm. Theodore de Bary. These scholars have themselves translated and edited classical texts but in the process have evidenced a real dissatisfaction with the existing formulae for central philosophical concepts, and have moved, through lengthy introductions, specific papers, and commentary, to correct this situation. But such redress is easier sought than realized, for it is presently unrealistic to expect a single individual to possess sinological *and* philosophical skills in sufficient degree to perform the task of both linguistic and conceptual translation in an adequate manner. We have, therefore, sought through our collaboration to complement the individual virtues of the sinologue and the philosopher by combining both sorts of expertise.

We are certainly aware that the collaborative effort in which we are engaged invites criticism from each of the two scholarly camps whose interests it is meant to serve. On the one hand, professional sinologists will be exercised by the apparent importation into the text of concepts and categories which, they believe, can only determine in advance (and therefore distort) the meanings of terms. Our reply should be obvious: sinologists often lack a full appreciation of the fact that, willy-nilly, interpretive categories are always at work in the act of translation. It is truistic to the point of cliché that "every act of translation is an act of interpretation." Raising to the level of consciousness the hermeneutical assumptions actually employed in such work must be counted as among the more responsible endeavors of comparative philosophers dealing with exoteric texts. Moreover, as the etymological work in the body of this book should evidence, although a Chinese term may, indeed, be served by a number of variant translations, the plausible translations are hardly functions of hermeneutical whim, but are determined by their textual and intertextual loci, as well as by their etymological roots.

A second group of critics might be as adamant concerning the opposite sort of criticism. Many philosophers who read this work will warm readily to the familiar concepts and categories drawn from the traditions of Chinese and Western philosophy. They might, however, become impatient with certain of the etymological discussions. They may want to "get on with it," believing after all (and here there is an ironic convergence between the sinologue and the philosopher) that since hermeneutical principles determine philological interpretations (so they would think), the philological work is superfluous at best and, at worst, represents a semantic smoke screen meant to dazzle the naive philosopher into believing that the meanings have in fact leapt full blown from the text itself.

To both groups of critics we may offer this biographical fact—namely, the two authors of this book, one working primarily out of Chinese sources, and the other from Western, discovered in each other's work important convergences that invited the sort of collaboration represented by this book. At the very least the intellectual engagement permitted by this collaboration has required a continual examination of the insights emerging from the thought of each of the two principals. This sort of engagement guaranteed that the determinations of the meanings of concepts and the character of arguments, along with the conclusions drawn therefrom, were always co-determinations.

Ideally, a collaboratively written work should be read collaboratively as well, but we realize this cannot be expected. The arguments and conclusions of this work must speak to individual sinologists and philosophers as well as to the general reader. All that this apologia can effect is to challenge the reader to remain open to the sort of interweaving of philosophical and sinological methods this book presents. The striking convergence of the conclusions drawn from these distinctive methodological procedures is, we believe, important evidence attesting to the validity of our interpretation.

Perhaps more than any other philosophic activity, comparative philosophy has suffered from its own excesses. Particularly is this so with respect to efforts at comparing Chinese and Anglo-European thinking, which in their early stages have celebrated the most naive sorts of similarities and divergences. At the extremes, one either begins with the assumption of irrevocable differences and demonstrates what is distinctive about each cultural milieu in the broadest of theoretical strokes or, alternatively, one assumes the existence of a single hermeneutical community which putatively includes every thinker of importance. From this comparative perspective, Chinese and Anglo-European philosophers are thinkers whose thought can be judged and compared transculturally in accordance with presumedly neutral criteria determining the nature and character of styles of philosophizing per se.

The classic example of the former approach is F. S. C. Northrop's description of the contrast between the Eastern penchant for "concepts by intuition" and the Western employment of "concepts by postulation."[1] The heavy-handedness of this contrast, particularly when employed by interpreters with less philosophic skill than Northrop, created a reaction against this sort of comparative methodology and a move toward the characterization of commonalities rather than differences. Thus the transition to the transcultural extreme.

The transcultural comparative program is popular among thinkers who believe that philosophical reflection can be delineated as a family of viable perspectives and that thinkers from apparently divergent cultures can be assessed in terms of the relatively neutral categories characterizing these perspectives. This metaphilosophical endeavor is informed by an urge to classify and organize thinkers as a means of making comparative judgments concerning the internal character of their speculations and constructions. These metatheorists are merely performing the task that Kant left undone in his *Critique of Pure Reason*—namely, providing a history of pure reason, a history of the ways in which thinking has been shaped by alternative theoretical schemes. As different as these two comparative approaches are, they both presume the irreducibility of differences, whether these differences be culturally grounded or are based in the sorts of theoretical commitments that transcend cultural boundaries.

The comparative method of this work shares commonalities with both the intercultural and transcultural perspectives. With the intercultural method we remain sensitive to those contrasting cultural emphases that establish real alternative approaches to significant theoretical and practical concerns. With the transcultural approach we share the search for a single hermeneutical community serving as the context of viable philosophic dialogue. We differ only in the sense that we are less sanguine than are these transculturalists as to the possibility of constituting such a community without considerably more work being done. That is, until we are capable of detailing certain fundamental presuppositions relevant to the understanding of alternative cultural contexts, this pursuit of a hermeneutical community will lead us inadvertently to foist upon an alternative culture a set of criteria drawn from our own tradition which are then chauvinistically presumed to characterize the determinants of philosophical thinking per se.

This present book is written in the belief, first, that in the enterprise of comparative philosophy, difference is more interesting than similarity. That is, the contrasting presuppositions of the Chinese and Anglo-European traditions are, for reasons soon to be rehearsed, a presently more fruitful subject of philosophic reflection than are the shared assumptions. Further, and this is abundantly clear from the situation of Chinese philosophy in Western institutions of learning, the sort of commonality that eventually will allow thinkers to engage in important conversations grounded in shared values and concerns is yet to be realized between Chinese and Western societies. One main consideration we are attempting to defend through this work is that the differences of emphasis that exist between the rich and diverse fabrics of Confucian and Anglo-European cultures are not merely meant to be charted or celebrated in some dispassionate manner. On the contrary, we hold that it is precisely this recognition of significant differences that provides an opportunity for mutual enrichment by suggesting alternative responses to problems that resist satisfactory resolution within a single culture.

The comparative method employed in this essay has led us to isolate a particular problem within our cultural milieu and then to employ the thought of Confucius as a means of clarifying precisely what is at issue with regard to that problem and to suggest approaches to its reconsideration. Thus our method cannot be predicated on either the irreducibility of cultural or of theoretical differences. It is transcultural in intent since it seeks to promote that sort of dialogue which eventually may result in a mutual recognition of both commonalities and differences as a means of addressing important issues of theoretical and practical concern. Herbert Fingarette's small book, *Confucius: The Secular as Sacred*, is an excellent example of a work employing the "problematic" approach.[2] Fingarette uses a language drawn from contemporary Anglo-European philosophy to illumine a distinctive aspect of Confucius' thinking in order to suggest ultimately that Confucian philosophy can make important contributions to our contemporary understandings of the nature of language and social praxis.

Though we shall have occasion to differ in some crucial instances with Fingarette's interpretation of Confucius, our principal purpose is quite similar to his. We wish to challenge the understanding of Confucius' *Analects* as a mere repository of culture-bound ethical norms relevant to the origin and development of classical Chinese culture, and to promote the relevance of his vision as a potential participant in present philosophic conversations.

The problem that serves to focus this essay may be discerned from its title, "Thinking Through Confucius." In this book we hope, first of all, to *think through* Confucius. Our goal will be to achieve relative clarity with regard to the principal issues in Confucius' thought. A second, equally important aim will be to provide an exercise in *thinking* using Confucius' philosophy as medium. It is here that the method of our work is best illustrated. The choice of "thinking" as the primary focus of our work is a considered one. For by reflecting upon the meaning of "thinking" and its relationship to "philosophy" in the Confucian vision, we shall be considering an issue of extreme relevance; perhaps the most urgently discussed philosophic problem in Anglo-European philosophy today is that of the character of the philosophic discipline and its status within general culture.

We have attempted to keep the methodological discussions at a minimum lest this work take on encyclopaedic proportions. But something needs to be said about the possible confusions of focus and intent that are all too likely in approaching a work of this sort.

Not the least of our methodological problems is the fact that we have been forced to exchange the hermeneutical circle for an ellipse whose twin foci are constituted by the cultural sensibilities of classical China and the West. The expositions of this work cannot exist without either of these interpretive foci. Resort to only one would effectively prevent any responsible assessment of the alternative member of the proposed dialogue. We do not, therefore, claim to have performed a purely *in situ* reconstruction of Confucius' thinking. Our claim, rather, is that the most accurate picture of Confucius can be obtained if we reject the possibility of such a reconstruction and instead attempt to change lenses and sharpen our focus in such a manner that we enhance our vision of Confucius from the perspective of the present.

The fact that we are predominantly influenced by the experiential and conceptual climate of Anglo-European culture does not mean that we are unable to assess responsibly the resources of alternative cultures. Alterations in the character of Western culture have called attention to unusual elements of our own milieu that strongly resemble the ideological mainstream of the classical Chinese. To the extent that we are able to shift our perspective away from the dominant toward some of the more esoteric of the elements of our cultural milieu we are in a position to recognize and appreciate the distinctive significance of classical Chinese thought.

Our comparative method will strike some readers, both sinologists and philosophers, as questionable. We have openly resorted to a method which we shall term (before our critics, with less constructive intent, have a chance to do so) "cross-cultural anachronism." That is to say, we have sought to understand the thinking of Confucius by recourse to issues originating within contemporary Western philosophic culture, issues which Confucius may well have not explicitly entertained. Although this method has required frequent resort to anachronistic references, our ultimate aim has been to provide the grounds for arriving at a more accurate picture of Confucius' thinking independent of such reference.

We are convinced that our exercise in cross-cultural anachronism will provide us a truer account of Confucius for the following reason: current Western understandings of Confucius are the consequence of the mostly unconscious importation of philosophical and theological assumptions into primary translations that have served to introduce Confucius' thinking to the West. These assumptions are associated with the mainstream of the Anglo-European classical tradition. In point of fact, as we shall demonstrate directly, these assumptions have seriously distorted the thinking of Confucius. Our thinking through Confucius, therefore, must be in its initial phases an *un*-thinking of certain of the interpretive categories that by now have come to be presupposed in understanding Confucius.

We cannot responsibly presume to stand above disputes that define the character of our culture or the relations between cultures. Even if Confucius himself did not explicitly concern himself with certain of the issues that now so exercise us, it is precisely by engaging his thought with these issues in mind that we discover the character and thrust of his philosophic enterprise. Thus, we shall argue that although Confucius was perhaps naive with respect to many of the contrasts we find pertinent to the comparison of Western and Confucian thinking, we shall come closest to a relevant assessment of his thought through the employment of just these contrasts. The facile assumption that one can simply make the quantum leap into another culture and deal with that culture on its own terms needs no further refutation from us; it has been pragmatically self-repudiating. We are content to leave our alternative expository and interpretive methods open to the same sort of pragmatic testing.

Certain difficulties will inevitably result from the fact that this volume has been written for both native Chinese and Anglo-European readers.[3] Doubtless many of our summaries of Western philosophic thinkers and trends will appear altogether too simple-minded to our Western audience. This cannot be avoided if we are to be at all successful in attracting Chinese readers who may not be expected yet to possess familiarity with the Western philosophical scene. Doubtless we have sometimes erred equally egregiously in reverse in our attempts to make Chinese thought understandable to Western readers unacquainted with the classical Chinese sources.

The character of our anticipated audience has also influenced the choice of those thinkers with whom to engage the Confucian sensibility. We have obviously not attempted to be exhaustive in our comparative discussion. Instead we have sought to find those points of convergence and divergence which might promote the most stimulating and rewarding interactions and to introduce those classical and contemporary Western thinkers who most cogently address those issues.

It is our belief that by thinking through Confucius we shall be able to make a contribution to the discussion currently defining the center of philosophic thinking. More specifically, our hope is that by presenting the thought of Confucius in its most dynamic aspects we shall promote a process of thinking which will not only be true to Confucius but will contribute to a renewed understanding of both the intrinsic and instrumental importances of philosophic activity.

Some Uncommon Assumptions

IN THIS ESSAY we have been bold enough to challenge both the principal understandings of Confucian thought and the traditional methods of articulating them. It behooves us, therefore, to begin by discussing certain of the fundamental background assumptions which characterize what we consider to be an appropriate interpretive context within which Confucius' thought may be clarified. The primary defect of the majority of Confucius' interpreters—those writing from within the Anglo-European tradition as well as those on the Chinese side who appeal to Western philosophic categories—has been the failure to search out and articulate those distinctive presuppositions which have dominated the Chinese tradition.

The assumptions we shall be considering are precisely those not shared by the mainstream thinkers of our own tradition. It should be of some real assistance to our Anglo-European readers if they have ready to hand some important cultural contrasts as a means of avoiding the unconscious translation of Chinese Confucian notions into an idiom not altogether compatible with them. We should caution, as well, Chinese thinkers trained within the Neo-Confucian tradition to keep in mind that we are here primarily attempting to explicate the thought of Confucius as it appears in the *Analects,* and not as his Neo-Confucian disciples, however distinguished, have envisioned it.

We must attempt to be as clear as possible at the outset concerning the nature and applicability of these uncommon assumptions. By "assumptions" we mean those usually unannounced premises held by the members of an intellectual culture or tradition that make communication possible by constituting a ground from which philosophic discourse proceeds. By calling attention to contrasting assumptions of classical Chinese and Western cultures, we certainly do not wish to suggest that the conceptual differences we chose to highlight are in any sense absolute or inevitable. The richness and complexity of the Chinese and the Western traditions guarantee that, at some level, the cultural presuppositions dominant in one culture can be found—if only in a greatly attenuated form—in the other milieu as well. Thus, our claims with respect to the assumptions uncommon to Chinese or Anglo-European cultures are to be understood as assertions as to their differential importance within the two cultures.

When we discuss the "uncommon assumptions" in the following pages we shall take the conceptual contrasts from the inventory of Anglo-European philosophy, but the meanings of these contrasts will be shaped in part by the fact that we are employing them to engage Confucius with the Western tradition. This is only to say that we shall often be employing our philosophic vocabulary in a fashion that stretches its traditional connotative bounds.

As we noted in our consideration of the necessary resort to cross-cultural anachronism in the Apologia above, by discussing concepts that Confucius did not explicitly entertain or by representing him as a defender of one of two contrasting assumptions grounded in a distinction he might not explicitly have recognized, we are attempting to provide an assessment of Confucian thought that openly accepts as inevitable that one always begins to think *where one is*. The naive assumptions that one can find a neutral place from which to compare different cultural sensibilities or that one can easily take an objective interpretive stance within an alternative culture, while comforting to those compulsively attached to the external trappings of objective scholarship, have led to the most facile and distorted accounts of exoteric thinkers.

1 An Immanental Cosmos

Perhaps the most far-reaching of the uncommon assumptions underlying a coherent explication of the thinking of Confucius is that which precludes the existence of any transcendent being or principle. This is the presumption of radical immanence. Our language here is somewhat misleading, since, in the strict sense, the contrast of transcendence and immanence is itself derived from our Anglo-European tradition. At any rate, it will become clear as we discuss Confucius' thinking in subsequent chapters that attempts to articulate his doctrines by recourse to transcendent beings or principles have caused significant interpretive distortions. Employing the contrast between "transcendent" and "immanent" modes of thought will assist us materially in demonstrating the inappropriateness of these sorts of transcendent interpretations.

Given the complexity surrounding the several applications of the term "transcendence" in the development of Western thought, it is essential that we be as precise as possible in what we intend by it. Strict transcendence may be understood as follows: a principle, *A*, is transcendent with respect to that, *B*, which it serves as principle if the meaning or import of *B* cannot be fully analyzed and explained without recourse to *A*, but the reverse is not true. The dominant meanings of principles in the Anglo-European philosophic tradition require the presumption of transcendence in this strict sense.

The prominence of the language of transcendence in considering the basic principles of Western philosophers tempts Anglo-European interpreters of Confucius' thinking to employ such language in their analyses of the *Analects*. This has been particularly true to the extent that the major burden of introducing the Chinese classics to the non-Chinese world fell initially to Christian apologists with an inescapable commitment to the notion of transcendence. The necessity to employ transcendent principles is, of course, quite obvious in the Platonic and Aristotelian traditions. In Plato's *Timaeus*, the ideas or forms are independent of the Cosmos and provide the models in accordance with which the Cosmos is made. Aristotle's Unmoved Mover is the primary substance which, as the eternal, immutable, immaterial source of all other things, is the principle that accounts for all change and motion and grounds our understanding of the natural world. This principle, by its very definition, remains undetermined by the Cosmos or any element in it.

Classical forms of materialism, drawn from the philosophies of Democritus and Lucretius, construe the world in terms of "atoms" as the independent and unchanging units of which everything else is comprised. In the strictest sense the atoms of classical materialism transcend the things of the world which they comprise since they are the determinants of these things while themselves remaining unaffected by that which they determine.

A fourth alternative source of philosophical categories among the traditions of Western philosophy is associated with the dominant forms of the existentialist or volitional perspective. Here principles have their ultimate origin in human agents. "Princes" provide principles; rules come from "rulers." In the most general sense the human world is an array of artificial constructs which places upon each individual the burden of achieving "authenticity" by making this world his own through acts of reconstruction and valuation. Although this characterization of the existentialist perspective may seem to echo the sort of human-centered contextual ethics that we choose to associate with Confucius, these are false resonances to the extent that, in the Anglo-European tradition, existentialists have tended to be less concerned with interdependence than with the independent realization of excellence. According to this view, individuals at the peak of self-actualization become transcendent principles of determination, independent of the world that they create.

The existentialist perspective can be adjusted toward classical Confucianism only to the extent that it recognizes the relativity of the individual with respect to the society that determines, as well as is determined by, him. Furthermore, this interaction with the social context cannot be in the form of a "war of each against all" but must be grounded in deferential relations within interdependent contexts.

In the project of comparative philosophy, we have no choice but to attempt to articulate the other tradition by seeking out categories and language found in our own tradition that, by virtue of some underlying similarity, can be reshaped and extended to accommodate novel ideas. The thought of Confucius can only make sense to the Western reader by appeal to analogous structures within the purview of his own cultural experience that, however inadequate, can provide some basic similarity through which to deal with the differences. Difference cannot be taken on wholesale. What we are at a loss to find in the classical Anglo-European philosophic tradition is any fully developed position within which the principles of order and value are themselves dependent upon and emerge out of the contexts to which they have intrinsic relevance. An appropriate and adequate explication of the meaning of Confucius' thought requires a language of immanence grounded in the supposition that laws, rules, principles, or norms have their source in the human, social contexts which they serve.

If contemporary comparative philosophic activity is any indication, it might be the pragmatic philosophies associated with Peirce, James, Dewey, and Mead, and extended toward a process philosophy such as that of A.N. Whitehead, that can serve as the best resource for philosophical concepts and doctrines permitting responsible access to Confucius' thought. This presumption, in fact, will be tested in the following chapters. This is hardly a controversial move, of course, since many from both the Chinese and Western contexts have pointed out the similarities between pragmatism and process philosophy, on the one hand, and classical Chinese philosophy, on the other.[1]

This immanental language necessary in the explication of Confucius' thought is of peculiar importance in articulating the Confucian concept of the self as an ethical agent. For there is a direct relationship between the Anglo-European language of transcendence and the necessity to construe the world, and *a fortiori* the *social* world, in terms of substances. Thus any recourse to transcendent principles inevitably leads to a substance view of the self. If the meaning of an agent or an action is to be discerned by recourse to a transcendent principle, then it is that principle which defines the essential nature of both person and context. Rational principles require rational beings to implement them. Moral principles require moral beings to enact them. Such beings are agents characterized respectively in terms of "rationality" and of "morality." And it is such characterization that renders the agent into a substantial being—that is, a being with an essence, an essential "nature."

Confucian philosophy, on the other hand, entails an ontology of events, not one of substances. Understanding human events does not require recourse to "qualities," "attributes," or "characteristics." Thus in place of a consideration of the essential nature of abstract moral virtues, the Confucian is more concerned with an explication of the activities of specific persons in particular contexts. This does not involve a mere shift of perspective from the agent to his acts, for such would still require the use of the substance language we have deemed inappropriate. Characterizing a person in terms of events precludes the consideration of either agency or act in isolation from the other. The agent is as much a consequence of his act as its cause.

The defense of the substantial self so prominent in the Judaeo-Christian tradition is to be contrasted with articulations of more diffuse senses of "self" in the Buddhist, Taoist, and Confucian schools of classical Chinese philosophy. The fact that these two disparate traditions have begun to interact constructively by dint of the recent growth of comparative philosophy raises some extremely interesting questions with regard to the distinctions within the various traditions. Criticisms of the notion of substantial selfhood within Anglo-European philosophy, beginning perhaps with Nietzsche and emerging most distinctively in the twentieth-century process philosophies of James, Bergson, and Whitehead, altered the problematic that had been presumed fundamental to the understanding of persons. The resort to exoteric cultures was therefore almost inevitable, for the theoretical context of Anglo-European thought was not conducive to the optimal expression of the nonsubstantialist insights.

The ontology of events underlying Confucius' thought is a most important implication of the immanental cosmos. Two other implications should be highlighted. These are the altered meanings of "order" and "creativity" in an immanental universe. Two fundamental understandings of order are possible: one requires that order be achieved by application to a given situation of an antecedent pattern of relatedness. This we might call "rational" or "logical" order.[2] A second meaning of order is fundamentally aesthetic. Aesthetic order is achieved by the creation of novel patterns. Logical order involves the act of closure; aesthetic order is grounded in disclosure. Logical order may be realized by the imposition or instantiation of principles derived from the Mind of God, or the transcendent laws of nature, or the positive laws of a given society, or from a categorical imperative resident in one's conscience. Aesthetic order is a consequence of the contribution to a given context of a particular aspect, element, or event which both determines and is determined by the context. It would be an error to suppose that order in Confucius' thinking meant anything like the rational order that results from the imposition of an antecedently entertained pattern upon events. As strange as this may seem to those still persuaded by the rigid stereotypes foisted on us by our received tradition, for Confucius order is realized, not instantiated.

It is also important that the Confucian sense of "creativity" be noted. In the Western philosophic tradition, informed by the Judaeo-Christian notion of *creatio ex nihilo*, creativity is often understood as the imitation of a transcendent creative act. In Confucian terms, creative actions exist *ab initio* within the world of natural events and are to be assessed in terms of their contributions to the order of specific social circumstances. In no sense are creative actions modeled after the meaning-closing actions of an extra-mundane creative event. Creativity in a Confucian world is more closely associated with the creation of *meaning* than of *being*.

2 Conceptual Polarity

The ubiquity of the concept of transcendence in the Western tradition has introduced into our conceptual inventory a host of disjunctive concepts—God and the world, being and not being, subject and object, mind and body, reality and appearance, good and evil, knowledge and ignorance, and so forth—which, although wholly inappropriate to the treatment of classical Chinese philosophy, nonetheless have seriously infected the language we have been forced to employ to articulate that philosophy.[3] The mutual immanence of the primary elements of the Confucian cosmos—heaven, earth and man—precludes the use of the language of transcendence and therefore renders any sort of dualistic contrast pernicious. The epistemological equivalent of the notion of an immanental cosmos is that of conceptual polarity. Such polarity requires that concepts which are significantly related are in fact symmetrically related, each requiring the other for adequate articulation. This is a truistic assertion about Chinese thinking, of course, and is usually illustrated with regard to the concepts of *yin* 陰 and *yang* 陽. *Yin* does not transcend *yang*, nor vice versa. *Yin* is always "becoming *yang*" and *yang* is always "becoming *yin*," night is always "becoming day" and day is always "becoming night." But having said as much, most commentators on the Chinese tradition simply leave it at that, without spelling out precisely the character of the presupposition that underlies the mutual immanence and symmetrical relatedness of classical Chinese notions.

The presupposition, abstractly stated, is simply this: the Confucian cosmos is a context that both constitutes and is constituted by the elements which comprise it. But an important clarification is necessary. An organism is generally conceived as a whole with parts that functionally interrelate in accordance with some purpose or goal.

In the West, Aristotelian naturalism is the most representative example where in an important sense the end or aim that characterizes the highest purpose or purposes transcends the natural world. The Unmoved Mover is an unconditional aim or goal. Where "organism" might be applied to the Confucian cosmos, an important distinction is that there is no element or aspect that in the strictest sense transcends the rest. Every element in the world is relative to every other; all elements are *correlative*.

If there is a true lack of correlativity even in naturalistic cosmologies such as the Aristotelian, then *a fortiori* there will be this same lack in philosophic systems influenced by cosmogonies of the *creatio ex nihilo* variety. Since the convergence of the Hebraic and Hellenic traditions in the West, *creatio ex nihilo* doctrines have had a profound influence in encouraging the language of transcendence and the dualistic categories which perforce must be employed to instantiate this language.

A dualism exists in philosophic vocabularies influenced by *ex nihilo* doctrines because in these doctrines a fundamentally indeterminate, unconditioned power is posited as determining the essential meaning and order of the world. This dualism involves a radical separation between the transcendent and nondependent creative source, on the one hand, and the determinate and dependent object of its creation on the other. The creative source does not require reference to its creature for explanation. This dualism, in its various forms, has been a prevailing force in the development of Western-style cosmogonies, and has been a veritable Pandora's box releasing the elaborated pattern of dualisms that have framed Western metaphysical speculations.

Polarity, on the other hand, has been a major principle of explanation in the initial formulation and evolution of classical Chinese metaphysics. By "polarity," we wish to indicate a relationship of two events each of which requires the other as a necessary condition for being what it is. Each existent is "so of itself" and does not derive its meaning and order from any transcendent source. The notion of "self" in the locution "so of itself" has a polar relationship with "other." Each particular is a consequence of every other. And there is no contradiction in saying that each particular is both self-determinate and determined by every other particular, since each of the existing particulars is *constitutive* of every other as well. The principal distinguishing feature of polarity is that each pole can only be explained by reference to the other. "Left" requires "right," "up" requires "down," and "self" requires "other."

Dualistic explanations of relationships encourage an essentialistic interpretation in which the elements of the world are characterized by discreteness and independence. By contrast, a polar explanation of relationships requires a contextualist interpretation of the world in which events are strictly interdependent.

Not only are the dualistic categories mentioned above inappropriate to the orientation of polar metaphysics, they can be a source of distorted understanding. Polarity requires correlative terminologies in order to explain the dynamic cycles and processes of existence: differentiating/condensing, scattering/amalgamating, dispersing/coagulating, waxing/waning, and so forth. Further, since everything that exists falls on a shared continuum on which they differ in degree rather than in kind, the distinctions that obtain among them are only qualitative: clear (*ch'ing* 清)/turbid (*cho* 濁); correct (*cheng* 正)/one-sided (*p'ien* 偏); thick (*hou* 厚)/thin (*po* 薄); hard (*kang* 剛)/soft (*jou* 柔); genial (*wen* 溫)/overbearing (*pao* 暴).

The polar character of early Chinese thought discouraged the interpretation of creativity in terms of *creatio ex nihilo*. The historian, Michael Loewe, goes so far as to assert that in the classical Chinese context, "in neither mythology nor philosophy can there be found the idea of *creatio ex nihilo*."[4] The *Chuang Tzu*, as an example of this tradition, explicitly challenges the principle of an absolute beginning:[5]

> There is a beginning. There is not yet begun to be a beginning. There is not yet begun to not yet begin to be a beginning. There is being. There is nonbeing. There is not yet begun to be nonbeing. There is not yet begun to not yet begin to be nonbeing. Suddenly there is being and nonbeing. And yet I don't know what follows from there "being" nonbeing. Is it "being" or is it "nonbeing"?

The implications of this dualism/polarity distinction are both many and important in the kinds of philosophical questions that were posed by the Chinese thinkers, and in the responses they provoked. For example, Loewe suggests that in that culture, "no linear concept of time develops from the need to identify a single beginning from which all processes followed."[6] The process of existence is fundamentally cyclical. There is no final beginning or end in this process; instead, there is cyclical rhythm, order and cadence.[7]

Again, the notion of a purposeful, anthropomorphic creator is certainly found in the classical tradition—the *tsao wu che* 造物者 of the Taoists, for example. However, the polar commitment which does not allow for a final distinction between creator and creature rendered this idea stillborn.[8]

If the Chinese tradition is grounded in conceptual polarities, a reasonable expectation is that this fact would be manifested in the main areas of classical Chinese thought: social and political philosophy. Benjamin Schwartz among others has observed that this is indeed the case. Schwartz identifies several "inseparably complementary" polarities which are grounded in classical Confucianism and which pervade the tradition: personal cultivation (*hsiu shen* 修身) and political administration (*chih kuo* 治國), inner (*nei* 內) and outer (*wai* 外), and the familiar knowledge (*chih* 知) and action (*hsing* 行).[9]

One of the most significant implications of this dualism/polarity distinction lies in the perceived relationship between mind and body. The dualistic relationship between *psyche* and *soma* that has so plagued the Western tradition has given rise to problems of a most troublesome sort. In the polar metaphysics of the classical Chinese tradition, the correlative relationship between the psychical and the somatic militated against the emergence of a mind/body problem. It is not that the Chinese thinkers were able to reconcile this dichotomy; rather, it never emerged as a problem. Because body and mind were not regarded as essentially different kinds of existence, they did not generate different sets of terminologies necessary to describe them. For this reason, the qualitative modifiers that we usually associate with matter do double duty in Chinese, characterizing both the physical and the psychical. *Hou* 厚, for example, can mean either physically thick or generous, *po* 薄 can mean either physically thin or frivolous. Roundness (*yüan* 圓) and squareness (*fang* 方) can characterize both physical and psychical dispositions. In fact, the consummate person in this tradition is conventionally distinguished by his magnitude: great (*ta* 大), abysmal (*yüan* 淵), and so forth. Similar yet perhaps less pervasive metaphors in the Western languages might hark back to a pre-dualistic interpretation of person. At the least, they reflect an interesting inconsistency between theory and metaphor, reason and rhetoric, in our tradition.

3 Tradition as Interpretive Context

The final assumption that gives access to the thinking of Confucius concerns the character of tradition as the interpretive context within which the foregoing presuppositions receive their literary and philosophic expression. As in the case of the two former assumptions, it will be helpful to characterize the Confucian position in terms of a conceptual contrast.[10]

History may be understood in distinctively different ways, of course, but there is a rather broad agreement concerning the centrality of the concept of *agency*. Whether history is construed directly in terms of efficient causal factors of an above all economic or military sort or is interpreted as the history of ideas, the concept of agency is indeed crucial. Ideas have consequences, if not in the same manner then certainly to the same degree as the arrangement of economic variables, for example. Even so, it would appear that neither idealist nor materialist conceptions of history would promote the notion of human agency to the same extent that, for example, volitional or heroic notions would. But there is little doubt that the materialist and idealist understandings are themselves constructions of individuals who lay claim to greatness. If not the historical figures themselves, then historians and philosophers, as authors of texts, become the efficacious agents determining the meaning of events. One has but to recall the manner in which the history of science, grounded in a materialist paradigm for most of its history, is celebrated in terms of the "great" scientists.

The situation is certainly no different with regard to intellectual history. We are still concerned with the import of our historical past construed almost exclusively in terms of the great minds. Ideas have discoverers, inventors, champions, and caretakers. And these individuals have names and careers. Their stories can be told.

All this is truistic and so much a part of our self-understanding as to be wholly taken for granted. Is there, after all, an alternative? The alternative that most readily contrasts with that of the preeminence of history as the defining context of cultural experience is one which finds tradition to be central. The terms "history" and "tradition" certainly have overlapping significances, but it is usually the case that one of these notions is more fundamental to a given social context. History is *made* by personages or events. Traditions possess a kind of givenness that defies or is at least resistant to the questions of originators and creators. History is rational and rationalizable in the sense that reasons and causes can be demonstrated for any given event or sets of events even though the whole complex of events may seem chaotic and irrational. With tradition just the reverse is true: it may be impossible to defend the rationality of this or that tradition, ritual or custom, but the rationality of the whole complex of traditions can usually be well-defended in terms of, for example, social solidarity and stability.

The different sorts of rationality associated with history and tradition indicate a great deal about the nature of the relationships that are most viable between them. Traditional cultures are ritualistic in the sense that the ritual forms associated with public and private praxis are employed in large measure as ways of maintaining institutional and cultural continuity with a minimum of conscious intervention. Those societies conditioned less by tradition and more by conscious history must resort to positive laws and sanctions to a greater degree.

This obvious and much advertised distinction between historical and traditional cultures is, of course, related to the fact that the former tend to stress morality in the sense of obedience and disobedience to principles and laws while the latter stress the aesthetic character of ritualistic participation. Rules are normative in the sense of external ordering principles with respect to historical cultures, while in traditional cultures rules are constitutive and immanent in the sense that, as ritualistic forms, they constitute the being or agent in the performance of the ritual. Also, given that a necessary and defining condition of ritual action is that it be personalized, there is a closer relationship between rituals and persons than between principles and individuals.

Rituals performed in accordance with tradition are readily contrasted with rules obeyed out of either rational deliberation or prudent self-interest. And the weight of this contrast is to be grasped in terms of the consequences it has for the exteriority of the person with respect to grounding principles characterizing his social matrix. As a constituting activity, ritual action provides form to the person and the means of his or her expression. On the other hand, laws, which transcend the individual, provide guidelines for actions since they serve as guiding norms which measure, and standardize. They are to be obeyed. As such, one may (indeed must) feel "outside" the laws and alienated to however slight a degree by them and from them.

In the West, the strength with which one feels one's individuality is a function of the exteriority of norms. Unless one exists over against and in tension with the norms of society, there can be little in the way of ego-centered existence. The blending with one's ambience associated with aesthetic, ritualized life does little to promote intense forms of individuality. One can easily understand this by recourse to the contrasting senses of individuality in Western and Chinese cultures.

The distinction between Western forms of individualism and the Confucian concept of the person lies in the fact that difference is prized in Western societies as a mark of creativity and originality, while in China the goal of personality development involves the achievement of interdependence through the actualization of integrative emotions held in common among individuals. Such an ethos is based upon a rejection of those idiosyncratic emotions and actions that are not expressible through immanent norms of custom and tradition. The actions of individuals who dare to stand away from and challenge tradition and the visions of the past are interpretable by the Confucian as consequences of self-serving effrontery in the face of the legitimate continuities of a received tradition.

The dominance of tradition as the source of practical and affective norms leads to a restriction of the novel contributions of persons as individuals who would break the continuities of the past and establish new directions in thought or institutional practice. History thrives on the actions of rebels, idiosyncratic creators and innovators. Traditional societies prize continuities as embodiments and elaborations of the thinking and action of the past. The history of theoretical disciplines in China and Europe illustrates this distinction extremely well. In Chinese philosophy, the mark of excellence is found in the manner in which the wisdom of the originating thinkers of the past is appropriated and made relevant by extension to one's own place and time. In the West, the history of philosophy may be read as a series of revolutionary visions forwarded by (to limit ourselves merely to modern times) Descartes, Hume, Kant, Hegel, Marx, Nietzsche, and so forth.

Tradition-oriented societies, like the persons who comprise them, do not tend to initiate dramatic cultural changes. Of course, this is not to deny change. On the contrary, the continued appeal to the authority of Confucius as sage in the Chinese tradition has masked a great deal of novelty. Doctrines significantly at variance with those of Confucius have been credited to him by virtue of the tendency to promote the continuity of traditional values. For example, although Confucius seems repeatedly to eschew the explicit treatment of metaphysical questions in the *Analects*, the profoundly metaphysical *Chung-yung* is nonetheless "attributed" to him via his grandson, Tzu-ssu. And Hsün Tzu, consciously flying under the banner of Confucius, does in fact represent a radical paradigmatic shift from his original teachings. Tung Chung-shu, the ranking Confucian scholar of the Western Han, is arguably more representative of Han syncretism than of Confucius or even pre-Ch'in Confucianism. And so on.

This relationship between the original teachings of Confucius and later interpretations can be understood in two ways. Either Confucius, for whatever reason, has been used as a medium to conceal the novel ideas of innumerable creative individuals, or he is in fact a "corporate" person who is continually being seen in a new way by virtue of the participation of later thinkers in the ongoing transmission of cultural values. Thus viewed, "Confucius" is a community, a society, a living tradition. We shall consider certain of the consequences of this "traditional" interpretation of Confucius in some detail later on.[11]

It is interesting in this connection to note the degree to which important historical changes in China have been occasioned by external forces. The so-called "Westernization" of China, particularly in its late nineteenth- and early twentieth-century phases, is a perfect example of such seeming historical passivity. This very historical passivity, however, masks the novelty and discontinuity of Chinese society. When Liang Sou-ming, one of the principal theoreticians of the Chinese May Fourth Movement, spoke of China's "accommodating will" in contrast to the "aggressive will" of the West, he was alluding to this characteristic of many traditional societies.[12] Such accommodation is a process of absorption taking place over a long period of time. It is, likewise, a process of transformation in which what is in its inception a novel element is provided a traditional interpretation. One of the arguments of this work will be that one must avoid the temptation to interpret Confucius' thought from a strictly historical rather than a traditional perspective. To do so would make of him an originator, a "great man," instead of the "transmitter" that he understood himself to be. On the other hand, unless one remains sensitive to the meaning of creativity in Confucianism, the understanding of Confucius as a transmitter of tradition will lead one to mistake him for a mere transmitter, and not the sage that he indeed is.

I

"At fifteen my heart-and-mind were set upon learning. . . ."

1 The Conditions of Thinking

William James characterized philosophy in this manner: "Philosophy is the unusually stubborn attempt to think clearly." The virtue of this understanding of philosophy is that it is altogether free of a host of theoretical accoutrements that would bind it to a particular history and tradition. For James, philosophy is an endeavor, always imperfectly realized, to achieve clarity by means of the process of "thinking."

The aim of clear thinking characterizes not only philosophy but science as well. But, paradoxically enough, science differs from philosophic thinking by virtue of its slightly less stubborn commitment to clear thinking. For the scientist, clarity is contextual; it always means "clear enough for now," or "clear enough given these particular hypotheses." In our culture it is the philosopher who has the aim of thinking things through to their most fundamental ground. The philosopher subjects the assumptions of the scientist (and ultimately his own philosophic assumptions as well) to critical examination.

This is but to say that philosophy has been characterized by a greater degree of self-consciousness with regard to the theoretical assumptions that constitute its various modalities than has scientific discipline. For the philosopher, clear thinking almost always leads to the reflexivity of thinking about thinking itself.

Obviously, clarity is approachable through other than strictly philosophic or scientific means. The poet's use of metaphor or the mystic's meditations are themselves aimed at a sort of clarity. In fact, in our tradition art and religion have often been distinguished from science and philosophy by virtue of the contrasting means employed to search for that elusive clarity so much desired by civilized human beings.

In the Anglo-European tradition, particularly since the advent of the modern period, neither artists nor religious virtuosi have been considered thinkers in the strictest sense. This tacit rejection of the cultural interests of art and religion as resources for the activity of thinking has entailed consequences for our contemporary cultural self-understanding that must be examined if we are to be open to possible reformulations of the meaning of thinking.

It is the dialectical character of philosophic thinking that has defined its history in Anglo-European culture. The term "dialectic" has a number of associations that are helpful in articulating the principal meanings of thinking. Dialectic has the character of a dialogue. Dialogue (*dia-logos*) is a "talking through" or a "thinking through" which requires the sort of reflective engagement best represented by Plato's early Socratic dialogues. Such thinking is presumed to be *aporetic*, and, therefore, open to continual clarification. The more modern association of dialectical thinking with opposition (thesis-antithesis) is a function of reading the history of philosophy, and of history in its broader senses as well, in terms of agonistic engagement. A philosopher's subjecting of predecessors to dialectical examination has more often than not constituted an effort to supplant those thinkers and to promote a new theoretical construction in place of the older mode of thinking. Historically, thinking has become associated with the dialectical process of discarding and reformulating ideas, the process of critique and reconstruction. The construing of thinking as a progressive activity in which the thought of the present supplants that of the past is a result of the particular manner in which the dialectical character of thought has come to be understood.

The association of thinking with an historic process involving measurable progress in the accumulation of knowledge may best be understood by reflecting on the contrast of "thinking" and "reasoning" in our tradition. The relative openness of thinking as an activity aimed at clarity may be contrasted with the exercise of reason, which searches for ideal values or ends and for the methods that promote their recognition and understanding.

The history of Anglo-European philosophy told in terms of theoretical systems, schools, and movements is more a history of reason and reasoning than of thinking in the broader sense. Further, the rather severe separation of values from the distinctive means of realizing them characteristic of philosophic thinking in the modern period has promoted a distinction between reasoning in relation to ends and reasoning in relation to means. This distinction is rooted in certain fundamental dichotomies long celebrated in our intellectual culture. The dichotomies of being and becoming, reality and appearance, idea and action, mind and body, and so forth, receive powerful support from the classical distinction between God and the world which entailed the belief that something Divine transcended absolutely the world which He had either created, and therefore had completely determined, or over which He maintained some telic and/ or efficient influence. Such transcendence requires that reason itself must transcend the given or created world if it is to comprehend what is most real. Thus, *as* thinker, the reasoning being transcends the structures of his world. Plato's realm of Eternal Forms, Aristotle's activity of self-reflective thought, Leibniz' Principle of Sufficient Reason render thinking detachable from the welter of concrete circumstance.

Reason can discover principles that may be held apart from praxis since they themselves do not originate in it. The discovery of proper ends, therefore, does not automatically lead to their implementation or actualization. Plato's urgent dictum, "to know the truth is to do the truth," has not been honored in our tradition. The separation of ends and means, principles and methods, has meant that we are more often forced to side with St. Paul against Plato: "The good that I would do I do not do; the evil that I would not do, that I do."

There is a greatness in our tradition, however, which is itself a direct consequence of the identification of thinking with reasoning in its two detachable modes. Our scientific reasonings and practice argue that, although there might well be moral and religious problems consequent upon the separation of principles and practice, there could be little if any scientific activity without precisely that separation. The hypotheses of the scientist establish conditions contrary to presently acknowledged fact, and the methods permitting experimental verification of these hypotheses are (surprisingly enough to the naive empiricist) often only indirectly connected to the hypothesis. Nor has verification of an hypothesis generally meant to the scientist or philosopher of science the demonstration of the correspondence of principles with the empirical flux they are believed to order. The paradigmatic scientific hypotheses were those of atomistic materialism. From Leucippus and Democritus to Nils Bohr atomic theory was developed in order to interpret the experienceable world in terms of nonexperienceable, "rational" constructs. Such constructs were fundamentally ad hoc. The question of Democritus, for example, was not the naive, "What kinds of things are there?", but the rather jaded question, "What kind of world must there be if we are successfully to defend experience against the logic of Parmenides and Zeno?"

Zeno's inexorable logic occasioned a crisis in thinking characterized by the general acceptance of the dichotomy of "reason" and "experience." Much of the greatness and the poignancy of the Anglo-European philosophic tradition has been the consequence of the bold attempts, both fruitful and futile, to resolve this dichotomy. Plato responded to this crisis by providing reason and experience distinctive realms of operation—those of Being and Becoming respectively. The latter was held to be but a pale shadow of the former. Aristotle grounded human reason in experience but maintained a separation between *theoria* and *praxis* which was overcome only at the level of a reflexive "thinking on thinking," that highest form of praxis vouchsafed to the Divine alone. In each of these paradigmatic responses to the problem of the separation of reason and experience the rational activity was ultimately warranted by that which transcended the empirical world.

The theological movements from the fifth to the fourteenth centuries, from Augustine to Scotus and Ockham, worked out their doctrines under the shadow of this problem now ramified by its expression in terms of the relation of a transcendent God to His created world. Theories of revelation supported the experiential side of the human enterprise, and the doctrine of incarnation sought to answer the need for mediation between two vastly distinct orders of existence. But the frantic disputes of the late Middle Ages, which ended in a flurry of nominalist and voluntarist theories, argued against the successful resolution of the problem which so exercised the philosophical spirits of the day.

René Descartes illustrates one of the boldest attempts at resolving the dispute between rational and experiential modes of knowing. He tried to begin and end his philosophic system by recourse to reason alone. The aim of reasoning is the discovery of truth. According to Descartes' familiar discussion of knowledge in the *Meditations*, truth and falsity are qualities or characteristics of judgments. A judgment involves an act of willing as distinct from an act of knowing. That we do not have the same capacity to know as does the omniscient being (God), the ultimate source of our ideas, means that false judgments are all too possible. Only to the extent that we withhold claims of truth and falsity until we have achieved the clearest and most distinct grasp of the ideas involved in our judgments may we be assured a reasonable degree of accuracy.

Underlying the Cartesian analysis is the claim that the source of understanding, the infinite ground of knowledge, transcends the finite knower. Knowledge cannot, therefore, be immediate but must be mediated through judgments which attempt to introduce ideas into the world of finitude and relative ignorance. The separation of knowledge and will which grounds the theory of judgments is a reflection of the distinction between *theoria* and *praxis*. The exigencies of our practical world require that we cannot indefinitely withhold judgments, but must decide. The act of withholding judgments in order to clarify and render as distinct as possible the ideas which we are striving to grasp is possible only if we can effectively separate our acts of knowing from the application or implementation of that knowledge in practice. Entertaining an idea must not in itself involve a tendency to judge or to act, for if it did then the process of meditation which aims at clarity and distinctness could not proceed dispassionately.

Descartes' philosophic and mathematical speculations were determining influences in the development of the mathematical sciences and technology. Contemporary critics of Descartes, of course, would claim that he perpetuated a pernicious separation of mind and body, making a virtue of the apparent necessity to hold reason and experience incapable of intrinsic union. Perhaps a more trenchant criticism of Descartes would be that his argument for the existence of the self was so much more cogent and immediately persuasive than his arguments for God and for the external world, that skepticism and solipsism were inevitable responses to his philosophy.

Hume clearly discerned this fact about Cartesian philosophy but, unwilling to follow his own reasoning to its ultimate conclusion, avoided absolute skepticism by appeal to the passions of one's "animal nature" and to "custom," the cumulative consequences of the passion of "belief." Hume's philosophy illustrated, at least to Hume's satisfaction, the irrelevance and disutility of Pyrrhonian skepticism. Even if it is the case that metaphysical thinking can lead nowhere except into the most radical sort of doubt, one is not, after all, bound to be a metaphysical thinker. Reasoning is ultimately a function of the passions, the strongest passion being that of belief. Radical doubt, the outcome of uncompromising thought, is unable to withstand the power of believing, that power which grounds custom and praxis.

Immanuel Kant, recognizing the destructive consequences of Hume's critique of causal connection for the rational ground of scientific thinking, developed a means of defending the autonomy of science by giving to the knower the power of constituting experience through the forms of perception and the categories of the understanding. This was accomplished, of course, by excluding "reality," things in themselves, from the sphere of potentially knowable things. Kant's solution further ramified the division between values and objective facts, by referring to ethics and aesthetics (as opposed to pure theoretical reason) all substantive questions of ultimate ends. The validity of scientific reasonings was guaranteed by making understanding into that which constitutes the principal objects of scientific investigation.

Despite a number of significant demurrers, Kant's solution to the reason-experience dichotomy provided the dominant impetus to reflections upon the nature and character of thinking until the end of the nineteenth century, after which the crisis of thinking originating with Parmenides and Zeno came to be illustrated from within science and mathematics itself. The emergence of conventionalism in science, the development of non-Euclidean geometries, and the discovery of physical relativity, revolutionized the conception of science and necessitated an approach to the meaning of thinking that no longer so blithely associated that enterprise with the narrower conceptions of reason and reasoning.

Within the philosophy of science, the crisis erupted decisively with the failure of the positivists' program. Wittgenstein's *Tractatus Logico-Philosophicus*[1] attempted to state a referential theory of language which established univocal relationships between "names" and "facts." Had he been successful, the goal of positivism to ground our knowledge of the external world in the language of physical description might have been realizable. Wittgenstein's recantation of that earlier work, and his subsequent speculations in the *Philosophical Investigations*,[2] were an important factor in determining the direction of the philosophy of language which, until recently, dominated contemporary Anglo-American philosophic activity.

Philosophers of language have generally been less inclined to consider the referential character of language and more interested in its practical and constitutive dimensions. Wittgenstein's later philosophy probed the consequences of construing language in terms of its use by variant linguistic communities operating in accordance with distinctively different linguistic rules. J. L. Austin's development of the pragmatic tendencies in Wittgenstein's later thought culminated in a rather sophisticated theory of the "performative" character of language which gauged its functions as a set of activities such as promising, judging, giving oaths, and so forth.[3] Several American philosophers—W. V. O. Quine, Nelson Goodman, and Wilfred Sellars—have considered some of the consequences of the *constitutive* functions of language, its capacity to constitute a world for its communicants.[4]

Each of these forms of linguistic philosophy refused the gambit offered by the theory-practice dichotomy. In place of the denotative character of language as providing names and descriptions permitting the thinker to characterize the nature and structure of an antecedently existing "objective" world, there is the celebration of language as a form of praxis, as a way of acting or making.

The general turn away from *theoria* to *praxis* and the claim found in the linguistic movements that philosophy as a theoretical activity has come to an end, was the central claim of Karl Marx as well. Marx's constantly quoted thesis announcing that the true aim of philosophy is to change the world, not describe it, was both a statement of general despair at the ability of philosophers to transcend present praxis in order to characterize the nature of the world in any but a grossly ideological manner, and a programmatic response promising such transcendence as a consequence of the proletarian revolution that would bring to an end the history of oppression and with it an end to ideological thinking.

Of all the academic philosophers who have sought to reformulate the meaning of thinking in the light of the claim that philosophy has come to an end, Martin Heidegger is perhaps best known. He is a particularly interesting example of both the strengths and weaknesses of Anglo-European attempts to reformulate the meaning of thinking, since he, more than any other contemporary philosopher, has been sensitive to the need to uncover a new vocabulary with which to characterize the cluster of concepts associated with the broader philosophic issues and, more specifically, with the meaning of thinking per se.

Heidegger has called attention to the consequences of attempting to maintain a distinction between ontological and technical forms of reason. That distinction, he claims, insures the victory of technical, means-oriented thinkers. Ontological reason requires a movement from *praxis* to *theoria*. But when, as more recent events in the history of Western philosophy have shown, ontological accounts of the process of thinking as reason prove unsatisfactory, the only alternative is to invert the priorities and construe thinking as a kind of practice or activity. Merely technical reasonings express the extreme forms of this inversion. The difficulty, of course, is that whereas theoretical reason without practice is vacuous and abstract, and practical reasoning without theoretical justification is unfocused and often blind, it is simply not an easy task to provide a parity of emphasis upon theory and practice.

Heidegger addresses the problem of the meaning of thinking in terms sufficiently comprehensive to encompass most of the issues that determine the focus of the current controversies concerning the character and fate of the philosophic enterprise. For Heidegger, the end of philosophy spells its "completion." That completion is the final consequence of the transition from metaphysics—the investigation of the Being of beings—to the special sciences which developed from out of philosophy.[5]

> The development of philosophy into the independent sciences which, however, independently communicate among themselves ever more markedly, is the legitimate completion of philosophy. . . . The interest of the sciences is directed toward the theory of the necessary structural concepts of the coordinated areas of investigation. "Theory" means now supposition of the categories, which are allowed only a cybernetical function, but denied any ontological meaning. The operational and model character of representational-calculative thinking becomes dominant.

The end of philosophy involves the movement away from the investigation of the Being of beings (metaphysics), to the consideration of the "necessary structural concepts of the coordinated areas of investigation" (science), to the full recognition of the consequence of denying ontological meaning to these concepts (the operational, calculative thinking of technology).

Thinking associated with metaphysics and the sciences can be characterized in terms of such alternative notions as representing, conceiving, reasoning, calculating. The sort of thinking that would constitute philosophic thinking in this age could not be any of these things, since there is no longer metaphysical thinking apart from that which is, and which must remain, implicit in the special sciences. These sciences, having taken over the activity of thinking in its traditional guises, have no need for any special mode of philosophic thinking.

Looking for a role for philosophic thinking under such conditions leads to the question, "Is thinking which is neither metaphysics nor science possible?" Heidegger answers this question with a qualified "yes." The later stages of Heidegger's career involved a search for novel evidences from which to develop a revisioned mode of thinking. The aesthetic and mystical resonances of Heidegger's later thinking suggested such a radical departure from the received meanings of philosophic thought that Heidegger, not without some ambivalence, resigned himself to the demise of philosophy.

Richard Rorty accepts the consequences of this Heideggerian argument, acceding to the end of philosophy as foundational thinking. The vision of philosophy as providing a ground for cultural consensus and a means, therefore, for the adjudication of knowledge claims must be abandoned. Philosophy is not to be identified with knowing in any strict sense.[6]

It would make for philosophical clarity if we just gave the notion of "cognition" to predictive science, and stopped worrying about "alternative cognitive methods." The word *knowledge* would not seem worth fighting over were it not for the Kantian tradition that to be a philosopher is to have a "theory of knowledge" and the Platonic tradition that action not based on knowledge of the truth of propositions is "irrational."

For Rorty, who extends the implications of Heidegger's apocalyptic vision, the sort of philosophic thinking that will take the place of foundational thinking (metaphysics) or some presumed "alternative cognitive method" (alternative to "scientific" thinking) is characterized as "edification." Edification involves the discovery of "alternative, more productive ways of speaking."[7]

The emphasis of Rorty upon the discovery of alternative ways of speaking seems to perpetuate the image of the philosopher as a thinker as distinct from an actor or maker. But clearly Rorty feels that edification is a means of aiding us to become new, although it is not altogether clear how this sort of thinking could have the power to transform. There is no argument to demonstrate that this hermeneutic conception of thinking derived from Heidegger and Hans-Georg Gadamer does in any sense get rid of the fact-value distinction, as Rorty claims. The "abnormal" discourse of the edifying thinker "is always parasitic upon normal discourse . . .; edification always employs materials provided by the culture of the day."[8] This fact highlights the element of Rorty's conception of thinking that we shall find most interesting and to which we shall have occasion to revert when we further consider certain contemporary Western philosophic perspectives on thinking in the final chapter of this work.

Existentialism and phenomenology, Marxism, pragmatism, and linguistic philosophy have all attempted to develop theories of human experience and expression that would overcome the abstractness of ontological reason by providing a ground for the activity of thinking in concrete praxis. That these have not been entirely successful, even considered in terms of their own criteria of success, is in large measure due to the fact that the dialectical tensions between theoretical and practical modes of analysis directed at the meaning of thinking have determined that the two contrasting modes cannot be synthesized in any adequate manner. The reason for this is obvious to anyone who rehearses the history of Western philosophy: the dichotomy of theory and practice has so long been presupposed in our tradition that the philosophical categories that form the inventory of our speculative notions are themselves constructed with reference to this dichotomy. The very concepts of "idea," "action," "intention," and so forth, tend to be one-sided, rooted as they are in one or the other of the two distinct modalities of human expression.

Our brief rehearsal of the problem of thinking in the Anglo-European tradition has been aimed at highlighting what surely is one of the central problems of Western intellectual culture. And if the meaning of thinking is in doubt, then the significance of philosophy as thinking in its most unqualified form, must also be questioned. Further, if the tendencies of recent philosophical writing are indicative, it is doubtful whether the resources available within our own cultural tradition are adequate to resolve successfully the crucial dilemmas associated with attempting to think one's way through to a sufficiently novel understanding of thinking.

In these preliminary remarks, we have attempted to describe historically what thinking has meant in the development of Western philosophy and how this definition in turn has determined what it means to be a philosopher. The fact that, in our tradition, the concept of thinking has gradually come to be construed in narrowly cognitive terms has had two very important consequences; first, it has both ramified and reified the disjunction of theory and practice, leading to the construing of practice or action in terms that cannot easily be associated with any putative ontological ground such as is explicitly or tacitly presupposed with respect to cognition. Second, forms of experiencing the world which answer to descriptions such as appreciating, evaluating, participating in, empathizing, and so forth, have not been given entirely respectable status as aspects of the activity of thinking per se.

Contemporary philosophy, whether it be existentialism, hermeneutics, pragmatism, analytic philosophy, or Marxism—or any of a host of other "isms" currently vying for intellectual commitment—expresses a surprising consensus on the subject of the inadequacy of our received meanings of philosophic thinking. A wholesale assault upon the fact–value, theory–practice dichotomies characterizes the vast majority of our philosophers. But the difficulty with all reconstructive attempts is, as we have already indicated, that they are infected by the tradition they seek to overcome. Attempts by reconstructive thinkers to revision the meaning of thinking have required, *per impossibile,* an avoidance of the cultural biases which largely sustain their efforts. Where *does* one stand when challenging a foundational claim of one's own intellectual milieu?

The most obvious answer to such a question would be that one stands in an alternative milieu, in another culture. Granted the difficulty of presuming to step into an alternative culture as a means of examining one's own, it is our intention to make a responsible effort to do just that. The justification of this effort will be pragmatic: if we do in fact provide a meaningful perspective upon our indigenous culture by recourse to the thinking of Confucius, one part of our project will have been vindicated. The implication of our claim to have done what we have set out to do is that we shall have presented far more than an introduction to Confucius' thought, or an impressionistic assessment of his relevance for our times. To do what we claim must be done requires that we present a coherent analysis and construction of Confucius' philosophy such that reflecting upon Confucius' manner of thinking will provide a model for that crucial activity by which the meaning of thinking itself may be investigated.

We are faced, as philosophers perennially are, with something of the problem of the chicken and the egg: we cannot be expected to understand Confucius' thinking unless we have some understanding of the process of thinking per se. But it is precisely this concept that we seek to reconceptualize by recourse to an understanding of Confucius. Such is the irony of even the most responsible enquiry: it presupposes what it seeks to understand. So be it. All we can do is to provide as clear and as cogent a characterization of the problem of philosophic thinking at the beginning of our essay, and then to see, at the close of our work, if there has been any significant progress toward the resolution of that problem.

Enter Confucius. This most prominent of all thinkers in the Chinese classical tradition may well serve Western philosophers as an alternative model of the activity of thinking. For in many respects his thought departs significantly from our too-familiar reveries; it directs our attention to novel and challenging approaches to the perennial problems and issues which, seen through refocused eyes, are themselves likewise transformed. To reshape the meaning of thinking by an analysis of Confucius, and a consequent reformulation of the character and responsibilities of the philosopher from such reflections, may serve as a timely contribution to our own philosophic culture.

It is our further hope, however, that whatever contribution our work may make will not only serve those Western philosophers relatively innocent of Confucius' thought, but will also be of value to the mainstream of the Confucian tradition and its (sometimes reluctant) contemporary heirs. In this respect we trust that there will not be occasion to accuse us of merely carting coals to Newcastle. The Confucius emerging from our analysis may well be a rather controversial figure, one who might meet with serious criticisms from certain traditional Confucian scholars. On this count, we believe that we shall have little to fear from those scholars willing to think through our interpretation of Confucius to its conclusion.

Our procedure in interpreting the dynamics of thinking in Confucius shall be a conceptual reconstruction involving a mutually corroborative philological and philosophical analysis: an analysis of the language in which his thinking is couched, and a verification of the direction established by this analysis through a consideration of its philosophical implications.

J. L. Austin once remarked that "a word never—well, hardly ever—shakes off its etymology and formation. In spite of all changes in and extensions of and additions to its meaning, and indeed rather pervading and governing these, there will persist the old idea."[9] The English equivalents most commonly used for the "thinking" or "philosophizing" process in Confucius are heavy with the connotations of our own tradition, and are, consequently, in many ways misleading. To settle upon an English equivalent for each major concept and then pursue the analysis through the equivalent rather than the original term is unquestionably the most problematic methodological pitfall of Western interpreters of Chinese philosophy. It is for this reason that it shall be necessary to begin from a philological and semantic analysis in order to excavate the "old idea" and establish a clear sense of what these concepts mean and what they do not mean within their own context. In this manner, we shall be moving towards a new, more philosophically sensitive set of equivalents for Confucius' philosophy while at the same time keeping the original concepts as visible as possible.

This activity will involve us in what only Peter Boodberg could be allowed to call a "philological semasiology."[10] Such an analysis observes and computes the etymologies of a given locution, its frequency of occurrence, range of meanings, and associations, in an effort to delineate the expression with some precision.

Our methodological approach attempts to take as its point of departure the following historical situation. Over the last century and a half, the classical Chinese corpus has been served well by philologically trained translators with adequate language skills, a significant number of whom have in fact been native Chinese. Many disciplines have participated fully in this enterprise: linguistics, history, economics, and others. However, most philosophers have not entertained the Chinese tradition as "philosophy." As a consequence, the major difficulty confronted by the reader in attempting to use and appreciate translations and discussions of the original sources lies not so much in the syntax as in the semantic content of core philosophical concepts. An obvious problem of translation generally is that when a concept is assigned an English equivalent, a certain depth of the concept is unavoidably lost: the word-image, its allusive effectiveness, its morphological implications, and so on. At the same time, of course, inappropriate associations are evoked by the translated term to the extent that the term is burdened by its own cultural history. This general problem of translation is exacerbated when philosophy is not translated and interpreted by trained philosophers.

There is a distinctive characteristic of specifically Chinese philosophy that aggravates this already troubled situation. A feature of the classical vocabulary is that a shared terminology is often used by rival schools to articulate significantly different conceptual content. This necessitates a subtlety of analysis that goes beyond the consultation of dictionaries. The methodology that we employ for conceptual reconstruction certainly uses the classical dictionaries and glosses, but we also utilize available concordances and indices in an effort to employ contemporaneous texts and later commentary for lexical benefit. Our argument is that the distinctions necessary to identify conceptual overlap and difference can best be established by defining a given terminology contextually as well as etymologically. There is an obvious check by approaching a concept both morphologically and genetically.

Let us face a probable methodological criticism head-on. As an example, some sinologist is sure to ask how we can use a concept as it is defined by the text of Tung Chung-shu's *Ch'un-ch'iu fan-lu* to elucidate its usage in the *Analects*. It would be equally irresponsible to say that the Confucian Tung Chung-shu (ca. 179–104 B.C.) is irrelevant as a resource for understanding classical Confucian vocabulary as it would be to accept his definition of these concepts uncritically. The problem, then, is to try to discover in Tung Chung-shu's presentation and elaboration of Confucian vocabulary that which is consistent with the *Analects* and that which deviates from it. This problem echoes a similar concern to distinguish a "process" reading of Confucius from a reading of Confucius where a process vocabulary is merely the most appropriate resource available to us to make Confucius clear to a Western reader. We are not presenting a Han Dynasty interpretation of Confucius, but rather, are attempting to use Tung Chung-shu's commentary critically where it sheds light on the idea being expressed in our record of Confucius. Tung Chung-shu typically elaborates on a concept paronomastically by explaining its content through cognate terms. There is in this approach certainly a playfulness, but it also acknowledges the profoundly organic nature of the Chinese language. Following Austin, it is in focusing in on the "old idea" of the concept that this kind of commentary can be most useful. The argument is that with the classical Chinese language, the "old idea" is often to be excavated from a cognate cluster rather than simply a discrete word.

Given the limited and uncertain data base and the generally speculative nature of this kind of philological analysis, the claims and conclusions derived from it can only be read as suggestive in their various parts. The credibility of our case depends rather upon the coherence of our strictly philosophic claims insofar as they are consistent with the results of our philological analyses.

A first step in this hermeneutical analysis should be careful examination of the etymology of the relevant characters, with attention to their cognates and homophonically related expressions. In this examination, we are inclined to treat the entire characters as meaning-indicative rather than analyzing them as phonograms constituted of discrete phonetic and signific elements.[11]

In our initial discussion, we shall be presenting Confucius' understanding of the activity of thinking as a set of interrelated processes associated with "learning" (hsüeh 學), "reflecting" (ssu 思), "realizing" (chih 知), and, entailed by the notion of chih, "living up to one's word" (hsin* 信). In so doing we shall hope to demonstrate that Confucius provides an understanding of thinking that avoids the disjunction of normative and spontaneous thought in a manner that has not been achieved in other major philosophic visions. If this is, in fact, the case, then it may be argued that his philosophy is directly germane to reconceptualizating one of the frustrating problems of contemporary Anglo-European speculation.

2 Learning (hsüeh 學)

The dynamics of "thinking" in Confucius can be explicated as a continuing interplay among "learning" (hsüeh) and "reflecting" (ssu), the consequence of which is "realizing" (*chih*) through "living up to one's word" (*hsin**). The "learning"/"reflecting" polarity might be roughly construed as the functional equivalent of reasoning in the dominant Western paradigm, "realizing" would correspond to "knowing," and "living up to one's word" would correspond to at least one meaning of "truth." We must hasten to add that while these categories are a starting point for the activity of "thinking" in Confucius, they by no means exhaust it. We must at every step guard against an impoverishing psychologization of Confucius which, in assuming commitments and concerns of our own tradition, can serve only to frustrate our understanding of the significant differences of the Confucian vision. In the discussion that follows, we hope to make it clear that thinking for Confucius is not to be understood as a process of abstract reasoning, but is fundamentally *performative* in that it is an activity whose immediate consequence is the achievement of a practical result. Far from being a means for lifting oneself out of the world of experience, thinking for Confucius is fundamentally integrative, a profoundly concrete activity which seeks to maximize the potential of the existing possibilities and the contributing conditions. Thus, in place of any activity that merely assesses an objective set of facts and/or values, thinking for Confucius is *actu*alizing or *real*izing the meaningfulness of the world.

It is significant that *hsüeh* 學 as "learning" refers to an unmediated process of becoming aware rather than a conceptually mediated knowledge of a world of objective fact. In fact, the character, *hsüeh* 學, is itself an abbreviated form of *hsiao* 斆, meaning "to teach," "to become aware." During the pre-Ch'in period, this "becoming aware" denoted the heightening awareness of the scholar engaged in both studying and teaching as he pursued the goal of becoming a learned person. It was only later in the tradition, perhaps with the accumulation of a more substantive cultural tradition, that the focus of *hsüeh* came to rest on studying.[12]

A second implication of *hsüeh* is that it involves the project of transmitting one's cultural legacy.[13] In the association of the character *wen* 聞, "to hear," with *hsüeh*, and in the verbal nature of the learning process, there is a clear sense of *hsüeh* as the appropriation and embodiment of the cultural tradition (*wen** 文) through pedagogical interaction and exchange (*wen* 聞).[14]

The objective of the exercise of *hsüeh* is the transmission of human culture (*wen** 文). The root meaning of *wen** is "lines" or "design," often associated with systematic themes in the decoration of pottery. It is the human organization and elaboration of the stuff of existence, the articulation of human values and meaning captured in symbol and then transmitted from generation to generation. In this process of accumulation and transmission culture undergoes gradual refinement (3/14): "The Chou surveys the two preceding dynasties. How resplendent is the culture! My choice is with the Chou." Confucius, perceiving himself from within the context of a traditional society, took the embodiment and transmission of his own cultural legacy as a personal mission.[15]

There are many modes and structures for the transmission of culture, perhaps the most obvious being the written word. To whatever extent the historical Confucius was actually responsible for compiling and editing the various classics attributed to him, it is clear that he placed considerable emphasis on a familiarity with, if not a rote memorization of, historical and cultural documents. This is not to say that books were regarded as the only repository of significances. Much of the traditional wisdom was transmitted orally or captured in social institutions, rituals and music. Although Confucius' commitment to a literary corpus as a basic curriculum is beyond question, learning was perceived as an enterprise which engaged a person both mentally and physically, both cognitively and experientially. From the "six arts" (*liu-i* 六藝) established by Confucius as the curriculum for his followers—ritual (*li* 禮), music (*yüeh* 樂), archery (*she* 射), charioteering (*yü* 御), writing (*shu* 書), and calculations (*shu* 數)—it is clear that learning was a project requiring a commitment on the part of the entire person, and that written documents were only one, albeit important, element in the scholar's career.[16]

Confucius emphasized learning to the extent that, in spite of his modesty, he unabashedly prided himself on his eagerness to learn,[17] and further described his favorite disciple, Yen Hui, in similar terms.[18] In his three-faceted philosophy of education rooted in the concepts of capacity, opportunity, and effort, he took the last, enthusiasm for learning, as his primary concern.[19] Confucius argues that human beings are similar by nature in their capacity to learn; this, in fact, is the distinguishing characteristic of the human being.[20] But the criteria of opportunity and effort present greater difficulty. Yet when, as in the case of Yen Hui, enthusiasm for learning is great enough, the opportunity to learn can be arranged.[21] Unquestionably the single most important criterion Confucius invoked in deciding whether or not to accept a student was the student's apparent desire to learn.[22] And consistent with this commitment to learning, Confucius' greatest source of disappointment was "the masses who will not learn even when vexed with difficulties" (16/9).

Confucius' perception of the importance of learning is expanded by his distinction between humanistic learning and the acquisition of practical skills. Anxious to distinguish the appropriation of culture from that of functional, instrumental knowledge,[23] Confucius regarded the enrichment of life through cultural refinement as an end in itself. For Confucius, then, learning is not a means to secure a livelihood; it is an end in itself, a way of life.[24]

In the terms that we have described it above, learning (*hsüeh*) denotes the acquisition and appropriation of the meaning invested in the cultural tradition by those who have gone before. As such, it provides persons in a society with a shared world on the basis of which they can communicate and interact. The extent to which participation in this shared world is perceived as a necessary condition of all the various dimensions of personal cultivation is clearly stated (17/8):[25]

> The flaw in being fond of acting authoritatively (*jen** 仁) without equal regard for learning is that it leads to stupidity; the flaw in being fond of acting wisely without equal regard for learning is that it leads to license; the flaw in being fond of living up to one's word without equal regard for learning is that it leads to antisocial conduct; the flaw in being fond of straightforwardness without equal regard for learning is that it leads to acrimoniousness; the flaw in being fond of courage without equal regard for learning is that it leads to unruliness; the flaw in being fond of strength without equal regard for learning is that it leads to rashness.

3   Reflecting (*ssu* 思)

To the extent that learning is strictly the appropriating of meanings— deferring to the excellence of one's cultural legacy—it does not engage the scholar himself in either the exercise of transforming the appropriated culture or in the activity of generating novel meanings. It is in this spirit that Confucius describes himself as a transmitter rather than an innovator.[26] There are further passages in the *Analects* that can support a conservative interpretation of Confucius (15/31): "I once went a whole day without eating and a whole night without sleeping lost in my reflections, but to no benefit. I would have been better off devoting the time to learning." In this passage certainly Confucius gives priority to learning (*hsüeh*) over reflecting (*ssu*). There can be no doubt that Confucius believes that the learning of traditional culture is a necessary condition for the effective development of the moral person.[27] And to the extent that reflecting (*ssu*) is critical and evaluative of something given, the learning of this given would, of course, have priority. But even though Confucius emphasizes personal appropriation of the cultural tradition, we shall argue that he held thinking to involve both the acquisition and entertainment of existing meaning and the creative adaptation and extension of this meaning to maximize the possibilities of one's own circumstances. In the dynamics of Confucian thinking, learning and reflecting are correlatives and have a polar relationship, neither being adequate in itself.[28]

The term "reflecting" (*ssu*) has several defining characteristics. It is generic in covering various modes of thinking: pondering, entertaining, imagining and so forth. Not unexpectedly, it is often associated with tolerance. It also connotes a directed concern. Further, *ssu* is not exhausted by its psychical dimension. That is, it does not exclude the physiological apparatus involved in the process of reflecting. We would argue that in the Chinese tradition generally, and with respect to *ssu* specifically, the psychical and physiological are perceived as aspects of a continuum.[29] In reducing classical Chinese discussions of the thinking person to assertions about the psyche which exclude reference to the physical, we might inadvertently be misconstruing or even impoverishing this concept in a serious way.[30]

In Confucius, then, the dynamic and holistic nature of the thinking process is apparent in the interdependence of the broad categories of reflecting and learning. The *locus classicus* for this relationship is *Analects* 2/15: "Learning without reflecting leads to perplexity; reflecting without learning leads to perilous circumstances." The point here is that if one simply learns without reflecting critically upon what one is learning, one will fail to act "properly," that is, to personalize what is learned in such a manner as to make it appropriate and meaningful in one's own unique circumstances. As a consequence, one will attempt merely to repeat what others have said or done. Further, any situation that requires him to go beyond his learning will leave him unprepared and hence, bewildered. Said another way, the processive vision of existence to which Confucius is committed requires that each event be the consequence of a unique set of conditions, precluding the precise repetition of what one knows as purely historical record. To some extent, then, the pedant is condemned to move through life in a state of bewilderment.

The interplay between "learning" (*hsüeh*) and "reflecting" (*ssu*)—between appropriating widely from the cultural tradition and elaborating on it through an investment of one's own creativity—is a recurring theme in the *Analects* (19/6): "Learn broadly yet be determined in your own dispositions; enquire with urgency yet reflect closely on the question at hand—becoming an authoritative person (*jen** 仁) lies in this." The principle that each event is sui generis requires that whatever is learned be creatively adapted to the new set of circumstances in order to be rendered appropriate (2/11): "He who in reviewing the old can come to know the new has the makings of a teacher."

One must be creative to take full advantage of appropriated culture, both in adapting it for his own place and time, and in using it as a structure through which to realize his own possibilities. He must labor assiduously to acquire the culture transmitted from ancient times but must also be able to take it a step further in maximizing the possibilities of the prevailing conditions (13/5):[31]

> If someone can recite the three hundred *Songs* but yet when you give him official responsibility, he fails you, or when you send him to distant quarters he is not able to act on his own initiative, then although he knows so many, what good are they to him?

The weight that Confucius placed on critical reflection is fully illustrated in his admonishment to his disciples to qualify even the instruction of their teacher with their own insights (15/36): "In doing what is authoritatively human (*jen**), do not yield even to your teacher."

Conversely, an imbalance in the thinking process in favor of reflecting at the expense of learning is even more threatening. If one reflects without taking advantage of the contributions of others who have gone before, he will not have the shared ground necessary to communicate with his society. A person who lives in his own separate world is generally perceived as mad and a threat to communal meanings and values. Further, to the extent that he is active, he will go off on tangents and pursue often fruitless and even dangerous pathways. Confucius describes this kind of absorption as nonproductive, and Hsün Tzu follows him in decrying this failure to benefit from accumulated wisdom:[32] "I once reflected for an entire day; I would have been better off learning. I stood on my toes to get a view; I would have been better off climbing a hill." The thrust of Confucius' attitude toward thinking as "reflection informed by learning" is captured in the *Chung-yung*:[33] "Learn the way broadly, question it in detail, reflect on it carefully, distinguish it clearly, and act on it with earnestness."

We have suggested above that thinking for Confucius is a process that engages the whole person. Just as the dualistic categories of mind and body are inapplicable, so a theory/praxis dichotomy would also be inappropriate. Throughout the *Analects*, Confucius describes the exemplary person as one whose words do not exceed his actions, as one whose words are authenticated in practice (2/13):[34] "Tzu-kung inquired about the exemplary person (*chün tzu*). Confucius replied: 'He first does what he is going to say, and only then, says it.' "

Even more specifically (14/27): "The exemplary person feels shame where his words go beyond his deeds." Ideas and their articulation in language are not simply academic and theoretical. They have real performative weight as promptings to act. Conversely, Confucius also denigrates the "local worthy" for going through the motions of moral conduct without having cultivated the proper attitude. He is concerned not only that words do not exceed action, but also that action does not exceed meaning (17/13): "The local worthy is the thief of virtue." The *Mencius* records Confucius elaborating on what he means by the "local worthy":[35]

> While their words and actions have no relevance to each other, they prattle: "Ah! the ancients, the ancients! Why did they walk through life alone and aloof? Born of this world, one must act on its behalf. If one can do a little good, he's fine." A person who is thus out to ingratiate himself with the world is your "local worthy."

Confucius himself denies being a pedant, one who "learns a great deal and remembers it all" (15/3), preferring to gauge the value of what is learned by the extent to which it has practical application in the service of others. As D. C. Lau reports, the project of becoming a person combines the sense of "placing oneself in another's place" (shu 恕) and that of "doing one's best" (chung 忠) to effect one's insight.[36]

4 Realizing (chih 知)

A third element in the "thinking" cluster of concepts that directly illuminate Confucius' understanding of thinking is chih 知, commonly translated as "to know," "to understand," but in the Confucian context, perhaps better rendered "to realize" in the sense of "making real." This character is used interchangeably with chih* 智, "wisdom," in the early literature, indicating an unwillingness to distinguish between theory and praxis adumbrated in the English distinction between "knowledgeable" and "wise."

Etymologically, chih 知 is constituted of shih 矢 , "arrow," and k'ou 口 , "mouth." We can only speculate about the "arrow" component which, being not at all clearly phonetic, might suggest the sense of "casting," or "directionality." The "mouth" component, on the other hand, indicates an unmistakable verbal association. Whatever it means "to know/to realize," the process entails verbal communication. Beyond the etymology of chih, semantic associations connote first the participation in a relationship where chih would contribute to the sense of mutual awareness or intimacy. Further, chih carries with it the active connotation of administering an office or station.[37]

These various etymological components and connotations of chih all come together in the following passage from Tung Chung-shu's Ch'un-ch'iu fan-lu:[38]

> What is it that is called chih? It is to predict accurately (lit., to first speak and then for events to happen accordingly). Persons who desire to get rid of certain conducts all act only after prescribing the situation with their chih. Where one's prescription is correct, he gets

his way in what he does and is appropriate in his undertaking. His actions are successful and his name is illustrious. His person is therefore benefited and free of harm. His good fortune reaches to his children and grandchildren, and his beneficence spreads to all the people. T'ang and Wu were like this.

Where one's prescription is incorrect, he does not get his way in what he does and is inappropriate in his undertakings. His actions are unsuccessful and his name is disgraced. Injury befalls his person, he breaks his lineage, he brings ruin on his kind and lays waste to his ancestral temple. Nations that have perished have been thus served. Thus it is said that nothing is as urgent as *chih*.

One who is *chih* can see calamity and fortune a long way off, and early anticipates benefit and injury. Phenomena move and he anticipates their transformation; affairs arise and he anticipates their outcome. He sees the beginnings and anticipates the end. When he says something, none dare dispute it; when he sets up something, it cannot be disregarded; when he takes up something it cannot be put aside. His course of action is consistent and has its proper order. He considers and then reconsiders something, and when he gets down to it, no one can take umbrage.

His words are few yet sufficient. They are brief yet instructive, simple yet explicit, terse yet comprehensive. Where they are few, they cannot be embellished, and where many, cannot be abbreviated. His actions fit the relationships and his words match the task. Such a person is said to be *chih*.

There are several implications of *chih* made clear in Tung Chung-shu's discussion. First, *chih*, commonly translated as "to know," and *chih**, commonly rendered as "wise" or "wisdom," are used interchangeably. There is no fact/value or theory/practice distinction to separate knowledge from wisdom in this tradition. Secondly (and a point to emphasize), *chih* refers to a propensity for forecasting or predicting the outcome of a coherent set of circumstances of which the forecaster himself is a constituent and participatory factor. This definition of *chih* as an ability to anticipate and predict the future on the basis of known conditions is common in the early literature. For example in the *Pai-hu-t'ung:*[39] " 'Wisdom' (*chih** 智) means 'to realize' (*chih* 知): simply on the basis of what one has seen and heard to have no doubts about events, to see a sign and realize what will ensue." Also, in the *Chung-yung:*[40]

The *tao* of the highest integrity (*chih ch'eng* 至誠) is being able to realize beforehand. . . . When fortune or misfortune approach, one is certain to realize beforehand whether it is good or not. Thus, the highest integrity is "god-like." . . . Integrity is not simply completing oneself, it is the means of completing things and events. Completing oneself is "person-making" (*jen** 仁); completing things and events is "realizing" (*chih* 知).

We have an example of *chih* being used in this performative manner in the *Analects* (15/4): "Rare indeed are those who realize their *te.*"

Many commentators interpret this passage via the frequently advertised Confucian commitment to the unity of knowledge and action. Given that authentication in action is a necessary condition of knowing, to understand *chih* as knowing with such a proviso is to interpret it as "realizing." There is another passage that provides a rather succinct statement of the relationship among "realizing" (*chih*), "authoritative humanity" (*jen**), and "ritual action" (*li*) (15/33):

> Where one realizes (*chih*) something but his authoritative humanity (*jen**) is not such that he can sustain it, even though he has it, he is certain to lose it. Where he realizes something and his authoritative humanity (*jen**) is such that he can sustain it but he fails to handle it with proper dignity, the masses will not be respectful. Where he realizes something, his authoritative humanity (*jen**) is such that he can sustain it, and he handles it with proper dignity, yet he fails to use ritual actions (*li*) to implement it, he will still not make good on it.

Without taking account of the performative force of *chih*, this passage is really quite impossible to interpret. Arthur Waley in his translation of the *Analects* despairs:[41] "This paragraph with its highly literary, somewhat empty elaboration, and its placing ritual on a pinnacle far above Goodness, is certainly one of the later additions to the book." And the characterization of the exemplary person (*chün tzu*) which follows makes considerably more sense where *chih* is something done as well as known (15/34): "The exemplary person (*chün tzu*) cannot undertake trivial things but can be relied upon for important responsibilities. The small person, then, is the opposite." As Waley observes, the standard renderings of this passage manipulate the grammar beyond recognition to force some sense out of *chih* here.[42] Because his *chih* (what he "makes real") is integrated and hence meaningful and enjoyable to him, the *chün tzu*, while certainly capable of "everyday" things, is not capable of "trivial things" (*hsiao chih* 小知 literally, "small realizations"). Since everything he does is funded with meaning and importance, his actions even when "everyday" always conduce to greatness.

Another suggestive passage is (6/20): "To be fond of it is better than merely to realize it; to enjoy it is better than merely to be fond of it." Confucius' point here is that a full realization requires a personal commitment and participation. Three categories are introduced: realization, realization that is a consequence of intention, and realization that effects harmony and enjoyment. The last, for Confucius, is the richest kind of realization. To make something real that is neither desired nor a source of enjoyment is to have undertaken trivial things. The fundamentally dynamic nature of realizing (*chih*) and its attendant enjoyment are highlighted in the metaphorically suggestive passage (6/23):

> Those who realize the world (that is, the wise) enjoy water; those who have authoritative humanity (*jen**) enjoy mountains. Those who realize the world are active; those who are authoritative as persons are still. Those who realize the world find enjoyment; those who are authoritative as persons are long-lived.

This passage focuses on two fundamental dimensions of being a person of significance. To the extent that one is making a world real with his performative wisdom (*chih*), he is creative and dynamic, comparable to water in that it too is fluid and productive. To the extent that one is an achieved person, he is a sustainer of values and meaning prominent and enduring like the mountain. The excellence achieved by the authoritative person is normative, influencing the world to become a continuing focus of deference and a resource for emulation. The categories of "being wise" (*chih*) and "being authoritative" (*jen**) are construed so as to reveal the creativity/ continuity distinction present in the relationship between "reflecting" (*ssu*) and "learning" (*hsüeh*). Just as traditionally both "mountain" (*shan* 山) and "water" (*sui* 水) have been considered necessary to achieve natural beauty in landscape painting (*shan sui* 山水), so both the continuous and the creative are necessary constituents of the complete person.

Another passage that stresses the continuity that wisdom affords the world is (17/3): "Only the wisest and the most ignorant do not move." The most ignorant person, unaware of his own limitations, maintains a cow-like intransigence; he is one "who will not learn even when vexed by difficulties" (16/9). The wisest person's ostensible immobility is not quite so easy to explain, especially against our argument that sagehood is open-ended and precludes any notion of final completion. We must understand the wise person as person-in-context, and must then understand motion in relative terms. This passage does not claim that the wisest person has ceased to grow; rather, in the process of growing, he represents the prevailing standard of constancy. He is the embodiment of the meaning and value that constitute the regularity and structure of human culture. Confucius himself, portrayed in the *Analects* as sage, says as much when he asserts (9/5): "If *t'ien* 天 (conventionally, "Heaven") is not going to destroy this culture, what can the people of K'uang do to me?" The passage in which Confucius compares sage-like rule to the pole star[43] makes this same point. It is not that the pole star is utterly stationary without its own motion. Rather, the motion of the other celestial bodies is measured against it. In spite of its own motion, it has constancy. In the dynamics of modeling, the wise person is by virtue of his excellence a relatively clear "order" that can be appropriated for analogical emulation.

In describing realizing in a holistic way that goes beyond the purely intellectual capacities of the human being, Confucius allows for the possibility of the less intellectually able to be purveyors of wisdom through realizing the world in alternative, equally valid directions. One might speculate that for Confucius, even the so-called "mentally retarded" can be contributors to the tradition to the extent that they are a source of significance and value, and occasion the realization of a world over which they exercise some power of selection.

Language has an important function in realizing the world. The claim to *chih* is based on an awareness of what is going to happen and an ability to articulate this understanding in language as a communal act (19/25): "Since the exemplary person *(chün tzu)* will be deemed wise *(chih)* or not because of one word, how could he be but careful about what he has to say?" Where an objective reality is concerned, the prediction of future developments involves little more than prophecy: the claim to speak with authority on behalf of that future reality. It is no more than a saying in advance of what must surely come to pass. The forecasting denoted by *chih*, as opposed to this mere saying in advance, involves two essential activities. First, *chih* involves the bringing into focus of selected possible future events along with the conditioning features of the past and present that form the context out of which these events may emerge. Secondly, *chih* entails a casting of the form of the future in such fashion and with such persuasive authority as to invite sympathy and participation.

The act of bringing into focus one possible future out of the welter of significances deriving from the interaction of received tradition and novel circumstances does not involve anything like speculative or hypothetical reasoning. In Confucius, there is no suggestion of the conscious entertainment of alternatives. The act of focusing is creative, more closely associated with the activity of artistic production than that of hypothetical-deductive reflection.

Chih is a process of articulating and determining the world rather than a passive cognizance of a predetermined reality. To *chih* is to influence the process of existence within the range of one's viable possibilities (12/22):

> Fan Ch'ih asked about authoritative humanity (*jen**), and the Master replied: "Love others." He asked about realization (*chih*), and the Master said, "Realize others." Fan Ch'ih did not understand and so the Master explained, "If you promote the straight over the crooked you can make the crooked straight."

Ch'en Ta-ch'i observes that the main function of *chih* is to distinguish between what is "appropriate/meaningful" (*yi* 義) and what is not.[44] What is appropriate and meaningful in any situation is relative to its specific circumstances. In order to distinguish and determine *yi*, therefore, *chih* must involve an evaluation of contributing conditions. In this regard, *chih* is frequently characterized as dispelling doubts (*huo* 惑) (9/29): "A person with *chih* is not of two minds. . . ." Being of "two minds" refers specifically to confusion over possible alternatives.[45] The character of this confusion, however, must not be thought to result from an inability to trace out the consequences of alternative propositions. The very existence of the alternatives is the source of the confusion. That is, a confused mind is one in which alternative courses of reflection and action are entertained. Hypothetical reasonings depend upon the entertainment of alternative possibilities and their consequences. But a person of *chih* is not of two minds and cannot, therefore, be said to exercise the sort of hypothetical reflections so prized in scientific cultures. This rather striking contrast between what we choose to call the rational and aesthetic models of thinking will be discussed in some detail when the function of language and communication in classical China is considered.[46]

4.1 *Living Up to One's Word* (hsin* 信)

A final concept pertinent to this introduction of Confucius' understanding of thinking is closely allied with the notion of *chih*. It is *hsin** 信 , "living up to one's word." As we have indicated, in a correspondence theory, cognitive knowledge involves the representation of a state of affairs as it really is. Knowing, then, is dependent upon the existence in fact (as opposed to appearance, thought, or language) of an objective reality, and the true correspondence between thought and this reality.

For Confucius, realizing *(chih)* is significantly different from this concept of knowing. Reality is immanent, relative, and contingent. It is something achieved rather than recognized. Since reality is not independent of a realizer, it follows that truth cannot be a consequence of simple correspondence. Rather, truth must involve something like "appropriateness" or "genuineness."[47]

Huston Smith attempts to contrast the dominant Western and Chinese paradigms of truth in the following manner:[48]

> Truth for China is personal in a dual or twofold sense. Outwardly, it takes into consideration the feelings of the persons an act or utterance will affect. . . . Meanwhile, inwardly it aligns the speaker to the self he ought to be; invoking a word dear to the correspondence theorists we can say that truth "adequates" its possessor to his normative self. The external and internal referents of the notion are tightly fused, of course, for it is primarily by identifying with the feelings of others (developing *jen*) that one becomes a *chün-tzu* (the self one should be). . . .

Smith highlights the personal nature of truth as a kind of sincerity in which one brackets his or her own private preferences in favor of "optimizing the feelings of all interested parties." He then goes on to define truth as something authored. This definition is quite consistent with our own explication of *chih* as "to realize." Smith describes truth as "a kind of performative":[49]

> It holds an act or utterance to be true to the extent that it "gestalts" (composes, resolves) the ingredients of a situation in a way that furthers a desired outcome— in China's case, social harmony. Truth thus conceived is a kind of performative: it is speech or deed aimed at effecting an intended consequence.

We would want to provide Smith's insight an even stronger performative meaning. Truth is speech and deed that *effects* an intended consequence. In order to trace this understanding of truth back to Confucius and demonstrate its appropriateness, we must begin with the *Chung-yung's* concept of *ch'eng* (誠), commonly rendered "sincerity."

A careful reading of the *Chung-yung* reveals that *ch'eng* 誠 is used in this basically Confucian-oriented text in a manner that would associate it functionally with *tao* in the Taoist texts. That is to say, *ch'eng* is the immanental source not only of man, but of all things:[50]

> *Ch'eng* means self-completing; and *tao* means self-*tao*-ing. *Ch'eng* is the full consequence of all things; to be not-*ch'eng* is to be nothing. It is for this reason that the exemplary person *(chün tzu)* prizes *ch'eng*. *Ch'eng* is not simply "self-completing," but is that whereby one completes things. To complete oneself is to become a "person" *(jen)*; to complete things is "to realize" *(chih)*.

As one would expect, the major distinction between the Taoist *tao* and this Confucian notion of *ch'eng* derives from the fact that the former interprets man through the structures of his natural environment, while the latter begins from human beings and tends to understand the cosmos through human categories. The focus of the Taoist is to understand humanity from the perspective of the unfolding pattern of existence, while the Confucian direction is to pursue an understanding of all existence from the human perspective.

The Taoists, being reluctant to rely exclusively upon the Confucian-laden term, *sheng jen* 聖人, "sage," as their comprehensive level of personhood, thus generate their own category, *chen jen* 真人, "authentic person." Similarly, the later interpreters of Confucius represented in the *Chung-yung* employ the term *ch'eng* 誠, "integrity," rather than the Taoist-burdened *tao* 道. Ch'eng, then, is the extending of the specifically human activity of actualizing genuine personhood from man himself to all constituents in the process of existence. As Tu Wei-ming remarks:[51] "To say that Heaven is *sincere [ch'eng]* seems to transform the idea of an honest person into a general description of the Way of Heaven."

We have above defined "to realize" (*chih* 知) as effective forecasting. Given the interdependent nature of this world and the co-extensive nature of realizer and that which is realized, the distinctions entailed in the correspondence between idea and reality are not operative. That is, not only is there no appreciable distinction between truth and reality as such, there is also no distinction among the event encompassing a subjective knower, an objective reality known, and the description of this relationship as truth. Fundamentally, to realize *(chih)* and to be true for oneself (that is, to have integrity) *(ch'eng)* are two ways of saying the same thing, both being open to valuation in qualitative terms.

The character translated "integrity," *ch'eng* (誠), is etymologically constituted by "to speak" (*yen* 言) and "to complete, to realize" (*ch'eng** 成). Its meaning, then, is "to realize that which is spoken." Thus, it would be expected that *ch'eng*, like *chih*, would refer to an accurate, self-fulfilling forecasting. It is so described in the *Chung-yung*:[52]

> The *tao* of the highest integrity *(ch'eng)* is being able to realize be-forehand: when the state is going to prosper, there are certain to be auspicious signs; when the state is going to perish, it is certain to be revealed in portents. It is manifest in the divining stalks and shells, and in the way that things comport themselves. When fortune or misfortune approaches, one is certain to realize beforehand whether it is good or not. Thus, the highest integrity *(ch'eng)* is "god-like."

The *Chung-yung*, in this way similar to the more metaphysical portions of *Mencius*, can be read as an attempt to establish a cosmological vision supportive of Confucius' social and political philosophy. It is not unexpected, therefore, to find *ch'eng* used in *Mencius* in a manner that anticipates its further elaboration in the *Chung-yung*:[53] "Everything is complete here in me. Can there be any greater joy than in plumbing oneself and finding oneself true *(ch'eng)*? In fact, *Mencius*, in a passage paralleled in the *Chung-yung*, describes the process of existence in terms of *ch'eng*.[54] We want to look closely at this passage because it provides us with an important insight into the way in which the meaning of *ch'eng* as "integrity," as "truth/reality," may have been derived from the *Analects:*

> If a person in a subordinate position does not have the support of his superiors, he will not be able to govern the people. There is a way of gaining the support of those above him: one who does not live up to his word *(hsin* 信 *)* with his friends will not gain the support of his superiors. There is a way of living up to one's word with friends: if one in serving his relatives does not give them pleasure, he will not live up to his word with friends. There is a way of pleasing one's relatives: if in plumbing oneself, he finds that he is not true *(pu ch'eng* 不 誠 *)*, he will not please his relatives. There is a way of being true to oneself *(ch'eng)*: if one is not clearly aware of what is good, he will not be true to himself. Therefore, truth *(ch'eng)* is the process of existence (lit., "the way of Heaven"), and to reflect on truth *(ch'eng)* is the process of being a person.

The *Chung-yung* passage that parallels *Mencius* here continues by describing the appropriate manner in which to cultivate the way of *ch'eng*:[55] "Learn about it (the way of *ch'eng*) broadly, question it exhaustively, reflect on it carefully, distinguish it clearly, and practice it with earnestness." Now, the focus of Confucius is on how to realize oneself as a human being in a social and political context rather than on metaphysical speculations about personhood. In fact, the *Analects* reveals on several occasions Confucius' profound disinterest in metaphysical questions.[56]

Confucius limits his concern to the way of the human being *(jen tao* 人 道 or better, *jen* tao* 仁 道 *)* as an achieved social and political "truth/reality," and how it can be effected in the medium of communication through "living up to one's word" *(hsin** 信 *)*. In this "way of *ch'eng*" described in *Mencius* and the *Chung-yung*, on the other hand, *ch'eng* covers both ontological as well as experiential truth. We would thus argue that the development of *ch'eng* as an ultimately ontological designation for truth in *Mencius* and the *Chung-yung* might best be construed as speculative extension of Confucius' conception of social and political truth. The language of the *Chung-yung* passage cited above which describes the proper manner of cultivating "the way of *ch'eng*" is reminiscent of if not in fact derived from a passage in the *Analects* which describes how to become a person (that is, how to become *jen**).[57] Where the *Mencius* and the *Chung-yung* take a turn towards the fundamental definition of personhood, this turn would still seem to have its origins in the more practical, sociopolitical dynamics of becoming a person emphasized by Confucius.

This intimate relationship between "living up to one's word" (*hsin** 信), as an aspect of effecting sociopolitical truth, and *ch'eng* 誠, as the process of ontological truth, is further suggested by the fact that in the *Shuo-wen* lexicon, these two characters are each defined by the other. The Tuan Yü-ts'ai commentary to the *Shuo-wen* underscores the "person-making" connotations of *hsin** which are so prominent in Confucius: "Since when a 'person' speaks there is nothing that he fails to live up to *(hsin*)*, this character is constituted of 'person' (*jen* 人) and 'to speak' (*yen* 言)." In fact, it is likely that Tuan's commentary is based on an *Analects* passage in which Confucius makes "living up to one's word" a necessary condition for achieving personhood (2/22): "I am not aware that one can become a person without living up to his word *(hsin*)*."

Living up to one's word *(hsin*)* is a major concept for Confucius, occurring some forty times in the *Analects*. In fact, it is said to be one of the four categories under which Confucius taught: culture (*wen** 文), conduct (*hsing* 行), doing one's best as oneself (*chung* 忠), and living up to one's word (*hsin** 信).[58] It is integrally related to the notions of "being sparing in one's words" (*chin* 謹)[59] and "doing one's best as oneself" (*chung* 忠).[60] Because living up to one's word is more than simply a willingness or even a promise to accord with what one says, it is perhaps close to the archaic notion of "plighting one's troth": the claim that one has the acquired ability, acumen and resources to enact and make real what one says.

If *hsin** were nothing more than a commitment to *try* to carry out what one says, the success or failure of one's actions would not be an issue, yet Confucius makes a lack of ability a condition of failing to be *hsin** (8/16): "I do not understand persons who are reckless and not straightforward, who are ignorant and not attentive, and who are lacking in ability and do not live up to their word (hsin*)." Confucius asserts that "living up to one's word" (hsin*) is the way to realize or "complete" (ch'eng* 成, cognate with ch'eng 誠, "integrity," "being true for oneself") one's own significance and appropriateness in the world.[61] Mencius reiterates this aspect of "living up to one's word" when he claims that "having it in oneself" is called hsin*.[62] It was because hsin* is more than simply a commitment that Confucius was pleased when his disciple, Ch'i-tiao K'ai, declined to take an official post, saying (5/6): "I do not think that I am yet able to live up to this (hsin*)." The disciple was certainly not admitting that he was less than trustworthy, as Arthur Waley's rendering of this same passage might suggest:[63] "I have not yet perfected myself in the virtue of good faith." Hsin* rather entails as a necessary condition being able to carry out what one says and thus being able to make it true and real. The fact that many of the occurrences of hsin* in the Analects are coupled with "doing one's best as oneself" (chung 忠) would suggest that hsin* is fundamentally performative. Hsin* 信 is the doing of what one says with earnestness.

Another feature of Confucius' emphasis on living up to one's word (hsin*) is that it seems to be a necessary condition for establishing the relationship of "friendship" (yu 友),[64] and for winning the continuing support of the people. [65] That is, living up to one's word is an essential factor in establishing interpersonal credibility which, for Confucius, is a precondition for realizing oneself as a person.

In spite of the fact that living up to one's word is necessary to qualify as a person, it does not follow that it is sufficient. Where living up to one's word is generally regarded as a positive trait, the appropriateness of this characterization really depends upon the "word" that one is living up to. In distinguishing three levels of the gentleman-scholar, Confucius attributes living up to one's word even to the third and lowest. This virtue in and of itself does not, it would seem, prompt an unqualified recommendation for promotion to higher levels. For Confucius, then, it is possible for someone to be morally retarded— to be a "small person" (hsiao jen 小人)—and yet still live up to his word (13/20):

> One who is certain to live up to his word and finish what he starts, even though this is no more than a small person being stubborn, can still qualify as a third level of the gentleman-scholar.[66]

Confucius, even in characterizing himself, tends to celebrate his love of learning (*hao hsüeh* 好學) over his concern to live up to his word, regarding the latter as a more common trait.[67]

Finally, there is an important relationship in Confucius between living up to one's word (*hsin** 信) and "signification" (*yi* 義) which requires brief elaboration. This concept, *yi*, discussed more fully below in the context of the notion of self-articulation, is a categorial notion in Confucius which locates the ultimate source of aesthetic, moral, and rational significance in the human being himself. It is with this capacity to significate that a person appropriates meaning from his cultural tradition and discloses his own creativity.[68]

Hsin* requires the articulation, disclosure, and realization of personal significance. If a person is true to his word, he has made himself a source of meaning in the world, meaning that can be realized and transmitted by others. Thus, the *Analects* records (1/13):[69] "Living up to one's word (*hsin** 信) comes close to significating (*yi* 義) in that these words (as articulations of significance) can then be repeated. . . ." Of course, where one's words are *not* grounded in, and informed by, significance (*yi*) and, as a consequence, are not lived up to, they hardly bear repeating.

The concept, *hsin**, is a necessary although not sufficient condition for the articulation and achievement of personal significance. To the extent that *hsin** is grounded in personal significating, the human being is capable of contributing meaning to his world.

5   An Illustration: The *Book of Songs*

The exegetical treatment of *hsüeh, ssu, chih,* and *hsin** above is, we believe, consistent not only with the substance of Confucian philosophy but with its method as well. For our treatment of the *Analects* accords with the manner Confucius himself was wont to treat the texts of his tradition. Our way of thinking through Confucius in the foregoing discussion is, therefore, consistent with Confucius' manner of thinking through his own tradition. We shall attempt to illustrate this fact by demonstrating how Confucius employed the classic, the *Book of Songs*. Several important implications of the activity of thinking may be clarified by appeal to an example of Confucius' own engagement in this enterprise.

The *Book of Songs* is the most frequently cited work in the *Analects*. In fact, the *Historical Records*[70] credits Confucius with having collected some three thousand songs from the archives of the feudal courts, and compiling the *Book of Songs* to include over 300 of them. Further, the tradition attributes the preface of the *Book of Songs* to one of Confucius' most prominent disciples, Tzu-hsia. Whether or not this is historical fact, it is clear that Confucius regarded this text as an essential element in his curriculum, and that his esteem for it helped to establish it as one of the Five Classics. It continued to have a central place in the writings of his later followers: *Mo Tzu*, *Mencius* and *Hsün Tzu*; from the Han dynasty on, the expression "the *Songs* and *Documents*" was used to characterize a Confucian education.

This anthology of songs dating from ca. 1200–600 B.C. is a mixed bag in many ways. There are folk songs which reveal the concerns and values of early Chou China, romantic odes about life among the nobility at court, political laments, festive ballads, ceremonial hymns, celebrations and dirges.[71]

Viewing the *Book of Songs* in terms of Confucius' curriculum, it may be said to serve several purposes. First, it is a repository of cultural values that can be learned by succeeding generations. It contains a wealth of important historical information about the cultural tradition, and lends stability to contemporary society by providing a sense of roots and context. As a work of art, it encourages refinement and aesthetic sensitivity. It is a source of vocabulary that can serve to improve oral and written skills and to provide a richer medium for organizing and articulating the human experience. Important in the whirlpool of Spring and Autumn Period political affairs, the *Songs* provided a currency for couching sensitive issues in an indirect manner. A close familiarity with the images and metaphors of the *Songs* was an essential background for any diplomat or would-be statesman. Confucius himself upbraids his students for neglecting the practical reasons for mastering the *Book of Songs* (17/19):

Why is it, students, that none of you master the *Book of Songs?* The *Book of Songs* can be a source of stimulation, can provide one with views, can contribute to sociability, and can be used to couch dissatisfactions. Close at home it can be used in the service of one's father, and at a distance in the service of one's ruler. And one can glean a rich vocabulary of flora and fauna from it.[72]

In reciting and mastering the *Songs* and reaching out for an ever-widening interpretation of their aphoristic contents, the scholar avails himself of a valuable apparatus for involving himself in the dynamic interaction between received tradition and novel circumstances. Yet if his "learning" (*hsüeh* 學) stops at unreasoning and unconsidered rote memorizing, his achievement is nothing greater than pedantry.

For Confucius, the *Songs* is not simply a repository of historical information to be learned (*hsüeh* 學), it is a primary source of creative reflection (*ssu* 思).[73] It stimulates one to pursue personal cultivation, to exercise one's creative imagination, to ascend to levels of heightened awareness, and to develop a deepened sense of sociability. The *Songs* is not to be read as a linear, sequential explanation of ethical imperatives, imitated in order to reproduce the moral man. Rather, it constitutes an authoritative structure of personal, social, and political experiences, which, given creative adaptation, can serve as a framework for constituting a harmonious community in the present. The main project of the *Songs* is practical: not simply to identify, define, and inform, but to engage and ultimately transform.

One extends and deepens his understanding of the *Songs* through action and reflection. The ambiguity of the text and the remoteness of the original intentions, far from being a failing, serve to extend its range of possibilities and make it readily adaptable to the unique circumstances of the present human condition. The Han commentators, for example, anxious to reinforce the rather stiff cultural values of their own age, were quite happy to read echoes of ribald fertility celebrations as metaphor for social solidarity. People of different ages with different concerns could use the text creatively to arrange and express their experiences, to structure their priorities and to argue for a specific point of view. In ostensibly unfolding the real meaning of the *Songs*, these interpreters would, in fact, make real their own meaning. Thus, the success of the *Songs* is in large part dependent upon the quality of its readers and the diversity of their experiences.

The fact that, dating back to classical times, the *Songs* and similar such cultural sources have been regarded as important resources for the characteristically proverbial expressions through which both diplomatic and interpersonal relations are negotiated helps reveal the nature of communication in this tradition. The invocation of an appropriate allusion to some aspect of the cultural legacy introduces into a situation the authority of historical record and a prompting to perpetuate its wisdom. The ambiguity of the allusion provides the flexibility for negotiation and disclosure. And the appropriateness of expression to situation, as a source of harmony and meaning, is not merely descriptive in characterizing the circumstances in their clearest light, but is fundamentally performative. If we contrast this function of the *Songs* as a repository of proverbial language with the desire for precision and accuracy of language often celebrated in our own tradition, we can locate an important difference in the nature of communication. Our more rationalistic tradition often simply eschews proverbs, regarding them as no more than hackneyed cliché.

In citing the *Book of Songs*, the *Analects* provides several instances in which the original intention of a song is adapted so as to render it appropriate to the present circumstances. For example, Confucius is delighted when Tzu-hsia uses a description of a handsome court lady to couch his own insight into the priority of content over form (3/8):

> Tzu-hsia inquired, "What does this passage from the *Songs* mean?
> Her knowing smile so lovely,
> Her gorgeous eyes so clearly defined,
> She enhances her natural color with cosmetics."
> Confucius replied, "The make-up comes after the natural color."
> "Do ritual actions (*li* 禮) also come after?" asked Tzu-hsia.
> "Precisely what I had in mind, Tzu-hsia. Only with a person such as yourself can I discuss the *Songs*."

On another occasion, Confucius praises Tzu-kung for similarly translating a lover's praise into the process of self-cultivation (1/15):

> Tzu-kung asked, "What do you think of the saying: 'Be poor without being ingratiating, be wealthy without being arrogant.' "
> Confucius replied, "It is fine, but it might be better to say: 'Be poor and yet find enjoyment, be wealthy and yet be fond of ritual actions.' "
> "The *Songs* have a passage," said Tzu-kung:
> " 'Like carving and then smoothing horn,
> Like cutting and then polishing jade.'
> Is this not what you mean?"

"Only with a person such as yourself, Tzu-kung, can I discuss the *Songs*," said Confucius. "You only have to be told what has happened to be aware of what is to come."

This passage illustrates the dynamics of "learning" *(hsüeh)*, "reflecting" *(ssu)*, and "realizing" *(chih)*—namely, an appropriated familiarity with the received text, a creative manipulation of its original meaning to some desired end, and the notion of realizing the future by refining it through existing structures.

The extent to which Confucius is willing to manipulate the putatively original intention of these two passages from the *Songs* can be more fully appreciated by reference to another observation that Confucius makes about human proclivities. On two occasions, Confucius is reported to have lamented (9/18): "I have never met the man who is as fond of *te* as he is of beautiful women."[74] In the two passages that we have cited from the *Songs* above, Confucius and his students are effectively turning a classical expression of man's fondness for beautiful women to communicate the importance that they invest in *te*. They are deepening the descriptions of female beauty to accommodate their own sense of value and importance in an effort to bring about a world in which an appreciation of *te* does in fact take precedence over sexual attraction. Confucius cites the one phrase that, to his mind, provides unity and coherence to the entire *Book of Songs* (2/2): "Do not deviate in your reflections *(ssu wu hsieh* 思无邪)." Even here, he is hardly being literal with a passage that, in its original context, means:[75] "(The stallions)—they do not swerve."

In Confucius' own appropriation and creative interpretations of the *Book of Songs*, we can see the interaction between learning *(hsüeh)* and reflecting *(ssu)* that leads to an ever-deepening understanding and a personal transformation. In that the *Songs* provides a source for appropriating meaning and an apparatus for disclosing one's novel significance, they serve the project of personal realization *(chih* 知) (17/10):

Confucius said to Po-yü, "Have you mastered the *Book of Songs* (lit. its first two sections, the 'Chou-nan' and 'Shao-nan')? Being a person and not doing so is like standing with your face right to the wall."

Personal growth is fundamentally creative; realizing oneself as a person is an art. Confucius' open, interpretive employment of the

Songs as cultural scripture dramatically demonstrates the extent to which personal creativity must be accounted for in a fair appraisal of his thought.[76]

Confucius' use of the *Songs* provides a peculiarly apt illustration of the epistemological dimension of thinking. One might be tempted to ask, however, "What, precisely, is so distinctive about his interpretation?" One approaches an answer to this question by pointing out that Confucius' method of thinking by recourse to traditional texts such as the *Songs* is not merely an illustration of one sort of thinking—textual or exegetical—which may be contrasted with, say, empirical or speculative thinking. Thinking per se always involves a grounding in tradition and may never be modeled after the direct investigation of "nature" or undisciplined, imaginative constructions.

For Confucius, knowledge is grounded in the language, customs, and institutions that comprise culture. Culture is the given world. Thinking is cultural articulation that renders this givenness effective. There is no knowledge to be gained of a reality which precedes that of culture or transcends its determinations. The "world" is always a human world.

To the majority of contemporary Western philosophers, thinking strictly within the delimitations of received culture would seem to be somewhat cramped and oppressive. In the Anglo-European tradition, richness and complexity have quite often been associated with the existence of a realm of abstract possibilities that constitute the fundamental source of conceptual and practical novelties. Confucius' thinking provides no such resource. Existentialism might offer some reason to believe that a humanly constructed world is sufficiently open to individual creativity and spontaneity so that the constraints entailed by the absence of transcendence need not occasion despair. But even the existentialist could hardly accept the extreme form of cultural positivism which Confucius' philosophy seems to represent. For such positivism appears to challenge overmuch the existentialists' regard for *individual* creativity.

Confucius is, in fact, such a cultural positivist. That is to say, he is one who posits the received cultural tradition as the authority sine qua non for all knowledge and conduct. Having said this, however, we must also note that one purpose of the following pages will be to indicate just how, within the presumed limitations of such a positivist orientation, Confucius adumbrates an extremely subtle

and complex vision of the personal, social, and cosmological implications of the process of philosophic thinking.

The preceding discussion of *hsüeh, ssu, chih,* and *hsin** introduces
Confucius' understanding of thinking as a complex activity involving
learning, reflecting, realizing, and living up to one's word. Our
consideration of this conceptual cluster is introductory in two important senses. First, thinking so far has been discussed primarily
from an "epistemological" perspective. That is, we have been concerned with the manner of achieving knowledge and the consequences
of knowing. Although a considerable number of Anglo-European
philosophers might believe the strictly epistemological dimensions of
thinking to be the only interesting or important ones, this is certainly
not true of Confucius. As a consequence, we shall be considering
the personal, social and cosmological dimensions of thinking as a
means of providing a full articulation of that activity.

The second reason this discussion must be said to be introductory
is due to the fact that the conceptual cluster outlined in this chapter
cannot be adequately understood until ramified with respect to those
concepts associated with the personal, social, and cosmological implications of Confucius' thought. The analogical relations obtaining
among all the principal notions in the *Analects* not only argue against
univocal understandings of Confucius but actually suggest alternative
criteria for the act of understanding which render undesirable the
sort of clarity associated with univocal definition. Although Confucius
would doubtless accede to William James's characterization of phil-
sosphy as "the unusually stubborn attempt to think clearly," we
shall not be prepared to grasp the distinctive meaning of clarity
presupposed by Confucius' philosophy until we proceed further with
our analysis.

II

". . . at thirty I took my stance. . . ."

1 Personal Articulation: Some Alternatives

In the Western tradition, the process of becoming a person has often been characterized in terms of the realization of ideals of a transcendental sort. The classical advice, "Become what you are," has been most influential in characterizing the activity of realizing personhood. Materialist and idealist thinkers have interpreted this advice to mean, "Recognize your essential nature and permit yourself to be determined by it." From Plato's educational program which sought to provide the means of gaining that recognition through insight into the unchanging essences that pattern existence itself, to Freud's *therapeia* which required a turning from the light to the darker reaches of the psyche, becoming a person involved the realization of what one in fact truly is. Naturalistic theories which consider the human being as a rational organism are no less possessed of a substantialist bias, for such an organism is defined by those ends or aims that characterize reason itself. To be a person is to function optimally with regard to rational ends.

An alternative to these substance notions of personality was adumbrated early in the Greek tradition by the Sophists. Here the understanding that persons are "makers" is introduced into our philosophic consciousness. The sense in which making has come to be understood in our tradition establishes the most appropriate connection (and contrast) with the idea of person making in the Confucian context. It is most essential, therefore, to understand in as precise a manner as possible the similarities and differences among the contrasting notions of making in the context of Confucius' China and of the West. For our purposes, the most efficient way of understanding this is to explore the intrinsic connection between person making and thinking in the two traditions.

In our rehearsal of the meaning of thinking in the Anglo-European tradition, we noted how significant was the distinction between reason and experience which found its initial expressions in the Parmenidean vision. The correlative distinctions between theory and practice, idea and action, ramified by that separation, provided the ground for the development of both ontological and technical sorts of reasoning. Technical reasoning, concerned with the resolution of practical problems associated with the demands of social praxis, has come to dominate our understandings of the process of thinking itself. Whereas, for the greater part of our history, the ideal of the person was characterized in terms of ontological reason, the activity of knowing defined as a grasping of the principles characterizing the essential nature of things, that ideal is now more often expressed in terms of psychic, socioeconomic, political, or scientific praxis. Marxian, Freudian, liberal democratic, and technological values determine the extrinsic rationales for the sort of person making celebrated in our contemporary culture.

This turn in Anglo-European philosophy suggests that the distinction between theoretical and practical modes of activity permits the ideals of "knowledge," "making," and "action" to be entertained in relative isolation one from the other. One of the more fruitful ways that this distinction has been exploited is in terms of the contrast between "education" and "knowledge" as the intrinsic aims of thinking. Rorty has discussed precisely this shift in the last pages of his *Philosophy and the Mirror of Nature*. Referring to Hans-Georg Gadamer's *Truth and Method*[1] as the basis for his remarks, Rorty notes that Gadamer substitutes "the notion of *Bildung* ('education,' 'self-formation') for that of 'knowledge' as the goal of thinking."[2] Gadamer, according to Rorty, recognizes (as did Heidegger) the search for objective knowledge as merely one legitimate project alongside others.[3] By noting the projective dimension of becoming a person we can recognize the variety of projects associated with becoming human and the fact that each of these projects is a sort of making. The implication is, clearly, that each of these kinds of making is comprehended in the concept of education as self-formation, self-articulation, self-creation.

The connection between freedom and self-knowledge emphasized by philosophers as diverse as Freud and Sartre suggests the different connotation that knowledge has when it no longer has as its paradigm instance the knowing of something essential about the external world, but rather refers to the description, articulation, and interpretation of oneself. The difficulty in fully endorsing such a connection between thinking and person making derives, of course, from recognizing the danger of defining the process of thinking as ego-centered self-knowledge so narrowly as to challenge any meaningful notion of interpersonal or social relatedness.

The connection of self-articulation with practice or action, evident in contemporary theories deriving from the existentialists, pragmatists, and Marxists, insures however, that intersubjectivity cannot be altogether ignored. The sort of self-understanding that one can rightly achieve once the ideal of an objective knowledge transcending persons has been given up is that which is grounded in the interaction of individuals in a personal or social context. That is to say, if we are no longer searching out the Mind of God or the inexorable laws of nature, we must search out one another. For, once the myth of objective knowledge has been laid to rest, the world ceases to be construed as an objective datum for dispassionate investigation and becomes the (relatively) articulated expressions of environing others. In other words, it becomes culture. And culture is rife with the personal creativity of the best representatives of the human community.

In our discussion of the conceptual cluster of learning (*hsüeh* 學), reflecting (*ssu* 思), and realizing (*chih* 知) in Confucius, it was clear that culture undergirds thinking in the sense that both the resources for learning and the articulated capacities for reflection are cultural attainments. In our consideration of Confucius' concept of person making, we shall be highlighting a dynamic relationship obtaining among ritual action (*li* 禮), signification (*yi* 義), and authoritative personality (*jen** 仁) which will likewise presuppose the cultural milieu as the fundamental matrix which grounds the process of becoming a person. Confucius' understanding of person making is, as we shall see, quite distinctive. Its closest analogues in the Western tradition are to be found among the existentialists and the American pragmatists.[4]

The insight that the human being is defined in terms of the process of making is rooted, as has been noted, in the thinking of the Greek Sophists. In our more recent history, this notion is most firmly entrenched in certain of the cultural anthropologists who, seeking a definition of the human being which would distinguish him from his biological kin, forwarded the notion of "man as toolmaker." The interaction between the human being as natural and as cultural is a function of the introduction of tools into nascent social contexts. Such tools are "cultural objects," ranging in variety and complexity from merely sharpened stones to linguistic signs and symbols. Culture—and distinctly human being as both the source of cultural objects and the most complex illustration of such objects— was born *pari passu* with the introduction of meaning into the natural world. On this view, then, making is the making of meaning. Thus, the human being, as cultural object, is primarily a maker of cultural objects and is, thereby, a maker of himself.

The contrast between nature and culture, employed as an interpretive tool for anthropologists and philosophers, is itself dependent upon culture as a complex of acts of signification. And understanding the passage from nature to culture, which the philosophical anthropologist Claude Lévi-Strauss[5] claims to be the central problem of anthropology, presupposes concepts and theories that could only have emerged after such a presumed passage had taken place. The human being as a maker of meaning has as his initial product, his self, his person.

This interpretation of human nature has been translated by contemporary existentialists and pragmatists into extremely subtle understandings of the activity of person making. Jean-Paul Sartre well represents the existentialist perspective. For Sartre the person is to be understood in terms of the relation between freedom and self-knowledge. But this relation itself must be understood by recourse to the concept of action. "To act is to modify the shape of the world; it is to arrange means in view of an end."[6] What is most important about an act for Sartre, however, is that it is intentional and that intention implies consciousness of something (that is, what is intended) as *not being the case*. Consciously to bring into being what is not is the purpose of action. This entails the freedom of the human being, for without a sense that bringing into being what is not is a real possibility, no intentionality is possible. "Man is the being through whom nothingness comes into the world."[7] That is to say, human consciousness is born out of a recognition of states of affairs that are not the case, and human freedom underlies the intentional acts that seek to bring into being what is not. "Man's relation to being is that he can modify it."[8]

That relation to being is, *a fortiori*, true of one's own being. As an object of intentional change, the self is a thing among other things—*en soi.* Only through actions directed by intentions can one be a person, a consciousness for itself—*pour soi.* The modification of an individual *en soi* by becoming *pour soi* is the means whereby persons are made.

The problem with such an approach to the meaning of persons is that whereas it overcomes quite handily the difficulties inherent in the characterization of the person as primarily a knower of abstract essences or principles, it greatly ramifies the difficulty of accounting for the social character of person making. Idealist theories of the person, for example, can demonstrate the social or communal character of human interactions by appeal to the transcendental structures of reason and experience that characterize the essential meaning of being human. Existentialist accounts of the sort provided by Sartre begin with individual consciousness and then perforce must interpret society as an accommodation and adjustment of individuals each of whom modifies and is modified by others. Such a vision doesn't quite lead us back to the Hobbesian "war of each against all," but clearly social interactions are agonistic. Because of this individualistic bias, the existentialists find themselves precluded from fully exploiting the sociocultural resources for the understanding of persons.

In Sartre's case, the basis of social and interpersonal relations lies in the distinction between *en-soi* and *pour-soi.* Only insofar as an individual is *en-soi* may he or she be the subject of external determination. Both the cooperative and the agonistic relations of individuals in society are functions of their autonomy and integrity *pour soi.* The difficulty with such a theory is that someone claiming to be *pour soi* has to decide precisely who is a candidate for determination.

The fact that in his later writings Sartre moved in the direction of Marxist theory suggests, first, that his existentialism could not itself generate a satisfactory sociopolitical theory and therefore had to have recourse to alternative philosophic resources and, second, that the specifications of *en-soi* and *pour-soi* in relation to individuals in society would be determined by a particular economic theory. On its own terms, Sartre's social theory seems to be a consequence of the same sort of "bad faith" that he finds so prevalent among others. He accepts determinations from the outside about the meaning of persons which are not authentic implications of his most fundamental views.

From the perspective of a vision that insists upon the social character of the self, such bad faith is to be found in any existential theory, indeed, in every individualistic view of the meaning of persons. What is missing in such theories is any important discussion of the contributions made to the meaning of persons and person making by the social context considered as a primary datum.

That the human being is a maker of meaning, and that the primary meaning he or she makes is related to the self-conscious appropriation of the world of experience, are views held in common by both the existential and pragmatic traditions. In pragmatism, however, the development of the person as a self-conscious being is dependent upon the more fundamental notion of social interaction. Contrary to the suggestions of individual absoluteness to be found in existentialist views, the individual (and this is true *a fortiori* of the developed person) must always be understood as relative to social contexts.

John Dewey characterizes the socially derivative character of consciousness and personhood in terms of the contrast between experiencing and being a self:[9]

> Experience, a serial course of affairs with their own characteristic properties and relationships, occurs, happens, and is what it is. Among and with these occurrences, not outside of them or underlying them, are those events which are denominated selves. In some specifiable respects and for some specifiable consequences, these selves, capable of objective denotation just as are sticks, stones, and stars, assume the care and administration of certain objects and acts in experience.

The self arises out of experience by the accepting of responsibility for certain consequences of experiencing. This acceptance is predicated upon an adoptive act. Such an act is "proclaimed in virtue of which one claims the benefit of future goods and admits liability for future ills flowing from the affair in question."[10] For Dewey, then, human beings are not the authors of experience; they are, rather, the responsive agents or actors who adopt experience and in so doing accept the consequences, good or ill, that flow from it.

The stress upon responsiveness and accepting the liability of one's adopted experience clearly suggests that the emergence of the self is from a social context, for the environment occasioning the experiences from among which one adopts one's own experience is not merely a world of sticks, stones, and stars; by far the most significant responses are occasioned by stimulations associated with other human beings. Thinking, believing, desiring are experiences usually occasioned by cultural stimuli. And although human beings are not strictly the authors of experience, they certainly are the most complex and refined occasions for the stimulation of experiencing:[11]

> Authorship and liability look in two different ways, one to the past, the other to the future. Natural events—including social habits—originate thoughts and feelings. To say "I think, hope, and love" is to say in effect that genesis is not the last word.

One of the more interesting questions for our purposes is the manner in which social habits author experience. Dewey stresses that "animals are connected with each other in inclusive schemes of behavior by means of signalling acts. . . . In the human being this function becomes language communication, discourse, in virtue of which the consequences of the behavior of one form of life are integrated in the behavior of others."[12]

Language, discourse as a "social habit," is one of the natural events that originate thoughts and feelings. The emergence of linguistic communication significantly challenges any denial to human beings the authorship of experience. "I think, hope, love," as addressed to another, is not only an adoption of experience, it is an evocation of experiencing in that other and a tacit request for an adoptive response. At its most sophisticated level, experiencing involves communication. It is, in fact, most often a consequence of communication.

It is not the case, for Dewey, that the self emerges out of natural experiencing solely by virtue of a prudent regard for the future consequences. Human beings are possessed of capacities permitting responses to the immediacies of experience:[13]

> Human experience in the large, in its coarse and conspicuous features, has for one of its most striking features preoccupation with direct enjoyment, feasting and festivities, ornamentation, dance, song, dramatic pantomime, telling yarns and enacting stories. . . . Direct

appropriations and satisfactions were prior to anything but the most exigent prudence.

The immediate satisfactions of experience are often accepted in spite of a realization of somewhat negative consequences. Drunken revelry usually carries some bad consequences which are accepted along with the adoption of the pleasurable experience. Aesthetic rather than instrumental satisfactions are the first choices of human beings. The powerful attraction of myths and rituals lies in their combining instrumental and aesthetic values. It is not going beyond Dewey's intent to say that the importance of ritualistic behavior in the formation of distinctly human beings lies in the fact that both pleasure and prudence are thereby given their due. One of the closest associations of enjoyment and utility is to be found in the institution of ritualistic celebrations.

Language, ritual—indeed, social habits of all sorts—intensify the enjoyment of experience while providing focus and order for experience as well. Individuals, in large measure, are themselves habits of acting and interacting, of participating, of communicating. Becoming a person is a process of adopting experiences and communicating the attitudes, desires, beliefs, and ideas which result from such adoptive activity. Given such a process, any attempt to consider a person as detached from the social matrix of communication among others is absurd. A person is parented by society. More precisely, a person is parented by social interactions of the sort that depend upon ideas, institutions, and attitudes comprising the most essential features of what we call culture.

The distinctions between Sartre and Dewey on the subject of becoming a person should be obvious, for they all relate to the contrasting meanings of "making" employed by each. For Sartre a person *(pour soi)* comes into being by virtue of actions which alter or remake those things constituting his or her environs. For Dewey the self arises out of a series of adoptive acts occasioned by the joint demands of pleasure and prudence. The existentialist takes as a virtue a sort of *creatio ex nihilo* that brings into being what was not. The pragmatist "makes" by rendering increasingly more subtle and complex the ways of adopting and transforming experience. Person making in the pragmatic tradition is essentially social. Society and persons arise in a mutually contributive manner.

There are advantages and serious disadvantages to both existentialist and pragmatic theories of the person with regard to their relevance as introductions to Confucius' idea of person making. The principal advantage of the existentialist is his humanistic bias, his refusal to construe the human being in naturalistic terms. For naturalism in Western philosophy since the sixteenth century has been understood in terms of the reigning paradigm of natural science—be it materialistic physics, evolutionary biology, or behavioristic psychology. The humanism of existentialists such as Sartre and the early Heidegger is fundamentally opposed to the importation into philosophical anthropology of the dominant cultural interest of natural science which in its classical guise was more than a little responsible for narrowing the concept of thinking to conform to scientific and technical reasoning.

From the perspective of this work, the fatal disadvantage of existentialism is its individualistic presuppositions, which make of society a derivative, and therefore abstract, notion. Pragmatism provides a corrective to the individualism of the existentialist, of course, but in doing so threatens to fall into the equally serious mistake of reducing the concept of person to naturalistic categories that owe altogether too much to the method of the natural sciences. Thus, for Dewey, scientific knowledge in its broadest sense:[14]

> signifies events understood, events so interpenetrated by thought that mind is literally at home in them. . . . What is sometimes termed "applied" science may then be more truly science than what is conventionally called pure science. For it is directly concerned with the instrumentalities at work in effecting modifications of existence in behalf of conclusions that are reflectively preferred. . . . Thus conceived, knowledge exists in engineering, medicine and the social arts more adequately than it does in mathematics and physics.

Dewey, as much as any of the other pragmatists (with the possible exception of William James), sought to expand the notion of instrumental understanding beyond the confines of technical reasonings, but the naturalistic bias of his theory militated against his being altogether successful in this endeavor. It is George Herbert Mead, Dewey's contemporary and sometime colleague, who provided a naturalistic theory the arguments and conclusions of which are most readily detachable from the scientific apologetic in which they are embedded. For this reason, it is to this relatively unheralded pragmatist we shall have recourse as providing perhaps the best introduction to the Confucian notion of person making. For unlike Dewey, whose use of "naturalism" is very nearly synonymous with "scientific" as well as "nonsupernatural," "worldly," "secular," Mead's form of naturalism is used primarily in the latter, humanistic sense. Thus Mead's "naturalism" is, as we shall see, closer to the kind of humanism that may be attributed to Confucius.

George Herbert Mead's work is primarily known by social psychologists and historians of American pragmatism. In essential agreement with Dewey, Mead's distinctive contribution to the subject of the meaning of person making and its relationship to thinking derives less from any strictly philosophic originality and more from the fact that his starting point is even more fundamentally social than is John Dewey's. Mead was a social psychologist at a time when this was still a nascent field of endeavor. Thus he himself provided much of the scientific speculations that undergird his arguments and conclusions. That is, he was one of the pioneers of the scientific discipline upon which he reflected philosophically. Further, his was a distinctly social, rather than a natural, science. For Mead, the natural sciences were themselves construed in terms of the principles of his social theory.[15]

The fact that Mead begins in the most radical manner with the concept of society renders his analysis of the emergence of the self within its social context extremely valuable as a resource for reflecting upon Confucius' understanding of person making. Mead is in essential agreement with Dewey as to the manner in which the self arises out of experience. Mead, however, provides a much more subtle analysis than Dewey of the precise character of that emergence. According to Mead, the person achieves unity or integrity as a self by virtue of internalizing the attitude of "the generalized other":[16]

> The organized community or social group which gives to the individual his unity of self may be called "the generalized other." The attitude of the generalized other is the attitude of the whole community. . . . Only in so far as [one] takes the attitudes of the organized social group to which [one] belongs toward the organized, co-operative social activities . . . in which that group as such is engaged, does [one] develop a complete self or possess the sort of complete self he has developed.

Taking the attitude of "the generalized other" begins with taking up the particular attitudes directed to oneself by those individuals with whom one interacts. Such attitudes include, as well, the attitudes of these individuals toward one another. The completion of this process involves its generalization to the social community as a whole. This generalization is performed in two ways: first, the greatest variety of relevant attitudes are entertained. And, second, the attitudes of the social group as a whole are internalized. It is these latter attitudes, those of "the generalized other," that are expressive of the most general features of "the world." Abstractly considered, these features are those found in the structure of discourse itself, the grammar and syntax of language, mathematical and logical relations, and so forth. Thus, for Mead the self is constituted by the internalization of alternative roles and attitudes and their organization into a coherent complex.

There is yet another phase in the complete articulation of self-hood. The self is not merely the individual and social attitudes of others in some organized form. This is only the "me." "The 'I' is the response of the organism to the attitudes of others":[17]

> The "me" represents a definite organization of the community there in our own attitudes, and calling for a response. . . . The "I" . . . is something that is, so to speak, responding to a social situation which is within the experience of the individual. It is the answer which the individual makes to the attitude which others take toward him when he assumes an attitude toward them. . . . The attitudes he is taking toward them are present in his own experience, but his response to them will contain a novel element. The "I" gives the sense of freedom, of initiative.

The response of the "I" to the "me" is always unpredictable in any precise manner. The dialectical process that goes on between the "I" and the "me," therefore, is not only creative of the developed self, it is also the means whereby novelty is introduced into the world. "The 'I' both calls out the 'me' and responds to it. Taken together they constitute personality as it appears in social experience."[18] The dialectic of the "I" and the "me" characterizes the activity of thinking itself. The self is "a process in which the individual is continually adjusting himself in advance to the situation to which he belongs, and reacting back to it. So that the 'I' and the 'me,' this thinking, this conscious adjustment, becomes then a part of the whole social process and makes a more highly organized society possible."[19]

This is a direct and explicit expression of the social basis of person making. It is also a straightforward statement of the relationship between thinking and becoming a person: if becoming a person is inexorably social, so is the act of thinking. There are no extra-mundane facts or truths to be discovered; no physical or mathematical doctrines, no metaphysical principles, no eternal verities—except these be articulated within the interaction of the "I" and the "me," each of which depends upon the other and both of which are rooted in the social character of experience.

In George Herbert Mead's concept of the emergence of the self from its social context we have, perhaps, some approximation in the Western tradition of the views of Confucius. Mead's naturalism is fundamentally a humanism, although the exposition of his views is burdened somewhat by the rhetoric of Darwinian and behavioristic science.

We have been attempting to uncover resources in the Anglo-European philosophic tradition permitting us more ready access to Confucius' concept of the relationship between thinking and person making. Our difficulty lies in the distinction between the theoretical and practical forms of life which have such widespread acceptance in our tradition. The consequent distinctions among thinking, acting, and making which pattern our classical philosophic theories make extremely difficult any attempt to interpret philosophies that do not depend upon such distinctions.

The turn toward praxis in twentieth-century Western philosophy does seem to make our task somewhat easier, but we must be cautious, nonetheless. While it is one thing to philosophize in innocence of any radical split between theory and practice, idea and action, it is quite another to construct one's philosophy in conscious revolt against that division. The reduction of theories to praxis with the consequent construal of ideas in terms of actions, found in existentialism, and to a lesser extent in pragmatism, cannot be wholly satisfactory to the Confucian who does not recognize a breach between the two.

As we have tried to demonstrate, thinking for Confucius contains elements of *theoria* and *praxis* inextricably combined. We shall now attempt to show the same sort of thing with regard to the meaning of persons. With appropriate caution, however, the concepts of Sartre, and particularly of Dewey and Mead, discussed in these pages can be helpful in attempting to understand Confucius' thought. In turn, Confucius' understanding of person making may be helpful in articulation and reformulation of the meaning of "making" in our tradition such as to avoid accepting too readily the narrowly technical senses of that term. If we are not prepared to accept such assistance from exoteric philosophies, we shall be led into repeating at the practical level the same mistake that was made at the level of theory: in place of the rationality of the theoretical sciences as the primary criterion by which we determine what it means to be a thinking person, we shall merely have substituted technological rationalization.

2 The Mutuality of Ritual Action *(li禮)* and Signification *(yi義)*

We have described personal articulation and realization in Confucius as a "thinking through." Since thinking entails an appropriation of the cultural tradition through the interpersonal activity of learning *(hsüeh 學)*, and culminates in the communal activities of realizing *(chih知)* and living up to one's word *(hsin* 信)*, thinking has a fundamentally social dimension. At the same time, to the extent that in thinking the person must adapt cultural consensus to his unique circumstances in the expression of his own creativity, it has the intentionality of the subjective agent as a constituent feature.

In the first chapter, we have delineated the dynamics of thinking in a discussion of education, reflection, and self-cultivation. The widening focus of the present chapter, then, is thinking through interpersonal activity. While we have indicated in the first chapter that, for Confucius, personal articulation requires the participation of others, in this chapter we want to continue to develop the thesis that person making can be described as a process of interpersonal communications and transactions whereby the emerging person pursues integration in the context of his social environs. The quality of this integration, as we shall discover, is a function of both appropriating from personal context and creatively altering that context through the expression of one's own appropriateness.

The dynamics of this process of extending the focus of "thinking through" to include personhood is captured in Confucius in the movement from "individual person" (*jen* 人) or "individual self" (*chi* 己) to "authoritative person" (*jen** 仁). An individual who, through some lack of effort or insight, fails to develop towards "authoritative personhood" is a "retarded individual" (*hsiao jen* 小人).

There is a development in this process of personal growth which legitimizes our choice of "authoritative person" as a fair rendering of this central concept, *jen** 仁. The *jen** person, by exercising his own judgment, sense of appropriateness, and capacity to invest selectively his importance in the world, that is, his *yi* 義, finds and appropriates meaning from the formal behaviors, customs, and institutions of his cultural legacy (*li* 禮). By enacting the formal structures of his tradition, he assumes the authority of consensus. At the same time, his personal *yi* is the capacity to adapt the tradition to his novel circumstances and intentions, and to recover these formal structures as an apparatus for developing and disclosing his own significance. From this perspective, the consummating person as "significator" engages himself in authoring his cultural tradition. It is this dialogue between his embodiment of the *authority* of consensus and his *authorship* of the emerging culture that makes him *authoritative*.

In this chapter, we shall attempt to justify our distinction between "individual" (*jen* 人) and "authoritative person" (*jen** 仁) by first analyzing the language in which the dynamic process of person making is couched and then unraveling the philosophical implications of our analysis. That is, at the philological level, we shall examine the emergence of "authoritative person" out of the movement between "ritual action" (*li* 禮) and "signification" (*yi* 義). From this conceptual analysis and reconstruction, we shall attempt to derive a coherent account of person making in Confucius.

It is important at this juncture to emphasize the irreducibly social context of person making in the philosophy of Confucius, and to encourage the reader to draw an interpretation from this chapter in tandem with the several chapters that follow. This caution is an effort to balance off the individualistic presuppositions that weigh so heavily in our contemporary attitudes toward personhood. We must at any cost guard against psychologization. Further, there is the very real danger of isolating what are only conceptual and explanatory distinctions, reading them for analytic clarity and losing at least some awareness of their intrinsic interrelatedness.

2.1 *Ritual Action* (li禮)

In Confucius' account of his own personal development, he states that " . . . at thirty I took my stance (*li* 立) . . . " (2/4). This notion of "stance" (*li*) is certainly related to the more formal and specific concept of "rank" or "position" (*wei* 位), and refers to the general posture that one strikes and pursues as a person. In the *Analects*, it is repeatedly stated that it is "ritual action" *(li)*—also frequently translated as "rites," "propriety," "ceremony," "decorum," "manners"—which enables one to determine, assume, and display his personal stance (16/13):

> Ch'en Kang asked the son of Confucius, Po-yü, "Have you been given any kind of special instruction?" "No," he replied. "Once when my father was standing alone, I moved quickly and deferentially across the courtyard. He addressed me, saying, 'Have you learned the *Songs?*' I replied 'no,' to which he remarked, 'If you do not learn the *Songs*, you will not have the means to speak.' I deferentially took my leave and learned the *Songs*."
>
> On another day when he was again standing alone, I moved quickly and deferentially across the courtyard. He again addressed me, saying, 'Have you learned the *Rituals?*' I replied 'no,' to which he remarked, 'If you do not learn the *Rituals*, you will not have the means to take a stance.' I deferentially took my leave and learned the *Rituals*. What I have learned, then, are these two things."
>
> Ch'en Kang, taking his leave, was delighted, and said, "I asked one question and got three answers. I learned the importance of the *Songs* and of the *Rituals*, and I also learned that an exemplary person does not treat his son as a special case.[20]

From this passage, the phrase, "if you do not learn the *Rituals*, you will not have the means to take a stance," can be used as a device to uncover several insights into the place and function of ritual action and its role in person making.

First, the social aspect of ritual action is an important constituent in the evolution of this concept. Consensus has it that originally ritual actions were formalized procedures enacted by the ruler in an attempt to establish and continue a relationship with the spirits and gods. These rituals were constituted in imitation of perceptible cosmic rhythms as a means of strengthening the coordination of the human being and his natural and spiritual environment. They were used to reinforce a sense of human participation and context in the regular processes of existence. Gradually, these ritual actions were extended outwards from the ruler himself to involve other members of the court and community, developing an increasing social significance. In these ritual activities, each participant would have his proper place, his *wei* 位. If one did not understand the ritual procedures, he would literally not know where to stand (*li* 立).[21]

A second feature of ritual action that is suggested by this passage is its disclosing and displaying function. The character *li* 禮 has the radical *shih* 示 as a component element, meaning, "show," "sign," "indicate."[22] Because these ritual displays were originally enacted in a religious context to make human intentions known to the spirits, *shih* as a constituent radical in a character is usually indicative of religious affairs. The "ritual vase" (*li* 豊) component of ritual action *(li)* further associates ritual with the sacred and sacrificial. Although changing conditions in Chinese society extended the range of ritual action from narrowly defined religious rites to include the various kinds of formal human conducts that structure interpersonal activity, this evolved notion of social ritual never lost the sense of sacredness and sacrifice. During the formative period of Chinese civilization in the Chou dynasty, society moved from a basically tribal–clan system to a more complex semi-feudal structure. The ritual actions which had originally constituted a code of rites and ceremonies governing specific religious observances came to embody the total spectrum of social norms, customs, and mores, covering increasingly complicated relationships and institutions. The focus of ritual actions shifted from man's relationship with the supernatural to the relationship obtaining among members of human society, and their application was extended from the court to all levels of civilized society.

The fact that the sense of sacredness which had always been associated with these formal structures persisted in the evolution of ritual action reveals an important characteristic of Chinese society and culture. Although the focus and application of ritual action shifted dramatically, the original religious function of integrating the specifically human sphere with the whole remained the same. Rather than just the court, the various strata of Chinese society sought, in ritual action, to regulate their lives in concert with the ordered patterns perceived in nature. From his context each person was free to seek a relationship with the whole through acculturation and interpersonal activity. If religiousness fundamentally involves an understanding and appreciation of a person's meaning-in-context and his relationship to the source of that meaning, then these evolving social rituals retained both their sacred and religious import in providing the members of society with an apparatus for spiritual development through social intercourse. While Confucius insisted upon confining his comments to the purely social implications of these ritual actions, later scholars were explicit in placing the human social structures within the broader context of the cosmological order.[23]

This evolution in the social dimension of ritual action is often described in terms of the emergence of a Chinese humanism, but such a characterization requires qualification.[24] Doubtless this period witnessed a transition from spirit-centered to human-centered ritual, from shaman–counsellor, to sage–counsellor, from authority by virtue of one's position to authority of one's person. But such a transition should not be understood as a movement away from religion and spirituality. As Robert Gimello observes:[25]

> One would do better to say that what was of ultimate and compre-
> hensive value to Confucius and his followers (and was therefore "re-
> ligious" in the truest, least culture-bound sense) was the process
> whereby one could live a rich and fulfilling spiritual life solely as "a
> man among other men." In this process, the *li* themselves came to
> be regarded less as modes of hieratic action than as paradigms of
> human relations.

A final and important insight that is suggested in Confucius' admonishment to his son to "learn the *Rituals*" in order to "take a stance" is the physical analogy that can be drawn between "taking a stance" and the "body" of a ritual tradition. Throughout the early lexicons, ritual action (*li* 禮) is defined with its homophone, "to tread a path" (*li*** 履), emphasizing the necessity of enacting and ultimately embodying the cultural tradition that is captured in ritual action.[26] A revealing association between ritual action and the body of the cultural tradition is the cognate relationship between the two characters, "ritual action" (*li* 禮) and "body" (*t'i* 體). As Peter Boodberg observes, these are the only two common Chinese char-acters that share the *li* 豊 phonetic, "ritual vase."[27] Further, he suggests that these two characters are related in their overlapping connotation of "organic form":[28]

"Form," that is, "organic" rather than geometrical form, then, appears to be the link between the two words, as evidenced by the ancient Chinese scholiasts who repeatedly used *t'i* to define *li* in their glosses.

The notion of formal *li* action overlaps with *t'i*, body, in that *li* actions are embodiments or formalizations of meaning and value that accumulate to constitute a cultural tradition. If we examine the notion of ritual in the classical literature in a way sensitive to its intimate relationship with the concept of "rightness/signification" *(yi)*, we find that these rituals can be more elaborately described as an inherited tradition of formalized human actions that evidence both a cumulative investment of meaning by one's precursors in a cultural tradition, and an openness to reformulation and innovation in response to the processive nature of the tradition. These ritual actions, like bodies, are of variable "shapes," appropriating much of their definition from their context. Ritual actions, invested with the accumulated meaning of the tradition, are formalized structures upon which the continuity of the tradition depends and through which a person in the tradition pursues cultural refinement. Like a body of literature or a corpus of music, these rituals continue through time as a repository of the ethical and aesthetic insights of those who have gone before. A person engaged in the performance of a particular formal action, taking meaning from it while seeking himself to be appropriate for it, derives meaning and value from this embodiment, and further strengthens it by his contribution of novel meaning and value.

Further, as suggested by the simplified version of "body" *t'i* as 体, constituted of "man" 人, and "root" 本, the body of ritual actions and institutions can be described as the "root" that supports and sponsors the innovation and creativity of a cultural tradition. Like the human body, it is an organic entity which must be nurtured and cultivated to preserve its integrity, and which must be constantly revitalized and adapted to prevailing circumstances in order to retain its influence. It is at once the fruit of the past and the ground out of which the future will grow.

This suggestive cognate relationship between "ritual action" (*li* 禮) and "body" (*t'i* 體) works both ways. As we have indicated, tradition has it that the Sage–rulers of antiquity observed regularity and order implicit in the natural process and sought to devise formal rules of conduct that would enable human beings to make the same cosmological patterns explicit in their own lives. These formal behaviors, serving to structure human life within and integrate it without, are a microcosm of the *li* 理 (veins, fibres) of the macrocosm. Similarly, throughout the early literature, the human form, with its "wind," orifices, circulation, and so forth, is treated as a microcosm which functions in a way analogous to the whole. Both ritual action and body as imitations of cosmic functions share a sense of mysterious power, sanctity, and efficacy.

Li, from its earliest meaning as those sacrifices whereby the ruler established a relationship with deity, has always had a strong relational import. Ritual action establishes, conditions, and bonds relationships at every level of human experience, from one's own introspective dialogue to the broadest social and political matrices. Similarly, the physical form is a means for the concrete particular's engaging, taking from, and contributing to its environs.

Ritual actions are certainly not perceived as divinely established norms. If they have normative force, it is because they have been generated out of the human situation, and hence render informed access to it. They are patterns of behavior initiated and transmitted in order to refine and enhance life in a community. Similarly, the human body is contingent. Neither fashioned in God's image nor informed by an immutable species character, the human body is a changing configuration of processes that have been embodied as a creative response to relevant circumstances. There is no ideal physical form; rather, the kinds of skills and faculties embodied are generated out of the situations with which they seek integration. The body is a variable statement of meaning and value achieved in an effort to refine and enhance human life within the changing parameters of particular contexts.

2.2 *Signification* (yi 義)

Having adumbrated the evolution and consequent implications of ritual action (*li* 禮) for Confucius, we can now proceed to the second concept relevant to the process of personal articulation. *Yi* 義 is frequently divided into two concepts and translated alternatively as "righteousness" or "meaning." It is because this specific concept is so important and yet has been so sorely misunderstood that we shall hold its translation in abeyance and, letting context speak for itself, pursue an adequate rendering that will reunite the two halves of an idea in one expression. We shall argue not only that a full appreciation of the meaning of *yi* is fundamental to an understanding of the dynamics of person making but that the value of recent liberalized interpretations of Confucius have been significantly reduced by the omission or misconstrual of this concept. In fact, from the very beginning of the Confucian tradition the problematic status of *yi* has made possible rigidly narrow and conservative interpretations of Confucianism. An ancillary but nonetheless significant argument entailed by this discussion is that the theoretical vocabulary employed in Anglo-European interpretations of classical Chinese thought tends to shape the conceptual cognates associated with the legitimate meanings of central philosophical concepts such as *yi* in such a way as to occasion serious misunderstanding.

The arguments and principal conclusions we shall present with respect to the meaning and function of *yi* in Confucius' thought will be both radical and conservative: radical in the sense that our semantic and conceptual analyses will permit the suggestion of a relatively novel set of meanings for *yi*, so we shall find ourselves somewhat at odds with traditional and contemporary interpretations of Confucius' philosophy; yet since our purpose is to move closer to an understanding of the original Confucius, the primary aim of our interpretation may be justifiably claimed to be a conservative one.

We may productively begin this analysis with the question of the etymological relationship between *yi* 義 and *wo* 我, "personal self." The first assertion that can be made with respect to that relationship is that *yi* in the classical Confucian tradition is perceived to be a natural condition, if not the distinguishing characteristic of the human being and his personal identity. In the *Analects*, *yi* is the "raw stuff" (*chih*** 質) out of which the exemplary person fashions himself (15/18):

> Having *yi* as his raw stuff, to practice it in ritual actions, to express it with humility, and to complete it in living up to his word: this then is the exemplary person (*chün tzu*).[29]

The *Mencius*, pursuing its project of bringing clarity and detail to the teachings of Confucius, repeatedly underscores the "internal" locus of *yi*. This is a major theme in Mencius' several encounters with Kao Tzu, who regards *yi* as the "external" *product* of human nature.[30] In fact, Mencius, discussing *yi* in terms of "an unlearned capacity of the human being" and "a prereflective realizing," internalizes it and locates it in the natural mind:[31]

> The basic nature of the exemplary person (*chün tzu* 君子)—his capacities for (*yi* 義) authoritative humanity (*jen** 仁), ritual action (*li* 禮), and realization (*chih* 知)—are rooted in his heart-and-mind and manifested in his countenance such that a sheen is seen on his face.

The problem as to how Mencius can locate these seemingly relational and actional notions such as "authoritative personhood" (*jen**) and "ritual action" (*li*) in the heart-and-mind only arises if one insists upon an atomistic or essentialist interpretation of the person. In fact, that Mencius chooses to locate the impetus of these relational notions within the particular person's heart-and-mind reminds us of Confucius' statement that "to discipline oneself and practice ritual action is to become authoritative as a person. . . . Becoming an authoritative person emerges out of oneself; how could it emerge out of others?" (12/1). Achieving quality as a person requires a social forum, but this is a social forum that must be informed in the fullest sense by one's own unique disposition. The capacity to significate (*yi*) is not restricted to the exemplary person, but like the five senses, is a natural characteristic incipient in the hearts-and-minds (*hsin* 心) of all people:[32]

> Could it be that the heart-and-mind alone is without any common ground? What is the common ground among hearts-and-minds? Rationality (*li* 理) and the capacity to significate (*yi* 義).

It is Hsün Tzu who specifically and explicitly identifies *yi* as the unique distinguishing characteristic of the human being:[33]

> Water and fire have *ch'i* 氣 but no life; plants and trees have life but no intelligence; birds and beasts have intelligence but no *yi*; man has *ch'i*, intelligence, and, moreover, *yi*.

The early Han philosopher, Tung Chung-shu, in an extended discussion on the relationship between authoritative person (*jen** 仁)

and *yi* 義, insists that *yi* is a personal concern directed at the proper disposition of one's own conduct:[34]

> The relationship of authoritative personhood *jen** 仁 to others (*jen* 人) and of *yi* 義 to the personal self (*wo* 我) should be carefully examined. Most people do not do this, but instead use *jen** to be self-indulgent and *yi* to demand a certain conduct from others. . . . The method of *yi* lies in making the personal self orderly (*cheng* 正), not in making others so. If a person is not able to make himself orderly even though he is able to make others so, the *Spring and Autumn Annals* would not designate this as *yi*.

Tung Chung-shu goes on to state that *yi* is the condition of personal identity and uniqueness inasmuch as conduct that expresses a person's *yi* is attaining it in oneself (*tzu-te* 自得), while conduct which does not disclose *yi* is self-negating (*tzu-shih* 自失):[35]

> *Yi* means appropriateness to one's own person. Only once one is appropriate to his own person can this be called *yi*. Thus, the expression *yi* combines the notions of "appropriateness" (*yi** 宜) and "personal self" (*wo* 我) in one term. If we hold on to this insight, *yi* as an expression refers to personal self. Thus it is said that to realize *yi* in one's actions is called attaining it in oneself (*tzu-te* 自得); to neglect *yi* in one's actions is called self-negligence (*tzu-shih* 自失). A person who is fond of *yi* is called a person fond of himself; a person who does not like *yi* is called a person who does not like himself. Considering it in these terms, it is clear that *yi* is personal self (*wo* 我).

The expression "attaining it in oneself" (*tzu-te* 自得) which occurs in this passage and is equated with "attaining *yi*" (*te-yi* 得義) appears frequently in the corpus of early Chinese literature in discussions that center on the achievement of personal identity, and the uniqueness of that achievement.[36]

The *Shuo-wen* dictionary also defines *yi* in terms of the positive achievement of personal identity: "*Yi* means one's dignity of demeanor." It would seem on the basis of these several definitions and discussions of *yi* that it is a notion of self-construing identity. It is important to bear in mind the contextualist ontology in which the teachings of Confucius are grounded, and that the conception of person operative in this context is "processive" rather than "substantial." Hence, there is no difficulty in asserting that *yi* is both a self-construing identity and what one does.[37]

The personal self (*wo* 我) seems to be the source, the locus, the impetus, and, at least initially, that which is determined by its own disclosure of *yi*. As we have indicated, it would seem that *wo* has two characteristics that are immediately relevant to our analysis: it is an exalted form of the first person denoting high status, and in Middle and Late Archaic Chinese its grammatical function seems to have shifted at least to some degree from a nominative to an objective role.[38]

Our reconstruction of this concept, *yi*, would suggest that *yi* as personal disclosure of significance is coextensive with the process of self-realization. That is to say, the paradigmatic person to be associated with *yi* is "exalted" or has achieved high "status" to the extent that he is actively engaged in the process of self-realization. This would, of course, account for the cognate of *yi* 義, *yi*** 儀, as an exemplary model by virtue of proper demeanor and comportment. Now, a major concern in Confucius' program of self-realization is "to discipline oneself" (*k'o-chi* 克己) and overcome the fixed perspective that this ego-self entails. This fixed perspective gives rise to the distracting "ego advantages" (*li** 利) which the ego as self seeks to appropriate from what it construes as "other." The tension between ego advantages *li** 利 and *yi* 義 is a persistent and recurring theme throughout early Confucian literature.[39] Where *li** 利 is to pursue the good on behalf of the interests of the ego-self (*chi* 己) and is associated with the conduct of the less developed individual (*hsiao jen* 小人), *yi* can be readily identified with the exalted-self (*wo* 我) and the conduct of the exemplary person (*chün tzu*) who pursues the broader good.

The process of becoming an exemplary person in Confucian thought entails both the dissolution of a delimiting and retarding distinction between self and other, and the active integration of this liberated self into the social field through the disclosure of *yi*. This process is described in an important and often misinterpreted phrase in the *Analects* (12/1): "To discipline oneself (*k'o-chi* 克己) and practice ritual action *(li)* is to become authoritative as a person."[40] The process of dissolving the barrier between the self and its social environment involves disciplining the ego-self and becoming a person-in-context. This process can alternatively be described as the objectification of self in that it recognizes the correlative and coextensive relationship between person making and community making, and ultimately, world making.

This interpretation of exalted self as person-in-context is implicit in Confucius' assertion (20/3) that: "A person who does not understand the causal conditions governing life (*ming* 命) has no way of becoming an exemplary person *(chün tzu)*." It is Mencius, however, who gives this notion fuller expression when he claims:[41] "The myriad things are here in me *(wo* 我). There is no greater enjoyment than to realize cosmic integrity *(ch'eng* 誠) through introspection." What we are calling "objectification" and hence integration of self is captured perhaps most profoundly by Mencius when he is asked about his notion of "flood-like *ch'i*" *(hao-jan chih ch'i* 浩然之氣):[42]

> I am good in nurturing my flood-like *ch'i*. . . . This *ch'i* is ultimately vast and resilient. Where it is genuinely nurtured and is not obstructed, it will fill the cosmos. This is *ch'i* which weds *yi* 義 with the *tao* 道. Without these, it starves. It is born and grows out of accumulating *yi*, and is not obtainable where *yi* is in short measure. Where conduct fails to match up to one's natural mind, this *ch'i* will starve.

The personal self *(wo* 我) that discloses *yi* is exalted in that it is a self-realizing person-in-context. It is objectified in that, no longer asserting merely one limited perspective in its interpretation of experience, it does not make any final distinction between self and other in construing the world. To express this another way, the person-in-context understands "self" as a dynamic and changing focus of existence characteristically expanding and contracting over some aspect of the process of becoming, the interpretation of which is grounded in and involves reference to the environing whole. This contextual orientation of the *yi*-disclosing, realizing person is immediately evident in Mencius' assertion[43] that: "The heart-and-mind of shame *(hsiu* 羞) and disgrace *(wu* 惡) is the starting point of *yi*." "Shame" *(hsiu)* and "disgrace" *(wu)* are context-dependent in that they presuppose someone else's evaluation. They entail public evaluation of oneself as interpreted and considered from one's own perspective.

We have determined that *yi* is something exclusively human that has its origins in and defines the unique "exalted" or "realizing" self, and that informs human action in some positive, normative way. At its most fundamental level, *yi* denotes the importation of aesthetic, moral, and rational significance into personal action in the world. It is from this that the sense of *yi* as "meaning" or "significance" arises. A person, like a word, achieves meaning in the interplay between bestowing its own accumulated significance and appropriating meaning from its context.[44]

An examination of early Confucian philosophical literature would indicate that a personal contribution of *yi* is a necessary condition for meaningful action. All of the various modes of moral, aesthetic, and rational action are ultimately traceable to and dependent upon this personal disposition of *yi*. Confucius, for example, insists that *yi* is a precondition for courageous action (2/24): "To fail to do something when one sees that it is *yi* is to lack courage."[45] It is *yi* which must qualify all moral actions such that, for the exemplary moral person *(chün tzu)*, "*yi* is taken to be paramount" (17/23). Mencius echoes this commitment to *yi* in giving it categorial status:[46] "The great person does not necessarily have to live up to his word or see things through to completion. He only concerns himself with what is *yi*."

Of fundamental importance in this analysis of *yi* is that the person-in-context imports significance to the world. Given the contextualist cosmology in which this Confucian conception of the realizing person is grounded, it follows that matters of human conduct within the process of existence characteristically represent novel situations which require a person to bestow his *yi* in perpetually changing and ever-unique sets of circumstances. This would have to mean that no two personal investments of *yi* in the world are ever the same and, further, that attaining *yi* (*te-yi* 得義) must be characterized by a flexibility necessary for a person to interact with and integrate into ever new situations. Ch'en Ta-ch'i terms this flexibility *pu ku* 不固. It is a central theme in Confucius, emphatically underscoring the creative and novel dimensions of *yi*.[47]

Because of the non-fixed, multivalent nature of the person-in-context, the person's construal of *yi* cannot be solely a matter of applying some externally derived norm. On the contrary, this realizing person cannot surrender to some set of determining principles, but must rather exercise his own judgment creatively in response to the uniqueness of his situation: "But I [Confucius] am different from these in that I do not have presuppositions as to what may and may not be done" (18/8). The realizing person must impel himself on a course of conduct informed by and engaging his own sense of *yi* (4/10): "The exemplary person *(chün tzu)* in his activity in the world does not have things that he invariably does or does not do, but rather is committed to *yi*."[48]

From this discussion, it is clear that *yi* entails some unique personal contribution serving to define a human becoming. But this is not the whole of it. Given the interdependent relationship between integrated person and his environment, it must also be the case that his environment in some sense contributes to and determines his emergence as a person. This leads us to an important philological observation.

Throughout the early philosophical and philological literature, *yi* 義 is consistently defined in terms of its homophone, *yi** 宜, "right, proper, appropriate, suitable."[49] The two characters diverge, however, in that whereas *yi* denotes appropriateness to one's own person, *yi** refers to appropriateness to one's context.[50] *Yi* is the active and contributory integrating of self with circumstances, where the self originates unique activity and construes itself on its own terms in a novel and creative way. It is the articulation and contribution of the self to the organism. The character *yi**, on the other hand, denotes the yielding or giving up of oneself and "appropriating" meaning from the context or circumstances. Where the focus of *yi* is one's personal self (that is, *person*-in-context), the focus of *yi** is on the environment (that is, person-in-*context*); where *yi* is fundamentally self-assertive and meaning-bestowing, *yi** is self-sacrificing and meaning-deriving.[51]

It is because personal self in the bestowal of *yi* requires consideration for the appropriateness to context, *yi**, that one must remain flexible in his personal assertiveness. This prompts Confucius to say (15/16): "There is nothing that I can do for someone who is not constantly asking himself: 'What to do! What to do!' " The reason that a person must remain flexible and cannot be instructed specifically in what he ought or ought not do is that he is always called upon to exercise his own moral sense in the uniqueness of his situation.[52] Thus, Confucius as the "timely sage" is timely both in what he contributes to the situation and what he appropriates from his context.[53]

Another way in which *yi* and *yi** can be associated is in their overlapping connotations of "sacrifice." According to the *Erh Ya,* "before setting off to initiate some important affair or before mobilizing the people, one must first make observances at the Altar of the Soil, and this is called *yi*.*" *Yi,* on the other hand, is cognate with *hsi* 犧: "sacrificial animal, pure victim." The "meaning-bestowing" and "meaning-deriving" distinction that we want to claim for *yi* and *yi** is immediately present in the several connotations of sacrifice. *Hsi* as a sacrificial victim is obviously the contributory "offering" or "giving" side of sacrifice, while the *yi** performed at the Altar of the Earth preliminary to some grand undertaking would reflect a willingness "to yield" or "to relinquish" something of one's own ambitions and authority in an effort to derive meaning and find congruency with this broader context.

We have established that *yi* represents personal investment of meaning in the world. What it means to be human is contingent, being ever redefined by man himself in the emergence of new circumstances. Not only does *yi* distinguish certain actions as uniquely human, but a particular human action invested with and conditioned by *yi* is called *li* 禮 "proper form, moral conventions, ritual actions."

It is *yi* which renders *li* actions distinct from nonsignificant human activity. Such being the case, it is significant that the character *li* 禮, "ritual action," is often rendered "propriety," derived from the Latin, *proprius,* "one's own," and cognate with "property." That is, *yi* 義, "appropriateness of personal self to context," is related to *li* 禮, "ritual action," as the disposition of making the ritual action one's own and displaying oneself in that conduct. The *Tso-chuan* describes the process whereby only those actions characterized by *yi* are designated *li*:[54]

> Now, nominal distinctions are what delineate *yi*, doing *yi* is what gives rise to ritual actions *(li),* these ritual actions are what embody political order, and political order serves to make the people right in what they do.

The Tuan Yü-ts'ai commentary on the Shuo-wen also defines *yi* with reference to its expression in ritual action: "The basic meaning of *yi* is each person's achieving his appropriateness *(yi** 宜) in the performance of ritual actions *(li).* Where one does so, he is good (shan 善)." Ritual actions are intimately related to yi, those overt human actions which give expression to the personal disclosure of meaning. This is evident in the increasing popularity of the expression li-yi 禮義 after the death of Confucius. In Hsün Tzu, for example, more than a third of the occurrences of yi are in the binomial expression of li-yi.[55]

The association of ritual action (li) and yi has given rise to a confusion between these two concepts which, in obfuscating the contributory nature of yi, has robbed classical Confucianism of considerable profundity. The failure to distinguish clearly between ritual action (li) and yi, and the consequent failure to appreciate fully the concept of person as an original source of meaningful action, is not only characteristic of current conservative readings of Confucius but dates back at least as far as the earliest Taoists who condemned Confucianism for its demand that the human being conform to an imposed and unnatural order. It is only by clarifying the distinction between ritual action (li) and yi and recognizing the essential function of yi in Confucius' philosophical reflections that we can appreciate the extent to which misinterpretation has detracted from it.

Whatever the import of yi, it would seem that in preclassical society, the expression of it was very much an individual matter. The Mo Tzu describes this situation rather vividly:[56]

In antiquity at the dawn of human existence when there was as yet no law or political order, it is said that people had different yi. Thus, where there was one person, there was one yi, where there were two persons, there were two yi, and where there were ten persons, there were ten yi. In fact there were as many yi as there were people, and each approved of his own yi and disagreed with everyone else's. Thus arose disagreement among people.

From this beginning, and in the process of socialization, these individual expressions of meaningful action were knit into a somewhat constant, somewhat changing fabric of social, political, and cultural institutions called ritual action (li). These ritual actions are the repository of the yi that past generations have invested in the world. The Tso-chuan characterizes literary portions of this tradition in the following terms:[57]

The Book of Songs and the Book of Documents are the repositories of yi, ritual actions (li) and music are the patterns of particular potency *(te)*. And it is particular potency and *yi* that are the root of all human advantage.

As the encapsulated cultural insights embedded in and inherited out of the tradition, these ritual actions have several functions. First, these ritual actions have a pedagogical, heuristic importance. A person in learning and reflecting upon these ritual actions seeks in them the *yi* contributed by his precursors, and in so doing, stimulates, develops, and refines his own sensitivities. Not only does a person perform ritual actions, but in the sense that ritual action evokes a certain kind of response, the ritual action can be said to "perform" or "accomplish" the person. As received wisdom, ritual actions are normative to the extent that they are counsel for the person living in the present, but are empirical in that what is appropriated requires one's own judgment.

The normative force of ritual actions gives rise to frequently encountered expressions such as "following or moving to *yi*" (*hsi yi* 徒義),[58] "prevailing *yi*" (*t'ung yi* 通義),[59] and the metaphor "road" (*lu* 路) often used in referring to *yi*.[60] The use of such expressions of course fuels the interpretation of *yi* as a normative principle or standard with which one must put oneself in accord in order to be moral. While the invested *yi* of past generations is impressed on the inherited cultural tradition and is a rich resource for the person who would cultivate himself, it is still incumbent upon this person to engage his own *yi* in evaluating and appropriating from his inheritance, and to contribute his own *yi* to the development and enrichment of this tradition. This is perhaps Mencius' distinction in saying:[61]

> Shun understood the way of things and had a keen insight into human relations. His actions proceeded *from* authoritative personhood *(jen*)* and *yi*. He did not simply act out his authoritative personhood and *yi*.

Yi can certainly be interpreted as a "road," but as Confucius states (15/29): "It is the human being who is able to extend the Way, not the Way that is able to extend the human being." Any interpretation of *yi* which exaggerates its normative force at the expense of its essential empirical aspect would reinforce the perception of Confucius' thought as a conservative, order-imposing philosophical system.

A second function of the ritual actions is their role as a formal apparatus for achieving and displaying one's *yi*. These ritual actions lack any real significance when they consist merely in baldly imitating the actions of others. It is ritual actions personalized so as to disclose oneself which constitute truly meaningful human activity.[62] Ritual actions achieve significance to the extent that the person, stimulated by the import given these actions in the tradition, infuses them with his own commitment. Of fundamental importance here is the primary role of the particular human being as the ultimate source and maker of meaningful action.

This leads to the third function of ritual action, a vehicle for reifying the creative insights of the self-cultivating person. This person is counseled by his tradition, but must evaluate and alter this tradition in pursuit of appropriateness. We must hasten to qualify this creative function of ritual action by underscoring the extent to which deference is paid to the inherited tradition. Below we shall suggest, in fact, that the respect shown this tradition might constitute an alternative form of religiousness. Even so, the changes that the person might introduce and the novelty that he might contribute to the tradition is couched in the currency of formalized actions. That is to say, new ritual actions are the reification of personal creativity that issues forth in the expression of *yi*.

Stressing the holistic nature of ritual action (*li* 禮), the cognate character, "body" (*t'i* 體), also reflects an intimate and important relationship with *yi* in that this can be interpreted as a physical rendering of meaning and value. By investigating and evaluating the physical dispositions inherited in the tradition, a person stimulates and refines his own sense of what is physically right, and can appropriate it for himself. At the same time, his own selection and embellishment of the physical constitutes a reformation and refinement of the tradition. Thus, the body, as a repository of *yi*, also has its heuristic function. And the body, like ritual action, is a formal apparatus for actualizing and displaying meaning and value. Physical dispositions communicate moral, rational, aesthetic, and religious sensitivities and commitments in their engagement with the world.

Finally, just as the ritual actions inherited from the traditions require appropriation and creative elaboration, so the inherited physical disposition is not definitive, but an achievement informed by the insights of those who have gone before. It is malleable—wax into which one's novelty can be impressed.

The foregoing philological and semantic analysis suggests a number of insights for interpreting Confucian philosophy. Among the more significant: First, the organic unity of heaven, earth, and man in Confucius' thought entails the strict immanence of rules and principles, and thereby precludes the use of any language of transcendence as a means of characterizing the significance of *yi*. Secondly, the necessity of explicating *yi* by recourse to notions of creativity, spontaneity, and context-dependence requires that a language of events rather than one of substances be employed. The necessity to eschew both the language of transcendence and that of substance in the interpretation of *yi* presents the philosopher with peculiar difficulties if he seeks to render Confucian insights in traditional Western categories, since overwhelmingly these Western categories are rooted in and have grown out of firmly held assumptions which require precisely such language. Both the inappropriateness of such philosophical language and the extreme difficulty of avoiding its use will be illustrated below with reference to three recent interpretations of the notion of *yi*.

One of the significant aspects of *yi* highlighted above is that it has ethically normative force. It is natural enough for philosophers employing Western philosophic vocabularies to characterize this normative forcefulness in terms of "principles." More often than not, this entails the assumption, tacit or explicit, that such principles are transcendently grounded.

In his interpretation of *yi*, Cheng Chung-ying seems to adumbrate some of the dimensions of our analysis of the meaning and function of *yi*. Cheng's uncritical resort to classical Western metaphysical language, however, reduces the value of some of his most important insights. Thus, he claims "*Yi* . . . determines the total significance of one's life and activities," and "*Yi* is a universal and total principle which applies to every particular case of judging the worthiness or unworthiness of an action."[63] Defining *yi* as "a universal and total principle" and employing language such as *"Yi determines"* and *"Yi applies"* to every particular case" suggests that *yi* is a standard of decision making or of conduct which exists in some sense prior to the decision or action that expresses *yi*. The evidence and arguments presented above challenge just such an interpretation.

Yi cannot be a principle in any of the classical Western senses of that term. *Yi* is context-dependent and hence comes into being with its context. It involves acts of signification which require more than the application of an antecedently existing meaning to an action or state of affairs. These acts of signification are meaning-disclosing actions that "extend the Way." *Yi* is thus intrinsically intertwined with the particular circumstances within which it is realized.

Yi has normative force without itself actually constituting a norm. The actions that realize *yi* are not performed in accordance with strict guidelines. Such actions are, at least to some degree, spontaneous, novel, and creative. This means that *yi* is as much the consequence of a particular decision or action as its cause. The normative force of *yi* exists in spite of its inchoate character at the beginning of *yi* acts. The articulation of *yi* with respect to a given situation involves the emerging awareness of what is or is not appropriate in that situation and how one might act so as to realize this appropriateness in its highest degree. This articulation occurs *pari passu* with the act itself. Neither determined nor determining, *yi* is actualized in the interplay between decision and circumstance; in this manner it achieves its appropriateness.

In the introductory essay to his translation of the *Analects*, D. C. Lau employs the distinction between agents and acts in an attempt to clarify the meaning of *yi*. Claiming that, whereas benevolence *(jen*)* is more a quality of agents than of acts, the reverse is true of *yi*:[64]

> Rightness *(yi)* is basically a characteristic of acts, and its application to agents is derivative. A man is righteous only in so far as he consistently does what is right. The rightness of acts depends upon their being morally fitting in the circumstances and has little to do with the disposition or motive of the agent.

In the light of our remarks on the mutuality of agency and act, it should be clear precisely why this sort of characterization of *yi* is misconceived. If *yi* is only derivately applicable to the person performing such *yi* acts, then any transforming effect of *yi* upon the person seems to be denied. Thus the consistently right actions performed by an individual, which lead to his being designated as righteous, are then in no real sense internal to the person. This makes *yi* an external, wholly objective measure by which actions are assessed. To whatever extent *yi* can be said to be characteristic of human conduct, its source clearly lies elsewhere. Such an analysis of *yi* leads directly to the separation of the dispositional, meaning-disclosing dimensions of moral activity from a person's actions. Far better to say, apropos the statement of Lau just quoted, *yi* actions render the person himself "morally fitting" and such actions performed with consistency make a person righteous by making him a consistent source of harmonious behavior. This mutuality of agent and act makes Lau's distinction unprofitable.

Closely allied to the distinction between agency and acts is Lau's employment of the distinction between ethical rules and ethical principles. Lau uses this contrast to organize his discussion of the relations between "rites" *(li)* and rightness *(yi)*. Ritual actions *(li)* as rules of behavior are to be judged in accordance with the standard of *yi*. *Yi* is thus a principle implemented by ritual actions *(li)* functioning as rules. The principle of rightness assesses the viability of the rules of ritual actions *(li)*. Such a distinction, which separates *yi* as a principle from the rules that seek to implement it, is as troublesome as the distinction between agency and acts. A person does fulfill himself at any given moment through ritual actions *(li)* performed with *yi*, just as Lau wishes to indicate. However, such actions are not *yi* simply because they conform to ritual actions *(li)*, nor are they *yi* because they conform to a principle of rightness instanced by ritual actions *(li)*. In other words, the referent of *yi* is not solely an "appropriate" principle expressed by a given *li*, nor is it to *yi* itself as the ultimate standard of conduct. For Confucius, the primary referent of *yi* is to the process comprised by the harmony of action and circumstance which constitutes the righteous person in the moment of realizing *yi*.

It would be quite misleading to speak of the moral person as one who conforms to a context simply by acting in accordance with a standard of *yi*. There is no principle of *yi* existing apart from persons-in-context. The appropriateness of ritual actions cannot be decided by comparing present rites with an intuition of *yi* as a standard or principle that subsequently can be employed as a criterion for discarding or maintaining these rituals. The person becomes *yi* in those contexts associated with his *yi* acts. And his decision concerning the appropriateness of present rites is itself always contextual and circumstantial.

Discussing Confucius' concept of *yi* by reference to distinctions between agency and acts and between rules and principles is misleading since it cannot but suggest that there are objective principles in accordance with which one can construct relevant ritual actions. Such a presumption would require ethical deliberations that could only find their justification in the context of a general theory. Different kinds of biases expressing themselves in different types of ethical reflection must lead to a plethora of ethical theories. In this way there is little hope that one may avoid either a conservative dogmatism that rejects alternative theories in favor of a single "correct" theory, or the skeptical relativism that arises from the inability to decide which theory is most adequate. This kind of ethical theory, with its arguments between absolutism and relativism, while familiar to us in our own tradition, is absent in Confucius. Within the bounds of traditional Confucianism, however, conservative interpretations such as that of Hsün Tzu have tended to read Confucius as theoretical and systematic, and have encouraged the development of an ethical dogmatism.

For Confucius himself, the process of forming an ethical vision bears little relation to the rationalization process described above. He does not search for principles that overarch the various rule-regulated contexts in human society. Instead he asks that one should remain open to the experience of authoritative humanity *(jen*)*; one must be sensitive to the manner in which such humaneness depends upon actualizing the self-in-the-moment at the intersection of action and circumstance, the harmony of which depends upon and is an expression of *yi*. Performing ritual actions with *yi* leads to this harmony, and in so doing, permits the expression of authoritative humanity through ritual action *(li)*. However, we must be careful in fleshing out these purely conceptual distinctions to avoid recourse to means/ends, method/goal categories. We can, for example, quite legitimately describe "authoritative humanity" *(jen*)* as a goal effected through meaningful and appropriate *(yi)* action. But we can equally well describe the significance and appropriateness of the *yi* action as the goal, and "authoritative person-ing" *(jen*)* as the means of attaining it. In this project we are burdened with the presuppositions of substance language.

The apparent strangeness of the language necessary for a more faithful characterization of *yi* is also due to the fact that, for Confucius, "rightness" has a distinctly aesthetic connotation. Perhaps the readiest illustration of the ethically normative force associated with *yi* is to be found in the "urge to create" experienced by the poet or painter. The artist does not have a created product in mind, nor is he usually at his creative best when acting in accordance with a plan. What has normative force for the artist is precisely that which achieves articulated presence at the culmination of aesthetic achievement. Only then is the meaning of the creation fully disclosed. This disclosure is felt as a sense of the rightness of the completed creation. An act of aesthetic creativity is achieved when, for the first time, its meaning stands forth. In our subsequent discussion of the Confucian project of becoming a sage, we shall have frequent occasion to revisit the aesthetic experience as the most illuminating model for thinking through the subtleties of his philosophical insights.

The event ontology that is presupposed in our analysis requires that we not consider *yi* as a static "virtue," but as dispositional. *Yi* involves persons disposing themselves in this or that manner within particular contexts. Thus *yi*, in so far as it involves acts of signification, means that persons dispose themselves in such a way as to insure the disclosure of appropriate meanings. Such disclosures of meaning arising from *yi* acts serve as both cause and consequence of the maintenance of harmony within a social context. As indicated above, meaning is disclosed in two directions. From those situations that call for a high degree of deference or acceptance, meaning is derived. On the other hand, those circumstances that call for positive actions which create novel situations require that meaning be bestowed. The objective in either case is the harmonious order occasioned by appropriate action and its attendant enjoyment. It is absolutely essential that we understand what such order entails.

Yi cannot be associated with the sort of order achieved by the imposition of antecedently existing patterns upon events, for *yi* acts involve the deriving or bestowing of meaning in such a way as to realize novel patterns uniquely suited to each concrete circumstance. Although this is more obviously the case in bestowing meaning, it is equally true in those cases where meaning is derived. For deriving meaning, if it is an *yi* act, is an act of appropriation constituting a novel instance of propriety which is, in a very real sense, unrepeatable.

To claim that *yi* acts are meaning-disclosing and thereby productive of a harmonious social order is only to say that they are creative actions. With a clear understanding of the fundamental meanings of creativity and order, it is possible to grasp the distinctive character of the moral person entailed by our analysis of *yi*.[65] The intrinsic relationship between the agent and his act enables the characterization of the ethical individual and his actions as co-creative foci of an ellipse defining the contours of the person in his truest sense. There is certainly a sense in which the agent authors his act. But it is only apparently paradoxical to state that the act authors the agent, as well.

Yao and Shun, and the Duke of Chou, are known through their deeds. They serve as models of *yi* by virtue of their deeds. Their persistent presence in the Chinese tradition is due to belief in the rightness of their actions. In fact, allusions to historical figures are more often than not allusions to specific acts as concrete instances of right behavior. And we can frequently observe a movement from allusion to attribution such that the historical figure and his repertoire of acts are recreated for subsequent generations. Neither the individual nor his action may be held in isolation one from the other, however. We model our actions upon the person who is constituted by both his agency and the act in which it culminates. The sage-kings and Confucius himself serve as models of *yi* because of the presumedly high degree of consistency with which they realized *yi* in their individual acts. They are thus authored by their deeds as well as being authors of them.

This may seem truistic, of course, unless one reflects upon the very real differences that exist between concepts of the person in traditional as opposed to relatively nontraditional societies. In societies that celebrate the heroic deeds of individuals as determinative of greatness, it is important that the individual be credited as author of his deed. In such contexts history is literally made by exceptional personages. In more traditional societies such as that of classical China, custom has a givenness that is resistent to the isolation of creators and innovators. Confucius' own claim that he was a transmitter of tradition rather than an originator is illustrative of this view of the relation of the person to his cultural context.

Among contemporary interpreters of Confucius it is perhaps Herbert Fingarette who has best appreciated the central character of custom and tradition in Confucian thought. This fact is quite surprising if one notes that he does not discuss the concept of *yi* at all in his small book and several articles on Confucius. Though clearly in sympathy with the sort of understanding of Confucius and Confucian thought that emerges from taking the concept of *yi* seriously, Fingarette does not seem to believe it essential to employ this concept in any explicit sense. By ignoring *yi* he has been forced to interpret authoritative humanity *(jen*)* and its relations with ritual action *(li)* in such a way as to overwork and thereby render equivocal these admittedly central notions.

Fingarette's very sensitive analysis of the philosophy of Confucius is organized around his discussions of this relationship between authoritative humanity *(jen*)* and ritual actions or rites *(li)*. Rites, the forms through which authoritative humanity is expressed, are seen as those "intelligent conventions" which distinguish the peculiarly human realm from the bestial and the inanimate and which illustrate "intrinsic harmony, beauty and sacredness." These intelligent conventions

> cannot be invented and accepted en bloc; they rest primarily on the inheritance by each age of a vast body of conventional language and practices from the preceding age. . . . The ultimate solemnity of which rite is capable, the deep, archaic response it evokes in man's soul is never present in so far as any pattern of conduct or gesture is felt as new, invented, or utilitarian.[66]

Thus the distinctly human realm is constituted by the ritualistic celebration of certain conventional practices grounded in tradition. These practices derive their authority from a sense of the sacredness of the inherited past.

This understanding of Confucius' insight into the stabilizing and harmonizing function of ritual actions permits Fingarette to argue for the origin of rites in inherited tradition rather than in either of two principal alternatives—command or consensus. Whatever his power and prestige, the Emperor cannot establish ritual actions in an ad hoc manner. Neither can ritual actions be established by the people through rational consensus. Ritual actions have their origin in the givenness of tradition. And this means that neither the specific origin of a particular rite nor its "rational" significance is of ultimate importance. In societies less oriented toward tradition, events and institutions are rational or rationalizable in the sense that originating causes are sought for any significant practice or institution. Quite the reverse is true of tradition-oriented societies: it is likely to be impossible to trace the historical origin of this or that tradition or rite, but the rationality of the whole complex may well be defined in terms of societal stability.

Understanding Fingarette's somewhat bewildering silence concerning *yi* in his interpretation of Confucius requires a consideration of his views on ritual actions and tradition. Given his views concerning the nonrationalizable character of *li*, Fingarette does not deem it appropriate, or even possible, to discover the origin of any given ritual action or its mode of alteration. And it is precisely with regard to these issues that *yi* is most obviously relevant. Indeed, understanding the importance of *yi* in the performance of traditional rites depends upon the sense of *yi* as the capacity to originate and/or alter ritual actions.

The most profound illustration of *yi* involves the establishment of ritual actions. As Fingarette himself notes, ritual actions are conventions; as such they must have a human origin. The fact that the origin of any particular ritual action is not traceable to this or that individual does not mean that the sources of ritual actions themselves are, in principle, different from the sources of the performance of these ritual actions—namely, personal *yi* acts. That we cannot trace the exact origins of *li* is due less to any inherent mysteriousness of tradition and more a function of the deemphasis upon the ego-self and the recognition of the person as context-dependent. Given that a person is as truly authored by *yi* acts as he is author of them, the question of the origin of this or that rite is of little intrinsic interest. Nonetheless, it is *yi* acts that establish ritual actions. To say otherwise is to be forced into searching for a transcendent origin for *yi* (which is, of course, wrongheaded) or to claim that ritual actions have an impersonal origin. This latter is Fingarette's claim. And, as he says, "the only candidates for an impersonal standard are tradition or a

Divine Command."[67] Finding the latter inappropriate, Fingarette discovers the "impersonal standard" in tradition.

Clearly there is a serious ambiguity in Fingarette's claim that the "intelligent conventions" which make us distinctly human have an impersonal origin. Far better to claim that the ritual actions inherited from tradition have their (for the most part untraceable) origins in *yi* acts, the very sort of acts which make us persons in the truest sense. The persistence of ritual actions through their continued inheritance from the past is an argument in favor of their continued viability as models and vessels for *yi* acts. But the persistence of ritual actions cannot in itself guarantee such viability.

Fingarette's interpretation does not give an adequate account of that personal creativity necessary to overcome the inertia of the past. Without personal creativity, ritual actions are reduced to the blind compulsion of repetition and continuity. This bondage to empty forms, far from enlivening persons, dictates the performance of meaningless actions as parodies of true rites. Fingarette is correct in claiming that tradition is the source of ritual actions. But it cannot be an impersonal source if it is to constitute a continuing impetus for the realization of social harmony. Understanding ritual actions explicitly as having their origin in *yi* acts permits insight into the importance of tradition as an (inter)personal source of harmonious relations in the social realm.

We said that, in addition to the pedagogical function of *li* and their function as formal means for displaying *yi*, they should be understood as the consequence of personal creativity expressed through *yi*. Understood in this manner, the concept of *yi* not only insures the personal investment of meaning in tradition, but it prevents agreement with any interpretation of Confucius which, like Fingarette's, would suggest that tradition could contain a single set of meanings articulated in accordance with a relatively unchanging set of ritual actions. Originating ritual actions through *yi* is the model for subsequent *yi* acts.

One might object that stressing to such a degree the function of *yi* in establishing ritual actions renders incomprehensible Confucius' concern to promote a coherent set of rituals, grounded upon tradition, as a context for human experience. But all our interpretation requires is recognition that the primary meaning of *yi* acts lies in their function of establishing ritual actions. That of course is *not* to say that establishing ritual actions is the most frequently illustrated function of *yi*. On the contrary, such novelty can only be appreciated against the continuity which long-established ritual conduct provides the tradition. Our concern is to suggest that formally recognized, socially sanctioned ritual actions are not the *only* shape that meaning takes in the public realm. One obviously may be presented with situations for which no ritual actions are specifically relevant. And, although the greatest number of *yi* acts that extend the way of mankind are novel realizations that accord with already established ritual actions, acts of signification which contribute to the establishment of new ritual actions cannot be ignored.

The concept of *yi*, so interpreted, adds a dimension to traditional understandings of Confucius that allows us to see him as something other than a rigid conservative. It enables us to put his formal commitments in some proper perspective. The foregoing analysis of *yi* precludes any particular set of ritual actions from functioning as an uncriticized source of human conduct. As the uneven history of Confucianism in China so well illustrates, when the inertia of formalized conducts is left unchallenged by spontaneous and creative actions which introduce appropriate novelties into the social world, the result is rigid and dogmatic moralisms. We have attempted to demonstrate that Confucius, as opposed to many of the Confucians, was on the side of *yi*, and in so taking his stand, articulated a most profound insight into the meaning and consequences of the process of becoming fully human.

3   The Authoritative Person

3.1   Jen* 仁 *as Authoritative Person*

We have above described the dynamics of ritual action (*li* 禮) and *yi* 義 in the production of the cultural tradition. In so doing, we have simply transliterated *yi* to avoid prejudicing our exploration and reconstruction of this very complex concept. At this point we are ready to suggest that *yi*, an investment of importance which is always personal and always communal, might tentatively be rendered "significating." The final concept that we are concerned to analyze in this chapter on personal articulation is the product and goal of this movement between ritual action *(li)* and significating *(yi)*, that is, the embodiment of the cultural tradition as authoritative person (*jen** 仁).

Whatever *jen** might mean for Confucius, several things can be said about it with reasonable certainty. First, it has a central role in the *Analects*, occurring some 105 times in fifty-eight of the 499 passages included in that text.[68] Followers ask Confucius specifically about this concept more than any other. Prior to Confucius it seems to have been a relatively unimportant term. Few instances of *jen** occur in the pre-*Analects* literature. *Jen** as found in the *Analects* has a richness and prominence that seems to depart significantly from its earlier usages.[69]

Although scholars generally agree in identifying *jen** as a central, if not *the* central, concept in Confucian philosophy, it is not unusual to find them pursuing their various analyses with trepidation, ruing that *"jen* is surrounded with paradox and mystery in the *Analects,"*[70] and that *"jen*, in the *Analects*, appears to be discouragingly complex."[71] While commentators despair in their attempts to focus in on the meaning of *jen**, this is certainly not because Confucius was being purposely obscure, as Tu Wei-ming points out:[72]

> It should be noted from the outset that the lack of a definitional statement about what *jen* is in itself in the *Analects* must not be construed as the Master's deliberate heuristic device to hide an eso- teric truth from his students: "My friends, I know that you think that there is something I am keeping from you. There is nothing at all that I keep from you. There is nothing that I do which is not shown to you, my friends" (7/23). On the contrary, Confucius seems absolutely serious in his endeavor to transmit the true sense of *jen*, as he understood and experienced it, to his students.

W. T. Chan, in his analysis of *jen**, argues that Confucius was the first to conceive of *jen** as general virtue.[73] That is, prior to Confucius, the Chinese tradition did not have a general, universal virtue under which all particular virtues could be subsumed. Con- fucius, in developing *jen** as this comprehensive virtue, established a ground that provided classical Chinese ethical theory with unity, consistency, and coherence. Much of the problem in interpreting the *Analects*, according to Chan, arises from the fact that *jen** is at times used in its pre-Confucian "particularistic" sense, and at other times used as general virtue.

Tu Wei-ming has been inclined to follow Chan in reading *jen**
as some inner character or virtue:[74]

> *Jen* is not primarily a concept of human relations, although they are
> extremely crucial to it. It is rather a principle of inwardness. By "in-
> wardness," it is meant that *jen* is not a quality acquired from out-
> side; it is not a product of biological, social or political forces. . . .
> Hence, *jen* as an inner morality is not caused by the *li* from outside.
> It is a higher-order concept which gives meaning to *li*. *Jen* in this
> sense is basically linked with the self-receiving, self-perfecting, and
> self-fulfilling process of an individual.

In his more recent work, Tu elaborates on his interpretation of *jen**,
describing it as: "a matter of inner strength and self-knowledge,
symbolizing an inexhaustible source for creative communal expression."[75]

Herbert Fingarette, in his interpretation of *jen**, is adamant in
rejecting what he perceives to be this unfortunate psychologizing of
this term. Among English language commentators, *jen** is variously
translated as "benevolence," "love," "agapé," "altruism," "kindness,"
"charity," "compassion," "magnanimity," "perfect virtue," "goodness," "human-heartedness," and "humanity." As these renderings
clearly indicate, Fingarette is right in suggesting that there has been
a tendency for scholars to "psychologize" *jen** as a "subjective"
feeling made manifest in "objective" social norms or mores which
we submit to or come into accord with in ritual conduct. *Jen** has
for the most part been interpreted as psychological dispositions of
which ritual actions are overt physical demonstrations. Fingarette
cautions us against this kind of reductionism:[76]

> *Jen* seems to emphasize the individual, the subjective, the character,
> feelings and attitude; it seems, in short, a psychological notion. The
> problem of interpreting *jen* thus becomes particularly acute if one
> thinks, as I do, that it is of the essence of the *Analects* that the
> thought expressed in it is not based on psychological notions. And,
> indeed, one of the chief results of the present analysis of *jen* will be
> to reveal how Confucius could handle in a nonpsychological way
> basic issues which we in the West naturally cast in psychological
> terms. . . The move from *jen* as referring us to a person on to *jen*
> as "therefore" referring us to his inner mental or psychic condition
> or process finds no parallel in the *Analects*.

Fingarette takes considerable pains to disassociate his interpretation of *jen** from its more conventional definition as an inner spiritual/moral condition:[77]

> We are tempted to go further than I have above and to say *jen* refers to the attitudes, feelings, wishes and will. This terminology is misleading. The thing we must *not* do is to psychologize Confucius' terminology in the *Analects*. The first step in seeing that this is so is to recognize that *jen* and its associated "virtues," and *li* too, are not connected in the original text with the language of "will," "emotion" and "inner states." . . . I must emphasize that my point here is not that Confucius's words are intended to exclude reference to the inner psyche. He could have done this if he had had such a basic metaphor in mind, had seen its plausibility, but on reflection had decided to reject it. But this is not what I am arguing here. My thesis is that the entire notion never entered his head. The metaphor of an inner psychic life, in all of its ramifications so familiar to us, simply isn't present in the *Analects*, not even as a rejected possibility.

Fingarette, as a corrective against the psychological, "inner" interpretation of *jen**, argues for what amounts to be an "outer" reading in which "*jen** is the aspect of conduct that directs our attention to the particular person and his orientation as the actor."[78] That is, *jen** is action: "*Li* and *jen* are two aspects of the same thing. Each points to an aspect of the action of man in his distinctively human role."[79]

We would argue that these disparate "inner" and "outer" interpretations of *jen** represented by Chan and Tu on one side and Fingarette on the other are an impoverishment of this concept. Not enough attention is paid to the term itself. As Peter Boodberg has observed:[80]

> *Jen* 仁, "humanity," is not only a derivative, but is actually the same word, though in a distinct graphic form, as the common vocable *jen** 人, "man," *homo*. That is no mere pun, as Professor Dubs believes; the consubstantiality of the two terms is part and parcel of the fundamental stratum of Chinese linguistic consciousness, and must be reflected somehow in the Occidental translation.

The important point that Boodberg is making here is that we must give more attention to the common definition of *jen** as "person" found in Confucian texts: the *Mencius* and the *Chung-yung*, for example, state explicitly, "*Jen** means 'person.'"[81] If *jen** 仁 and *jen* 人 both mean "person," it follows that the distinction between these two terms must be qualitative: two distinguishable degrees of what it means to be a person. This same kind of distinction is captured in the familiar kind of expression: "There are persons and there are *persons.*"

That *jen** refers to an achieved state of humanity manifested as a signatory feature of all one's behaviors, and identified as a source of admiration from and inspiration for one's community is expressed metaphorically in a passage from the *Analects* (6/23) cited above in our discussion of *chih* 知 (realizing):

> Those who realize the world [that is, the wise] enjoy water; those who have authoritative humanity (*jen**) enjoy mountains. Those who realize the world are active; those who are authoritative as persons are still. Those who realize the world find enjoyment; those who are authoritative as persons are long-lived.

The prominence and visibility of the authoritative person is necessary to continue and foster those meaningful activities that are constitutive of society (15/23): "Where one realizes (*chih*) something but his authoritative humanity (*jen**) is not such that he can sustain it, even though he has it, he is certain to lose it. . . ." But this description of *jen** as solely the quality of a person can be misleading.

Boodberg, in his analysis of *jen**, goes on to register a second feature of this term:[82] "It must be observed in addition that the term *jen** in Confucian texts is used not only as a noun and an adjective, but also as a transitive verb. . . ." That is, *jen** should be regarded as a qualitative transformation of person which embraces not only the achieved person, but also the process whereby this quality of humanity is realized. This definition of *jen** as the process of human realization is found specifically in the early Confucian literature:[83] "The realization of oneself is called *jen**."

3.2 Jen* 仁 *and Person Making*

If *jen** is in fact a process term denoting qualitative transformation of the person and achievement of authoritative humanity, the seeming

ambiguity surrounding it is at least partially explicable. First, the
holistic concept "person" is so complex and can be approached on
so many levels that any assertion about it is necessarily only partial
and hence can easily give rise to distortion and even contradiction.
Second, since "person" (like all such generic categories) violates the
principle that all particulars are sui generis, whatever is asserted is
not necessarily true in all cases, and must be explained relative to
concrete conditions. That is, what might be *jen** under one set of
circumstances is not necessarily *jen** under another. And for each
unique person the way of achieving humanity is necessarily going
to be different. Third, Confucius in stating that "it is the human
being who is able to extend the Way" (15/29) indicates clearly that
"person" is self-defining. Since as we have seen, Confucius' philosophical orientation does not tolerate a strict agent/act distinction,
"jen*" is a process term that has no specific *terminus ad quem*. The
authoritative person is perpetually self-surpassing, to be evaluated
in open-ended, qualitative, terms rather than in terms of "completion"
or "fulfillment." As such, the achievement of authoritative humanity
is a "fiction"—like the Nietzschean *Uebermensch*—which is approx-
imated in the "doing," and at the same time, lies forever beyond
one's grasp. Finally, Confucius' interpretation of personhood as pro-
cessual requires that the past be constantly recast in the present.
Historical influence is bidirectional as is evidenced in Confucius
himself; not only does a person's influence in the world continue as
the past gives birth to the present, but also the historical past is
being revised and reshaped by the continual introduction of new
perspective. As the significance of Confucius' own speeches and
actions continues to swell with the passage of time, his project of
attaining authoritative humanity remains profoundly open and transitive.

We have argued that *jen** is the same term as "person" (*jen* 人),
but reflecting a degree of qualitative achievement. The difference in
the graphic form representing this qualitative achievement is the
simple yet significant addition of the numeral, "two" (*erh* 二). The
implications of this symbolic amplification are several.

Jen* is fundamentally an integrative process. It is the transformation of self: the disciplining of the "small man" (*hsiao jen* 小人),
with his disintegrative preoccupations with selfish advantage, towards
the sensibilities of the profoundly relational person. The fact that

"two" is attached to the notion of "human being" would indicate that authoritative humanity is attainable only in a communal context through interpersonal exchange. Confucius is adamant that qualitative development of the human being is only possible in a human world (18/6): "We cannot commune with the birds and beasts. Am I not one among the people of this world? If not them, with whom should I associate?"[84] Confucius' disciple, Tzu-lu, goes on to insist that personhood must be pursued in a social environment in which one has the occasion to express that which is most essentially human: "signification" (yi 義) (18/7):

> To refuse office is to withhold one's contribution of significance (yi). The appropriate distinction between young and old cannot be abandoned. How could one think of abandoning the appropriate relationship between ruler and subject? This is to throw the most important human relationships into turmoil in one's desire to remain personally untarnished. The exemplary person's opportunity to serve in office is the occasion for him to effect what he judges important and appropriate.

The force of this emphasis on interpersonal action is captured in what D. C. Lau rightly calls the "methodology of jen 仁": altruism (shu 恕).[85]

> Shu is the method of discovering what other people wish or do not wish done to them. The method consists in taking oneself—"what is near at hand"—as an analogy and asking oneself what one would like or dislike were one in the position of the person at the receiving end.

This intimate relationship between authoritative humanity (jen* 仁) and what Lau translates as "altruism," shu 恕, is underscored by the classical lexicons which repeatedly define shu specifically as "jen*."[86]

Fingarette refines this sense of "analogy" by underscoring the fact that in the process of extending oneself into the circumstances of another, one retains his own cultivated judgment.[87] It is not simply abandoning one's own person in assuming the persona of another; rather, it is projecting oneself personally into the circumstances of another, and responding to those circumstances as one deems most appropriate. One acts by extending the perimeter and the parameters of one's own person to embrace the defining conditions, perceived attitudes, and the background of the other person in order to effectively become "two" perspectives grounded in one judgment. Further, this one judgment is continually conditioned and refined by the relationship between it and the changing circumstances with which it is engaged.

The fact that in *jen** actions one always retains one's own cultivated judgment and one's own values is easily lost in those interpretations of Confucius in which *shu* is rendered "altruism," for such interpretations emphasize the "disciplining oneself" (*k'o-chi* 克己) aspect of this methodology by interpreting it as "overcoming oneself." Confucius does insist that the dissolution of the limiting ego-self is a necessary precondition for *jen** action[88] and rejects the pursuit of ego-grounded interests (*li** 利) as the unworthy concern of the "retarded individual" (*hsiao jen* 小人).[89] But Confucius regards the disciplining of the ego-self as preliminary to the extension of one's range of concern and the appropriate application of one's own intentionality to this broader context. The ego-grounded individual, like the authoritative person, pursues the good; the difference lies in that the authoritative person exercises himself in seeking a general good that evidences a concern for the widest possible range of interests. Although the authoritative person is distinguished by a general regard for the interests of others, this concern falls far short of self-effacement. As *Mencius* observes:[90]

> The authoritative person is like an archer. The archer shoots only after having set himself properly. When he misses the target, far from resenting those who have bettered him, he turns inward to examine himself.

That is, although *jen** conduct is generally directed "outward," the ground of this action is always one's own sense of significance and appropriateness (*yi* 義).

In explaining the dynamics of person-making, Tung Chung-shu despairs that people have a tendency to reverse the function of *jen** and *yi*, wrongly interpreting *yi* as a means of projecting oneself outward as a standard on which to evaluate others, and *jen** as a way of bringing others in to make much of oneself. In fact,[91]

the difference between *yi* 義 and *jen** 仁 is that while *jen** is out-
ward-directed, *yi* means proceeding inward; while *jen** emphasizes
what is distant, *yi* stresses what is close at hand; while love invested
in others is *jen**, being appropriate to one's achieved personhood is
yi; the focus of *jen** is mainly on others while that of *yi* is one's
person.

The process of person making entails both the taking in of other
selves to build a self, and the application of one's own personal
judgment *(yi)*. And personal judgment is refined and developed in
the process of appropriating the meanings and values of other persons
and taking them in as one's own.

The process of person making entails inner- and outer-direct-
edness. In this process one both influences one's environing others
and is influenced by them. As we noted above, the social psychologist
George Herbert Mead often employs language which is helpful in
interpreting Confucius' understanding of person making. For example,
Mead argues:[92]

> The organized structure of every individual self within the human
> social process of experience and behavior reflects, and is constituted
> by, the organized relational pattern of that process as a whole; but
> each individual self-structure reflects, and is constituted by, a differ-
> ent aspect or perspective of this relational pattern from its own
> unique standpoint.
> The response of the "I" involves adaptation, but an adaptation
> which affects not only the self but also the social environment which
> helps to constitute the self; that is, it implies a view of evolution in
> which the individual affects its own environment as well as being
> affected by it.

Wayne C. Booth describes interpersonal "self-building" with a
vocabulary that highlights certain implications of Mead's concept of
the self:[93] "What an adult man or woman is, in all societies, is in
large degree what other men and women have created through
symbolic exchange. Each of us 'takes in' other selves to build a self."
The self, for this disciple of Mead, is thus a "field of selves" that
results from taking in other selves and making them a part of our
communal self. Self-articulation is a process in which a field of selves
is constituted by a confluence of historical and contemporary selves

reified in the formal structures of tradition and engaged through social interactions.

Reflecting on the human being as a focus of meaning unbounded by a notion of discrete and discontinuous selfhood, person is then an indivisible continuum between "self" and "other," between "I" and "we," between "subject" and "object," between "now" and "then." The boundaries between psychology and sociology,[94] between ethics and politics become vague. The importance and influence of a person becomes measurable in terms of the extension into and integration with the selves of others. That is, a person is meaningful and valuable as a function of his participation in the field of selves that constitutes his community, and the quality of his own person in turn is a function of both the richness and diversity of the contributing selves that he has brought into his particular focus, and the extent that he has been successful in maximizing their creative possibilities. Thus, the degree of one's extension and integration would seem to be the basis for determining one's quality as a person, for distinguishing the sage (*sheng jen* 聖人) from the authoritative person (*jen** 仁) (6/30):

> Tzu-kung said: "If there were a person who extended beneficence broadly to the masses and was able to assist the multitude, what would you say? Could he be called an authoritative person (*jen**)?" The Master replied, "Why stop at authoritative person? Certainly he is a sage (*sheng*). . . . "

Authoritative personhood is a calculus of "taking in" the selves of others and exercising one's own developing judgment in trying to effect what is most appropriate for all concerned. There is a second important feature of this process that may add increased clarity to the meaning of person making.

In the *Shuo-wen*, *jen** is defined by the character *ch'in* 親, which carries the basic meaning of "extending affection to those close at hand." Given that person making involves the taking in of other persons in the building of oneself, it is not surprising that *ch'in* can refer not only to the affection that is extended to others, but also to the person extending the affection ("personally") and the recipients of that affection ("parents," "kin," "intimates").

The question that arises here is that if Confucius himself at least on one occasion defined "person making" explicitly as "loving others" (*ai jen* 爱人),[95] why did he choose to make this love graduated rather than universal, beginning with one's family members and extending by degree out into one's society? As Confucius himself says (1/2): "The exemplary person works at the roots, for where the roots are firmly set, the *tao* will grow forth. Filial piety and fraternal deference—these are the roots of becoming a person." One reason, we believe, lies with the important role of personal judgment (*yi*) in this process of person making. The function of this personal judgment poses an insurmountable problem for those Christian interpreters of Confucius who, given the "un-self-ish" implications of *jen**, would equate *jen** with agapé. For *jen** cannot be agapé. As the highest form of Christian love, agapé originates with God. Persons are channels of agapé and can only approximate it in their relationships to the extent that they are vehicles for God's love. *Jen**, by contrast, originates with personal judgment (*yi*) exercised in community.

Jen* is the integrative process of taking in and subsuming the conditions and concerns of the human community in the development and application of one's own personal judgment. This is certainly what Confucius means when he says "becoming an authoritative person emerges out of oneself; how could it emerge out of others?" (12/1). And the fact that the ultimate source of *jen** is the communal application of one's own personal judgment rather than something external leads Confucius to remark (7/30): "How can becoming an authoritative person be at all remote? No sooner do I seek it than it appears." Because *jen** always entails the application of personal judgment to the concrete circumstances of environing persons, it follows that one is most fully constituted by those relationships nearest at hand in the naturally defined social structure. *Jen** is always immediate, that is, unmediated.

An interesting question here is whether the classical notion of family is a necessary or a contingent factor in Confucius' project of becoming authoritatively human. Given what we have said about the malleability of the context-dependent structures and institutions through which human life is experienced and refined, it would follow that no specific formal structure, even family, is necessary. Of course, the various kinds and qualities of love that can be elaborated through the traditional institution of the family have an unquestionable richness: filiality (*hsiao* 孝), paternal affection (*tz'u* 慈), fraternity (*t'i* 悌), camaraderie (*yu* 友), and so forth. To begin with, the institution of family is itself an abstraction from particular concrete relationships that are themselves always unique. But even as an abstraction, given the need to adjust structure to circumstances and the wealth of possible worlds, the family is perhaps best regarded as a contingent institution that could, under different conditions, be replaced by a different, more appropriate, more meaningful communal organization. One need only reflect on the gross distance between the clan-oriented extended family of Confucius' own world and the nuclear family of contemporary China to entertain this sense of contingency.

Confucius, and subsequently many of his followers, defined authoritative humanity in terms of loving others (ai jen). This concept of love in the classical Chinese tradition, consistent with the "taking in" aspect of person making, conveys a sense of appropriation. Ai is to take someone into one's sphere of concern, and in so doing, make him an integral aspect of one's own person. Where this taking in is reciprocated, ai is a bond that allows one's own person to be defined by reference to those he loves.[96] The Hsün Tzu records a suggestive passage in which Confucius questions his favorite disciples on the meaning of "authoritative person" (jen*):[97]

> Tzu-lu came in and Confucius asked him, ". . . What is an 'authoritative person?' " He replied, ". . . An authoritative person is one who causes others to love him." Confucius remarked, "Such can be called a refined person."
>
> Tzu-kung came in and Confucius asked him, ". . . What is an 'authoritative person?' " He replied, ". . . An authoritative person is one who loves others." Confucius remarked, "Such can be called a consummately refined person."
>
> Yen Yuan came in and Confucius asked him, ". . . What is an 'authoritative person?' " He replied, ". . . An authoritative person is one who loves himself." Confucius remarked, "Such can be called the truly enlightened person."

At least for the Hsün Tzu's interpretation of Confucius, the love originated by the authoritative person is a ground of mutual incorporation between the self and the other. The lowest level entails conducting oneself in such a manner as to occasion other people taking one's concerns as their own. While this is praiseworthy conduct, there is a selfishness here. The next level is for one to take the concerns of others as one's own. This is perhaps higher, but is self-effacing: one's own legitimate concerns are not served. The highest level, then, is necessarily reflexive, incorporating in one's own person the entire field of self–other concerns.

We have defined "authoritative person" (jen*) as a process of integrative person making in which one incorporates the interests of others as his own and conducts himself in a manner that addresses the general good. It is now possible to return to the more specific statements on "authoritative person" contained in the *Analects* to test our understanding of this concept. Most of the passages describing the authoritative person in the *Analects* focus on a process which entails both deference to others and an authored excellence of one's own. For example (17/6):

> Tzu-chang asked Confucius about authoritative humanity. Confucius replied, "A person who is able to promote the five attitudes in the world can be considered authoritative." "What are these?" Tzu-chang asked. Confucius replied, "Respect, tolerance, living up to one's word, diligence, and generosity."

These "five attitudes" can be factored into either deference to established meaning or the articulation and realization of one's own novel significance. They are, however, heavily weighted towards the former.

This process with its accent on deference to transmitted wisdom is a consistent feature of the *Analects*. For example (13/19):

> Fan Ch'ih asked about authoritative humanity. The Master replied, "Be respectful wherein one dwells, be reverent in the handling of official duties, and do one's best in dealing with others. These cannot be abandoned even in life among the barbarians."

The authoritative person is one who not only extends his sphere of concern to embrace and serve the interests of his community, but who literally extends himself to take in this community. Because he is himself irreducibly communal, he must conduct himself with seriousness in coordinating his own sense of rightness with the demands that he is ready to make on others (12/2):

> Chung-kung asked about authoritative humanity. Confucius replied, "In public life conduct yourself as though you are entertaining an

important guest, employ the masses as if carrying out an important sacrifice. Do not impose on others what you yourself do not desire . . ."

The concern that Confucius has for the relational self and the communication that effects it is a major theme throughout the *Analects*. The identification and articulation of interests and importances is the basis for person building and the inclusion of others in one's field of selves. The authoritative person inherits the values and significance of his culture and contributes to it in a process of symbolic exchange dominated by the medium of language. This language is performative in the sense that, for the authoritative person, saying requires the enactment of what is said in order to be true. Because speech necessarily entails action, being circumspect in what one says is a necessary although not sufficient condition for being authoritative (12/3).

> Ssu-ma Niu asked about authoritative humanity. Confucius said, "Being authoritative is being circumspect in what one says." "Can one be said to be authoritative simply by being circumspect in what he says?" Ssu-ma Niu asked. Confucius replied, "Given the difficulty of doing things, how could one not be circumspect in what he says!"

An important consideration in Confucius upon which we shall expand in the following chapter is the coextensive and correlative nature of personal, social, and political development. Because, as we shall elaborate below, person making requires a taking in of others into one's field of concern, it follows that there is a close relationship between the advancement of the interests of others and the cultivation of oneself (6/30): "The authoritative person establishes others in seeking to establish himself, and promotes others in seeking to get there himself." The final definition of authoritative person that we find in the *Analects*, while perhaps the most explicit, is also the most controversial (12/1).[98]

> To discipline oneself and practice ritual action is to become authoritative as a person. If for the space of one day one were able to accomplish this, the world would turn to him as an authoritative person.

Most of the controversy centers on the expression, *k'o chi* 克己, alternatively interpreted as "to overcome the self," "to control oneself," "to master oneself," "to discipline oneself," and "is able himself to."[99] Our interpretation of this passage is consistent with that of Tu Wei-ming, who states:[100]

> The concept of k'o-chi may be rendered as "to conquer oneself," but the special connotation in English is quite misleading. The Confucian idea does not mean that one should engage in a bitter struggle with one's own corporeal desires. It suggests instead that one should fulfill them in an ethical context. The concept of k'o-chi is in fact closely linked to the concept of self-cultivation (hsiu-shen). Indeed, they are practically identical.

Tu is surely correct in identifying the disciplining of one's ego-self with "self-cultivation" (hsiu-shen 修身).

In this respect, "to discipline oneself" and "to practice ritual action" amount to the same thing. Both are positive aspects of person making that involve deference to the meaning and value of tradition as embodied both in the cultural legacy and the "importances" of one's contemporaries, and in the creative contribution of one's own personal judgment in construing and realizing what one deems most appropriate in the circumstances. It is profoundly personal in that it is reflexively transformative, profoundly active in that one's own capacity to "significate" (yi) is the source of novelty and appropriateness, profoundly influential in that there is a symbolic relationship between personal and communal realization: authoritative humanity and authoritative community are coextensive.

If we survey passages from the Analects that characterize authoritative humanity (jen*), we find that, contrary to Fingarette, becoming jen* does involve something like "attitudes, feeling, wishes and wills."[101] Jen* person making engages the whole person: his "public," "active," and "outer" self[102] as well as those dimensions that are "private," "contemplative," and "inner." Further, contrary to Tu Wei-ming, this authoritative "personing" goes far beyond "a principle of inwardness,"[103] and requires reference to one's environing conditions. The limitations that both Tu Wei-ming and Fingarette encounter in their discussions of jen* can be overcome once it is understood that claiming both an "inner" and an "outer" reference for jen* makes sense provided one employs the appropriate model for understanding that relationship. Below, when we introduce the model of "focus" and "field" as a means of interpreting the part-whole relationship in Confucian terms,[104] our claims concerning *jen** will be rendered clearer.

4   An Illustration: Po I and Shu Ch'i

In the preceding chapter, we used Confucius' attitude to and use of the *Book of Songs* to illustrate the dynamic relationship that obtains among "learning" (*hsüeh*), "reflecting" (*ssu*), and "realizing" (*chih*). Confucius made much of the assiduous effort necessary in becoming an authoritative person (*jen**)[105] to the extent that while he was proud of his own love of learning, he did not allow that he himself had achieved this level of personhood.[106] Even so, Confucius was willing to attribute this quality to a few historico-legendary figures. An analysis of two brothers, Po I and Shu Ch'i, who were so described, might provide us with at least one concrete illustration of what it means to Confucius to act authoritatively.

The account of the lives of Po I and Shu Ch'i is one of the stories most frequently alluded to in Chinese literature, appearing everywhere from the *Book of Documents* to the Ch'ien Lung Emperor's poem on the temple dedicated to the two brothers.[107]

Po I and Shu Ch'i were the first and third sons of the ruler of the state of Ku Chu, whose location is in dispute. Before his death, the ruler made Shu Ch'i, his third son, heir-apparent. However, on the death of the father, Shu Ch'i insisted that he abdicate in favor of his eldest brother. Po I, refusing to accept the throne on the grounds that Shu Ch'i's appointment was a paternal injunction, fled the state. Shu Ch'i, however, was adamant that he not deprive his eldest brother of his rightful place, and so followed him in flight. In the meantime, the people of Ku Chu enthroned the second brother as ruler in their stead. Po I and Shu Ch'i grew old in self-imposed exile.

King Wen, founder of the Chou dynasty, had a reputation for caring for the aged, and so Po I and Shu Ch'i sought him out, but by the time they arrived at his court, he had passed away. Wu, carrying his father's sacrificial tablet and honoring him as "king," had set out eastward to attack the tyrannical imperial overlord. Po

I and Shu Ch'i seized the bridle of his horse and admonished him, saying "Your father is not yet buried and you are taking up arms—can this be called filial? A subject assassinating his ruler—can this be called being authoritatively human?"

Wu's retainers wanted to kill them on the spot, but Duke T'ai intervened, saying, "These are men doing what they believe to be right." He protected them and sent them on their way. When Wu had conquered the Shang empire and overthrown its dynasty, the people paid homage to him as founder of the Chou dynasty, but Po I and Shu Ch'i regarded his investiture as a source of shame. In accordance with their sense of what was right, they refused to eat the grain of Chou, secluded themselves on Shou-yang Mountain, and lived on wild beans. They recorded their grievances in a song which has been passed on to posterity:

> We have climbed Shou-yang Mountain
> and gather wild beans.
> They replace a violent ruler with a violent subject
> and do not realize their wrong.
> The succession of the ancients has continued,
> but now is done.
> Where can we turn?
> Alas! We depart.
> Such is the unhappy tide of circumstance.

They starved to death on Shou-yang Mountain. The Grand Historian remarked: "Viewing the situation so, have they done anything to incur ill-will? Yet is what they call 'wrong' really wrong?"

Confucius' attitude toward Po I and Shu Ch'i discloses what he considers to be an illustration of two human beings conducting themselves authoritatively through the interplay between ritual action and personal judgment. Po I and Shu Ch'i demonstrate a commitment to ritual action in their reasons for refusing their father's throne, in their unwillingness to challenge their brother's appointment, in their fearless remonstrance to King Wu's several violations of ritual action and finally in their protest against King Wu's regicide. In each of these cases, Po I and Shu Ch'i acted in accordance with established values as couched in ritual action, often at the expense of what could be construed as their own self-interest. In that they overcame their own self-interests in the service of those values embedded in ritual action, they conducted themselves with the authority of consensus and thus neither harbored nor incurred ill-will.[108]

But Confucius' high regard for these two exemplars is due only in part to their championing established values. He reserves his highest praise for their willingness to exercise their own personal judgment (18/8): "Po I and Shu Ch'i were two men who were unwilling to compromise their dispositions or bring disgrace on their persons." Po I and Shu Ch'i are contrasted favorably with the wealthy ruler of a large state who, because of his preoccupation with self-interest, has been forgotten. Po I and Shu Ch'i, on the other hand, are remembered to the present day because they were able to achieve authoritative humanity (16/11): "They dwelled in seclusion to pursue their ends, and acted on their personal sense of importance (*yi*) to extend their way."

The fact that Confucius allows that Po I and Shu Ch'i were doing what was right (*yi*) in withholding their support for King Wu, while at the same time himself reserving high praise for King Wu,[109] certainly suggests that Confucius regarded *yi* as the exercise of personal judgment rather than the reflection of some objective standard of rightness. That Confucius does not think in terms of categorical imperatives or universal ideals is clear inasmuch as Confucius readily describes Po I and Shu Ch'i as authoritatively human (*jen**)[110] and yet chooses to distinguish himself from them by virtue of his own commitment to tolerance (18/8): "I differ from these [Po I, Shu Ch'i, et al.] in that I do not have presuppositions as to what may and may not be done." Confucius is at once praising Po I and Shu Ch'i for the quality of their humanity and distancing himself from what he regards as their lack of flexibility. Perhaps Confucius, given his singularly high regard for the Chou, would have exercised his personal judgment under similar circumstances to a different end. And yet, rather than demanding that others be like him, he extends this same tolerance to Po I and Shu Ch'i in deference to the way in which they choose to act authoritatively.

III

". . . at forty I was no longer of two minds . . ."

1 The Primacy of Aesthetic Order

Modern social and political theory in the West has in large measure revolved about questions such as the relation of the individual to society, the realms of private and public activity, the status of natural and of positive law, the character of rights and of duties, the sanctioning power of the state (legitimate authority), the meaning of justice, and so forth. It would not be possible to employ such a list of issues in the analysis of Confucius' philosophy without distorting it beyond recognition. A representative list of subjects relevant to a discussion of Confucius' "social" and "political" theory would include a rather different set of items: the cultivation of personal life, ritual activity (*li* 禮) as the foundation of penal law (*fa* 法), social roles and institutions, the ordering of names, the official as model, and so forth.

What is immediately evident from a comparison of these two lists is the degree to which what might be construed as distinctly ethical phenomena enter directly into reflections upon social and political thinking for Confucius. The association of political order with "cultivation" and the demand that the ruler be "sage within and kingly without"—that is to say, that he be an exemplary person (*chün tzu* 君子)—provides a distinctly different coloration even to those topics in political theory that overlap between the Chinese and Anglo-European traditions.

The principal reason for the radical differences in problems and priorities between the Confucian and Western traditions can be accounted for in terms of the contrasting understanding of order dominating each tradition. Significant contrasts between social and political vision in Western intellectual culture and the thinking of Confucius are to be found not only in presumed differences in the procedures for realizing social order, but in the contrasting meanings of "order" as well. Our initial task in this present discussion, therefore, is to come to some understanding of the contrasting notions of order presented by Confucius and the historically dominant forms of Western social and political theories of order. The most efficient way to perform this task may appear initially rather indirect. The analysis of the contrasting meanings of social order requires that we gain some understanding of the problem of praxis in classical Western philosophy.

1.1   The Aesthetics of Praxis

As we have indicated before, the tendency to separate *theoria* and *praxis* or to construe the latter almost wholly in terms of the former is both cause and consequence of the belief in a transcendent normative dimension with respect to which individual and social behaviors are to be assessed. The actual form of that separation or reduction is, of course, dependent upon the particular cosmological assumptions grounding the theory.

The dominant theoretical interpretations of praxis in the Western tradition include the Platonic and idealist approaches which characterize praxis as activity in accordance with normative principles of knowledge. The sophistic and existential rejoinder to this view attempts to identify praxis with the volitional component of the individual human agent. The consequence of such a view is the celebration of heroic individuals whose power and influence have determined our understandings of the natural and social worlds. These beings actually function as transcendent principles themselves, as normative measures of human thinking and conduct. The naturalistic tradition associated with contemporary pragmatism defines praxis as actions stimulated by problematic situations from which guiding principles may be abstracted. In American pragmatism, the scientific method elaborated in the works of C. S. Peirce, John Dewey and, to a lesser extent, George Herbert Mead has functioned as the normative dimension of the theory.

It is important here to note that none of these distinct visions of praxis permit us to challenge the disjunction between the maker of order and those who enjoy the benefits of order. There is, however, a concept of praxis which has not been exploited in our tradition and which promotes just such a challenge.[1]

The distinction between the economic and the artistic understandings of "making" is the key to a novel conception of praxis. If we extend the meaning of "needs" beyond the strictly economic interpretation to include aesthetic "enjoyments," we have the beginnings of a conception of *praxis* (πρᾶξις) as *aisthesis* (αἴσθησις) construed in terms of aesthetic creativity. In a tradition such as ours which has stressed the domination of nature by *techne*, such an understanding of *praxis* may seem both irrelevant and futile. It is definitely the case, however, that the conception of *praxis* as *aisthesis* permits a more appropriate interpretation of Confucius' social and political theory.

Aisthesis in ancient Greek meant simply "perceiving the external world through the senses." *Aisthetikos* (Αἰσθητικός) carries the sense of "being preoccupied." The sense of being preoccupied with the sensuously perceived external world relates the concepts of *theoria* and *aisthesis*. John Ruskin first made this connection specific when he characterized *theoria* as "the perception of beauty regarded as a moral faculty," in contrast with *aisthesis*, which is "the mere animal consciousness of pleasantness."[2] Each was construed as a form of preoccupation related to a mode of entertaining the world of sense experience. For Immanuel Kant, aesthetics was the science that treats of the conditions of sensuous perception. Aesthetics considers the perception and function of *aestheta*, or "material things" as contrasted with *noeta*, "things immaterial."

Aisthesis has become increasingly relevant as a philosophic notion due to the fact that many contemporary characterizations of sense experience depend on an analysis of perception which stresses phases of experience more primitive than consciousness. In such characterizations, the objects perceived are the facts of experience, while the manner in which they are perceived defines the subjective sense of the world. The data of experience are received in accordance with a form of feeling that characterizes the manner of the perceiver's preoccupation with the world. And it is precisely this mode of preoccupation that largely determines the nature and direction of one's interpretation of the world.

Aisthesis as *praxis* requires a world composed of the termini of aesthetic acts. *Praxis* as *aisthesis* is fundamentally to be understood in terms of processes of self-creativity grounded in perspectives defining the forms of preoccupation with the world. We have considered such processes above in our discussion of *yi* (義) acts as significating.

The relevant issue in this context is whether Confucius' social and political philosophy depends upon notions of praxis which approximate the aesthetic interpretation outlined above. This aesthetic perspective can be made most clear if we proceed to a discussion of the meaning of order within the Confucian sociopolitical context. The question we shall ultimately address is whether Confucius' concept of order is one which requires the coordination of individuals in conformity with objective laws and modes of relatedness or if his thinking presupposes a preference for "aesthetic order," involving the emergence of a complex whole by virtue of the insistent particularity of constituent details.

The contrast between "rational" or "logical" and "aesthetic"[3] orders must be explicated in some detail since doing so demonstrates the coherence among the several dimensions of Confucius' social and political thought and can further be used with considerable effect to organize many of the notions that have characterized the development of both Western and Chinese social and political theory. Our initial considerations will require rather abstract language. We shall be able to descend to a more concrete level as we employ this contrast to interpret certain of Confucius' specific doctrines.

We may introduce the distinction between "logical" or "rational" order, on the one hand, and "aesthetic" order, on the other, by contrasting forms of social organization. To the extent that our social interactions are limited by appeal to a preestablished pattern of relatedness, be it political or religious or cultural, and to the extent that we conform to and express this pattern as containing habits, customs, rules, or laws determinative of our conduct, we are constituted as a "rational" or "logical" order. On the other hand, to the degree that we interact without obligatory recourse to rule or ideal or principle, and to the extent that the various orders which characterize our modes of togetherness are functions of the insistent particularities whose uniquenesses comprise the orders, we are authors of an "aesthetic" composition.

Thus, there are two perspectives one may assume with respect to the subject matter given in experience: One attends to the manner in which the experienced items instance a given pattern or set of formal relations, the second notes the manner in which just those experienced items constitute themselves and their relations to one another in such a way as to permit of no substitutions. Each perspective involves abstraction. The first abstracts from "actuality," the second from "possibility." The first observation is governed by the aims of logical orderedness; the second is concerned with aesthetic orderedness. Aesthetic order obtains when any items except those comprising the order fail to meet the conditions for the order or harmony in question. At the other extreme, that of the primary instance of logical or rational order, pure uniformity is guaranteed by the condition of absolute substitutibility. That is to say, in a logical order one abstracts from the particular characteristics of the ordered items.

Metaphysics in the West has been presumed to be the science of order. In fact, it has most often advertised itself as the science of uniformities. Both as *scientia universalis* and as *ontologia generalis*, speculative philosophy has sought to articulate those characteristics or relationships that allow us access to the uniformities of existence and experience. As "universal science," metaphysical speculation has uncovered those principles of order which together permit the organization and classification of the elements of the World and our experience of them. The "general ontologist" searches for the meaning of the *be-ing* of beings expressed by the set of uniform relations that qualify everything that is. What is missing in Anglo-European notions of order is the *aesthetic* perspective.

It is important to recognize that the ambiguity in the meaning of order suggested by the contrast of rational and aesthetic order does not seem to be easily reconcilable. At best aesthetic and rational orders are related to one another as figure and ground of a gestalt. We can bring one sort of order into focus only at the expense of shifting the alternative order to the background.

A rational or logical order consists in a pattern of relatedness which is, in principle, indifferent to the elements whose mutual relatedness comprise the order. The particular ingredients in the order register importance only to the extent and in those respects necessary to satisfy a requisite pattern. Thus, if one wishes to construct an isosceles triangle, one can do so using any items whatever to represent the three points whose relations form the figure. The particularity of these items is overlooked, and only their characteristic of representing points which locate them in a predetermined relationship to one another is significant. The direction of logical or rational construction is always away from the concrete particular towards the universal. The act of closure required by logical construction is readily recognizable in those philosophical positions in which realization instances a transcendent form or actualizes a given potential.

Aesthetic order begins with the uniqueness of the one thing and assesses this particular as contributing to the balanced complexity of its context. Because the aesthetic order celebrates the disclosure of the insistent particularity of each detail in tension with the consequent unity of these specific details, plurality must be conceived as prior to unity and disjunction to conjunction. The focus of an aesthetic order is the way in which a concrete, specific detail discloses itself as producing a harmony expressed by a complex of such details in relationship to one another.

The concepts of aesthetic and logical order are inversely related. Aesthetic order presses in the direction of particularity and uniqueness; logical order toward generality and absolute substitutibility. Aesthetic disorder exists to the extent that there is a loss of particularity. A complex of elements reaches the maximum of aesthetic disorder with the realization of absolute uniformity. But this is the highest degree of rational *order*. The Second Law of Thermodynamics promises the universe will end when the lowest degree of aesthetic disorder, the highest degree of logical order, has been reached.

The notion of "orderedness" as we usually understand it is ambiguous. What we normally call order is a mixture of the logical and aesthetic varieties. The value of the distinction between logical and aesthetic order is that it calls attention to contrasting tendencies in the production and maintenance of "order." The process of rationalization tends toward uniformity and pattern regularity; the aesthetic tendency challenges this direction through its preference for uniqueness and pattern nonregularity. As long as one does not think too much about the subject of order, it doesn't seem to present great difficulty. However, considerations of the character of the order and orderedness sought by differing individuals—artists as against engineers, for example—can sometimes lead to the recognition of the serious ambiguity hidden by the apparently straightforward term "order."

It is simply not the case that uniquenesses establish no orders. The composition of a work of art is, of course, abstractable from the unique items that compose it, but its greatness in large measure lies with the comprehension of just those particular items comprising the work. And although our enjoyment of the harmony of a work of art is both aesthetic and rational, and thus is based upon an appreciation of the uniformities (the compositional elements) as well as the diversities (the irreplaceably unique characteristics that constitute the work), we find it difficult to discover a coherent notion of order that accounts for this fact.

The understanding of orders as functions of the particular, idiosyncratic items which in fact comprise them provides a much more complex conception of order than that of rational orderedness. Aesthetic consistency is not bound by putative reference. The orders established by aesthetic particulars include at their least ordered levels (aesthetically) those selected orders that will in fact meet the demands of logical consistency, but also include myriad others that will not. Logical or rational order is the sort of order grounding the search for those uniformities in nature constituted by compatible sorts of uniformities that are of particular interest to individuals.

The orders of social organization provide the best illustration of the manner in which aesthetic and rational orders interact. For human societies per se are "mid-range" phenomena which do not permit resort to the extremes of either logical or aesthetic interpretation. Persons in society are construed rationally to the extent that their idiosyncrasies are abstracted and their general or universal characteristics are made relevant. Concepts of "human nature," "human rights," "equality under the law," and so forth, signal the resort to logical or rational orderedness. Even the major forms of individualism are consequences of rational or logical interpretations, as we shall soon see.

A society rooted in the preference for aesthetic orderedness will not be open to the employments of rules, standards, or norms that are presumed to be generalizations or instances of essential defining characteristics of human beings and of their modes of togetherness. Neither will consensus be used as objective grounds for social order. The uniformities and continuities evident within an aesthetically ordered society originate in specific acts of deference on the part of individuals whose focusing perspectives offer the variety of orders possible at any given moment.

The contrast of what we are calling logical and aesthetic orders is one that has, surprisingly, been little stressed within the Anglo-European tradition. This is, perhaps, due in large measure to the fact that paradigm instances of order have been drawn from notions of "the created order" or from "the order of nature." With regard to such notions we are more concerned to account for uniformities than irregularities. Thus we seek causal laws or patterns of meaning that normatively measure our natural world.

In the Western tradition, belief in a single-order cosmos reinforces the search for natural and social uniformities. Laws as external determining sources of order provide the grounds for the perpetuation of a sense of rational orderedness. On the other hand, if there is little or no recourse to the concepts of a created order or a world obedient to natural laws, such order that exists must be conceived as contingent. This contingency in itself does not provide the grounds for an alternative to rational or logical order. Rules and laws, as external determining principles of order, can originate in the arbitrariness and contingency of individual rulers, or in the inertia of unquestioned tradition, or in shifting patterns of consensus unthinkingly realized. The distinctive feature of aesthetic order is that, whereas rational order permits one to abstract from the concrete particularities of the elements of the order and to treat these elements indifferently, aesthetic order is constituted by just those particularities. That is to say, the variety of aesthetic orders is a function of precisely those features that distinguish one ordering perspective from another.

We introduce this characterization of rational and aesthetic orders here in anticipation of the treatment of Confucius' social and political theory and, ultimately, of his implicit cosmological vision. The contrast will make sense only gradually as it is employed in subsequent discussion. In the context of Confucius' social philosophy and its comparison with Western social theory, the distinction of rational and aesthetic order will permit us to better understand the origins and implications of Anglo-European concepts of "the individual," and the distinction between "principles" and "models" as means of achieving social harmony.

2   The Masses (*min* 民)

2.1   *Min* 民 and *Jen* 人

The distinction between "the masses" (*min* 民) and "persons" (*jen* 人) that we find in the *Analects* and other classical texts has been a focus of some debate, especially with Marxian concerns in recent years being expressed through traditional categories.[4] The question as framed is whether or not this distinction entails a conscious class distinction between the masses *(min)* who have no right to office, and the upper classes *(jen)* who do have political status and privilege. The first response that a reader might have is that this distinction is imported wholesale from the Marxian notion of class contradictions, yet D. C. Lau, himself a conservative interpreter of Confucius, allows that it has a certain plausibility. At the same time, Lau is quick to point out that the seemingly unsystematic use of these terminologies in the *Analects* goes a long way toward blunting the force of the contrast.

Following Lau, we believe that a credible case can be made for a perhaps blurred yet significant contrast between the amorphous, indeterminate mass of peasants *(min)*, in themselves having little by way of distinguishing character or structure, and particular persons *(jen)*. The distinction, however, as we understand it, is fundamentally cultural rather than political. That is, political privilege and responsibility are simply conditions which attend higher enculturation. Although economic and social status would certainly affect one's opportunities for edification, birth in itself is not a warrant for the distinction. A person is not entitled to political participation because he is born into an exclusive *jen* class. Rather, he becomes *jen* as a consequence of that personal cultivation and socialization that renders him particular. Being a person is something one does, not something one is; it is an achievement rather than a given. This argument can be made by appeal to the language in which the distinction is couched.

The character *jen* 人 has many connotations, and is only rarely used in contrast with *min*. In its broadest sense, *jen* can mean "human being" as a generic term for those persons who constitute the human species.[5] It is perhaps because the human being was widely perceived as "the most noble among the natures in the cosmos"[6] and "the heart-and-mind (*hsin* 心) of the cosmos"[7] that this same character was used to designate the "heart" or "kernel" of a fruit or nut.[8] In the *Analects, jen* is most frequently used in this general sense of "a particular person qua human being," where the contrast lies with those phenomena that are not persons. Because the human being is implicitly contrasted with other less worthy creatures, *jen* unless otherwise qualified, carries a positive import. This is most clearly in evidence where *jen* itself means a superior person (6/14):

> Tzu-yu was the chief official of Wu-ch'eng. The Master asked him, "Have you found any able people (*jen* 人) there?" He replied, "There is T'an-ta'i Mieh-ming. He does not take shortcuts in carrying out his duties, and never comes to my private quarters unless on official business."

This positive connotation of *jen* is further suggested by its cognate relationship with *jen** 仁, "authoritative person." In the *Analects*, there are even cases where these cognate characters are used interchangeably.[9]

The second most frequent use of *jen* in the *Analects* is in its meaning of "other persons" in contrast to oneself (*chi* 己).[10] The fact that it is used to designate "other" as opposed to "self" is consistent with the suggestion of exalted status.

A third, relatively uncommon use of *jen* is when it is set in opposition to "the masses" (*min* 民). We can examine this *jen/min* distinction, our major concern here, by detailing the primitive implications of *min*, and setting them in contrast to the more positive connotations of *jen*.

The character, *min* 民, is the root from which a large field of cognate characters derive. These characters almost uniformly convey refinements on the primitive meaning of "blindness and confusion": *min* 泯 "troubled, confused, disorderly"; *hun* 殙 "blinded, distracted, confused"; *hun* 昏 "dusk, darkness, benighted, blinded, mentally dark"; *hun* 惛 "darkened in mind, stupid"; and so on. Another cognate, *min* 珉, which denotes "jade," is in fact an abundantly available pseudo-jade which, because it lacks the luster of real jade, is disdained by the exemplary person.[11] This core meaning of dark and undiscriminated chaos that is reflected in the term "masses" (*min* 民) is underscored by the several classical texts that define *min* paronomastically as "dark" (*ming* 冥), or its cognate, "shut the eyes, troubled sight" (*mien* 瞑). Tung Chung-shu is a ready example:[12]

> The designation for "the masses" (*min* 民) is derived from "closed eyes" (*mien* 瞑). If by natural tendency the masses are already good, why should "closed eyes" (*mien*) be taken as their designation?

. . . It can be likened to the eye. When the eye is sleeping, it is closed. . . . Just as the closed eye needs to be awakened, so the masses need to be instructed before they can be good. Before they have been awakened, we might say they have the potential, but we cannot say that they are good. . . . The way we express "the masses" (*min* 民) is certainly similar to "closed eyes" (*mien* 瞑). We can get at this meaning when we pursue its conceptual structure by analyzing the term.

One of the primitive forms of the character *min* 民 given to us on the earliest Chou inscriptions is 𠂤 which has been interpreted as a pictograph of an eye blind because it lacks a pupil.[13] In contrast to *jen* 人 as the kernel of the fruit, *min* 民 is the eye lacking in its most essential element, the pupil. Tuan Yü-ts'ai is insistent that the *Shuo-wen* dictionary in defining *min* as *chung meng* 眾萌 uses the character *meng* 萌 specifically to indicate an attitude of mental darkness and ignorance: hence, "the ignorant masses." The second meaning of *meng* 萌 as "sprout" resonates clearly with Tung Chung-shu's description of the *min* 民 as sleeping with the potential to be awakened.

The low status of *min* is clear in the *Analects* where it is frequently contrasted with "those above = superiors" (*shang* 上). For example (14/41): "The Master said: 'When superiors (*shang*) are fond of ritual action, the masses (*min*) will be easy to employ.'"[14]

The *min* as *min* tend to be passive. The language that is used to characterize the appropriate attitude of their superiors to them is generally condescending: they are to submit (*fu* 服)[15] to those above whose posture in administering to them is to oversee (*lin* 臨)[16] them and treat them with magnanimity (*hui* 惠).[17] It is the superiors on behalf of the masses, rather than the masses themselves, who work on what is appropriate (*yi* 義) for them;[18] the masses as masses are generally governed by the rule of law and its attendant punishments.[19] The masses should be reverent (*ching* 敬) in their attitude to those above, and model themselves upon them.[20] The virtue and potency of the masses is to be expressed in the proper execution of their everyday occupations (6/29): "Taking hitting the mark in common affairs as their *te* 德 is of the utmost importance, yet it has been lacking in the masses for a long time." Yang Po-chün in his interpretation of this passage argues that "*min* here does not exclusively refer to the common people, and for this reason I have rendered it 'everybody.' "[21] But it is precisely because they are *min* that they ought to exert themselves in common affairs. And given the association between *min* and the proper seasons, [22] it would appear that their proper employment (*shih min* 使民) is specifically tilling the land and performing corvée duties at the appropriate times. The employment of the *jen* (*shih jen* 使人), on the other hand, can often refer to public office.[23]

The *Analects* uses several different expressions to designate the people: "the multitude" (*chung* 眾), "the hundred surnames" (*pai hsing* 百姓) and "the many" (*shu jen* 庶人) among them. These terms have important differences in connotation; but they may share one common difference from *min* itself in that while they all suggest an assembly of discrete persons, or at least discrete clans, *min* would seem to connote the common people as an undiscriminated mass. A second important difference would be that these alternative designations would not necessarily exclude the upper echelons of society, while *min* almost certainly would.

When Confucius uses *min* as the amorphous mass of commoners, he can be deprecatory.[24] These are the blind who will not see: "the masses who will not learn even when vexed with difficulties" (16/ 9). That Confucius uses the expression, "the *te* of the masses" (*min te* 民德), if we understand *te* to be a "particular focus,"[25] might further suggest that the *min* can be treated as a whole.[26] We have seen above that the distinguishing characteristic of ritual action is that it requires a personal investment of significance (*yi* 義). To the extent, then, that the *min* act en masse rather than as unique persons, their capacity for performing ritual actions is compromised.

To be a particular person (*jen* 人) is difficult, and to become an authoritative person (*jen** 仁) is profoundly difficult (6/22): "The authoritative person (*jen** 仁) reaps his reward only after dealing with the difficulties."[27] By contrast, the masses are simple, and are to be treated as such (6/2):

> Chung-kung asked Confucius about Tzu-sang Po-tzu. Confucius replied, "His simplicity was indeed all right." Chung-kung responded, "In administering to the masses would it not be all right to be reverent in one's own mind and yet to be simple in dealing with them? Is not being both simple in one's own mind and simple in dealing with them in fact being too simple?" Confucius replied, "Yung, you are right in what you say."

The masses are dependent upon the culture of their superiors for a meaningful mode of living (19/19): "Those above have lost the way *(tao)*, and the masses have been dissipated for a long time." Because the common people are lacking in personal cultivation, they do not have the resources to deal critically with the way of life provided for them (16/2): "When the *tao* prevails in the empire, the common people do not debate political issues."

Social and political harmony, as the coordination of differences, requires individual participation. As a body of people who do not contribute meaning and value as individuals, the *min* are unable to express their potential as particular human beings, and cannot function as an important source of *tao*. They may be able to follow the *tao*, but certainly cannot be made to realize it.[28]

But Confucius also provides a positive sense for the notion of *min*. The *min* represent a potential source of humanity. In Chapter II, we argued that the qualitative development from particular person *(jen 人)* to authoritative person *(jen* 仁)* occurs as the particular person integrates himself with his human context to bring it into an increasingly meaningful harmony. We would argue that this same movement is evident in the emergence of the particular person *(jen 人)* from the indeterminate masses *(min 民)*. For Confucius, not only is the emergence of particularity *(jen 人)* from the masses possible, the masses can even give rise to authoritative humanity *(jen* 仁)* (8/2):

> When the exemplary person *(chün tzu)* treats his relatives with earnest affection, the masses *(min)* will be aroused to authoritative humanity *(jen* 仁)*; when he does not abandon his old associates, the masses will be encouraged to pursue substantial relationships.

The potential for becoming truly human is in fact of critical importance for the masses (15/35): "Authoritative humanity *(jen* 仁)* is more vital to the masses *(min)* than fire or water." Indeed, the possibility of authoritative humanity is, for Confucius, the possibility for human life in its fullest sense.

Confucius was part of a tradition which regarded the masses, although simple and uncultured, as having this potential for growth. In the *Book of Documents*, an important resource in Confucius' curriculum, we read:[29]

> The masses ought to be cherished,
> Not oppressed,
> For it is only the masses who are the root of the state,
> And where this root is firm, the state will be stable.

In Mencius, perhaps Confucius' most prominent interpreter, the relationship between the ruler and the masses is repeatedly cast as analogous to that of parents to their children.[30] The masses, as his children, are dependent upon the ruler to ensure their economic well-being and their security.[31] Even more essential than sustenance and safety, however, is their confidence in the ruler's ability to effect a meaningful society (12/7):

> Tzu-kung asked about effecting sociopolitical order. The Master replied, "Give the masses enough food, enough arms, and make sure they have confidence in their ruler. . . . If the masses do not have this confidence, the society will not endure."

The intervention of cultured superiors is necessary if the masses are to exploit their potential as a resource out of which particular human beings can emerge. The Han Confucian, Chia Yi, describes this relationship:[32]

> The expression "masses" (*min* 民) means "closed eyes" (*mien* 瞑); the expression "populace" (*meng* 萌) means "blind" (*mang* 盲). Therefore, it is only on the basis of the support that those above give the masses in employing them that they are really transformed. . . . The masses are the raw timber for both superior and inferior persons; both are contained therein.

The relationship between the cultured superiors and the masses, then, is reciprocal and interdependent. Just as the masses are dependent upon their superiors as concrete examples of excellence available for emulation, so the superiors are dependent upon the masses as the ground out of which the society and state can grow. It must be understood, of course, that the superiors have a vested interest in the condition of the people. Given that personal, social, and political realization are coextensive, the possibilities for those above are very much a function of the richness of their cultural context. Hence, their concern for the people ought not be construed as a selfless altruism. In fact, in listing the most important concerns of the state, the *Analects* places the masses first before food, mourning, and sacrifices.[33] They are to be employed with the same devotion and care that is expressed in the performance of important sacrifices. For like the appropriate performance of the sacrifices, the proper treatment of the masses leads to a harmonious future.[34] To attract a large population is to accumulate a vital resource.[35] It is only once the ruler has provided circumstances conducive to material prosperity, however, that he can turn to the project of edifying and transforming them (13/9):

> When Confucius went to Wei, Jan Yu drove for him. Confucius remarked, "What a teeming population!"
> Jan Yu asked, "Now that the population is teeming, how can they be further benefited?"
> The Master said, "Make them prosperous."
> "And once they are prosperous, what more can be done?"
> "Instruct them."

One final point needs to be made with respect to *min*. In the Confucian tradition, there is a frequent association between *t'ien* 天, conventionally rendered "Heaven," and the masses *(min)*. The *Book of Documents*, for example, states:[36] "*T'ien* has compassion on the masses *(min)*: whatever they desire, *t'ien* is sure to effect."

Perhaps the best known passage, repeated in the *Mencius*, is:[37] "*T'ien* sees as the masses *(min)* see; *t'ien* hears as they hear." This association between *t'ien* and *min* will become clearer as we explore the meaning of *t'ien* in Chapter IV, below. At this juncture, we shall only note that *t'ien* and *min* overlap in representing available fields of possibilities. Just as *t'ien* can be construed as the indeterminate field in which the myriad things, including the human being himself,[38] articulate themselves and grow,[39] so the masses *(min)* can be regarded as that field of possibilities from which the particular person emerges as a cultured human being (6/18):

> When raw stuff overwhelms refinement, the result is coarseness, but when refinement overwhelms the raw stuff, the result is a hollow formality. The exemplary person *(chün tzu)* emerges from a complementary measure of both raw stuff and refinement.

That Confucius employs distinctions between cultured persons and the uncultured masses is clear. But this attitude is qualified by his egalitarian approach to the source of this difference, education (15/39): "In instruction, there is no such thing as social classes." Confucius explicitly celebrates his favorite disciple, Yen Hui, for pursuing refinement in spite of his poverty.[40] His primary criterion for accepting a student and participating in his education was perceived commitment (7/8):

> In instructing students, I do not open the way for them until they are struggling for clarity; I do not elaborate for them until they have given it their best effort. If I give a student one corner and he does not return with the other three, I will not go over it again.

For Confucius, then, edification is necessary for difference and distinction. Edification permits one to move from the indeterminate masses (min 民) to the expression of one's particularity (jen 人) and, ultimately, to the expression of one's authoritative humanity (jen* 仁).

2.2 Individual Absoluteness and Individual Relativity

The manner in which the classical Confucian understands the relationship between the masses and particular persons has some interesting parallels with classical Western views. Initially, however, it is the contrasts that stand out most clearly. What gives the discussion of Confucius' "sociopolitical theory" such an unfamiliar ring is the absence in his thinking of certain distinctions that Western social and political thinkers have deemed fundamental. The most important of these distinctions is that of the "private" and "public" realms. Allied with this distinction is the equally important division between the "social" and "political" modes of organization. The acceptance of these distinctions is both cause and consequence of the bias toward "individualism" in the West.

The classical Confucian is loath to make a distinction between the social and political forms of togetherness. When in the *Chung-yung* the five relationships are discussed, the relation of father and son is employed as the pattern for the relationship between the ruler and the masses. One of the nine principles of government involves the ruler treating the masses (*min* 民) as his own children.[41] The basic relationships of father and son and ruler and people are isomorphic. This fact determines the manner in which social and political relationships are intertwined. The ruler, as exemplary person, is a model for his people in much the same manner as the father is a model for his children (sons). Thus, the authority of the ruler is moral authority in its primary form.

The analogy between the family and the state is certainly not absent in the Western tradition. Aristotle had recognized the family as the basis of moral education in which the father would provide moral training for the son until the entrance of the son into the public sphere. The state itself, according to Aristotle, was an association of families. The distinction between this view and that of the Confucian is dramatic, however. Aristotle and the majority of the Greeks held that the family has its roots in the private sphere, and the state fundamentally concerns the sphere of public praxis. This division of the life of the individual into public and private dimensions is in no way echoed in early Confucianism. The notion, which Aristotle sometimes appears to suggest, that the father is surrogate for the state in the moral education of the child, does not resonate with the Confucian position in which the obligations to the father continue essentially unchanged throughout the life of his child. For Confucius, the moral function of the father-son relationship is not a preparatory one, but is a permanent part of the life of both son and father.

The Greek distinction between public and private life, a mainstay of our political tradition, finds its justification in the distinction between the theoretical and practical activities, between the contemplative life and the active life. Both Plato and Aristotle found *theoria*, (θεωρία), contemplation, to be the highest type of existence. And, although Plato (in the *Republic*) required the return of the philosopher-king from meditation to the affairs of the state, it is clear that this was thought to be a particularly painful responsibility.

The importance of the *vita contemplativa* continued into modern times through the emergence of the Christian tradition in the West. Christianity institutionalized the contemplative sphere through the construction of monastic orders and the emphasis upon prayer as a private meditative event. The importance of the theological doctrines that emphasized the personal relationship of the individual to God cannot be overemphasized in this context. The seeds of modern liberal theories of individualism are found here. Having a soul or consciousness that has as its primary referent "God" or "principles of conscience" guarantees that something of absolute significance occurs in the privacy of one's cell or study.

This form of individualism results from the presumption that the most fundamental forms of life are associated with the private sphere in which the individual relates to a transcendent Being or principle. The private self is the true self and the public self is in fact only a *persona*. The importance of this outlook can be understood by reflecting upon the widespread fascination with the private lives of our famous celebrities. It is as if knowing about their private lives tells us what they "really" are like, beyond the "appearances" of their public personae.

There is a more celebrated form of individualism associated with the nominalist tradition. This atomistic individualism is grounded in the wholly secularized view that the member of a society or state, while autonomous in the "state of nature," is nonetheless patterned by needs and interests which if expressed in any unqualified manner would lead to "a war of each against all." This concept attains its classical expression in the thought of Thomas Hobbes.[42]

> All men in the state of nature have a desire and will to hurt. . . . The most frequent reason why men desire to hurt each other ariseth hence, that many men at the same time have an appetite to the same thing; which yet very often they can neither enjoy in common nor yet divide it; whence it follows that the strongest must have it, and who is strongest must be decided by the sword.

Society arises, therefore, from mutual fear and is constituted for either gain or glory, the fundamental gain, of course, being that of relative security from the violence of the state of nature. Further, society is not formed by choices, it is inevitable:[43]

> Every man is desirous of what is good for him and shuns what is evil, but chiefly the chiefest of natural evils which is death; and this he doth, by a certain impulsion of nature, no less than that whereby a stone moves downward.

If the chiefest natural evil is death, the chiefest natural good seems to be glory or honor.[44]

Whatever is good, is pleasant, and relates either to the senses, or the mind. But all the mind's pleasure is either glory (or to have a good opinion of oneself) or relates to glory in the end; all the rest are sensual, or conducing to sensuality, which may be comprehended under the word conveniences. All society is either for gain, or for glory; that is, not so much for love of our fellows, as for love of ourselves.

The first type of individualism is not, by intention, individualistic at all. The Greeks, preeminently Aristotle, held man to be *zoon politikon* (ζῷoν πoλῑτῐκoν), a political animal. Persons could not be conceived of as existing outside the context of the *polis*. Language, the basis of rational intercourse, is a gift of society; social togetherness is a sine qua non of rational existence. But that same rational activity for the sake of which society exists achieves its most fundamental expression in *theoria*, contemplation. And the reasoning creature par excellence is one whose existence refers to values transcending society. Atomistic individualism, being the more obvious form of individualism, is often held responsible for some of the consequences of rational or transcendental individualism. Both are equally responsible, however, for maintaining a separation between the private and public realms.

Hobbes and classical liberalism reject the theory of man as *zoon politikon*. Hobbes presents a classic theory of the ameliorative origin of the state—that is, its origin in the attempt to secure oneself against the hurtful actions of others. A trace of the positive form of organic naturalism remains in Hobbes, however. The desire for glory that he attributes to human beings echoes aspects of the Greek conception of the *polis*. The public sphere is the realm in which honor can be achieved. It is the appreciation of glory, honor, and greatness that has provided the public realm with its particular appeal throughout the ages and has intensified the privative sense of privacy.

The desire for fame is, perhaps, the reflected desire for immortality. It is the wish to live on in the memories of one's fellows and their descendants. One leaves the sphere of the private and enters the public realm in order to have his existence certified through recognition by others and, thus, to become fully human. But as common sense would suggest, the desire for fame and honor, like the desire for economic profit, is predicated on their relative scarcity. If everyone could realize these aims they would not constitute such powerful motivations. Fame is one of those desirable things which cannot be enjoyed in common, nor yet divided. The desire for fame, honor, pleasure, and profit can only lead to an intensification of the individualistic temper.

There are strong motivations toward individualism to be found in both the conception of the human being in terms of the public as well as the private sphere. In the Western tradition, both the *vita contemplativa* and the *vita activa* conduce toward varieties of individualism.

The majority of attempts to mitigate the more negative consequences of these sorts of individualism have involved either the reduction of the public to the private realm, or vice versa. Plato's abolition of the family in his *Republic* effectively cancelled the private realm. The *polis* was the only home of individual citizens. Each member of this ideal society served the state. Even the philosopher who achieved the final intuition of the Good in the supreme act of *theoria* was expected to return to the world of public praxis in order to serve as enlightened ruler. Much of the poignancy of the *Republic* lies in the fact that Plato's proposals, however seriously intended as political statements, were made against the background of the distinction between the practical and the contemplative lives and the clear preference for the latter over the former.

Hegel made the strongest claims on behalf of the dominance of the public over the private sphere. The power and authority of the state over its citizens was effectively absolute for him. But even this absolutist theory which gave such unqualified expression to the importance of the state was motivated by the presupposition of individuality as the aim of existence.[45]

> Since the state is mind objectified it is only as one of its members that the individual himself has objectivity, genuine individuality, and an ethical life. Unification pure and simple is the true content and aim of the individual, and the individual's destiny is the living of a universal life.

Considered apart from the state, citizens are mere abstractions without true individuality. And the unity of the state, its individuality, assures the individuality of its members precisely to the degree that they live "a universal life." For Hegel and the idealist political tradition, the reality of the human being is apparently determined by his sociality. But this sociality is itself an expression of a transcendent principle, the Absolute, which is the fundamental reality instanced by individual citizens living a universal life. Thus, even in this reduction of the private to the public sphere, of the individual citizen to the state, it is individuality that serves as the true standard of reality.

The alternative reduction of the public to the private sphere was originally associated with religious and theological motivations that served as ground for the Christian ideal of community. St. Augustine's *Civitas Dei* promoted a distinction between the City of God and the City of Man which provided arguments for subsequent champions of spiritual communities as the ideal mode of human togetherness. The complete abandonment of the public, secular sphere of social existence has hardly ever been achieved although it has been attempted from time to time in our tradition under the inspiration of eschatological and apocalyptic motives.

In contemporary Western societies, the reduction of the public to the private sphere is largely a function of what are considered to be negative forces. Political and social life in the West has been constituted by a peculiar balance of the private and the public realms of existence. The increased importance of economic determination in the contemporary world has seriously threatened the public sphere by focusing upon the private economic motivations of the individual as "consumer." Allied with this is the increased importance played by technological processes in defining the character of social and political life. The automation and regularization of the public realm has taken some of the prestige from public life. The public sphere is less and less a political arena and more a home for the burgeoning class of technocrats.[46]

The classical distinction between the public and the private spheres of existence, and the ubiquitous acceptance of individualism as a fundamental given of social existence together exacerbate a crisis in social and political philosophy in the West. Political individualism is viable only if there is in fact a public realm within which an individual can exercise his desire for fame and greatness. Without such a realm within which to act, individualistic motivations lead to egoistic demands for economic gratifications which contribute little to social and political viability.

By contrast, the Confucian distinction between the masses (*min* 民) and particular persons (*jen* 人) is predicated neither upon a contrast of private and public spheres, nor upon a distinction between social and political modes of togetherness. Apart from the intrinsic interest of Confucius' sociopolitical thinking, it is of importance by virtue of its constituting a significant alternative rendering of the meaning of human togetherness. Reflecting upon Confucius' views on this subject might well stimulate thinking of the sort that can contribute something worthwhile to contemporary Anglo-European discussions of social and political issues.

According to Alfred North Whitehead:[47]

> One of the most general philosophic notions to be used in the analysis of civilized activities is to consider the effect on social life due to the variations of emphasis between Individual Absoluteness and Individual Relativity. . . . In one of their particularizations those ideas appear in the antagonism between freedom and social organization. In another they appear in the relative importance to be ascribed to the welfare of the state and the welfare of its individual members.

It is certainly true, at least on the surface, that the contrast between individual absoluteness and individual relativity is relevant to the organization of classical Confucian and dominant Western political understandings. Confucian sociopolitical thought can easily be understood to be based in notions of social interdependence. And the concept of individual autonomy is presupposed in the most influential discussions of social and political issues in the West. Applied with appropriate caution, this contrast between absoluteness and relativity can permit us to avoid some rather serious misunderstandings of the differential importance of the Confucian and the Western visions of social life.

Western social theories are weighted in favor of the notion of individual absoluteness which suggests that they have difficulty making an appropriate case for social interdependence without challenging the viability of the notions of freedom and autonomy. The case is the opposite for the classical Confucian view. There the preference for individual relativity is quite evident. Any attempt to shift that view in the direction of individual absoluteness threatens the very structure of the Confucian social vision.

Of course, we cannot forget that there are striking contrasts between the notions of "person" in the dominant strain of Anglo-European thought and that deriving from the Confucian view. The very notion of "individual" in the strictest sense is suspect from the Confucian perspective. "Sociality" is at the very root of existence. Our presentation of the contrast between logical and aesthetic interpretations of order in this chapter should promote an initial understanding of the distinctive meaning of individuality in the Confucian sensibility. Later, when we introduce the model of "field and focus" to articulate the Confucian understanding of the relations of "parts" and "wholes,"[48] greater clarity will be possible. Suffice it to say here that the sort of individualism prized in Anglo-European societies would be wholly undesirable to one informed by the classical Confucian perspective.

An appropriate balance of individual absoluteness and individual relativity is not easily attained. What needs to be clarified here is that there are distinctly different models operating in the contrasting social visions which, if not recognized, lead to mutual confusion. Neither the Chinese nor Western thinker can afford to reduce the other to his own particular model without perpetuating the most pernicious misunderstandings. If the Chinese thinker looks to the West presupposing the aesthetic model of orderedness, then the principal forms of Western individualism must appear to be almost horrifying in their disdain for what, aesthetically, are the fundamental facts of social togetherness. And the Westerner, armed with the notion of rational order as the paradigmatic understanding of social togetherness, cannot but believe that the Confucian sensibility is destructive of the fundamental notion of individual autonomy.

The Confucian thinker would hold that the Western preference for rational orderedness creates an inappropriate interpretation of social life in which equality is abstract and freedom is quantitatively construed. What makes us equal is that we are "the same," what insures our freedom is that we have choices. These choices are too often among merely quantitatively distinct sorts of items. We can choose among a number of kinds of cereal on the grocery shelf or among a variety of different automobiles. But are not our choices mainly quantitative? The many things from among which we make our choices are seldom possessed of true qualitative differences.

Significant freedom would require choices among a variety of qualitatively distinct items.

It should be noted here that a host of analyses of Western society, from those inspired by Marx[49] to that of the ostensibly aristocratic anti-Marxist, José Ortega y Gasset,[50] are in essential agreement about the crucial problems of societies dominated by quantitative considerations. Due to their implicit assumption of rational order as the sole basis for social togetherness, however, programmatic suggestions for the amelioration of these problems are not expressed in altogether appropriate categories. Nonetheless, it might be helpful if we draw rather loosely upon certain of these critiques as a means of highlighting the sort of contrasts between models of social togetherness upheld by the classical traditions of China and the West. Having discussed certain of the important questions in language familiar to the Anglo-European, we will then be prepared to consider the subject from the distinctly Confucian perspective.

In the West, as in Confucian China, the health of a society has been a function of an appropriate balance between elites and masses. Some critics of modern Western societies find the most pressing political problem to be the "massification" of societies and states. This phenomenon is associated with the theoretical and practical employment of quantitative criteria in determining social and political value. Such criteria are primarily economic.

The masses and the elites of a modern Western society are found to be distinguished less by qualitative and more by quantitative differences. The first reason for this development is associated with modern forms of individualism which we have considered above. Individualist theories promote a rather abstract sense of equality and freedom. Our equality is a function of our sameness; our freedom is defined in accordance with quantitative choices among items of little qualitative difference. The second reason is that which is associated with the phenomenon of technological society, which exacerbates this promotion of such abstract freedom and equality. Each of these is, at base, a function of the assumption of rational order in the world and society.

Technological society, as the complex organizational form given to industrial and scientific technique, came into its own in the nineteenth century. Since then rapid technological development has given the masses of Western society material resources hitherto unobtainable. Liberal democracy has contributed to an increase in the power of the masses, and technology has increased their level of security. This increase in power and security yields an unanticipated consequence: the deferential relations that might obtain between the elites and masses are threatened by the fact that the distinction between the two social elements is felt to have been largely cancelled by the general rise in the standard of living. That is, the masses accept their increase in living conditions as warrant for the claim that they are equal in every significant respect to anyone else. Further, technology has so emphasized the need for specialization that the necessity to remain in contact with the general theoretical schemes that contextualize and render coherent the variety of specialized tasks is insufficiently appreciated.

By narrowing the scope of endeavor necessary for intellectual achievement, modern technology has made financially rewarding positions available to individuals with constricted talents and skills. It is much easier to qualify for a specialized task than for one which requires the understanding of the principles of coherence underlying such tasks. And since much of the work of science and technology is routine, the specialist is qualified to be considered a "scientist," one who *knows*. The specialist who knows more and more about less and less is the product of technological sophistication. He is the epitome of "the mass-man."

Civilization lives by the grace of men of effort who understand the principles upon which it was built and who are willing to sacrifice themselves to its maintenance and development. The masses in Western societies no longer function as the indeterminate field of potentiality from which true humanity emerges but rather are considered and consider themselves the source of power and the locus of decision making.

Individuals in a liberal democratic society feel themselves to be equal to their fellow citizens. Indeed, the belief in such equality is built into the constitutional structures of most Western nations. And it is a belief that should not casually be challenged. But social forms of togetherness cannot easily survive without appropriate deference paid to those in society possessed of true excellences. Such individuals are responsible for the introduction of meaning into their social context. They are the individuals who perform the acts of signification that uncover and transmit the values of the tradition. The stress upon quantitative criteria for assessing social value has had the effect of making qualitative assessments for acts of deference altogether suspect.

The Confucian vision of social theory offers, as we shall see, an alternative conception of social order grounded on qualitative criteria. The distinction between the masses (*min* 民) and the elites (*jen* 人 and *chün tzu* 君子) is rather more severe than might be comfortable for the contemporary Anglo-European proponent of liberal democracy, but the deleterious effects of the massification of society by virtue of the mere quantitative distinctions among social classes is not present. To the extent that the masses serve as the field of potential humanity out of which authoritative persons emerge, the aesthetic interpretation of social order is maintained. One could certainly challenge any given instance of such an aesthetically ordered society if it ignored quantitative considerations to such a degree as to threaten the welfare and security of its members. But promoting a rise in the general level of existence of the masses in a Confucian society would not lie in the implementation of quantitative rather than qualitative criteria for the assessment of social welfare.

3   Effecting Sociopolitical Order (*cheng** 政)

3.1   *Cheng** 政 and *Cheng* 正

Peter Boodberg, perceptively yet somewhat vaguely, hovers about the logical/aesthetic distinction in his philological analysis of *cheng** 政, "effecting sociopolitical order."[51] First, he seeks to distinguish *cheng** from its common rendering as "government" on the grounds that "government" derives from the Greco-Latin etymon *guberno*: "to steer (as a helmsman)." *Cheng** on the other hand derives from "right, correct." Boodberg then goes on to identify a positive and a pejorative sense of *cheng**. The positive sense is "rectitude" in which "effective government was to be achieved in a happy medium between the correctness of the rulers and correction of the subjects."[52] The negative sense, Boodberg relates to the cognate, *cheng*** 征, which he reads as "to compel submission." In this case, *cheng** politically would mean "compulsory enforcement of a standard."

In distinguishing between voluntary modeling and imposed authority, Boodberg seems to associate the former with aesthetic order, yet his distinction is not clear enough. First, by insisting on the inseparability of *cheng** 政 from its two cognate characters, *cheng* 正 and *cheng*** 征, "to effect (personal) order" and "to compel submission," respectively, he suggests that it might be too restrictive to identify *cheng** 政 with the political sphere alone. We shall see below that ritual action (*li* 禮) functions as a method for effecting order in the personal, the social, and the political dimensions of human life, and that any separation among these in the Chinese context is an abstraction. Thus, *cheng** 政 is better understood as "effecting sociopolitical order" (interpersonal order in its broadest sense), rather than the more politically specific "administering government." That Confucius understood it in this way is made clear in his response to an interlocutor who uses *cheng** restrictively in the sense of formal government (2/21):

> Someone asked Confucius, "Why are you not in government?"
> Confucius replied, "The *Book of Documents* says: 'Filiality! Simply extend filiality and fraternity into government.' This filiality then is also taking part in 'government.' Why must one take part in formal government?"

Secondly, there is indeed a positive and a negative sense of *cheng** 政 as it occurs in the *Analects*. The former refers to an aesthetic order that involves the participation of both rulers and people in an emergent harmony defined by the personal display of meaning and value in the performance of ritual action. Ideally, this order is effected by a modeling process in which personal cultivation above inspires emulation below. The specific disposition of a society's order, although grounded in the continuity provided by tradition, is qualified by the meanings invested by its specific participants, and hence, is always novel and unique.

The negative sense of *cheng** arises because personal cultivation requires commitment and effort. As we have seen, ritual actions, to be meaningful, require that particular people exercise their capacities to "significate" (*yi* 義). Even with the influence of the ruler's exemplary conduct on the people, there will inevitably be a recalcitrant fringe who, for want of wit or refinement, will pursue their own personal advantage without concern for the consequences of their actions. For the sake of general harmony, these persons must be

held to a minimum standard of orderly conduct described and enforced as the rule of law. This then is the second, derived meaning
of *cheng**: articulated (and hence formal) social and political measures
taken to insure a minimum degree of compliance with the prevailing
sense of order. This second, ancillary, order is negative in that it
does not require "signification" *(yi)* from those whom it most immediately affects. The assumption is that these persons have failed
to participate voluntarily, and hence must be compelled. Although
Confucius' sympathies clearly lie with participatory ordering, as we
shall detail, he was realist enough to acknowledge the need for
enforced compliance as a backup measure.

The *Analects* contains frequent discussions of *cheng** 政, commonly translated as "governing" or "government," but rendered here
as "effecting sociopolitical order." These discussions pointedly ad-
vertise the relationship between this concept and its homophonous
etynomic root, *cheng* 正, "to order" (12/17 and 13/13):[53]

> Chi K'ang Tzu asked Confucius about effecting sociopolitical order.
> Confucius replied, "Effecting sociopolitical order (*cheng** 政) means
> 'ordering' (*cheng* 正). Where one leads with the example of order,
> who would dare be otherwise!"

> The Master said, "If one is orderly *(cheng)* in his own person, what
> problem would he have in administering sociopolitical order *(cheng*)*?
> But if he is unable to order himself, how can he bring order to
> others?"

In what follows, we shall present several arguments in support
of the claim that Confucius' social and political philosophy gives
priority to aesthetic over rational ordering. In so doing, we shall
further attempt to clarify some of the important implications of this
commitment.[54]

It has been the argument of this work so far that Confucius'
philosophy makes no resort to any concept of transcendence, that a
systematic implication of employing an immanental vision is a commitment to explaining the world in terms of events rather than substances, and that a primary emphasis on particularity is necessarily
entailed by process and immanence. Rational order prizes continuity
and consistency, and eschews disjunction and novelty. By contrast,
aesthetic order, with its concern for concrete particularity, is most

fully realized in an event ontology in which the degree of disjunction and inconsistency that characterizes process permits a corresponding degree of creative possibilities.

As we have seen above, the primacy of the particular that we find in an aesthetic order is a distinguishing characteristic of Confucius' epistemology. The realization (*chih* 知) accomplished in living up to one's word (*hsin** 信) generates an emergent world contingent upon the conditions and capacities of the specific persons engaged in the dynamics of enacting reality. As such, truth and reality are ultimately personal categories, unique for each participant.

This primacy of the particular has also been evident in our discussion of authoritative person (*jen** *che* 仁者) where personal realization is a process qualified by one's own peculiar disposition and circumstances. That this focus on the unique particular is further an important dimension of Confucius' social and political philosophy is readily apparent in the character of the relationship between personal ordering and the attainment of sociopolitical order. This correlativity between "part" and "whole" stands in rather vivid contrast to any reductionist political theory. Hsiao Kung-chuan makes this point, albeit in rather overdrawn language:[55]

> The relationship of the world and the self, . . . while conditioned by distinctions of proximity and of priority, was not a distinction of the internal versus the external or of the unimportant versus the important. If we were to attempt a comparison of Confucius' understanding of *jen* with European theories, then we would have to note that this concept is on the one hand different from that of emphasis on groups and the de-emphasis of the individual as encountered in collectivism, and simultaneously is dissimilar to the aggrandizement of the self and the restraining of the state in individualism. For both of these acknowledge the antithesis of the individual and society, whereas Confucius obliterated such boundaries and effected a unity of mankind with the self.

For Confucius, then, neither person nor society is subordinated as an instrumental means to serve the realization of the other. Rather, they stand as mutually implicatory ends. Any and all semblance of order in society and the state is ultimately traceable to and is an integral feature of the personal ordering of its constituents. On the other hand, personal order would not be possible except for the context provided by social and political life. Confucius emphasizes the role of personal order in his analogy between social order per se and the language used to characterize it: just as the character cheng*政, "sociopolitical ordering," is derived from cheng 正 (used frequently by Confucius as "personal ordering"), so sociopolitical order itself is traceable to the concerted achievement of personal order among the people. Confucius on numerous occasions moves to underscore the interdependence of sociopolitical order and the ordering of the particular person (13/6): "The Master said, 'Where one is orderly in his own person, people will accord with him without need of command. But where he is not orderly himself, even when he commands he is not obeyed.' "[56] For this reason, the pursuit of social and political harmony must always begin from personal cultivation (14/42):

> Tzu-lu asked about becoming an exemplary person (chün tzu).
> The Master said, "In cultivating himself he inspires reverence."
> "Is that all there is to it?" Tzu-lu asked.
> "In cultivating himself he brings peace and stability to others."
> "Is that all there is to it?"
> "In cultivating himself he brings peace and security to the common people. Even Yao and Shun were not able to accomplish this."

The coextensive relationship existing among the dimensions of personal, social, and political order has the effect of precluding the employment of categories familiar to us from the vocabulary of Western philosophical theory. Confucius, given his distinctly social perspective with regard to the project of person making, does not perceive a corresponding degree of difference between private and public interests, between ethical and political concerns, between social and political structures.

There are important consequences of the fact that in Confucian social theory a person is irreducibly communal, especially when weighed against the concerns of our own tradition. For the majority of Western philosophers since Descartes, perhaps the most perplexing problem has been how to account for intersubjective experience, given the autonomy and absoluteness of individual consciousness. For Confucius this issue does not arise since experience is, ab initio, intersubjective.

In recent Western philosophy this problem of intersubjectivity has received perhaps its most urgent formulations in the writings of representatives of the hermeneutical tradition.[57] By stressing the need for empathic understanding of literature as a means of comprehending historical actions and institutions, Wilhelm Dilthey celebrated the insight that was later to serve as ground for a social hermeneutics. The pattern of intersubjectivity established by the historian between himself and the subject of his interpretive skill creates a psychic and spiritual contemporaneity of interpreter and interpreted. The brilliance of his position is to highlight the fact that history may best be understood as a society defined temporally, sequentially. And the art of historical interpretation establishes or exploits a virtual inter-subjectivity, transitive and reciprocal, indifferent to temporal distance.

The principal difficulty these subsequent thinkers in the West have had in appropriating the insight that the primary datum of social theory, the social unit, is to be found in intersubjective ex-periencing, is that social philosophers have allowed their theoretical visions to be dominated by categories deriving from the political rather than the distinctly social sphere.

A perennial difficulty in Western political theory involves the fact that for a variety of not altogether understandable reasons the desire to enjoy the benefits of order so often exists separately from the desire to create or maintain order. This (primarily) psychological distinction has given rise to differences of a social and political kind between "rulers" disposed to create or maintain order and "the ruled" who are disposed to enjoy its benefits. The various classical attempts to overcome this disjunction, from socialism to participatory democracy, have met with only limited success. The disjunction between ruler and ruled continues to qualify our social and political life.

An issue of much greater importance than the means of dis-tributing the functions of rule in a society is the question as to whether the distinction of ruler and ruled is not a questionable ground for the promotion and maintenance of civilized order. For the most part, this question has been academic in the West, for the distinction has persisted well into modern times as most broadly problematic for social and political philosophy. Even socialist and liberal democratic visions in which the "rulers rule themselves" require the detachment of norms and rules from the social and political conduct they enjoin. The subject who rules himself, rules by the light of reason or the immutable principles promoting social order. That is to say, he rules himself by recourse to objective rules. Underlying the distinction between ruler and ruled, therefore, is a distinction between rules as procedures for promoting and maintaining social order, and those elements of a society which require ordering.

The speculations of Max Weber constitute a primary illustration of the continued dominance of social theory by political categories. With Weber, social theory as theory of society, rather than as cosmology or political ideology casually and uncritically applied to social phenomena, began to come into its own. But Weber's conception of *verstehen* social theory does not quite measure up to Dilthey's original vision. The architectonic of Weber's social theory as contained in his magnum opus, *Economy and Society,* is shaped in part by his distinction between *verhalten* and *handeln,* behavior and action, the former characterizable in terms of external measurement, the latter requiring some resort to an interpretation of the meaning of the behavior which takes account of the values and intentions of the subject. The social theorist must seek to explain that which can be behaviorally described, and to interpret that which can only be considered, at least in part, through an internal reference to a locus of meaning. Comprehension *(verstehen)* results from an organization of the interpretation of actions which is, in fact, an organization of subjective meanings. But if we consider the problematic of Weber's social theory, as distinct from its architectonic, we discover an internal tension that ultimately precludes Weber's understanding the concept of *verstehen* in terms of intersubjectivity.

Weber's social theory is heavily influenced by his philosophy of history, the principal theme of which is that the story of Western (or Anglo-European) culture is one of increasing organization defined by bureaucratic rationalization. The creative element in this historical development is associated with charismatic individuals who have the power to interrupt and partially shape and/or redirect the rationalizing trend. In the concepts of rationalization and charismatic influence, we find the threads which together bind the social modalities of science, politics, and religion. The aim of the scientist in his classic guise is to further the development of bureaucratic rationalism.

Over against this dynamic in society is that which introduces spontaneous values and ideals. These values Weber identifies largely with the religious dimension of society, particularly insofar as religion has served as a fundamental source of value orientations. But it is to politics that Weber looks for the guiding forces of society. The social unit is the individual agent. The essential relation is that of ruler and ruled. Like Aristotle, whose social problematic was shaped by the context of the *polis* as a political structure, Weber is a political sociologist. Intersubjectivity, considered in terms of community *(Gemeinschaft)* as over against society *(Gesellschaft)*, is a notion of secondary importance in Weber's social philosophy.

Only quite recently has the difficulty involved in attempting to appropriate the insights of Dilthey for developing a social theory been recognized. As the example of Weber so well illustrates, the notion of intersubjectivity cannot be properly applied to social theory as long as it is felt necessary to construe social praxis in terms of political praxis. Classical political theory, bound as it is by the ruler–ruled distinction, cannot move beyond the notion of consensus. And, as Charles Taylor has so trenchantly noted, whereas consensus concerns meanings that may be entertained by individuals in abstraction from their social relations, intersubjective meanings "are rooted in social practice" and are, as such, "constitutive of social reality."[58]

The present challenge to Western social theory, in fact, may involve giving up the apparently futile quest for a free, rational consensus, to seek instead to discover what value intersubjective experiencing might have for explicating the notion of authoritative action, and how such action is germane to the understanding of personal and interpersonal cultivation. The insights derived from Confucius regarding the relations between personal and social ordering may prove an important resource for addressing this issue.

In reviewing the relevant citations from the *Analects* regarding the mutuality of personal and social order, one might well respond that Confucius is not suggesting that "personal ordering" *(cheng)* has political efficacy for all people, but only for those in positions of power. A radical example of this limitation is the seeming focus on the ruler as a preeminent source of order (16/2):

> Confucius said, "When the way *(tao)* prevails in the empire, ritual actions, music, and punitive expeditions come from the Son of

Heaven; when it does not, they come from the various nobles. . . .
When the way prevails in the empire, responsibility for effecting sociopolitical order does not lie with the ministers; when the way prevails in the empire, the common people do not debate political issues."

This limitation must be understood, however, against the participatory nature of the achieved harmony in which each person has
his own privileges and their attendant responsibilities (14/26):

The Master said, "Where one does not have the position, he does
not plan its contribution to sociopolitical order." Tseng Tzu said,
"The reflections of the exemplary person do not go beyond his position."[59]

That is, the range of a person's contribution is determined by his
political station. And for Confucius, "personal ordering" and a position of significant social and political influence are mutually im-
plicative. Personal ordering can only take place in the context of
social and political participation, and social and political station are
only justifiable as attendant upon the achievements of personal
cultivation.

As we shall discover in our discussion of exemplary person (*chün
tzu* 君子) below, Confucius eschewed the essentialist notion of
quality by birth. *Chün tzu* is a nobility of refinement rather than
blood. This same attitude of Confucius marks his distinction between
the civilized and the noncivilized world. As Hsiao Kung-chuan observes:[60]

Of greatest interest to us, however, is the fact that Confucius used a
cultural standard in deciding who was a barbarian and who was a
Chinese. . . . Since the distinction between them was not one of any
fixed line, but one that fluctuated according to rising or falling cultural levels, it therefore entirely lost its racial significance and became
a purely cultural term.

For Confucius, social and political distinctions are a reflection of
personal cultivation and one's consequent contribution to the sociopolitical harmony.

Confucius' insistent rejection of factionalism further signals the
priority of aesthetic order. In a social and political process in which

formal construction has precedence, "sameness" is prized over "difference," "agreement" over "harmony." To take an example from the classical Chinese tradition, in Legalism (*fa chia* 法家), a political philosophy based on obedience to established standards, the concept of "accountability" (*hsing ming** 刑名) is an attempt to insure conformity to a preestablished definition of office and responsibility. Any deviation from prescribed form is met with fatal displeasure. This contrasts sharply with Confucius' perception that appropriate political contribution presupposes the ability of the office holder to adapt existing policy to changing circumstances.[61] Confucius, scoring the limits of human solidarity, makes it clear that although one is usually able to rely on the opinions and good intentions of others, one must be able to act alone when the contingencies of circumstances require it (9/30):

> The Master said, "You can learn with him, but cannot necessarily share his accomplishments; you can have his accomplishments, but not necessarily share his stature; you can have his stature, but not necessarily share the contingencies of his circumstances."

In fact, Confucius regards political conformism to be characteristic of persons who have no business serving in positions of authority. Repeatedly Confucius describes social and political participation in terms of pursuing a harmony among differences (13/23): "The exemplary person (*chün tzu*) pursues harmony rather than agreement; the small person is the opposite." The commentator, Yang Po-chün,[62] in explanation of this rather cryptic passage, refers us to the *Tso-chuan*:[63]

> The Marquis of Ch'i said, "Only Chü is in harmony with me!"
> Yen Tzu replied, "All that Chü does is agree with you—wherein is the harmony?"
> "Is there a difference between 'harmony' (*ho* 和) and 'agreement' (*t'ung* 同)?" asked the Marquis.
> Yen Tzu replied, "There is. Harmony is like making broth. One uses water, fire, vinegar, sauce, salt, and plum to cook his fish and meat, and burns firewood and stalks as fuel for the cooking process. The cook blends these ingredients harmoniously to achieve the appropriate flavor. Where it is too bland, he adds flavoring, and where it is too concentrated, he dilutes it with water. When you partake of

this broth, you feel most content. The relationship between ruler and minister is the same.

"Where the ruler considers something workable and yet there are problems, the minister should indicate what is problematic, and carry out what is workable with zeal. Where the ruler considers something problematic and yet there are workable elements, the minister should indicate what is workable and shunt aside what is problematic. Accordingly, political affairs will function harmoniously without violating ritual observances, and the common people will not be rebellious. Thus, the *Book of Songs* states:

> Where there is harmoniously blended broth, one has already cautioned the kitchen to bring out a harmonious and even flavor. The gods will come and partake of it without rancor, and above and below will be free of contest.

The Former Kings blended the five flavors and harmonized the five notes to bring contentment to their hearts and completeness to political affairs. ... Now Chü is not acting accordingly. Whatever you say is right, Chü also says is right; whatever you say is wrong, Chü also says is wrong. If you add water to flavor water, who can eat it? If you keep playing the same note on the lute or *se*, who can listen to it? The failing of 'agreement' lies then in this."

The difference between *ho* 和 , translated here as "harmony," and *t'ung* 同, "agreement," is the difference between "attuning" and "tuning." Attuning is the combining and blending of two or more ingredients in a harmonious whole with benefit and enhancement that maximizes the possibilities of all without sacrificing their separate and particular identities. "Tuning" is finding agreement by bringing one ingredient into conformity and concurrence with an existing standard such that one ingredient is enhanced possibly at the expense of others.

That this *Tso-chuan* passage is a fair elaboration of Confucius' meaning is clear from several other passages in the *Analects* in which Confucius specifically condemns factionalism in political service (2/14 and 15/22):

> The exemplary person *(chün tzu)* associates openly with others, but does not caucus; the small person is the opposite.
> The exemplary person *(chün tzu)* ... gathers together with others, but does not form cliques.

Perhaps the most specific example of Confucius' pursuit of aesthetic harmony rather than formal agreement is found in 13/15:

> Confucius replied, "... People have a saying: 'I find no enjoyment in being ruler, except that no one contradicts what I have to say.' If what he has to say is good and no one contradicts him, that's good. But if what he has to say is not good and no one contradicts him, is this not almost a case of one dictum bringing about the downfall of the state?"

In these passages, Confucius is advocating a social and political harmony that can take account of the disparate opinions of its participants.

We have highlighted the importance that Confucius invested in tolerance and the extent to which he truly "detested inflexibility" (*chi ku* 疾 固).[64] The conduct of the authoritative person is free of preconceptions and inviolate rules. This tolerance is, of course, a necessary condition in a conception of sociopolitical order that strives to allow the fullest possible disclosure of particularity. As Confucius states (15/37): "The exemplary person (*chün tzu*) is orderly[65] but not punctilious." This sense of tolerance necessary in an aesthetic ordering of human society is a primary qualification of those who would exercise influence in the community.[66] This notion of tolerance, expressed in many different ways, is a major ingredient in Confucius' conception of appropriate social organization, and is certainly a necessary qualification for those who would seek to inspire the emulation of others (3/26):

> The Master said, "What is there to look at in a person who in holding a position of influence is not tolerant, who in performing ritual actions is not reverent, and who in performing funeral rites does not grieve?"

Given that Confucius' program for person making presumes the disciplining of oneself and the practice of ritual action (*k'o chi fu li* 克己復禮), attitudes such as respect, tolerance, and deference are precondition for any kind of personal growth. Just as the definition of one's person emerges communally, so the disposition of the society and the state unfolds in a dialogue between received

tradition and present circumstances, between inherited meaning preserved in ritual structures and the contribution of the present participants.

Taken to its ultimate degree, this sense of allowing social and
political order to emerge from below renders the ideal ruler "non-
active" (wu-wei 無為): clear of any impositional or coercive activity.
Confucius so described tradition's most exemplary rulers (15/5):

> The Master said, "If anyone could be said to have effected political
> order while remaining nonactive (wu-wei), it was Shun. What was
> there for him to do? He simply made himself respectful and took up
> his position facing due south."

This wu-wei posture is a function of the ruler's respectfulness and
tolerance. And this passage is not an odd, unrepresentative excerpt
from the Analects; rather, it can fairly be regarded as a succinct
characterization of the appropriate attitude of those responsible for
coordinating social order. In Chapter IV, we explore the concept of
particular focus, te 德, at some length, describing it in terms of both
individuation and of synthesis and integration. The ruler who is fully
able to realize his particularity through aesthetic integration with the
whole is indeed wu-wei in that he exerts no impositional force over
those around him (2/1):[67] "The Master said, 'A ruler who effects
social and political order through his te can be compared to the pole
star which merely lodges in its place while the other stars pay it
homage.' " The accomplished ruler, far from exercising coercive power
over his people, grounds his pursuit of order in the richness of
diversity and orchestrates his subjects' impulses toward quality in
the direction of an aesthetic harmony that maximizes their possibilities
for creativity (20/1): ". . . Where one is tolerant, he will win over
the multitude. . . . Where he is impartial, he will win their appro-
bation."

3.2 Law and Ritual Action: Hsing 刑 , Fa 法 , and Li 禮

Confucius' recognition of the value of models as guiding norms
is illustrated in his comparison of ritual action (li 禮) and penal law
(hsing 刑) as a method of achieving social order. Ritual action (li)
permits the spontaneous exercise of harmonizing actions. Law (hsing)

only controls external behavior. The existence of law, particularly penal law, however necessary it might be, suggests the failure of ritual action. Ritual actions *(li)* are models for Confucius. They are objects of imitation. And they only exist as such objects in their institutionalized form. Primarily they exist as significating patterns informing the actions of the exemplary person. Ritual actions *(li)* are models in a manner that law *(hsing)* cannot be, for law cannot serve, as do ritual actions, to express the significating actions of the exemplary person.

Since in each case, the exemplary person is himself a unique achievement made possible through the appropriation, personalization, and creative extension of the meaning encapsulated in ritual actions *(li)*, it would follow that meaningfully enacted ritual actions, like exemplary persons, must also take precedence over established law. In fact, Confucius does advocate persuasion and transformative education rather than forced-order discipline (12/19):

> Chi K'ang Tzu asked Confucius about effecting sociopolitical order, saying, "What if I kill those without *tao* in order to encourage those with *tao?*" Confucius replied, "You are the sociopolitical order. Why must you use killing? If you want to be good, the masses will be good. The *te* of the exemplary person *(chün tzu)* is wind while that of the small person is grass. As the wind blows, the grass bends."

The personal focus *(te)* which the exemplary person uses to engage the uncultivated person, far from being impositional or coercive, is his potential for integrating with and participating in the intersubjective person making of his people. The "wind" of his influence nurtures and encourages the people toward a condition wherein the application of law is unnecessary to achieve the desired social order. The wind is informing, not coercing, and the grass is receptive, not submissive. That is, they interact in a natural and mutually beneficial way.

Confucius' ideal is a society in which the application of laws is not necessary (12/13): "In hearing litigations, I am as good as anyone. What we must do is make it so there are no litigations."[68] In noting these passages, we must be careful not to misconstrue Confucius' attitude toward penal law. There can be no question that the Confucius depicted in the *Analects* advocated social and political order through a process of suasion and example. This preference for and emphasis on education and transformation did not, however, prevent the eminently practical Confucius from assigning penal law a place in his political thought as an unfortunate but necessary challenge to the threat of disintegrating order.[69]

In the Western tradition, laws as divine commands, whose transcendent source provides their strongest justification, or laws as rational principles articulating norms of behavior and interaction characterized by fairness and productive of the greatest social stability, are products of lawgivers. God gave the laws to Moses for promulgation to the Jews. Hammurabi and Solon codified the laws for their respective societies. But there was, clearly, a spiritual sanction for law in these cases as well. In each case a transcendent source empowers the laws and sanctions their authority.

As we have seen in our discussion of ritual action (li) and signification (yi), the origins of ritual action (li) for Confucius are personal acts of signification (yi), and the continued justification for any given ritual lies in its power to elicit significance (yi) in its performance. Those specific acts of signification (yi) which are the foundation for traditional ritual (li) are, for the most part, lost in the past, but the continued viability of any given ritual requires that it continue to be performed with significance (yi).

The contrast between law (hsing) and rites (li), therefore, is to be found in the meaningfulness of ritual performed with personal significance (yi) and the mainly coercive function of nonpersonal law (hsing) which originates in expediency. In the Western tradition, law, insofar as it is revered, has been regarded as having an extra-human origin. One of the consequences of the claim[70] that the strength of one's individuality is a function of the exteriority of norms, is that transcendent laws, laws as external determining sources of order, are necessary to societies patterned by individualism in its stronger sense. This is the case because communal consensus is well-nigh impossible to achieve in a highly individualistic society. Under such circumstances, then, law must apply primarily to external behavior and must have a sanctioning power which guarantees conformity by threat of punishment. Whatever the cost of subscribing to the existence of these externally imposed laws or norms, the sort of individuality which requires and is reinforced by them has come to be held at a premium within the Western tradition.

What is principally at issue here is the character of social harmony, and that leads us back to the contrast of aesthetic and rational
order. The assurance of the latter type of order depends upon already
existing patterns of relatedness which are in some very real sense
independent of any particular instances. Here we can speak of social
order as a function of obedience to, or conformity with, principles
or norms. The ultimate source of these norms must be the mind or
will of God, or human reason, or a commonly recognized sense of
enlightened self-interest. Social order, in its rational form, cannot be
made to depend solely upon the emergence of virtuous models.

Joseph Needham, in his comparison between Chinese and Western concepts of law, associates the Western notion of natural law
(jus naturale) with the Chinese idea of ritual actions *(li 禮)*, and
positive law with the Chinese conception of penal law *(fa 法)*. He
observes:[71]

> This 'positive' law partook of the nature of the commands of an
> earthly ruler, obedience was an obligation, and precisely specified
> sanctions followed transgression. This is undoubtedly represented in
> Chinese thought by the term *fa*, just as the customs of society based
> on ethics . . ., or ancient tabus . . ., are represented by *li*, a term
> which, however, includes in addition all kinds of ceremonial and sac-
> rifical observances. . . . Now in the Chinese context there could
> hardly be a *jus gentium*, for owing to the 'isolation' of Chinese civil-
> isation there were no other *gentes* from whose practices an actual
> universal law of nations could be deduced, but there was certainly a
> natural law, namely, that body of customs which the sage-kings and
> the people had always accepted, i.e., what the Confucians called *li*.

Although such a broad comparison among these categories is at some
level justifiable, it is their differences rather than similarities that are
most interesting. Confucius in his attitude toward law is certainly a
fair representative of the early Chinese tradition. He did not specifically use the character *fa 法* as "penal law;" this would have been
anachronistic. "Penal law and punishment" is represented by the
concept *hsing 刑*, which anticipates *fa* in the tradition.

In the classical Chinese tradition, ritual action derives from the
attempt to imitate the regularity and order of nature. We have stressed
that this imitation does not entail obedience to any presumably
universal norm or law. In fact, the early Chinese tradition simply

acknowledged a spontaneous harmony in nature with which human beings, through concerted effort, can effect integration, thereby enriching both their natural environment and themselves. The harmony which exists in nature, far from being predetermined by some abstract natural law, is a negotiated and open-ended achievement of those intrinsically related elements that constitute the process of existence.

Similarly, the harmony achievable in human society is not reducible to "universally acceptable ethical principles."[72] Man, like nature, must constantly, although usually imperceptibly, shift his ground to accommodate the emergence of ever-novel circumstances. Hence, the Chinese notion of ritual action must be distinguished from the classical Western concept of natural law in that it is an order that emerges out of past circumstances, to be altered by the exigencies of the present moment. It is irreducibly personal, in that it always bears the signature of particular participants.

There is no claim in Confucius that ritual actions either constitute or are responses to universal ethical norms. On the contrary, Confucius makes it clear that the ultimate source of ritual actions is the human being striving to achieve appropriateness in his social and natural context. In service to this appropriateness, the particular person has the right if not the obligation to alter and extend the content of these structures. Above we have defined ritual action (li) as a means of developing and displaying one's own capacity to significate (yi) and as an apparatus for fostering personal refinement. It is intersubjective in that it is laden with the meaning invested by one's precursors in the tradition and by his contemporaries who constitute his cultural ambience. To enact ritual meaningfully, it is further necessary that one exercise his own capacity to significate (yi) in order to gain access to this inherited meaning and to appropriate and extend it.

The association between the Western notion of positive law and Chinese fa 法 (or Confucius' hsing 刑) is certainly problematic. In the classical Chinese tradition, fa overlaps ritual action (li) in that it too represents a formalized investment of meaning. That is, li and fa share a common starting point. Furthermore, like ritual action, fa is directed at organizing and ordering society. Fa differs significantly from ritual action, however, in that it is neither intersubjectively integrating nor personal. The enforcement of fa in a given situation does not require the active participation of the object of enforcement.

For this reason, in its project of bringing order to society, it is not able to register the same degree of insistent particularity or contingency as ritual action (li).

The value of litigation for a defendant is fundamentally extrinsic and coercive. In the tradition, where fa has been evoked to maintain order, there has been an effort to ameliorate its inability to deal with cases in a way sufficiently sensitive to their singularity by entrusting the cultivated person with the responsibility of arbitration. Even so, this only allows the adjudicator to exercise his own yi in determining what is most appropriate to the circumstances. Because the use of fa to effect order does not require the active participation of those most affected by it, it can have little transforming or refining influence on the people. On the contrary, because it is fundamentally restrictive and imposed, it constitutes a real limitation on their possibilities for person making.

In the Chinese tradition, ritual action (li) and fa represent a qualitative choice. The need to invoke fa presupposes the failure of those concerned to achieve the harmony possible by recourse to ritual action. Fa can be fairly described as being derived from li but lacking the meaningful participation of those involved which can insure optimum appropriateness. Hence, Confucius asserts (13/3): " . . . When the use of ritual action and music does not prevail, the application of laws and punishments will not be on the mark. . . . "

In the employment of ritual action (li) to effect order, these li and the people who perform them are mutually determining and refining. Li permits and in fact encourages an emergent harmony that is expressive of the demands of insistent particularity. The society in its reliance upon li maximizes its possibilities for qualitative harmony. Where ritual action fails, however, fa simply serves as a coercive means to prevent decline into social discord from a level at which the more effective and enduring methods of ritual action can again be applied. In this vision of social order, the harmony which can be achieved through ritual action is an end in itself, whereas the imposed order achieved by fa has only functional, instrumental value as a temporary means to the higher end.

3.3   Shame (ch'ih 恥) and Guilt (tsui 罪)

There is another distinction that helps to illustrate the distance between the Western obedience to law and the Chinese commitment to the pursuit of aesthetic harmony. Given the importance that Confucius places on ritual action (li) as a means to sociopolitical order he seeks energetically to cultivate a sense of shame (ch'ih 耻) in the people. It is significant that Confucius is concerned with shame (ch'ih) rather than guilt (tsui 罪) in that these two concepts parallel the ritual/law distinction. Guilt is law-oriented in that it signals a personal acknowledgment that one has committed a breach of established conduct. Shame, on the other hand, is ritual-oriented in that it describes a consciousness of how one is perceived by others. Guilt tends to be individual as a condition of one's relationship to law; shame tends to be communal as a condition of one's relationship to others.

The concept, guilt (tsui), occurs infrequently in the Analects, and always indicates a transgression against some established standard (5/1):

> Confucius said that Kung-yeh Ch'ang could be allowed to marry his daughter. Even though Kung-yeh Ch'ang had spent some time in jail, it was not because of any guilt (tsui) on his part. On that, Confucius gave his daughter to him as wife.

If, by contrast, we examine the many passages in which shame (ch'ih) occurs in the Analects, it is always used with reference to a lapse of responsibility, often accompanied by insult, estrangement, and humiliation at the hands of others (1/13): " . . . Being respectful to others is close to ritual action in that it keeps one at a distance from shame (ch'ih) and humiliation."

The importance of shame in this tradition can be illustrated by reference to Brian McKnight's recent study of amnesties and pardons, *The Quality of Mercy*. This study presents a clear inference that litigation in China functioned as much to find a plaintiff "shameful" as to find him "guilty." That is, the courts and prison system, probably for economic reasons, were not prepared to incarcerate criminals for lengthy periods as punishment for wrongdoings. Amnesties and pardons of one order or another opened the prison gates literally every two or three years and sent the inmates home. Under these circumstances, the courts had to act harshly in cases of heinous crime, and to rely on the shame entailed in the process of litigation to discipline the more minor and marginal offenders and restore their commitment to social responsibility. "Shame" was also an important consideration in sentencing. Punishment by amputation or dismemberment would be used to bring shame on the criminal by rendering him an offender against the filial injunction to return one's body to one's ancestors intact.

Important to an understanding of Confucius' social and political philosophy is that his preference for and pursuit of an aesthetic harmony does not preclude an awareness of the functional value of some order which, having been established and defined, can be applied as a reinforcement where intrinsically generated order breaks down. This qualitative tension between the preferred status of aesthetic harmony and an acknowledged functional value of rational order is well illustrated by reference to a central yet frequently misconstrued passage in the *Analects* (2/3):

> Lead the people with administrative policies and organize them with penal law, and they will avoid punishments but will be without a sense of shame. Lead them with *te* and organize them with ritual actions, and they will have a sense of shame and moreover will order themselves harmoniously.

In this passage, imposed order based on regulation and edict is contrasted with political harmony effected through example, participation, and moral edification.[73]

This passage is all too frequently interpreted as offering two exclusive alternatives for government. It should be remembered, however, that for Confucius, society is a creative achievement. As such, established political policies and penal laws are not in themselves a sufficient condition for achieving the richest possibilities of social and political organization. Confucius establishes a clear line between indoctrination and education in his belief that to achieve truly effective and enduring political harmony, transformative "education" in its original sense of "drawing out from" the particular person himself, must be given priority. This immediate participation of the particular person can be maximized by generating a self-sustaining, self-regulating society out of that commitment to self-cultivation which results in personal focus *(te)* and allows for integrative modeling and the meaningful performance of ritual actions which can structure and sustain such a society.

The characteristic Confucian priority of the plurality and diversity
of the concrete particulars is expressed by reliance upon the modeling
made possible by a particular focus (*te* 德), rather than the use of
enforced policy and edict to effect social and political harmony. It
is evidenced in Confucius' preference for personally performed ritual
actions as against the application of largely external laws and punishments. It is illustrated by the absence of telling distinctions between
the private and public interest, social and political spheres, and ethics
and politics. It is exemplified in the concern with cultivating a sense
of shame in the people. It is further evidenced in the fact that, from
the perspective of the people, sociopolitical order is something that
they accomplish rather than have created for them. The disposition
of the society and state is signatory, displaying the character of the
specific participants, their diversity, and the quality of their participation. Finally, the preference for aesthetic order is found in the
contrast established between order by the exercise of power and the
emergent order of creative actions.

4 The Exemplary Person: *Chün Tzu* 君 子

The immanence of principles in Confucius' philosophical understanding precludes resort to social and political norms that are not ultimately grounded in immanent forms of personal and social action
(*li* 禮). This serves as the primary reason why models are of such
importance in Confucius' social thought. Norms or ideals in abstraction from the sort of concrete model instances in personal and
institutional situations would be useful only, if at all, as a stopgap
measure for imposing order, but would ultimately be of little service
to the educative project of self-cultivation.

The distinction between the functions of abstract principles and
of traditional models in the realization of social stability is quite
important. In the Confucian claim that it is the latter, not the former,
which best serve the personal and social needs of human beings we
discover a principal explanation for Confucius' metaphysical agnosticism.

In the Western tradition, it is God, or a transcendent realm of
forms, or the structures of rationality or the order of nature, that

most often constitute the source of guiding values, norms, and principles. Persons or institutions existing within the concrete, historical world may be seen as obedient, in greater or lesser degree, to such principles, but the primary reference of ethical activity is generally to the principle, not the person or institution itself. Exceptions to this generalization are rare. One thinks immediately of Jesus Christ and of Socrates as persons serving as models for Western culture.

Jesus Christ does appear to be a model in some sense, although we must be extremely careful in trying to decide precisely what that sense may be. For Christ was "the word *(logos)* made flesh." He was the instance of a transcendent *logos*, the referent of which was an eternal, unchanging world. Socrates, at least as Plato presented him, was the embodiment of *eros*, the desire for completeness of understanding, a drive which ultimately led him to choose an unjust death in obedience to his principles rather than a life that would have compromised them. It was the desire for knowledge and the hope for immortality that patterned the mortal existence of Socrates. Both Socrates and Jesus were characterized by lives lived in reference to a norm, standard, ideal, or principle that transcended this world. In Christianity one may in the strictest sense imitate Christ only up to a point. The purely divine character of his nature is more than human and transcends utterly the human realm. Jesus is more mediator than model and his salvific function is expressed ultimately in terms of doctrines of grace and atonement rather than by recourse to any urgings toward imitation.

Socrates comes closer to illustrating a model in the Confucian sense. The imitation of Socrates is the imitation of a life lived in pursuit of knowledge, a life lived without compromising the values and ideals which together have come to define the philosophic spirit. Socrates, as a historical personage, however, is shrouded in obscurity. And Plato's literary invention is more often than not employed by the later tradition as illustrative of Platonic principles (*eros*, the dialectic, intuiting the Form of the Good) than as a model for actual imitation. Here again, as in the case of Christ, it is the eternal, immutable world beyond this actual world that is the true object of "imitation." That is, both Jesus and Socrates are mediatorial and, to that degree, instrumental. Confucius was a sage. As such, he serves as an object of imitation in his own right.

It might be suggested that certain charismatic figures in the Western tradition do in fact function as virtuous models, but the argument against this claim is rather straightforward: the charismatic is, as the term suggests (*charisma* = "gift"), one who is "gifted" with a message deriving from a source beyond himself. The charismatic individual is often a prophet who may be said to serve, in his messenger function, as a mediator, but is in no full sense a model. Which of us would feel constrained to emulate Isaiah or Jeremiah? Such a thought would be completely misplaced. The prophets and charismatics are not models, but mediators of norms and principles. The greatness of these prophets and charismatic individuals is such as to create a distance between themselves and the ordinary human being and thereby to suggest that they are "more than human." In this way any exemplary role they might have had is seriously undercut.

What, more specifically, is Confucius' understanding of the function of serving as a model? For Confucius, to be is to be in a certain way. A model, therefore, is the actualization of a mode of being (*modus essendi*), not in the sense of instancing an antecedent "way," but rather, as the emergence of a novel way (*tao* 道). The *modus essendi* is equivalent to *modus operandi*. In its most fundamental sense a model is a new mode of being which adds to the *tao*. The model is a particular institutionalization of significating acts. The authoritative person, the person of *jen**, realizes or creates ritual (*li*) through personal signification (*yi*). The *modus operandi* of the authoritative person (*jen**) provides a model for others who would be authoritative (*jen**). But the dynamics of modeling require both deference and personal creativity. That is, one cannot imitate the model in any literal or formal sense and still achieve the sort of originative thinking and acting associated with the authoritative person. What precisely does one imitate in the model?

Imitation (*mimesis*) is associated with the notion of representation. To imitate is to re-present. Both Plato and Aristotle discuss art as the imitation of nature. Their significantly different characterizations of nature, however, certainly suggest different consequences of such imitation. For Plato it is the form or structure of a thing that is to be imitated; for Aristotle the object of imitation is organic functioning. The latter notion of imitation is more nearly relevant to the concept of imitating a model. Also, Aristotle's discussion of tragedy as a mimetic art form, in which the arousal and subsequent catharsis of pity and fear serves as the primary goal, suggests something of the modeling activity. Imitating a model entails imitating functions, processes, actions, and events. And such imitation has evocative consequences.

This, of course, leads us again to the expressive and evocative function of ritual action *(li)*. The enactment of ritual *(li)* with personal significance *(yi)* is not bare imitation of an abstract form; it is the representation of a model, the reenactment of concretely embodied *li*. Such imitation involves more than repetition; it requires the realization of the model in one's own person and thus requires that one become a person of authority *(jen*)*, a significating being.

Two points must be emphasized with respect to the understanding of models in the Confucian tradition: first, the model is not only a means of maintaining continuity with the sages of the past, he is a means of stimulating novelty, as well. The imitation of the model does not involve replication, but is rather an example of introducing novel meaning into one's social circumstances. Obedience to or instancing of principles involves the realization of what we have called logical or rational order; the imitation of a model entails, by contrast, the realization of aesthetic order. The realization of aesthetic order requires the emergence of a novel, complex meaning that is a function of the unique particularity of the imitating being. One need only consider the relations of learning (*hsüeh* 學) and reflecting (*ssu* 思) in the realization (*chih* 知) of wisdom to get the specific sense of how the modeling activity can lead to knowledge that is expressive of both continuity and novelty. Perhaps an even more obvious example is the relationship between ritual action *(li)* and personal significance *(yi)* in the achievement of authoritative personhood *(jen*)*. The performance of ritual action *(li)* with personal significance *(yi)* requires the sort of imitation that eschews mere repetition in favor of the re-presentation of ritual that both derives and bestows novel meanings.

This leads us to the second important point concerning the function of models: models may, indirectly, take the form of institutions *(li)* as well as persons. Thus Confucius' appeal to the Chou institutions is an appeal to appropriate models of human behavior. It is essential to realize, however, that these model institutions, as *li*, have efficacy only if there are persons, such as the Duke of Chou, who may be seen as having realized these *li* through appropriate acts of signification (*yi*). That is to say, the fundamental sense of model is grounded in exemplary persons who serve, for Confucius, as instances of authoritative humanity.

One of the most interesting and dramatic consequences of the resort to models rather than principles in the Confucian tradition is the manner in which it has served to shape the meaning of authority. The primary meaning of authority is discovered in the individual acts of self-actualization associated with creative experiencing. "Authority" means, ultimately, to be the author of oneself. There is no justifiable sense in which one ought to author or to be authored by another.

In authoring oneself, one also authors an ambience, an order, within which one finds one's environmental resources for life and activity. One construes a world and thereby creates a cosmos of possibilities for self-actualization. In so doing there emerges a world potentially alien to others. No one, on these conditions, has a right to authority over others, so the problem that arises in the authoring of a world in the process of self-actualization is one of insuring insofar as possible that one's creative actions do not have disruptive consequences. In accordance with the vision that one eschews power relations grounded in dualism in favor of creative relations grounded in polarity, the authoring of self and world includes the offering of self and world for the enjoyment of others.[74] In the authoritative act of self-creativity one lays claim to excellence. And the offering of self and world for the enjoyment of others involves the anticipation of others' deference.

A fundamental consequence of this conception of authority is that traditional moral norms governing social action may be more properly understood when seen as fundamentally aesthetic achievements reflective of the relations of excellence and deference in social interactions. That is to say, the social condition necessary for the realization of legitimate authority involves the existence of myriad and fluctuating deference patternings grounded in intersubjective experience. Patterns of deference require that "humility" characterize social interactions, where humility is understood as the appropriate sense of one's relevance in a given context of experiencing. This is the sense of one's intrinsic excellence and its pertinence within an intersubjective context. A primary condition for this quality of humility is a sense of one's excellence and the differential excellences of others.

It is important to recognize that both the claims to excellence and the exercise of deference have their basis in the notion of self-creativity. Deference is not self-sacrifice, although apparent acts of self-sacrifice could be illustrations of deferential activities. Deference is a response to recognized excellence. It cannot be forced. Deference is *ec-static* in the sense that it leads one to experience in and through another. The object of one's deference experiences *en-statically*, experiences him or herself as a locus of value. Artificial, conventional, or otherwise insincere acts of deference result in alienation. For example, ritual action performed frivolously or insensitively is at best ineffective, and more likely alienating. This alienation is the result of false enstasy or forced ecstasy. The attempt to reduce the alienating consequences of a particular social context is predicated upon the recognition of individual self-creativity as the model for social interactions.

Even in the most fortunate of circumstances, claims to excellence and the exercise of deference will doubtless involve error. We continually risk mistaking our own or others' excellences as distinctively relevant to a given situation. In addition, authoritative actions can involve us in risks of status, convenience, well-being—even our lives. These kinds of risk are part and parcel of the types of social interactions we are describing. Such failures will inevitably lead to the loss of value. Some freedom will be forfeited, some efficacy will be misdirected, some beauty will suffer decay, some truths will slip away, some importances will be trivialized, some things sacred will be ruined. Finitude, ignorance, insensitivity, and perversity are among the more important of the contingencies of our individual and social existence.

That we risk failure in order to author our own existence is obvious. We ought to expect suffering, the proof of risk, as a consequence of such authority. We might seem to carry Confucius' thinking to extremes to say that it enjoins the practice of risk and suggests that one ought to learn how to suffer. But these are indeed implications entailed by the vision of authoritative action at the center of Confucius' philosophy.

The most obvious risks are those associated with what has come to be known as civil disobedience. The refusal to obey a law on the grounds that it usurps one's authority or the authority of others is an expected outcome of adherence to the aesthetic vision of social and political order. The risks involved in such an action are many; one might, of course, wrongly assess the character of the law; or, through an exercise of civil disobedience, one might influence others to commit acts of violence against the law in question. But allowance for civil disobedience is compelling for Confucius, since it is essential that there be continued and direct testimony to the fact that authority is indeed vested in authoritative persons.

In the Chinese context, both classical and more recent, this notion of civil disobedience reflects the conception of person as being fundamentally coextensive with his social and political environments. For this reason, civil disobedience is a major phenomenon during the establishment of a new dynasty. From Shu Ch'i and Po I of the Shang dynasty to the heroes of the Sung (Wen T'ien-hsang 文天祥 and Lu Hsiu-fu 陸秀夫) and Ming dynasties (Shih K'o-fa 史可法 and Wang Fu-chih 王夫之), civil disobedience has been directed against a political force with which one is unable to identify.

One risks as much in alienated obedience to a law. The authoritative individual may legitimately "obey" a law only in the most Pickwickian of senses. For in acting freely in accordance with a law, the authoritative person defers to the excellence of the law as suggestive of a given action, and in so doing cancels its otherness. The authoritative person is one who, on his own authority, does as he pleases. Of course, it is all too easy to rationalize oneself into believing in the excellence of a law the disobedience to which would entail a great deal of inconvenience. In such manner one risks a kind of creeping alienation which could ultimately undermine the courage that would permit one to risk conflict with legal structures. For Confucius the continued investment of significance (yi) in both ritual actions and actions in conformity with law serves to preclude such alienation.

4.1   The Chün Tzu 君子 as Model

The Shuo-wen lexicon defines chün 君 with the rhyming tsun 尊, meaning "of high rank," and then derivatively, as "to honor." Interestingly, chün 君 and tsun 尊 both have cognates meaning "many together" (群 and 傳), and tsun 尊 has a homophonous cognate, 摶 , meaning "to moderate, to regulate." The *Shuo-wen* further isolates the etymonic elements of *chün* 君, suggesting that it is a *hui-yi* 會意 character derived first from *yin* 尹 "to order, to manage, regular," and then, because the person who "orders" issues commands, it is further constituted by *K'ou* 口 , "mouth." The *Hsi-chuan t'ung lun* commentary on the *Shuo-wen* states:

> *Chün* 君 means "to regulate, to order," a generic name for leaders; one whom the empire can take as its model for uprightness and order. Where the model is upright, so is the shadow it casts; where it is bent, so is the shadow. His mouth is his means of issuing commands. . . . The *chün* 君 is the one to whom the crowd below 群下 repairs.

The *yin* 尹 component in *chün* 君 is significant, defined in the *Shuo-wen* as *chih* 治 "to regulate, to direct, well-governed, in good order," and further, as "one who handles affairs."

To summarize, the etymological data on *chün* 君 provides the following associations: (1) noble rank, (2) a term of respect, (3) a model of order, cultivation, and refinement whose personal character attracts the emulation and participation of those below, and (4) one whose personal order is extended to a wider context through political responsibility and communication. *Chün* 君 is a source of order in a decidedly sociopolitical frame of reference. This order is not a preassigned pattern that the *chün* himself instances and then imposes on others, but is meant to be an order that ultimately derives from his engagement with his sociopolitical context.

It is frequently adverted that in the literature prior to Confucius, the expression *chün tzu* 君子 , a diminutive form of *chün* meaning "son of *chün*," had strong political connotations. That is, *chün tzu* was a term that specifically denoted nobility of birth and rank, and had no application as a category of personal achievement.[75] In a manner characteristic of the development of classical Chinese philosophy, Confucius then appropriated this political designation and redefined it for his philosophy, sociopolitical participation becoming a necessary component in the process of personal cultivation, and personal cultivation becoming a necessary qualification for sociopolitical status and influence. This correlative relationship between personal achievement and political responsibility has frequently been described in the not wholly appropriate terms of "means" and "end." Hsiao Kung-chuan, for example, observes:[76]

> The old meaning of the word [chün tzu] contains the general implication that the man who possessed rank should cultivate his virtue, while Confucius tended toward an emphasis on the cultivation of virtue in order to acquire rank.

H. G. Creel discounts the political connotations of chün tzu altogether:[77] ". . . chün tzu has been used, especially by Confucius to mean 'gentleman' (or in Legge's well-known rendering, 'superior man') in a moral sense, without any other connotation." These analyses, however, obscure the mutuality of personal cultivation and political responsibility, education and the sociopolitical order. As Tu Wei-ming rightly suggests, there is no private/public separation that can justify a moral/sociopolitical distinction:[78]

> The moral integrity of the ruler, far from being his private affair, is thought to be a defining characteristic of his leadership. He must realize that what he does in private is not only symbolically significant but has a direct bearing on his ability to lead. . . .

Confucius did not replace with new moral qualifications the political ones that had previously defined chün tzu; what he did was to insist that political responsibility and moral development are correlatives. The cultivation of one's person necessarily entails active participation both in the family and in the sociopolitical order, not simply in service to others, but as occasions in which to evoke the compassion and concern that leads to one's own personal growth and refinement. Stated another way, it is inconceivable that full personal growth and disclosure could be achieved in the absence of political responsibility. Confucius himself states clearly (18/7):

> To refuse office is to withhold one's contribution of significance (yi 義) . . . . The exemplary person's (chün tzu) opportunity to serve in office is the occasion for him to effect what he judges important and appropriate (yi).

Now there can be at least two objections to the claim that, for Confucius, personal cultivation and political responsibility are mutually implicated. First, Confucius states on several occasions that when the *tao* does not prevail, the *chün tzu* withdraws from involvement in administration (8/13): "When the *tao* prevails in the empire, reveal yourself; when it does not, hide. . . ." But withdrawal from formal participation in the administration of bad government does not mean the abandonment of responsibility for the sociopolitical order. On the contrary, it is precisely to serve sociopolitical order at its more fundamental level of family that the *chün tzu* withdraws from office (2/21): ". . . Filiality, then, is also taking part in government. Why must one take part in formal government?" Sociopolitical order is ultimately derived from and hence must be restored at the most immediate level, moving from the more distant political order toward its ground in familial and personal order.

A second objection that might be raised is that Confucius' own limited political experience is a rather compelling argument against the correlativity of political position and personal achievement. However, considering that the career of the historical Confucius was revisioned by his followers as having occupied increasingly important political positions,[79] culminating in the status of "uncrowned king",[80] suggests that growing recognition of his personal worth required a concomitant attribution of political stature.

In the *Analects*, *chün tzu* stands in contrast to a list of alternative categories of personal achievement: sage (*sheng jen* 聖人), authoritative person (*jen* che* 仁者), good/adept person (*shan jen* 善人), person of superior quality (*hsien jen* 賢人), complete person (*ch'eng* jen* 成人), scholar-official (*shih* 士) and great person (*ta jen* 大人). To understand the content of *chün tzu*, we must take advantage of these alternative categories as a source of contrast and clarification. What are Confucius' grounds for establishing such distinctions? D. C. Lau observes:[81]

> For Confucius there is not one single ideal character but quite a variety. The highest is the sage (*sheng jen*). This idea is so high that it is hardly ever realized. . . . Lower down the scale there are the good man (*shan jen*) and the complete man (*ch'eng jen*). . . . There is no doubt, however, that the ideal moral character for Confucius is the *chün tzu* (gentleman). . . .

Ch'en Ta-ch'i 陳大齊 analyzes these several categories of personal achievement in the *Analects*, and, by a close scrutiny of the text in which they occur, argues that they express various degrees of achievement which can be ranked in a specific relative hierarchy.[82] He suggests that, for the most part, there is a difference in level that clearly distinguishes the three most prominent designations, sage (sheng jen), authoritative person (jen* che), and exemplary person (chün tzu). Sage (sheng jen) is higher than either jen* che or chün tzu (7/25 and 6/30):

> The Master said, "As for a sage, there is no chance for me to meet one. I would be happy with meeting an exemplary person (chün tzu). . . ."[83]
> Tzu-kung said, "If there were a person who extended beneficence to the masses and was able to assist the multitude, what would you say? Could he be called an authoritative person (jen* che)?"
> The Master replied, "Why stop at authoritative person (jen* che)? Certainly he is a sage (sheng jen). . . ."

And, according to Ch'en Ta-ch'i, it is equally clear that the jen* che ranks second, above the chün tzu (14/6): "The Master said, 'Whereas you might find an exemplary person (chün tzu) who on occasion fails to act with authoritativeness (jen*), you will never find a small person who succeeds in acting with it.' " Confucius is unwilling to allow that he is either a sage (sheng jen) or an authoritative person (jen* che),[84] but in spite of the fact that he explicitly denies that he is an exemplary person (chün tzu),[85] the text does imply that he can be called one.[86] Also, where he is most reluctant to call any of his disciples authoritative persons (jen* che),[87] he does designate even some of his lower-order disciples as chün tzu.[88]

This translation of qualitative difference into a hierarchical ranking seems to have some textual justification, and certainly has a ready consonance with analytical scholarship. But, at the very least, it is not very illuminating, and at worst, it can be misleading.

First, the Analects, insisting that these several categories for personal achievement are intrinsically related, will not accommodate an exclusivity among them (19/12):

> In the tao of the exemplary person (chün tzu), what is to be conveyed first and what is to be placed last? The tao is analogous to the plant world in that category distinctions can be made. But how could

there be any "error" in the *tao* of the exemplary person *(chün tzu)*? It is just that it is only the sage *(sheng jen)* who knows the route from first step to last.

Apart from the comprehensiveness of the sage *(sheng jen)* category, the ranking of these other distinctions does not seem to hold. For example, although there might be an exemplary person *(chün tzu)* who "on occasion fails to act with authoritativeness *(jen*)*" (14/6), authoritative humanity is elsewhere clearly described as a defining condition that qualifies the *chün tzu* as such (4/5):

> Wherein does the exemplary person *(chün tzu)* who abandons his authoritative humanity *(jen*)* warrant that name? The exemplary person *(chün tzu)* does not leave his authoritative humanity *(jen*)* even for as long as it takes to eat a meal. In moments of haste and excitement, he sticks to it. In situations of difficulty and confusion, he sticks to it.

Contrary to Ch'en Ta-ch'i, it is not at all clear that *jen* che* is a category of personal achievement higher than *chün tzu*. For example, in the following passage, authoritative person *(jen* che)* and exemplary person *(chün tzu)* are used interchangeably (6/26):

> "If the authoritative person *(jen* che)* were informed that there was another person in the well, would he jump in after him?" The Master replied, "How so? An exemplary person *(chün tzu)* can be sent on his way, but he cannot be entrapped. You can cheat him, but not confuse him."

Far from being separate categories, authoritative person *(jen* che)* and exemplary person *(chün tzu)* entail each other (12/24): "Tseng Tzu said, 'The exemplary person *(chün tzu)* gathers friends through his refinement, and strengthens his authoritative humanity *(jen*)* through his friendships.' " In fact, we can readily identify a whole list of passages in which authoritative person *(jen* che)* and exemplary person *(chün tzu)* are described in strikingly similar terms.[89] Of course the real problem with Ch'en Ta-ch'i's analytical approach is that it provides us with little more than a bald ranking without being specific as to the content and criteria that justify these various distinctions concerning the achieving person. Further, and more dangerously, it obscures the relatedness of these categories to the point of suggesting that we are dealing with different models of personal achievement.

An alternative and perhaps more profitable way of explaining these several categories of personal realization is to begin by allowing that Confucius is using them all as different aspects of the one organic process of personal growth: the pursuit of sagehood. The category of sage (sheng jen) ranks highest because it describes the culmination of the whole process of achievement at its most comprehensive level. The other categories can be differentiated inasmuch as each of them represents a distinctive focus or emphasis in this project. At the same time, these categories are fundamentally correlated in that they are all contributing to and exhausted by the achievement of sagehood. The indistinctness that obstructs an analysis of them as separate categories can thus be accounted for by the fact that they are not only correlative, but at times even coextensive. As we have seen, even though this exemplary person (chün tzu) is a category with important sociopolitical references, it necessarily entails the strongly interpersonal category of authoritative humanity (jen*).

The overlapping of authoritative humanity (jen*) and exemplary person (chün tzu) as two dimensions of the project of becoming a sage accounts for the fact that many characteristics of the authoritative person (jen* che) are also distinguishing features of the exemplary person (chün tzu). To the extent that both are specific aspects of the general project of personal growth, the characteristics of commitment to learning, cultivation, and refinement are held in common.[90] Sagehood as a category is strongly associated with political influence as well as personal worth. What is peculiar and distinctive about sagehood, taking it beyond the category of exemplary person (chün tzu), is that the quality of one's achievement is a source of meaning, value, and purpose to the extent, both in the excellence one manifests and in the deference one evokes, that one becomes god-like, a person of cosmic proportions and influence.[91]

For Confucius, then, the exemplary person (chün tzu) is a qualitative term denoting someone who has an ongoing commitment to personal growth as expressed through the activities of self-cultivation and sociopolitical leadership. In that "the exemplary person (chün tzu) is not a functionary" (2/12)[92] describable in terms of specific skills or expertise, a person qualifies as chün tzu by virtue of the quality of his contribution to the fabric of human order, not by what he specifically does. As a device for underscoring this qualitative basis for identifying the exemplary person *(chün tzu)*, Confucius repeatedly draws a contrast between the integrative and self-disclosing characteristics of the exemplary person *(chün tzu)*, and the disintegrative and retarding characteristics of what he terms "the small person" *(hsiao jen* 小人).[93] This "small person," far from making a qualitative contribution, detracts from social harmony. Even when his conduct is tolerable, it contributes nothing more than simple conformity *(t'ung* 同) rather than qualitative enhancement *(ho* 和).[94]

It is the sociopolitical frame of reference for this *chün tzu* aspect in the overall process of personal realization that makes this category distinctive and warrants its translation as "exemplary person." And since personal realization can only emerge in the process of social experience and activity, the exemplary person's *(chün tzu)* form of communication is an important stimulus for attracting sympathy with and participation in an emergent order. Hence, Confucius, believing that what is said is a prompting to act, is very much concerned about the exemplary person's *(chün tzu)* responsibility for his speech.[95] Correspondence between what is said and what is done is the basis for one's integrity, one's capacity for "making whole." Thus, integrity is the ground for social integration.

The exemplary person *(chün tzu)* serves as the primary agent of sociopolitical ordering. He performs this function by virtue of his role as a model of cultivation. This modeling function is of such importance to the Confucian sensibility that we must take some pains to clarify it further.

For Confucius the exemplary person's *(chün tzu)* role as sociopolitical model is to be construed along aesthetic lines. Modeling is a qualitative activity. And the response to the model is qualified by the uniqueness of the respondent's resources, circumstances, and interests. Throughout the *Analects*, we are referred to particular examples of excellence: Yao and Shun, Wen and Wu, Kuan Chung and Yen Hui. Confucius' selection of curricular materials evidences a high regard for historical chronicles and classical songs that dramatize specific events in the evolution of Chinese culture. Reliance upon historical examples and poeticized personal accounts suggests that the kind of sociopolitical order that Confucius envisions begins with specific instances of desirable conduct. And even while referring us to these historical exemplars worthy of emulation, Confucius makes it clear that modeling is more than a passive reiteration of some established behavior. The student is, in fact, required to evaluate the model's conduct critically and adapt it to his own conditions. Recalling words of Confucius cited earlier (18/8):[96]

> The Master observed, "Po I and Shu Ch'i were two men who were unwilling to compromise their dispositions or bring disgrace on their persons." With respect to Liu Hsia Hui and Shao Lien, he observed, "They compromised their dispositions and suffered disgrace, but were reasonable in what they had to say and thoughtful in what they did. That was all there was to it." As for Yü Chung and Yi Yi, he said, "They lived in seclusion and said what came to mind. They were unsullied in their persons and what they abandoned was expedient under the circumstances. But I am different from these in that I do not have presuppositions as to what may or may not be done."

The text of this passage is undoubtedly corrupt, yet the sense of it is clear: the conduct of historical models is a resource that must be scrutinized and evaluated, and deferred to only to the extent that these actions are appropriate to oneself. This necessity of exercising critical judgment in the project of extending oneself through the embodiment of models is a recurrent theme in the *Analects*, applying not only to historical models, but also to popular figures in contemporary society (13/24):

> Tzu-kung inquired, "What do you think about someone whom everyone in the village likes?"
> Confucius replied, "That is not good enough."
> "What if everyone in the village disliked him?"
> Confucius replied, "That is still not good enough. Better if all the good people in the village were to like him and all of the bad people were to dislike him."[97]

In fact, Confucius suggests that the dynamics of model emulation should be a concern of the cultivating person in all of his interpersonal encounters (7/22 and 4/17):

> The Master said, "Walking in a company of three, I will surely find a teacher. Selecting out their good points, I follow them; identifying their faults, I improve myself accordingly."

The Master said, "In meeting someone of superior quality, reflect on how to become his peer; on meeting someone who is not of superior quality, turn inward and examine yourself."[98]

In Confucius' perception of sociopolitical order as coextensive with personal order achieved through interpersonal modeling, the focus upon particularity is prominent, both in the specificity of the model and in the need to appropriate from the model in a selective manner qualified by one's own personal disposition.

The model qualifies as model not on the basis of what he can do, but by virtue of the quality of his actions: how he does things. Thus Confucius rejects accumulated skills as a basis for according someone the title of exemplary person *(chün tzu)*. Confucius himself, anxious to distinguish menial skills from sagacity, regards his own collection of miscellaneous and sundry abilities to be little more than evidence of a misspent youth (9/6):

> The High Minister asked Tzu-kung, "Surely the Master is a sage, is he not? How is it then that he has so many skills!"
>
> Tzu-kung replied, "Indeed, *t'ien* is going to let him attain sage-hood, and in addition, has given him many skills."
>
> The Master heard of this and said, "The High Minister certainly knows me well! When I was young, we were poor, and hence I became skilled in many menial occupations. But should an exemplary person *(chün tzu)* have these many skills? No, he should not."

A person is to be adjudged a model on the basis of the quality of his achievement as a person. Behind the frequently cited assertion that "the exemplary person *(chün tzu)* is not a functionary" (2/12) is the assumption that a cultivated person by virtue of his refinement is able to perform any task better than the technician. He can do so because he is able to understand the implications of the technological undertakings for the overall quality of the human experience. This presupposition has directed the traditional Chinese education for government service, and training directed specifically toward the accumulation of specialized skills has been generally assigned an ancillary role. Furthermore, any survey of Chinese history, from Confucius himself to figures of the Republican era, reveals a tendency to represent the exemplary person as excelling broadly in whatever area of human endeavor he might choose to address himself, from statesman to athlete, from aesthete to philosopher.

The exemplary person *(chün tzu)*, as a performer of *yi* 義 acts, as a concrete embodiment of ritual action, and as a model of personal and sociopolitical order, is both a source of continuity and a ground for creativity in the tradition. He is a model who engages the members of society in his achieved order, providing them the occasion for personal refinement and for creative self-disclosure. At all levels of engagement, he has an educative function in that his influence evokes the participation and qualitative transformation of others. His existence is in pursuit of the fullest disclosure of the concrete detail as a contribution to the harmonious order of the whole. As such, it reveals his uniqueness and novelty and serves as a warrant for the fullest expression of the uniqueness and novelty of others.

The exemplary person *(chün tzu)* is one who models both the activity of realizing *(chih* 知 *)* and of personal articulation *(jen** 仁 *)*. He achieves his status as a model by a particular manner of focusing the events of his tradition and context so as to show and transmit what is excellent about them. As we suggested in our discussion of thinking, the act of realizing *(chih* 知 *)* does not involve the conscious entertainment of alternatives; it is not grounded in hypothetical reflection. The modeling activity of the *chün tzu* depends upon the fact that personal articulation leads to a condition in which one is no longer troubled by doubts. This is not achieved by selecting the best from among a set of alternative paths for thought and action; it is realized by attaining a particular focus in the field of possibilities such that one is no longer of "two minds." Just how one achieves this sort of focus will be better understood after we have considered the notions of *t'ien ming* 天命 , *te* 德, and *tao* 道 in the following chapter.

IV

"... at fifty I realized the ming of t'ien. ..."

1 The Question of Confucius' Cosmology

In his classic analysis of the development of modern scientific culture, Whitehead wrote:[1]

> When you are criticizing the philosophy of an epoch, do not chiefly direct your attention to those intellectual positions which its exponents feel it necessary to defend. There will be some fundamental assumptions which adherents of all the variant systems within the epoch unconsciously presuppose.

Our attempt to uncover certain of the fundamental cosmological assumptions of Confucius' thinking will involve us in a consideration of the sort of cosmology presupposed by the family of philosophers contemporary with Confucius and the principal disciples of Confucius who themselves extrapolated cosmological doctrines from the views of the Master. Equally we shall be concerned to make Confucius' philosophy relevant to certain issues characterizing contemporary Western philosophical discussions. Thus, in this consideration of Confucius' implicit cosmological vision we shall confront the problem of anachronism most dramatically. For by drawing out the cosmological implications of Confucius' thinking, implications in which Confucius himself was little interested, we shall be excavating Confucian thought with distinctly contemporary issues in mind. We offer no apologies for this fact since one of the announced purposes of this work is to demonstrate the contemporary relevance of the substance and direction of Confucius' vision, and this simply cannot be done without recourse to extrapolation.

Another reason we should not attempt to avoid anachronism is that Anglo-European readers are likely to approach the thinking of Confucius equipped with explicit or implicit assumptions many of which stand in severe contrast to those supporting classical Chinese philosophical thought. Unless we uncover the parallel presuppositions of Confucius we are apt to invite radical misunderstanding. Our introductory discussion of some "uncommon assumptions" addressed this situation in a general manner. Here we must pursue the task of apologia in somewhat greater detail.

The same necessity applies within the Chinese context. Beginning as early as Mencius and continuing into the Neo-Confucian period, many of Confucius' disciples extrapolated and ramified the principal insights of Confucius in cosmological directions: this makes it necessary for subsequent interpreters of the *Analects* to assess those cosmological traditions that claim Confucius as their source. This is particularly so if, as is the case here, a rather novel interpretation of Confucius' thinking is offered.

The desire to characterize a cosmological dimension of Confucian thought presents us with serious difficulties. Unlike the personal, societal, and political levels of his philosophy, this stratum is not readily accessible from even the most careful reading of the available materials. In fact, Confucius as portrayed in the *Analects* seems to express an ambivalence toward, if not a cultivated disinterest in, cosmological speculations. In this respect, he is characterized in what seems to be a rather puzzling if not even inconsistent way.

On the one hand, Confucius is made to eschew any discussion of cosmological concepts (5/13; 9/1):

> One cannot get to hear the Master talking on natural tendency (*hsing** 性) or the *tao* of *t'ien* 天道 .
> The Master seldom spoke on personal profit (*li* 利), causal conditions and their possibilities (*ming* 命) or authoritative humanity (*jen** 仁).[2]

Although he remained open to novel situations and possibilities, he was not given to surmise or speculation (9/4): "There were four things the Master abstained from entirely: he would not conjecture, he did not demand certainty, he was not inflexible, and he was not self-centered." Concerning the unknown realm of gods and spirits, Confucius maintained an attitude of respectful detachment (6/22): "Keep a distance from gods and spirits while showing them due reverence. . . ."

He shunted aside questions which required him to go beyond empirical understanding and carefully limited his discussions to those things within the bounds of immediate experience (11/12):

Chi-lu asked about serving the gods and the spirits of the dead, but the Master replied, "If you are not yet able to serve other people, how can you serve the spirits of the dead?" He then asked about death, but the Master replied, "If you do not yet understand life, how can you understand death?"

And again (7/21): "The Master did not talk about strange phenomena, feats of strength, disorderliness, or gods."[3] The portrait that emerges from these passages is that of a philosopher concerned only with those aspects of life that he can understand through personal experience and on which he can have some effect. This impression of a self-imposed limitation on Confucius' range of interest is further reinforced by the paucity of information available to us regarding his attitude towards *t'ien*, conventionally rendered "Heaven." His position is so profoundly unclear, in fact, that interpreters, in the service of their own disparate hermeneutics, have been able to construe him as both theist and atheist with their competing claims to incontrovertible textual support.

Confucius' reticence about discussing cosmological questions was not an unwillingness to reveal and share his deepest insights. He claimed explicitly to make available to his students the full substance of his reflections (7/24):

The Master said, "Gentlemen, do you think there is something I am not telling you? I really have no secrets from you. There is nothing I do not share with you; that is the kind of person I am."

Balanced against Confucius' unwillingness to speculate on cosmological problems is his insistence that an understanding of *ming* 命—often rendered (inappropriately, as we shall see) "fate" or "destiny"—is a necessary condition for becoming an exemplary person (*chün tzu* 君子) (20/3): "A person who does not understand *ming* has no way of becoming an exemplary person (*chün tzu*)."

When Confucius goes on to claim for himself that "at fifty I understood the *ming* of *t'ien*," a clear inconsistency emerges. If he understands *ming*, and he is always ready to share his insights, why did he "seldom speak on . . . '*ming*' . . .," especially since in his own terms an understanding of *ming* is essential for one's training towards the *chün tzu*?

One partial answer to this question might be that given the focus of Confucius' thought on sociopolitical questions, it was in this area that he developed his most innovative insights. For him, the cosmological ground of his elaborated philosophy was a starting point derived from tradition, largely absorbed intact and simply assumed in his discussions with his followers. His contribution was not the elaboration of a novel cosmology, but rather the application of an existing set of premises to his particular social and political circumstances. These premises were to a large extent implicit in the philosophical reflections of most members of his philosophical tradition.

Were this true it would perhaps justify the commentarial approach of Ch'en Ta-ch'i who, tacitly accepting Confucius' range of interests, limits his own interpretations to those questions of immediate human concern: personal, social, and political realization. Nowhere in his extensive and important contribution to studies on Confucius does Ch'en Ta-ch'i analyze and attempt to explicate the cosmological level of Confucian thought. Since Confucius himself refuses to elaborate on his own cosmological commitments, a credible interpretation of Confucius can be constructed without recourse to these distant and abstruse concepts. In fact, to yield overmuch to speculation might threaten to obscure Confucius' emphasis on the issues surrounding personal realization.

Further, Confucius seems to share a characteristic common to many teachers designated as wise men or sages—namely, a reticence to employ formally abstract language. In this manner he is not unlike the Buddha Gotama, who eschewed explicit treatment of abstract metaphysical issues, or Jesus, who spoke in parables which pointed away from the abstract generalities of theological doctrine and toward the concrete immediacies of experience. Each of these wise men in communicating their wisdom evidenced a clear mistrust of literal language and a preference for the more poetic modes of articulation. Given the central role that communication plays in Confucius' philosophy, we shall have occasion in Chapter V to investigate this attitude in some detail and suggest why this might be the case.

Confucius' reticence about speculating on what he perceived to be problems beyond the purview of immediate concerns should not be interpreted to mean that his efforts to organize human experience with consistency and coherence are free of cosmological presuppositions. Although Confucius did not discuss speculative questions, there are tacit intuitions that underlie and serve as ground for his articulated philosophy. We may safely assume that the implicit cosmological vision of Confucius was equally tacit among his chief disciples.

Most of us who approach Confucius' thinking today, however, possess a quite different cosmology. If only as a corrective to our own presuppositions, we must articulate the characteristics of the cosmological climate within which Confucius thought and taught. The sources available to us on Confucius are decidedly fragmentary, but at least at the level of social and political philosophy, it can be claimed that his philosophical reflections are presented as a consistent and adequate program for effecting order and harmony. He insists primarily that there is a coherence to his thought, both implicitly in describing it as a way *(tao)*, and explicitly in saying (4/15): "Ts'an, my way is bound together with one unifying thread." Our previous consideration of the meaning of "order" presupposed by Confucius' social and political teachings was an attempt to articulate some of the lineaments of that unifying thread. Here we shall address the most formally abstract dimensions of that idea.

In the Western tradition, cosmology has carried two principal connotations. First, *ontologia generalis*, general ontology, which is concerned with the question of the be-ing of beings. The second sense is that associated with the term, *scientia universalis*, the science of principles.[4] The first type of cosmology is well represented by the project of Martin Heidegger, who pursued the question, "Why is there something rather than nothing at all?" The second type of speculation addresses the question: "What kinds of things are there?" Whitehead represents this sort of philosophic activity. In this mode philosophers seek to delineate the principles underlying the character of things and their relationships to each other. The principle(s) of beings is the subject matter of *scientia universalis*, whereas the subject of *ontologia generalis* is the being of principles *(archai)*—that is, the being of the original and originating entities comprising that which is.

Traditionally, these two types of speculation have not been as distinct as might be suggested by the above description. Most thinkers have attempted to address both sorts of question, although one of the two has almost always been given express priority within a given philosophic project.[5] The important point to realize is that both *ontologia generalis* and *scientia universalis* are functions of the *mythos–logos* dialectic, about which we shall have more to say in the following chapter.[6] Each depends upon the assumption of the transition from Chaos to Cosmos as the basis for the development of rational order. Whether with regard to the transition from the chaos of "nothingness" to the order of "beings" and of "Being" or from the chaos of "confusion" to the "principles of order," Western cosmological speculation has, at root, been cosmogonic.

The problematic of classical Chinese thought is quite distinct, however. The relative absence of a strong cosmogonic tradition in classical China militated against the sense of reason as rationalization, as the construal of order from antecedent chaos. The influence of anything like a *mythos–logos* contrast is not readily discernible in classical Chinese thought. For this reason, it is unlikely that either of the two traditional Western understandings of metaphysics and cosmology could serve as models of Confucian cosmological speculation or interpretation. This being the case, do we have a model that would permit responsible understanding of the Confucian project at its most fundamental level?

In fact such a model has been adumbrated from the very beginning of this book. Starting with our discussion of uncommon assumptions and continuing through the consideration of the distinctions between logical and aesthetic order in our discussion of Confucian social theory, we have described an *ars contextualis*,[7] a general aesthetic vision, which can serve both to characterize the content of Confucius' "cosmology" and to delineate the principal components of his manner of thinking. It is this *ars contextualis* we wish to elaborate in the following pages.

The principal notions grounding Confucius' aesthetic cosmology are *t'ien*, or *t'ien ming* 天命, *te* 德 , and *tao* 道. In accordance with our classificatory model, *t'ien* or *t'ien ming* functions as the "authorial" concept, *te* as the "authoring" concept, and *tao* as the "authoritative" notion. Our elaboration of this conceptual cluster will provide the basis for an understanding of the peculiarly aesthetic perspective of Confucius' thinking. We shall begin with the notion of *t'ien*.

2   T'ien 天 and T'ien Ming 天命

2.1   The Historical Development of T'ien 天

The etymology of the character, *t'ien*, is the subject of much speculation. Karlgren represents the popular interpretation, suggesting that *t'ien* is an ideograph of an anthropomorphic deity: human being writ large.[8] A second theory suggests that it is a combination of the character for "great" (*ta* 大), itself a drawing of a mature human being, and a square representing the firmament over his head. The *Shuo-wen* dictionary follows the recurring practice of defining the character with a second character that is similar in pronunciation: *tien* 顛, "top of the head," following this with "the highest or supreme." It then interprets the graph as being comprised of the combination of "one" (*yi* 一) and "great" (*ta* 大), leading some commentators to suggest that it is a *hui-yi* 會意 character in which both components of the character contribute to its meaning. It is significant that the *Shuo-wen* defines *t'ien* as a conflation of "the one great." In the *Tao Te Ching*,[9] the *tao* is described in the following way:

> I do not know its name;
> Constrained, I would style it "*tao*,"
> And if forced to assign it a name,
> I would call it "great" (*ta*).
> "Great" means "passing" (*shih* 逝). . . .

Further, in the *Tao Te Ching*, the *tao* is frequently referred to as "the One."[10] A remote yet functional correspondence can be registered between this description of the *Lao Tzu's tao* and the representation of *t'ien* in the *Analects*. Confucius remarks that "only *t'ien* is truly great (*ta*). . . ." (8/19). On another occasion Confucius becomes uncharacteristically speculative, describing the cadence of existence in the same language that the *Tao Te Ching* passage above uses to describe the *tao* (9/17): "So it passes (*shih* 逝), never ceasing day or night."

The fact that these several theories concerning the etymology of *t'ien* lend themselves to an interpretation of this character as both an anthropomorphic deity and as a general, nonpersonal description for the process of existence, has helped to fuel a conflict that has been waged around this character by Western interpreters of the Chinese classics.[11] Is *t'ien* properly conceived as an anthropomorphic deity, or is it a nonpersonal force? We shall argue that this debate is fundamentally wrongheaded. While adequate translation certainly does demand that the important differences between *t'ien* and Western conceptions of deity be established, these differences center on the question of transcendence rather than on that of anthropomorphism. To make our argument we must consider what is known of the historical origins and development of *t'ien* prior to its appearance in those documents most closely associated with Confucius.

An analysis of extant historical records reveals that there are several important alterations in the concept of deity during the formative period of Chinese civilization. Archaeological evidence on the oracle bones and bronzes indicates that the people of the Shang dynasty did not conceive of *t'ien* as a deity. Rather, their religious observances—at least those of the royal house—were centered on *ti*, or *shang-ti* 上帝, a concept intimately associated with ancestor worship. *Shang-ti* was cast as an anthropomorhphic, personal deity ruling over the human and natural worlds in a manner analogous to the earthly ruler. He could and would intervene in human affairs with regularity and with decisiveness.

The fact that deceased rulers, also accorded the title *ti* 帝, would join the realm of *shang-ti* reinforced the perception of deity as an intimate and personal extension of the known world which, with similar structures and conditions, operates in much the same manner as the human community. In fact, the realm of *ti* was construed as a living, functioning aspect of *this* world, providing society with an additional dimension of context and meaning.

This concern for and reliance upon a world populated by human predecessors was a basis for the development of ancestral worship. And the focus of religious observances was on their capacity for influencing events in this world. Important in this respect is the emphasis placed on divination, perhaps interpretable as a formal apparatus for high ministers to provide counsel to the ruling powers without breaching their claim to political authority.

T'ien seems to have had some religious significance for the Chou people who conquered the Shang at the end of the second millennium

B.C. Given that the Chou was a federation of militant, semi-nomadic border tribes prior to their conquest of the Shang, there is no written basis for determining whether or not, or to what extent, *t'ien* was held to be a personal deity. The fact that *t'ien* also means "sky" might suggest that in this prehistoric period it was seen as a non-personal, unifying force of considerable dimensions at some distance from the human world.

This conjecture is reinforced by the fact that in the philosophical literature of Chou, there is a gradual tendency towards the depersonalization of *t'ien*, first in the relatively early identification of the will of *t'ien* with popular consensus, and further in a gradual redefining of *t'ien* as a designation for the regular pattern discernible in the unfolding processes of existence. The former attitude already had its beginnings in the *Book of Documents*,[12] and its development is adequately represented by *Mencius*; the latter interpretation of *t'ien* is certainly present in the Taoist literature, and its culmination in the Confucian literature is a major feature of the *Hsün Tzu*. In his study of the *Yi-ching*, Helmut Wilhelm remarks that, with respect to their status and nature, *ti* and *t'ien* are used almost interchangeably in classical times,[13]

> but at the time when the *Book of Changes* originated, the use of the word *t'ien* preponderated. In those passages, however, where something very concrete is to be expressed about God, *ti* is used, as, for example, in the statement that God battles in the sign of the creative.

Still, whether this tendency to read *t'ien* as a nonpersonal force should be construed as the resurrection of the original Chou idea can only be a matter of speculation.

A further reason to believe that *t'ien* was perceived as a non-personal force is the fact that somewhere in this period the notion developed that the sum of existence is a unity of *t'ien*, earth, and human being, each force having its peculiar characteristics, and each existing correlative to the other two. It is important to recognize that there is no final beginning or end in this process; rather, it has the identifiable rhythm, immanent order, and cadence of a cycle.

With the Chou domination of the Shang, there is ample documentation of a concerted effort on the part of the culturally inferior

Chou rulers to identify their indigenous notion of *t'ien* with the more personal deity of their sophisticated Shang subjects. *T'ien* and *shang-ti* are used interchangeably in parts of the *Book of Documents* and the *Book of Songs*. In this context, we might speculate that the Chou people imitated the personal relationship of *ti* to the royal house of Shang by claiming a similar familial relationship to *t'ien*. This assertion is reflected in the description of the Chou ruler as "son of *t'ien*" (*t'ien tzu* 天 子) mandated to power by his ruling "father." There is no reason to believe that prior to this identification of *t'ien* with *ti* that *t'ien*, like *ti*, was perceived as a dimension populated by human ancestors. Whatever the original contours of the Chou *t'ien* might have been, it assumed indisputable anthropomorphic characteristics during the Western Chou period, being described in the literature as rewarding and punishing at will, and exercising itself generally in ways associable with a human ruler. Whereras the impact of the Chou would seem to have had the effect of elevating the status of the ancestor spirit deity, *shang-ti*, to a higher level as a primeval cosmic force, there is little doubt that the influence of Shang seems to have been to contribute to the personalization of *t'ien*. Significant for our analysis here, however, is that although there is an unmistakable anthropomorphic interpretation of deity in this period, neither *ti* nor *t'ien* is ever presented as a transcendent deity. It is this distinction in the emergence and development of the Chinese and Western traditions that has had inestimable weight in determining the categories and conceptual structures that have served to define them.

2.2   T'ien 天 and Transcendence

There is considerable confusion among commentators concerning the applicability of "transcendence" to the classical Chinese tradition. For example, although the unity of *t'ien* and man is a central feature of Tu Wei-ming's interpretation of early Confucianism, he insists on numerous occasions that *t'ien* has a transcendent dimension.[14] Mou Tsung-san, using Kant to illuminate the distinctive characteristics of Chinese philosophy, observes:[15]

> The way of *t'ien* as . . . high above denotes transcendence. When the way of *t'ien* is invested in the human person and resides inter-

nally in him as human nature, it is then immanent. On this basis, we can use an expression that Kant liked to use, and say that in one sense the way of *t'ien* is transcendent, and in another it is immanent (immanent and transcendent are opposites). When the way of *t'ien* is both transcendent and immanent, it can be said to have both religious and moral import: religion stresses the transcendent meaning, and morality stresses the immanent. . . .

Given the immanental characterizations of *t'ien* that emerge in both Mou and Tu's analysis, both of whom underscore the inseparability of *t'ien* and *jen* (*t'ien-jen ho-yi* 天人合一), the term "transcendence," to the extent that it connotes independence, seems inappropriate.

One explanation for the willingness to employ the notion of transcendence in interpreting classical Confucianism is that the standard, rather ambiguous, rendering of "transcendence" as *ch'ao-yüeh* 超越("to go beyond") masks the fundamentally independent status of a strictly transcendent being or principle. On the other hand, the Chinese translation of "dualism" which purports to describe those categories necessary to relate transcendent principle and world—*erh-yüan lun* 二元論 (literally "two-source theory")—captures the connotation of independence rather well.

The case of Mou Tsung-san is not simply a problem of translation, however. He asserts that[16]

> the concept of *t'ien ming* as expressed in its transcendent aspect has imperceptibly within it an immutable, unchangeable standard which causes us to feel that under its sanction we must not err or transgress at all in our conduct. To have a sense of *t'ien ming*, one must first have a sense of transcendence, a possibility only when one accepts the "existence" of the transcendent.

He goes on to say that "this is a moral order which corresponds to 'justice' in Greek philosophy."[17] Mou Tsung-san is clearly attempting to attribute a strict transcendence to the early Chinese tradition, and it is precisely with this attribution that we wish to take issue.

In the *Analects*, *t'ien* is unquestionably anthropomorphic. There is, however, a gradual yet clearly discernible depersonalization of *t'ien* from its identification with the anthropomorphic deity, *shang-ti*, in the early Chou to its delineation as natural regularity and order in several philosophers of the late Chou. Although an important contribution of Confucius was his emphasis on man's responsibility for himself and for his circumstances, there is no doubt that his conception of *t'ien* retains a residue of anthropomorphism evident in *t'ien*'s capacity for conscious intervention in human affairs. Confucius' perception of himself as performing a divine charge in transmitting his cultural legacy is proof enough (9/5):

> When Confucius was surrounded in K'uang, he said, "Since King
> Wen has already passed away, does not culture thus reside here? If
> *t'ien* is going to destroy this culture, those who follow us will not be
> able to participate in it. If *t'ien* is not going to destroy this culture,
> what can the people of K'uang do to me!"

T'ien is also variously described as the maker of sages,[18] and as the determiner of social status and wealth.[19]

Since it is a power that has the capacity to understand human beings[20] to such an extent that it cannot be deceived by them,[21] we do well to stand in awe of it.[22] In fact (3/13): "Where one offends against *t'ien*, he has nothing to which to pray." Beyond these specifically anthropomorphic characterizations, *t'ien* is further described as the source of all phenomena and of the processes of natural change (17/19): "The Master responded, 'What does *t'ien* have to say? And yet the four seasons turn and the myriad things are born and grow within it. And what does *t'ien* have to say?' "

The portrait of *t'ien* that emerges from an analysis of relevant passages in the *Analects* is one that clearly has some anthropomorphic characteristics. But it does not follow that, because of this, *t'ien* is equatable with the Western conception of the deity. On the contrary, any comparison that this similarity might encourage is blunted when measured against their profound differences. These differences center first on the contrast between the transcendence of the Western deity and *t'ien* as unqualifiedly immanent. A further important consideration in this disparity is the fact that the Confucian conception of "person," entailed by the seemingly shared characterization as "anthropomorphic," is in fact significantly different. It is precisely these differences that are most germane to Confucius' concept of "religiousness," to be considered shortly.

The classical Chinese tradition generally evidences a strong interest in explaining existence by reference to immanental and naturalistic concepts. Such concepts preclude the development of theories that propose to explain the origin and birth of the cosmos per se. Phenomena are *tzu-jan* 自然 : "so of themselves." The only occasional references to theories of genesis are eclipsed by the far more prominent discussions of transformation. The passage from the *Analects* (17/19) cited above ("What does *t'ien* have to say? And yet the four seasons turn and the myriad things are born and grow within it.") is a case in point. In this context, *t'ien* is not a preexisting creative principle which gives birth to and nurtures a world independent of itself. *T'ien* is rather a general designation for the phenomenal world as it emerges of its own accord. *T'ien* is wholly immanent, having no existence independent of the calculus of phenomena that constitute it. There is as much validity in asserting that phenomena "create" *t'ien* as in saying that *t'ien* creates phenomena; the relationship between *t'ien* and phenomena, therefore, is one of interdependence. The meaning and value of *t'ien* is a function of the meaning and value of its many phenomena, and the order of *t'ien* is expressed in the harmony that obtains among its correlative parts.

The projection of the classical Chinese feudal structure on to *t'ien*, making it the ultimate ruler, is not inconsistent with our explanation of *t'ien* as the cosmological whole. *T'ien* as primitive ancestor of his deputy, the "son of *t'ien*," has an intrinsic relationship with his progeny. The father is the source and model of the son in life, and his counsel and guardian in death. The offspring, for his part, is the psychophysical embodiment and continuation of his progenitor. They are correlatives, requiring each other for explanation. *T'ien* as ruler has an analogous relationship with his empire. The ruler *is* his "empire" (or "command"), and the "empire" *is* the ruler.

In exploring this notion of *t'ien*, it is imperative that we examine it in the light of the polar categories of mind and body appropriate to this tradition. That is, it should be fully expected that any explanation of *t'ien* within the parameters of Confucius' thought which makes reference to physical characterizations necessarily entails a tacit if not explicit correlative psychical aspect.

Tu Wei-ming underscores this radical correlativity in asserting that "the quest for self-knowledge may thus be construed as corresponding to a search for an understanding of Heaven."[23] This can be read as commentary on Mencius' assertion, "He who realizes his natural tendency *(hsing*)* realizes *t'ien*."[24]

The particular phenomenon in this classical Chinese paradigm is not predetermined by some preexistent ideal which the particular must strive to instantiate. Since the particular both determines and is determined by the whole, its growth and maturation is a contingent act to be characterized in the qualitative terms of disclosure: sincerity, focus, integrity, appropriateness, harmony, intensity.

2.3 T'ien Ming 天命

Our speculations on *t'ien* 天 have been informed by several considerations. We have undertaken a philological analysis of this concept and pursued its original sense etymologically. By an examination of its usage in the corpus of early literature, we have sought to establish a historical context for Confucius' thought. Although the *Analects* itself does not provide us with an altogether clear statement on *t'ien*, by combining this historical orientation with an examination of relevant passages in the *Analects*, we have reconstructed a definition which accommodates its usage in this primary source. In addition, we have attempted to extrapolate from other dimensions of Confucius' thought in pursuit of a cosmological structure that could render this notion in a coherent manner. After having discussed the concept of *t'ien ming* 天命 and *te* 德, it will be possible to make some general statements about the fundamentals of Confucius' cosmological vision.

The classical lexicons are of some assistance in unfolding the various dimensions of meaning conveyed by *ming*. Etymologically, the *Shuo-wen* analyzes the character into its two components, *ling* 令, "to command," and *k'ou* 口, "mouth," and defines it as *shih* 使, "to command," "to cause." There are numerous examples in the early texts of *ling* and *ming* being used interchangeably. It is clear then that the fundamental idea represented by *ming* is "to command," "to cause to happen."

In its association with language and communication, *ming* seems to share a significant characteristic with several of the other core concepts that constitute the infrastructure of Confucius' thought. The importance of the *k'ou* 口 "mouth" to qualify *ming* as a verbalized and communicated command is reinforced by the several definitions of *ming* found in other early lexicons. The *Erh-ya* has *kao* 告 "to inform," *Kuang-ya* has *hu* 呼 "to call," and "to speak." Perhaps most significantly, *ming* not only means "to name," like *ming** 名 , but on occasion is actually used interchangeably with this character.

At some point which is not entirely clear, *ming* came to designate certain specific conditions that define existence in the world: lifespan, social and economic status, physical health—not only one's "lot" in life, but one's "life" itself. At least as early as the Chou conquest of Shang, the concept *t'ien ming* 天命 , "the command of *t'ien*," emerged as a condition for the ruler's political continuance in office. In the early corpus, this "command" of *t'ien* is frequently described as contingent upon and responsive to the particular character of the ruling authority.

T'ang Chün-i, in a survey of the early philosophical literature, concludes that:[25]

> The term *"ming"* represents the interrelationship or mutual related-ness of Heaven and man. . . . [W]e can say that it exists neither externally in Heaven only, nor internally in man only; it exists, rather, in the mutuality of Heaven and man, i.e., in their mutual influence and response, their mutual giving and receiving.

In this analysis, T'ang reflects the *Tso-chuan* definition of *ming* which states:[26] "That the people receive the context of the heavens and earth in being born and growing is what is called *ming*." The *Mencius* observes, "There is nothing which is not *ming*. . . ."[27] *Mencius* clarifies the ubiquity of *ming* and attempts to distinguish it from *t'ien*:[28] "Those things that are done (*wei* 為) without anything doing them are *t'ien*; those things that occur without anything causing them (*ch'ih* 致) are *ming*." From this passage, it would appear that while *t'ien* designates the process itself of the natural and human worlds arising spontaneously, *ming* represents those conditions and possi-bilities of a particular phenomenon which provide the context for its arising. There is not something "other" that makes *t'ien*.

As the causal conditions defining a particular event, *ming* is both its possibilities and its limitations. *Ming* is a possible future negotiated within the limitations of the sponsoring circumstances. As such, *t'ien* itself can be described in terms of its defining conditions. The *Chung-yung* cites the *Book of Songs*:[29] "Ah! The *ming* of *t'ien*—so profound and unceasing," and then provides the following commentary: "This (that is, *ming*) then describes what makes *t'ien* what it is." This does not mean that *t'ien* is made by something "other," but that there are certain causal conditions that define it in a certain way.

If *t'ien* is indeed a designation for a particular perspective on the whole process of existence, T'ang Chün-i is not wrong in defining *ming* as "the interrelatedness or mutual relatedness of Heaven and man."[30] That is, *ming* might be compared to a notion such as *shih* 勢, "conditions or circumstances," in that both can describe a calculus of existing conditions—physical, moral, environmental—that constitute the matrix for a given event. As T'ang Chün-i's definition would also indicate, the two notions have important differences, however, in that *ming* always seems to involve the human perspective.

If *ming* is to be understood as the conditions and possibilities that define a particular human perspective in the world, this is but to say that it involves an interpretation of the causal matrix for each particular phenomenon that arises in it. Moreover, without the concept of a cosmogonic act on the part of some transcendent source of meaning and value, it is precisely the interpretation of one's conditioning environs that is the creation of one's world. Thus *ming* is nothing less than one's *created world*. This explains the apparent relationship between "naming" (*ming**) and *ming*: to *ming* is to "articulate" the world. Robin Yates, in his work on the Mohists, arrives at a similar conclusion:[31]

> It is not the case, in my opinion, that the Chinese once had elaborate creation myths that were lost in the course of transmission. The demarcation of boundaries and relationships, geographical, political, religious and social, by naming, described as though it was an historical event, *was* the creation of the Chinese world.

Ming entails viewing the process of existence in a discursive way. The discrimination of the particular entails both a "naming" of it and a perception of it as emerging out of a certain context. And the extent to which this context is construable as "self" and as "other" is a function of the particular focus achieved in the act of naming. Where a person leads a fundamentally passive existence, deriving his order and meaning from his physical and cultural context, he is largely a product of external authority. Where a person diffuses his order and meaning throughout the world, he can be a significant factor in authoring the physical and cultural constitution of his environment. Such "world making" is, of course, a co-authored interpretation that emerges out of the range of possibilities represented by *t'ien* with the individual's ability to understand, select and effect certain of these possibilities.

There is an important analog to *ming* in the relational concept, *li*, "ritual action." The cosmological dimension of *ming* as "causal conditions" seems to have been an historical development from the *ming* of "command" in a ruler-centered world. This development parallels the extension of *li*, "rites," from its early restricted usage as a relationship obtaining between ruler and deity to the generalized notion of pervasive social structures. The concept *ming* embraces *li* inasmuch as cultural consensus itself is a premier set of causal conditions. It extends beyond *li* in that *ming* includes all conditions— biological, social, economic, geographical, historical, and so forth.

Another parallel between *ming* and *li* is that they are both alterable. Since the human being is the ultimate source of meaning and value, cultural consensus is always open to reformulation and reinterpretation. In fact, although *ming* sets certain limitations on possible futures, none of the given factors are in any sense incontrovertible. Each of the factors, insofar as it has bearing on the human world, has a human meaning. Since the human being is the source of discursive naming, he can alter his world by altering its meaning. The fact that, historically, a basically similar environment has sponsored such a vast range of cultural structures for the human experience is evidence of the flexibility of conditions as influenced by acts of interpretation.

Before turning to specific examples of *ming* as it appears in the *Analects*, we shall first qualify several assertions concerning *ming* that are shared by many commentators on Confucius, but which are perhaps most clearly and systematically advanced by D.C. Lau in the introduction to his translation of this text. Lau states:[32]

> Whether *ming* was simply used as an abbreviation for *t'ien ming* in early texts, there is no doubt that by Confucius' time, it had developed into a term with a different and independent meaning.

Lau goes on to clarify this distinction, venturing that *ming* is "Destiny": "things which are brought about, not by human agency," things "over which human endeavour has no effect." As such, *ming* is a mystery which we do best to leave alone. This attribution of fatalism to Confucius has historical precedent as far back as the *Mo Tzu*, which criticizes him with verve:[33]

> The Confucians think that there is an ultimate determination of men's long life or premature death, poverty or wealth, order or disorder [in the world] by *ming*, which can neither be decreased nor increased.

For Lau, *t'ien ming*, in contrast to *ming*, is a moral imperative "concerned with what man ought to do." As such, it can be understood and obeyed. Lau's argument here is basically that Confucius is a "soft determinist," separating determined and determinable along the lines of fact and value:[34]

> Whether or not a man is going to end up with wealth, honour and long life is due to Destiny. No amount of effort on his part will make any difference to the outcome. Thus, in the context of the fortunes of an individual, *ming* is his lot.

Lau contends that it is only an understanding of the predetermined and hence inescapable nature of the "factual" aspects of human existence that will persuade man of the futility of opposing them and will instead encourage him to "bend his efforts to the pursuit of morality." Although man does not control the facticity of his existence, he does have control over his own compliance or noncompliance with those predetermined moral imperatives which are embedded in *t'ien ming* as *yi* 義, which are (for Lau) given principles of rightness.

Lau's claim that a radical distinction between *t'ien ming* and *ming* in the *Analects* is "vital to the understanding of Confucius' position" may be unwarranted. As Lau himself allows, *ming* is frequently used as an abbreviation for *t'ien ming* in the early texts. It is also used in this way in the *Mencius* and later texts. It would seem rather improbable that the *Analects* would be the sole exception to this usage. Although there is a clear tradition of *t'ien ming* being used specifically in the early literature as a political justification for dynastic succession and continuity, as we have observed above, by the time of Confucius this notion of causal conditions had been extended from the ruler and his court to be applied to human beings generally.

In the *Analects*, *t'ien ming* and *ming* are both used in this more general sense, and if there is an appreciable difference between them, it may lie principally in the fact that *ming* can be used in both a narrow and an extended sense. Where *t'ien ming* means the causal conditions constituting the whole of existence as perceived from a particular perspective, *ming* can mean the same, or can also mean the causal conditions constituting a particular phenomenon, without necessary reference to the whole.

Secondly, to translate *ming* as Fate or Destiny, and to explain *t'ien ming* as a moral imperative strongly hints at transcendence. The verb "to destine" in the Anglo-European tradition means "to make fast or firm," "to fix beforehand," "to predetermine." "Fate" similarly means "that which has been spoken"—the doom of the gods. Making proper nouns of these terms reinforces the sense that some principle, power, or agency independent of the human being legislates at least certain aspects of his existence. To thus cast *t'ien ming* as an external, objectively existing moral imperative is to challenge the integrity of the *t'ien–jen* relationship. We would argue that *ming* constitutes the causal conditions that sponsor the emergence of a particular human being, or any other phenomenon, and that these conditions are neither predetermined nor inexorable. That is, inasmuch as a human being is himself a determining force in the world, existing conditions and specifically his own circumstances are alterable through his own participation. An individual's maturation is the result of responding to possibilities which are themselves determined in the interchange between his actions and the emergence of yet other phenomena.

The strongest case in favor of a deterministic interpretation of Confucius can be made from passages such as (6/10):

> Po-niu was ill. Confucius went to look in on him, and, grasping his hand through the window, he lamented, "It is due to the force of circumstances *(ming)* that we are losing this man. That such a man could have such an illness! That such a man could have such an illness!"[35]

This passage makes it clear that at the very least, man does not have complete control over his circumstances. However, this is not the same as saying that he exercises no control at all over them. In fact, the *Analects* describes Tzu-kung in revolt against his economic and social conditions (11/19):

Yen Hui has almost made it, but he is consistently in poverty. Tzu-kung does not accept his circumstances (ming) and has gone into business. And in his ventures he is consistently on the mark.

The exemplary person is portrayed as one who chooses to determine the duration of his own lifespan (14/12):

But to be a complete person in these times one need not go so far. He need only consider what is appropriate at the sight of personal profit, be willing to lay down his life (ming) at the sight of danger. . . .[36]

Clearly, if his *ming* were predetermined and inexorable, Tzu-kung could neither refuse it nor alter it, and the exemplary person's time of death would not be under his own sway. Further, there is the following passage (12/5):

Ssu-ma Niu lamented, "Everyone has brothers except for me."
Tzu-hsia said to him: "I have heard the saying:
    Life and death are a matter of *ming;*
    Wealth and honor lie with *t'ien.*
The exemplary person (chün tzu) is deferential and faultless, respectful of others and refined, and everyone in the world is his brother. Why would the exemplary person worry about not having brothers?"

This passage is frequently cited to support the contention that *ming* means Destiny. Lau calls it his best illustration. But in fact this passage seems to have precisely the opposite meaning. Confucius' disciple, Tzu-hsia, repeats a popular maxim which suggests that there are circumstances that are commonly perceived as being beyond human influence. He then takes one of these circumstances (a man having no brothers) which would seem to be positively unalterable and explores a condition under which this situation can be changed. First, we know that historically Ssu-ma Niu did in fact have a brother, Huan T'ui[37]—the man who threatened Confucius' life.[38] Here Ssu-ma Niu disowns him and alters the apparently unalterable by refusing to interpret "brotherliness" in terms of "facticity." Tzu-hsia then does him one better by demonstrating that the reverse can also be effected—a brotherless person can alter the conditions (that is, his *ming* 命) which cause him to be brotherless by redefining what it means to have brothers (that is, by changing its meaning and frame of reference, its "name," *ming** 名). He asserts that the criterion of brotherhood can be moral (fraternal) rather than biological (born of the same womb). This passage, far from justifying fatalism, demonstrates the fluidity of *ming* and the inseparability of fact and value in the description of one's causal context, one's *ming*.

The problem of the relation between *t'ien ming* and *ming* might be solved in such a manner as this: the individual who has attained a high degree of integration of the sort associated with the exemplary person *(chün tzu)* or the sage *(sheng jen)* has established a peculiarly immanent relationship with *t'ien* which permits him access to the *ming* of *t'ien* both in terms of understanding and of influence. The less intensely focused an individual is, the greater is his sense of *ming* as determining conditions over which he seems to exercise no control; the more intensely focused he is, the greater is his awareness of the role he can play in determining those conditions. Where the world defers to his excellence, he "speaks" for the world; that is, he speaks for *t'ien*. The distinction, then, bears on the meaningfulness of one's context both in the sense of its given meaning and in the sense of one's capacity to introduce meaning into it.

Such an interpretation, admittedly speculative, in part sustains the position of Lau, with the following important qualification: although *ming* might best be understood as contextual conditions over which one has initially less control than those represented by *t'ien ming*, this lack of control is largely a function of the degree of self-realization possessed by a given individual. Also, it is partly a measure of the extent to which a given context is deemed worthy of one's best efforts. There are, after all, some battles one simply will not choose to fight in order to save energy for the truly important tasks. In principle there are no limits to the ability of the authoritative person, *chün tzu* or sage, to meaningfully influence his conditions. A truism of the Western philosophic tradition has it that "philosophy is nothing more than learning how to die." One's ability to respond meaningfully to even the most "fated" of circumstances renders them significantly alterable.

When all qualifying remarks have been made, however, it remains true that Confucius' understanding of *ming* and *t'ien ming* is much less conservative than has traditionally been believed. Recalling the discussion of *yi* (appropriateness/significating) within the context of the activity of person making, it is clear that the interrelations of ritual action *(li)* and *yi* require something like our interpretation of *ming* and *t'ien ming*. For to perform ritual action *(li)* with *yi* is a paradigmatic instance of responding to one's given context in a meaningful manner.

3   Te 德

3.1   A Characterization of Te 德 from Early Literature

The concept *te* is painfully recondite. Confucius states rather specifically that few are able to understand or realize it.[39] In fact, this concept, *te*, is an uncomfortable puzzle in the early texts in that many scholars have not really determined what to make of it, and as a consequence, give it short shrift. In Lau's translation of the *Tao Te Ching*, for example, Lau dismisses the notion of *te* with a short paragraph, asserting that "in the *Lao Tzu* the term is not a particularly important one and is often used in more conventional senses."[40] We would contend, on the contrary, that a proper understanding of the relationship between *tao* 道 and *te* 德 is the key to Taoist cosmology and the entire philosophical edifice that this cosmology supports. It is precisely for this reason that the text is called *Tao Te Ching—The Classic of Tao and Te*. Lau is undoubtedly right in contending that *te* in the *Tao Te Ching* is used in its conventional sense. But to interpret the conventional sense as "the nature of a thing"[41] in a philosophy that denies essentialist self-nature and the finality of "things," and that establishes *tzu-jan* 自然, "uncaused self-arising," as a major precept, introduces a concept of nature that would be inappropriate, if not outright misleading. Both the *Tao Te Ching* and the "authentic" *Chuang Tzu* seem to consciously avoid the term "nature" (*hsing** 性) in explaining their ideas—we would do well to follow their lead.[42]

Both the prominence and the ambiguity of *te* in the wider corpus of pre-Ch'in literature is adequately illustrated in Mote's translation of Hsiao Kung-chuan's *A History of Chinese Political Thought*, in which he renders *te* in the following ways: "ethical nature," "spiritual powers," "Power," "moral excellence," "power imparted from the

Tao," *"virtus"* (in the sense of a thing's intrinsic and distinctive character), "moral force" (citing Waley), "the powers native to beings and things," and frequently, perhaps in despair, simply as *"te."*[43] Beyond the meaning of "virtue" or "power" that is cultivated and increased in the thing itself, *te* also has the sense of "favor" or "bounty" extended outwards, and further the gratitude that it evokes. For the Confucians and Mohists, it is generally translated "virtue," while for the Taoists it is usually some order of "power."

We would certainly not fault Mote for the latitude in his renderings; it is common in, if not characteristic of, the early Chinese thinkers to rework a shared set of locutions that come to have very different values in each of their respective philosophies. On the other hand, we would suggest that the various dimensions of meaning taken on by this concept are grounded in and related at some more fundamental level.

There are scholars who have so stressed the disparate meanings of *te* for the Confucians and Taoists as to separate them entirely.[44] While the interpretations of *te* advanced by these schools clearly differ in emphasis, we would suggest that the radical nature of the distinction that they draw reflects different levels of meaning rather than different conceptual content. The focus of the Taoists' discussions is predominantly a cosmological account of the cyclical process of existence where *te* is regarded as categorial: the presencing of a particular. In the *Analects*, on the other hand, *te* would seem to be specifically social and moral in its applications: the extent to which, through patterns of deference, the influence of the particular takes on normative force. When we lay bare the cosmological presuppositions underlying Confucian social theory, however, or when we draw out the social and political implications of *te* in the Taoist texts, we find that the distance between their interpretations of *te* closes significantly. In fact, we would claim that underlying the obvious disparities is an unadvertised commonality that both the Confucians and Taoists shared in their use of *te*.[45] It is the existence of this core idea underlying the many connotations of *te* that justifies our appeal to texts beyond the *Analects* in our attempt to reconstruct the concept *te*.

Before going to the literature to deal with *te* at a conceptual level, we want to explore the term philologically. In the *Shuo-wen*, significantly, *te* is defined as an event "arising" or "presencing itself" (*sheng* 升). Although traditional commentators flex some philological muscle in their struggle to discipline this explanation into something more conventional—namely, the cognate of *te* 德 meaning "to get" (*te*** 得)—their arguments are decidedly unconvincing.[46]

The character *te* is comprised of three elements: *ch'ih* 彳 "to move ahead"; a second element which most etymologists take as a representation of the human eye 直 ; and *hsin* 心 , the "heart-and-mind." The eye and heart-and-mind elements would suggest that the unfolding process of *te* is disposed in a particular direction. It is the transforming content and disposition of an existent: a self-construed "arising."

There is another twist in the philological analysis. It is general scholarly opinion that the character *te* 德 is a later variant of the character *te** 悳 (at times found as *chih* 直).[47] This earlier alternative form of *te* is constituted by *chih* 直 , commonly used in its derived sense as "straight," but perhaps better understood in its more fundamental meaning of "to grow straight without deviation" in the context of organic issuance.[48] The organic dimension of *chih* is underscored by its cognates, *chih* 稙 , "to sow," and *chih* 植 , "to plant." The heart-and-mind element in this variant character would again contribute a sense of disposition to the basic meaning of organic germination and growth. The *Shuo-wen* has a separate entry for the variant *te** 悳 , taking advantage of the homophonous cognate *te*** 得, "to get," in defining it as "to get from oneself within and from others without."[49] Finally, of some philological significance is the fact that both *te* 德 and the earlier variant *te** 悳 belong to the phonetic category deriving from *chih* 直 , "to grow straight without deviation."

To regard the data in the foregoing analysis as anything more than suggestive would be to overstate their importance and ignore their very tentative nature. In spite of their limitations, however, these data can serve us in two ways. First, they can indicate several dimensions of meaning to which we can be alert in the analysis of their various philosophical applications. Secondly, they can provide us with a structure and vocabulary for excavating content in reconstructing this concept of *te* from the available literature.

Across the corpus of pre-Ch'in literature, *te* seems to have a fundamental cosmological significance from which its other connotations are derived. In the Taoist literature, it denotes the arising of the particular as a focus of potency in the process of existence. As a total field this dynamic process is called *tao;* the individuated existents in this field, its various foci, are called *te*. The *Tao Te Ching*, for example, states: "The Great *tao* is so expansive. It reaches in all directions. All of individuated existence arises because of it. . . ."[50]

It is critical at this juncture to make it clear that *te* and *t'ien* do not differ ontologically. They are differentiable only as a matter of focus or emphasis. *Te* denotes any particular disposition of the whole. In those early texts in which the emphasis is primarily on the human condition, *te* is most frequently and not unexpectedly used in discussing human beings. However, even in texts such as the *Analects* and the *Tao Te Ching*, it is applied to a wide range of particular phenomena such as the common people,[51] horses,[52] dynasties,[53] neighborhoods,[54] families,[55] and empires.[56] Its most conventional usage is to characterize some variable focus of the whole. And since all foci relate to each other through patterns of deference, alternative interpretations can expand or contract the range of concern.

In distinguishing one aspect of and constituting one perspective on *tao*, *te* serves an individuating function. It is this function that underlies the frequent association between *te* and "natural process" (*hsing** 性).[57] The concept *hsing*, commonly translated as "nature," is a possible source of misleading associations. There is an unfortunate tendency to read *hsing** as something like an "essential nature" upon encountering passages such as:[56] "The *ming* of *t'ien* 天命 is called *hsing** 性 ; to lead out and accord with this *hsing** is called *tao* 道 . . . ." *Hsing** is not an inborn nature, a predetermined potential that is actualized and completed. Rather, given the process orientation of Confucian philosophy, and taking the *sheng* 生 signific ("life process, growth") literally, *hsing** is to be understood as a process in which nature is necessarily and irreducibly "nature-in-context." That is, a discussion of "individual nature" that seeks to separate "thing" from "environment" is an abstraction.

The concept *hsing** further asserts that although each particular focus in the process of existence is unique, it can be grouped with other particulars on the basis of similarities. Those differences that obtain among the members of these foci which are expressive of their uniqueness can be suspended, and a name can be assigned to represent their similarities. Since differences are more pronounced at a developed state, *hsing** is frequently associated with undeveloped potential. Of course, the concept *hsing** has a functional value, but is limited by the fact that no two particulars are identical. Even for Confucius, "People are similar (not the same) by natural tendency *(hsing*)*; they vary greatly as a matter of practice" (17/2). Where the whole is characterized in terms of unique particulars, it is called *te;* where it is characterized in terms of similarities among its components, it is called *hsing**. It is possibly because *hsing**, so interpreted, violates the Taoist insight that each thing has a unique *te* that both *Lao Tzu* and *Chuang Tzu* avoid it.

While *te* is most often used to denote a selected perspective on the whole, it is elastic, and can be extended through integration to overcome any presumed disjunction between part and whole, and in this sense, embraces the entire complex of existence. In the *Tao Te Ching*, for example, locutions such as "constant *te*" (*ch'ang te* 常德), "perpetual *te*" (*heng te* 恆德), "dark *te*" (*hsüan te* 玄德), and "superlative *te*" (*shang te* 上德) all denote the coincidence of *tao* and *te*. The *Tao Te Ching* states:[59]

> If you are a ravine to the empire,
> The constant *te* will not desert you.
> When the constant *te* does not desert you
> You will again return to being a babe. . . .
>
> If you are a model to the empire,
> The constant *te* will not deviate.
> When the constant *te* does not deviate,
> You will again return to the boundless. . . .
>
> If you are a valley to the empire,
> The constant *te* will be sufficient.
> When the constant *te* is sufficient,
> You will again return to being the uncarved block.

The *Yi-ching* describes the extension of one's person in similar terms:[60]

> The greatest person is one whose *te* is coincident with the heavens and earth, whose brilliance is coincident with the sun and moon, whose ordering is coincident with the four seasons, and whose fortune is coincident with the ghosts and spirits.

When *te* is cultivated and accumulated such that the particular is integrated utterly with the whole, the distinction between *tao* and *te* collapses and *te* as an individuating notion is transformed into *te* as an integrating notion. The *Tao Te Ching*, again, states: "One who possesses *te* in abundance is comparable to a new-born babe."[61] In these passages the infant, the uncarved block, the great person are metaphors for a condition in which one does not distinguish oneself from one's environment. There is no circumscription or separation from one's whole. Such being the case, because the babe is a matrix through which the full consequence of undiscriminated existence can be brought to focus and experienced, it can be used as a metaphor for the *te* which is *tao*. Metaphors frequently seen in the Taoist literature alluding to this extension and coincidence of *te* with *tao* are the uncarved block (*p'u* 樸), darkness (*hsüan* 玄), and water in its various forms. These metaphors underscore the notion that any particular when viewed in terms of its intrinsic relatedness entails the full process of existence, and as such focuses *tao*. Throughout the early literature, this collapse of *te* into *tao* is often expressed as a paradox:[62]

> Where one is *te*, he is without *te*.
> The person of superior *te* is not *te*
> And that is why he has *te*.
> The person of inferior *te* does not lose his *te*
> And that is why he has no *te*. . . .
> Hence, *te* arises after the *tao* is lost;
> *Jen** arises after *te* is lost. . . .

The *Chuang Tzu* also describes *te* as a unifying principle:[63]

> This man and this kind of *te* will extend things in all directions to make one.
> If you look at things in terms of how they differ, the gap between liver and gall is as great as the distance from Ch'u to Yüeh; if you look at them in terms of their sameness, everything is one. A person who is like this, totally oblivious to what is appropriate to each sense, sends his heart-and-mind rambling in the harmony of *te*. As for things, he sees wherein they are one and fails to see what they lose.

There is a harmonious order, a regularity, a pattern realized in the process of existence that is empirically evident and which brings a unified perspective on diversity, oneness to plurality.

3.2 Te 德 : A Philosophic Reconstruction

The early Confucian tradition sought to limit its concerns to the social and political problems that characterized its period. At this level, then, the cultivation of *te* serves the function of integration (4/25): "*Te* never is isolated, but necessarily has neighbors." In the opposite direction, to be small-minded and selfish leads to isolation (4/26): "To be petty in serving one's lord will incur humiliation; to be petty with friends will lead to estrangement." As we have seen above, for Confucius, the activity characteristic of a human event that leads to integration with the whole is called authoritative humanity (*jen* 仁*). Of course, this term is homophonous with and equivalent to the notion of person (*jen 人*). This kind of activity overcomes discreteness and discontinuity in the direction of integration and harmony. That is, the extension and focusing of particular *te* can be described in terms of *jen**. As we have outlined above, the *jen** person is fundamentally intersubjective, definable in terms of his human community. As his person is extended, his range of possibilities and the influence or power of his person are proportionately extended. He becomes a "large" person in that he focuses a sphere that goes far beyond the range of any ego-self. Given that a human being is a particular focus of meaning-creating and meaning-disclosing, his capacity for valuation is proportionately increased. His transvaluation, however, is not random; rather it is tempered and guided by the pursuit of an appropriate construing of conditions. As we have repeatedly stressed, Confucius believed that the human being is a world maker, and the greater his proportions, the greater his efficacy as world maker.

For Confucius, on the political level, the relationship that obtains between the ruler and his people can be described in terms of *te*. To the extent that his person reaches out to become coextensive with their natural direction, one might speak in terms of "getting them" (*te** 得*), or "winning them over." On the other hand, in his becoming coextensive with them through deference, they also come to share his values and moral insights. This is the "giving" or "bounty" (*en* *te* 恩德) aspect of *te*. As their *te* is embraced within his own, his potency is enhanced and becomes a wind that bends the weaker *te*,[64] the north star around which the other stars revolve,[65] the maker and transmitter of culture to which other persons subscribe.[66] By virtue of his achieved excellence, he becomes an object of deference.

In the Taoist tradition, which moves beyond the human world and extends its sphere of concern to all of existence, the activity which integrates the particular *te* with the *tao* is called "acting naturally" (*wu-wei* 無為) or "self-so-ing" (*tzu-jan* 自然). The Taoist texts, like their Confucian counterparts, see the repudiation of discriminating ego-self as a precondition for integrative natural action and the concomitant extension of *te*:[67]

> Yen Hui said, "I have sat and forgotten."
> Confucius, noticeably flustered, inquired: "What do you mean by 'sitting and forgetting?' "
> "I have demolished my appendages and body, expurgated my perceptiveness and perspicacity, abandoned my physical form and repudiated wisdom to identify with the Great All," said Yen Hui. "This I call 'sitting and forgetting.' "

In dissolving the boundary between "self" and "other," Yen Hui's *te* is integrated with and serves to focus what had been construed as "other." The early texts speak of "accumulating" *te*, "cultivating" it, "piling it up," and "extending" it.[68] Confucius defines this process of "accumulating *te*" (*ch'ung te* 崇德) in the context of overcoming poorly directed and ill-determined judgments, and actively producing meaning and value in the world (12/10):

> Tzu-chang inquired about "accumulating *te*" and sorting things out when one is of two minds. Confucius replied, "To regard doing one's best, living up to one's word, and accommodating oneself to what is appropriate as one's most important concern, is to accumulate *te*. You love something and want it to live; you hate it and want it to die. To want something to die when one already wants it to live is a case of being of two minds [that is, of muddled judgment]."

The association between "accumulating *te*" and the resolution of muddled judgment here and elsewhere in the *Analects* is significant if we recall from our philological analysis that the character *te* implies both impetus and the pursuit of appropriateness.[69] That is, the extension of *te* entails both an act of intending and the attraction of the support necessary to effect what is intended. The particular initiating the direction focuses this support as coextensive with its own particularity. At the same time, the particular becomes coextensive with "other" by overcoming its particularity and accommodating the natural direction and volition of "the other" to integrate that into its own field of interpretation.

This coextensiveness is rather clear politically in that the ruler expresses the people through his government by accommodating their natural proclivities and thus orchestrating an interpretation of culture that is both his and theirs. There is always, in this conception of *te*, a tension between attempting to maximize the possibilities for harmony provided by attending conditions, and the expression of an interpretation that does justice to one's own uniqueness and sense of appropriateness. This integration enables the person who is extending *te* to focus the whole and thus to be everywhere responsive and efficacious.

As this person extends his *te*, his sphere of presencing becomes more influential and his capacity for focusing an interpretation becomes more pronounced. As artist, as political leader, as teacher, he is able to organize his natural environment and disclose its possibilities for harmony—to manifest, interpret, and display its culture.

A most helpful metaphor in understanding *te* is that of the tally in the Taoist texts. The *Tao Te Ching* states:[70]

> The person of *te* takes charge of the tally;
> The person without it looks after collecting.

The meaning of this rather obscure passage is illumined in the fifth chapter of the *Chuang Tzu*, the title of which is "*Te* Satisfies the Tally." This chapter is a series of anecdotes about mutilated cripples who, under normal circumstances and the sway of conventional values, would be ostracized from their communities. Their mutilated physical forms, often the result of amputatory punishment, would be certain grounds for societal rejection. Having overcome ego-self and extended their *te* to integrate themselves with the spontaneous unfolding of their social environs, however, they "satisfy the tally" and not only blend harmoniously with their respective societies, but come to exercise considerable influence in them., The extent and quality of their *te* is such that they are important factors in the ongoing process of defining values and establishing an ethos. This new order is determined by and reflects the natural direction of its constituent *te*.

The person of pervasive *te* in the Taoist tradition is called *chen jen*真人 The character *chen*, meaning "true" or "real," is classified under the radical *hua* ヒ , meaning "to transform." In the *Chuang Tzu*, the process of existence is frequently referred to as the "transformation of things" (*wu hua* 物化). As the Taoist *chen jen* extends himself to become coextensive with the natural direction of his context, he becomes an increasingly influential "transformer" of things. Viewed as a discriminated focus, he is transforming something other than himself; from the perspective of his diffusion throughout his context, he has become a larger focus of what it is that is self-transforming. To the extent that his broad presencing has possibilities for creativity and novelty, so too does he. To the extent that he embraces the *te* of the whole within his particularity, he is integrated and efficacious at whatever he does. What might be perceived as his interface with "other" is in fact coincident *te* such that he facilitates and interprets the natural expression of whatever he encounters: his hands express the clay, and the clay expresses his hands.

The *chen jen* embraces the *te* of his natural as well as his human environment. By becoming coextensive with the *te* of the ox, for example, the person of pervasive *te* is able to express and interpret the natural impetus of the ox in such a manner as to become an efficacious butcher;[71] by becoming coextensive with the *te* of the clay, he is able to express and interpret the natural impetus of the clay to become an efficacious craftsman.[72] The absence of a "dis-integrating" ego-self makes him open to the *te* of his whole natural environment, so that the environment contributes to him, making him potent and productive, and he contributes to his environment, strengthening, enhancing, and interpreting its natural direction. His presence in the world is coincident with the *te* of his whole environment, extending out to ultimately focus all of existence.

Knitting the several strands of these philological and conceptual data together, it would seem that *te* denotes the arising of the particular in its context. For the classical Chinese philosopher, the world of particulars is "alive" in the sense that they are aware of and hence "feel" or "prehend" other particulars in their environment. The expression "self-so-ing" (*tzu-jan* 自然) is both a physical and psychical characterization that means that reality is self-causing and self-aware. And to be aware is to invest interest and thus value in other things. The notion of a particular and its "nature" in this tradition needs to be broadly understood not in terms of essential differences, but as specific perturbations and transforming configurations in *ch'i* 氣, the hylozoistic vapor that constitutes the process of existence. The range of the particular is variable, and is contingent upon the ways in which it interprets itself and is interpreted. The particular is a specific "focus" because its context, in whatever direction and degree, can alternatively be construed as "self" or as "other." The presencing of particulars is not random and chaotic. Rather, it is characterized by an inherent dynamism which, through its own disposition and self-direction, interprets the world. It has the possibility of making a direction appropriate by expressing itself in compromise between its own disposition and the context which it makes its own. Just as any one ingredient in the stewpot must be blended with all of the others in order to express most fully its own flavor, so harmonizing with other environing particulars is a necessary precondition for the fullest self-disclosure of any given particular. It is thus a calculus of the appropriate directions of the particulars that constitutes the unifying harmony and regularity observable in the world.

The potency of the arising event as innovative interpreter is dependent upon the range and quality of its self-construing. The particular, through harmonizing patterns of deference, can diffuse to become coextensive with other particulars, and absorb an increasingly broader field of emergent particulars within the sphere of its own particularity. As a particular extends itself to encompass a wider range of "presencing" or "arising," its potency for self-construal is proportionately increased.

4 Tao 道

4.1 Confucius' Understanding of Tao 道

Tao, occurring some one hundred times in the *Analects*, is of central importance for the interpretation of Confucius' thinking. And, as we shall see directly, a philological analysis of the character supports the plausibility of our particular interpretation of Confucius' cosmology thus far expressed in terms of *te* and *t'ien ming*.

The character for *tao* is comprised of two elements, *ch'o* 辵, "to pass over, to go over," "to lead through," and *shou* 首, "head," "foremost," both of which contribute significance to this "combined meaning" *(hui-yi)* character. Given these components, *tao* would seem to be fundamentally verbal. First, almost all characters constructed with the *ch'o* component are verbal. Furthermore, in the *Shu-ching*, *tao* is used a significant number of times in the context of cutting a channel and "leading" a river to prevent the overflowing of its banks. Even the *shou*, "head," component has the suggestion of "to lead" or "to give a heading." Taking the verbal *tao* as primary, its several derived meanings emerge rather naturally: to lead through; road, path; way, method, art, teachings; to explain, to tell.[73] As its most fundamental level, *tao* seems to denote the active project of "road making," and by extension, to connote a road that has already been laid and hence can be travelled.

Commentators upon the Confucian *Analects* often nominalize *tao*, explaining it as a preexisting ideal to which conformity is enjoined. Although the *Analects* does make specific mention of this kind of *tao* and a passive attendance upon it, this is done in a deprecating way (8/9): "The masses can be made to travel along it, but they cannot be made to realize it." That is, to simply be led along an existing roadway is to be distinguished from the rather different and more difficult task of "making a roadway real." We shall argue that to realize the *tao* is to experience, to interpret, and to influence the world in such a way as to reinforce, and where appropriate extend, a way of life established by one's cultural precursors. This way of living in the world, then, provides a road map and direction for future generations. Thus, for Confucius, *tao* is primarily *jen tao* 人道.

Confucius frequently describes the *tao* as a legacy received from preceding generations (19/22):

> The *tao* of Wen and Wu has not fallen to the ground—it exists in people. Those of superior quality have grasped its essentials, while the inferior have grasped a bit of it. Everyone has something of Wen and Wu's *tao* in him. Who then does the Master not learn from? Again, how could there be a single constant teacher for him?

Tao lives in the people, is carried forward by them, and is to be learned from them.[74] And individuals receive and embody *tao* in unique and qualitatively different ways. *Tao* inherited out of the cultural tradition is at times identified with representative historical persons: for example, Wen and Wu.[75] At other times it is identified with historical periods such as the Three Dynasties or "antiquity".[76] Since these persons and periods are really symbols of a certain quality of human experience, there is in fact little difference between this kind of historical attribution and the association of *tao* with abstracted levels of exemplary human beings: the exemplary person *(chün tzu)*, the good person *(shan jen)*, the sage *(sheng jen)*.[77] Although Confucius chooses at times to identify *tao* with distant historical figures and lofty exemplars of human achievement, he is adamant that it is also to be found close at hand, in one's contemporaries, one's teachers, and even one's family members.[78] *Tao* is frequently attributed to Confucius himself, either as "my *tao*" or the *tao* of the Master.[79]

An important consideration in understanding Confucius' concept of *tao*—limited as it is to the human world—is that the human being is not only heir to and transmitter of *tao*, but is, in fact, its ultimate creator. Thus we shall argue that the *tao* emerges out of human activity. As the metaphor "road" would suggest, *tao*, at least for Confucius, is ultimately of human origin.

The peculiarly human capacity for significating *(yi* 義 *)* has an important role as the primitive source of *tao*. The inherited *tao* embodied in the cultural tradition is transmitted and further extended by the exemplary person *(chün tzu)* through his propensity for generating meaning and value (16/11):[80] "They dwelt in seclusion to pursue their ends and acted on their personal sense of importance *(yi)* to extend their *tao*." In fact, where *tao* does not prevail in the empire, the exemplary person *(chün tzu)*, rather than becoming a recluse, may attempt to continue the *tao* and to revitalize it by personally exercising his capacity for imbuing the world with significance (18/7): "The exemplary person's *(chün tzu)* opportunity to serve in office is the occasion for him to effect what he judges important and appropriate. As for the fact that the *tao* is not prevailing, he is well aware of it."

The metaphorical characterizations of the *tao* used in the *Analects* disclose its two-sided nature as both appropriated inheritance and personal contribution. The received *tao* is regarded as a doorway which provides the concerned person with a direction (6/17):[81] "Who can go out without using the door? Why then does no one go out from this *tao?*" The *tao* is a door framed by one's cultural ambiance and through which one emerges to make his own way. It is a starting point and a heading, not an ultimate destination.

The world is like an artisan's workshop in which one is schooled in the skills and experience of the past as preliminary to achieving the *tao* creatively for one's own place and time (19/7): "The various craftsmen stay in their workshops so that they may master their trades; the exemplary person *(chün tzu)* learns that he may effect his *tao.*" The *tao* is generated and nurtured out of the efforts of the accomplished person, and is ultimately dependent on human action for its coming into being (1/2):

> The exemplary person *(chün tzu)* works at the roots, for where the roots are firmly set, the *tao* will grow forth. Filial piety and fraternal deference—these are the roots of becoming a person.

It is this often overlooked creative dimension of advancing the *tao* that is underscored in the assertion that becoming human is more than simply following in the footprints of others.[82] The human being has an active, creative role in continuing, broadening, and extending the *tao*, such that the *tao* is historically composite and cumulative, the human unfolding of chosen areas of importance (15/29): "It is the human being who is able to extend the *tao*, not the *tao* that is able to extend the human being."[83]

The immediate relationship between *jen** 仁 as "person making" and *tao* 道 as "world making" does much to clarify this contingent nature of *tao*. Throughout the *Analects*, *tao* is repeatedly associated with, if not defined in terms of, *jen** (8/7):

> The gentleman-scholar must be strong and determined, for his task is a heavy one and his way *(tao)* is long. Where he takes as his task becoming authoritatively human, is it not a heavy one? And where his way ends only with his death, is it not indeed long?![84]

It is because a person is both defined and defines himself in the dynamic interaction between his unique person and his unique circumstances that the frequently adverted *jen** remains obscure and indeterminate. The *tao* is a thoroughfare between birth and death that is determined by the exchange between an emerging humanity and a changing world.

Ultimately derived from particular efforts at person making, *tao* embraces all aspects of the historical process of organizing and structuring human experience. It is a process of world making unified by the basic coherence of all humans' ongoing achievements in the areas of the various cultural interests.

Yen Yüan (Yen Hui), Confucius' favorite disciple, describes the personal effort required to make one's way along the elusive *tao*, underscoring his debt to Confucius for leading him as far as possible, and preparing him to continue his journey (9/11):

> Yen Yüan heaved a deep sigh: "The more I look up at *tao*, the higher it soars; the more I penetrate into it, the harder it becomes. I am looking at it in front of me, and suddenly it is behind me. The Master is good at drawing a person forward one step at a time; he broadens me with culture and regulates my behavior with ritual action. Even if I wanted to quit, I could not. And when I have exhausted my abilities, and seem to have established myself, it rises up. Even though I want to follow it, there is no road to take."

Not unexpectedly, in the *Mencius*, we have reference to the *tao* of Yen Yüan and the assertion that his *tao* is the same as that of the ancient sages, Yü and Hou Chi.[85] What there is of a clearly delineated roadway was forged by cultural precursors and has been kept open by persons using it to make their way from one end of life to the other. But circumstances change, and generations will pass where the way has been overgrown and lost (14/36): "Whether the *tao* will be possible or in a state of neglect is a matter of circumstances. . . ."

Confucius himself lived in a period where the ancient heading had been lost and circumstances conspired against passage through a life of quality. As such, it was incumbent upon the particular person to clear what could be cleared from the path to make a new beginning for future travellers (3/24): "The empire has long since lost its way *(tao)*. T'ien is going to use the Master as a wooden bell-clapper." This responsibility of the particular person to locate the old road, cut it back, and make a new beginning is a major theme of the

Analects.[86] Where one cannot further *tao* by participation in govern-
mental service, one may withdraw to continue the project within the
confines of a private existence (15/7):

> How straight is Shih Yü! When the *tao* prevails in the state, he is
> like an arrow, and when it doesn't, he is still like an arrow. And
> what an exemplary person *(chün tzu)* is Ch'ü Po-yü! When the *tao*
> prevails in the state, he serves in office, and when it doesn't, he
> rolls himself up to be tucked away.

The *tao* is the continuous progress of human civilization, an
interpretation of human experience surveyed and laid down by succeeding generations. Although the embodiment of the *tao* always
entails a unique perspective, unqualified distinctions among historical
persons and their periods collapse in the syncretic extension of the
tao. The unity of *tao* is expressed by the fact that each present
perspective is a function of all past events, and is the ground of all
future possibilities. Not only does the past cast the present and
future, but the past itself is constantly being revisioned and recast
in light of the achievements of the present. Thus Confucius served
to fashion the present cultural product of Chinese civilization and
is himself constantly being remade by the succeeding perspectives
of human experience and their shifting investments of importance.

The *tao* may be described in qualitative terms as a collocation
of cultural vectors integrated and brought to a focus of intelligibility
by successive perspectives. Because there are various areas of importance and varying degrees of achievement with *tao*, its lower
levels can be described as trifling[87] if not even conflicting,[88] while
its central, more elevated dimensions are the proper concern of a
person's life.[89] The *tao* of the "good person" *(shan jen)* and the
exemplary person *(chün tzu)* both fall short of sageliness *(sheng jen),*[90]
and yet the text seems quite clear on the point that we are dealing
here not with entirely different *tao*, but rather with the quality of
the perspective measured in terms of differing degrees of focus and
comprehension (19/12):

> In the *tao* of the exemplary person *(chün tzu)*, what is to be con-
> veyed first and what is to be placed last? The *tao* is analogous to the
> plant world in that category distinctions can be made. But how could

there be any "error" in the *tao* of the exemplary person *(chün tzu)*? It is just that it is only the sage alone who knows the route from first step to last.

The *tao* is multifaceted in that it construes what is of importance in each area of our cultural interest. There is a *tao* of music,[91] a *tao* of archery,[92] a *tao* of the government minister,[93] a cosmological *tao*.[94] Given the special concern of Confucius for sociopolitical problems, the *tao* of proper government occupies a central place in the *Analects*.[95] Each important cultural figure in each historical period not only embodies *tao* in a particular manner appropriate to his unique circumstances, but also, with the energy of his own original contribution, is able to set the dynamics of *tao* on a novel course.

We can emphasize the uniqueness of the individual *tao* or the continuity of the *tao* as a resource for potential. While underscoring the much neglected pluralistic and individually created dimension of *tao*, we do not wish to overlook its fundamental continuity. Our point is simply that enthusiastic service to this continuity has inhibited an appreciation of an equally fundamental level of Confucius' thought, the novelty and originality inherent in the *tao*.

4.2   Tao 道 *and Transcendence*

We have gone to some pains to outline and argue the central, creative role of particular human beings in Confucius' conception of *tao*. This has been done by interpreting his *tao* as the peculiarly human way of focusing the world. Perhaps the most effective way of highlighting the implications of our interpretation is to deal with the rival position, that Confucius' *tao* is some order of transcendent principle. Since we are arguing against an established, if not the prevailing, reading of Confucius, there is no shortage of prominent representatives of that position.

Arthur Waley, in the introduction to his translation of the *Analects*, defines *tao* as the "one infallible method of rule:"[96]

> Thus, "when *tao* (the Way) prevails under Heaven" means when a good method of government prevails in the world; or rather "when *the* good method prevails," for Confucius "believed in the ancients," that is to say, he believed that the one infallible method of rule had

been practiced by certain rulers of old, and that statecraft consisted in rediscovering this method.

Waley is aware that this narrow definition cannot account for all instances of *tao* in the *Analects*:[97]

> There seem to have been other "Ways"; for Confucius speaks of "this Way" and "my Way." In general, however, the word *Tao* in the *Analects* means one thing only, the Way of the ancients as it could be reconstructed from the stories told about the founders of the Chou dynasty and the demi-gods who had preceded them.

Lau, unwilling to limit the jurisdiction of *tao* to the political sphere alone, construes it as "the sum total of truths about the universe and man:"[98]

> The importance Confucius attached to the Way can be seen from his remark, "He has not lived in vain who dies the day he is told about the Way" [4/8]. Used in this sense, the Way seems to cover the sum total of truths about the universe and man, and not only the individual but also the state is said either to possess or not to possess the Way.

Like Waley, Lau also registers a contingent, personal usage for *tao*:[99]

> There is another slightly different sense in which the term is used. The way is said to be someone's way, for instance, "the way of the Former Kings" [1/12], "the way of King Wen and King Wu" [19/22], or "the way of the Master" [4/15]. When thus specified, the way naturally can only be taken to mean the way followed by the person in question.

Still, Lau chooses to associate the more important usage of *tao* with the notion of transcendent principle so prominent in the development of Western thought:[100]

> The Way, then, is a highly emotive term and comes very close to the term "Truth" as found in philosophical and religious writings in the West.

The fullest, most elaborate, most sustained statement of this interpretation of *tao* must belong to Herbert Fingarette. In his explication of *tao*, he defines it as a "way without crossroads."[101] By this, he means that the *tao* is a "single, definite order":[102]

> This Confucian commitment to a single, definite order is also evident when we note what Confucius sees as the alternative to rightly treading the true Path: it is to walk crookedly, to get lost or to abandon the Path. That is, the only "alternative" to the one Order is disorder, chaos.

For Fingarette, the *tao*, capitalized as "the Way," "the Path," "the one Order," is necessary and absolute. It is a transcendent moral principle in the sense that it has an objective existence independent of the contingent particulars which it informs:[103]

> The *tao* says that *any* person in my present position should do thus and so—my proper name is not built into the *tao*, or the *li*. In all aspects of the *tao* there is an inherent generality, an absence of essential reference to a unique individual. My personal existence is contingent; not so the *tao*. The *tao* is not only intelligible independently of such reference, its moral authority is surely independent of reference to me as the unique existent that I am.

While many of the commentators who interpret *tao* as a transcendent notion would balk at some of the consequences of Fingarette's interpretation, it does appear that Fingarette is doing little more than unfolding in a systematic manner the consequences of attributing transcendence to Confucius. And the most serious ramifications of this attribution lie in what we believe to be an impoverishment of Confucius' conception of the human being.

For Fingarette, the applications of this objectively existing standard of right and wrong are a matter of recognition:[104]

> One may suppose that the notion of equally valid alternatives is not implied, that there is presumed to be only one right thing to do and that the question then means in effect, "What about this, *is* it right, is it the Way?" Put in more general terms, the task is not conceived [of] as a choice but as the attempt to characterize some object or action as objectively right or not. . . . The task is not posed as one

of *choosing* or *deciding* but of distinguishing or *discriminating (pien)* the inconsistent inclinations. . . . In short, the task is posed in terms of knowledge rather than choice.

This certainly suggests that the human being is to be shaped and informed in accordance with some objective standard:[105]

> The basic conception of man in the *Analects* is that he is a being born into the world—more especially into society—with the potentiality to be shaped into a truly human form. . . . If there is a failure to shape according to the ideal, then by virtue of this defect he will deviate from the Way.

The existence of this *tao* constricts the concept of human being, precluding the personal autonomy necessary for him to make life meaningful of his own accord:[106]

> Man is not an ultimately autonomous being who has an inner and decisive power, intrinsic to him, a power to select among real alternatives and thereby to shape life for himself.

The human being "walking the *tao*" for Fingarette requires the exorcism of one's particular will and the yielding of one's "self" to the dignity of the Way:[107]

> This outcome . . . sharpens and steadies a person's "aim" or orientation to the point where he can undeviatingly walk the one true Way: he is a civilized human being. Walking the Way incarnates in him the vast spiritual dignity and power that reside in the Way.

Fingarette's interpretation of *tao* renders the human being a conduit or medium through which the spirituality resident in the *tao* is made manifest. The ultimate source of meaning and value is this objective *tao*, and the greater the human achievement, the less particular the human and the more impersonal the *tao* becomes:[108]

> Since the *chün tzu's* will is thus ideally the medium by which, and through which, the *tao* is allowed and enabled to work and to be actualized, the "I" of the *chün tzu*, as purely personal, has become, as it were, transparent. . . . For it is a way of expressing, less preg-

nantly but in one respect more precisely, the spirit of the phrase, "Not my will, but Thine be done."

In fact, for Fingarette the notion of *particular* person in any important sense, is lost in the *tao*. Either a person deviates from the *tao*, and in so doing fails as a human being, or he succeeds in becoming human by surrendering his particularity to a higher ideal:[109]

> To understand the content of the *chün tzu's* will is to understand the *tao*, not the *chün tzu* as a particular person. The ego is present in the egoist's will. The *tao* is present in the *chün tzu's* will. . . .
> There is no imposition of personal will at all, whether by physical, psychological, legal, or political means. Instead, all cooperate spontaneously in a mutually respectful harmony defined by *tao*.

We believe that this interpretation of *tao* fails to give full value to Confucius' conception of the human being. It reduces human realization to the satisfaction of some externally existing schema, depriving the human being of his role as the ultimate creator of human meaning and value. In so doing, it renders the project of human fulfillment a basically logical proposition where one must fulfill necessary conditions to complete a predetermined product. Self-determination becomes obedience and imitation; novelty is defect. Human realization is more industry than art, more reproduction than creation. Fingarette's interpretation contradicts Confucius' perception of person making as an open-ended activity in which true qualitative growth is a function of cultural accumulation and the attendant enrichment of possibilities.

Using Fingarette's own metaphor, the human symphony is already scored and orchestrated, and becoming human is to play it such that "the spirit of the original music is creatively displayed."[110] Although Fingarette does allow that the performer must interpret the score "in a creative, artistic, dynamic way," he distinguishes his meaning of creativity from that of the post-Romantic Western celebration of "the highly original composer, who creates not only new works within old forms but also creates new forms."[111]

If Fingarette's analysis is a fair representation of Confucius, and for Confucius the human being is to be properly understood as performer rather than composer, one would expect Confucius' presentation of the "score" to be somewhat different. One would expect some explanation of the origin of *tao*, a clearer articulation of its content, and a more straightforward characterization of the person who performs in accord with it. One would expect a code of conduct reflecting a truth that, once discovered, would have universal application. And one would anticipate that a "way without crossroads" would be clearly delineated and would have a specific destination.

Contrary to Fingarette's understanding of *tao* is the fact that Confucius' instructions for appropriate conduct vary according to his audience. A pervasive attitude of tolerance and flexibility is a hallmark of the Confucian vision. Also, *tao* is significantly indeterminate, its multiplicity and multivalence evident in its association with various historical figures, varying levels of human achievement, and a broad range of cultural interests. Further, the internal structure of *tao*—the pattern of formal ritual actions (*li*)—itself is variable. Ritual actions have their ultimate source in the significating capacity of the human being, and owe their reformulation and appropriate application to the uniqueness of the individual. Finally, the polar relationship for Confucius between agent and act, and the inseparability of knowledge and action, demand that *tao* be something accomplished rather than simply obeyed. All these are evidence that renders Fingarette's master musical performer "following the predetermined path of the musical score"[112] an inadequate analogy for understanding *tao*.

5   T'ien-jen 天人

5.1   Field and Focus

Several models of part/whole relations exist in our conceptual inventory. A part may be simply a piece of a greater whole in the sense of being one of its constituents. Or the part may be a functionally interrelated element helping to constitute an organism. In the first instance parts are extrinsically related; in the second case the parts are intrinsically related in accordance with the aim or function of the organism. A third model presents a whole as a universal or archetype and the part as a particular or instance. In this case the particular is one of the class of items instantiating the universal. But the model most relevant for our considerations is yet another, in which a part reflects or contains its whole in some adumbrated sense. This model is that of the hologram.

In the hologrammatic view, the relations of "part" to "whole" are best characterized in terms of the notions of "focus" and "field." A particular is a focus that is both defined by and defines a context— a field. The field is hologrammatic; that is, it is so constituted that each discriminate "part" contains the adumbrated whole. Ultimately, a given part and its whole become identical when the field is focused in an especially intense manner. In terms of this model, *te* names the peculiar intensity of focus identifying the manner in which a discriminated "part"—an individual human being, for example— construes a "whole"—that is, its social context. *T'ien* 天, as discussed above, is the field of existing things for which *te* can serve as determinate focus.

By particular focus we mean to stress the notion that each focus is the focus of an alternative whole that constitutes its distinctive context. Alternative foci entail the notion of alternative wholes. In this model there is no overarching whole, no single context that contains all foci. Relationships among individual foci are defined by the differential perspectives each focus provides on the totality. The "totality" per se, abstracted from its alternative characterizations, is merely the additive sum of all orders defined by the alternative foci.

Tao 道 (a designation for the whole) is a functional equivalent of *t'ien* 天. In both Taoist and Confucian traditions, existence is understood either explicitly or implicitly as an ongoing process containing and generating its own motion by the interaction of complementary forces. This process is described in the language of cycles: growing and declining, waxing and waning, condensing and rarifying, concentrating and dissipating. All existence is a continuum on which every aspect is constituted within a process of transformation determined by its own impetus and the matrix of conditions that sponsor it. The particular focus (*te*) is not understood in terms of discrete and essentialistic self-nature; rather, it is a focus in the process of existence. When disclosing its uniqueness and difference, it is apprehended as a particular; when considered in terms of the full complement and consequence of its determining conditions, it is a field of existing things.

Our basic claim is that the early Confucians and Taoists in large measure share a common process cosmology defined in terms of "focus" and "field." In the Taoist tradition, this cosmology is explicitly articulated in the polar relationship between *tao* and *te* in the *Tao Te Ching*—*The Classic of Tao and Te*— and elsewhere in the literature. The process or field of existence viewed in toto and as integrated from a particular *te* perspective is called *tao*. When viewed in terms of the integrity of individual entities, however, this field is a collocation of particular foci, or *te*.

In the early Confucian tradition, a similar implicit cosmology is captured in the relationship between *t'ien* as field and the determinate world as focus. Since the Confucians restricted their concerns largely to the human world, the functional equivalent of the Taoist *tao–te* polarity is *t'ien–jen*, that is, *t'ien* and particular human beings. The polar relationship between *t'ien* and particular human beings is reflected in the underlying commitment to *t'ien-jen ho-yi* 天人合一 : the unity of *t'ien* and determinate human beings.

It is certainly not necessary to use technical terms such as "focus" and "field" to explicate the relations between *t'ien* and *te* or *t'ien* and *jen*. We might as appropriately employ a model drawn from Chinese Buddhism, provided we are careful to make the necessary qualifications. Consider Fa Tsang's Hall of Mirrors:

In the T'ang dynasty, at the request of Empress Wu, the Buddhist sage, Fa Tsang, provided an illustration of the Hua-yen doctrine of Totality. Covering the walls, floor and ceiling of a room with mirrors, Fa Tsang placed a statue of the Buddha in its center. A reflecting crystal in his hand, Fa Tsang demonstrated how each image of the Buddha reflected from the mirrors was contained in the crystal and was in turn reflected back into each mirror, ad infinitum. The reciprocal focusing of all things illustrated in this manner provided the basis for the Hua-yen interpretation of the traditional Buddhist notion of "codependent arising."

We are not claiming that Confucius should be considered a proto-Buddhist. Our claim is much simpler, although perhaps equally dramatic: the "reciprocal focusing" illustrated by Fa Tsang's Hall of Mirrors is characteristic of the classical Chinese language, which we shall discuss in some detail later on. Confucius' understanding of social relationships, which leads him to characterize individuals in terms of rituals and roles, is congruent with the functional character of Chinese language per se. And though we certainly grant that Confucius had little interest in explicating the cosmological implications of his thinking, we would claim that were he to have done so, his vision would not have been radically distinct from that of the Taoist or Hua-yen Buddhist.

We should not overemphasize the importance of this commonality at the level of cosmological presuppositions. The fact that Confucius chose not to be explicitly speculative in his pronouncements has significant sociological implications. Metaphysics is a time- and energy-consuming activity. The soteriological dimension of Confucian thought stresses the concretely interpersonal and social context for self-realization. It is not through speculation that Confucius offers "salvation." Idle speculation is not only vain but actually harmful insofar as it militates against the commitments of the would-be sage. Having said this, the apologetic concerns that we have outlined above nonetheless require that we attend to the cosmological commitments implicit in the philosophy of Confucius.

Although the *Analects*, given its primary concern for social and political problems, does not provide us with an altogether clear statement of this continuous relationship between part and whole, "focus" and "field," there are strong suggestions to this effect. For example, the exemplary Yao is described as becoming *t'ien*-like in the quality of his achievements as a ruler and person (8/19): "How great indeed was Yao as ruler! How majestic! Only *t'ien* is truly great, and only Yao took it as his model." Confucius himself is described in cosmic terms (19/24): "Confucius was the sun and moon which no one can go beyond. Were a person to cut himself off from the sun and moon, how could this detract from them?" As a person becomes *t'ien*-like, he becomes increasingly visible in the world (19/21): "The excesses of the exemplary person are like an eclipse of the sun and moon. When he strays, everyone sees it, and when he corrects his course, everyone looks up to him."

It is the description of Confucius in the *Chung-yung*, however, that provides us with perhaps the clearest expression of the coincident relationship between *t'ien* and the accomplished human being. Just as a specific human being becomes increasingly *t'ien*-like as he achieves excellence and inspires the deference of those in his community, so *t'ien* becomes increasingly Confucius-like as the whole which he construes from his perspective, through the same patterns of deference, assumes prominence as the reigning interpretation of the world in which men live:[113]

Confucius looked back to and carried forward the tradition of Yao and Shun, emulated and illuminated the ways of Wen and Wu. He modeled himself above on the seasons of the heavens and below he accorded with the patterns of earth and water. He is comparable to the heavens in that there is nothing that they do not overarch and cover, and again with the earth in that there is nothing that it does not bear up and support. He is comparable to the succession of the four seasons and the alternations of the sun and moon. . . . Only the most sagacious in the world . . . are expansive like *t'ien* and are profoundly deep like an abyss. . . . Thus they are said to be the complement of *t'ien*.

The sage is the complement of *t'ien*, in that the quality of his integration with the world reaches out to foster and enhance the integration of all phenomena:[114] "Great indeed is the way of the sage. Teeming, it spawns and nurtures the myriad things till they reach up to the heavens."

As has been the case with respect to a number of other concepts, our interpretation of Confucius here resonates somewhat with the Western existential tradition.[115] We accept the similarity but caution that Confucius' "existentialism" loses much of its typical character when qualified by the focus/field model of the relations of the individual to society. *T'ien ming*, as the most general expression of meaningfulness, is constituted by all correlative foci in the field of existing things. While it seems to be the case that the *ming* of *t'ien* may refer to any individual focus, Confucius seems to have believed that *t'ien ming* will be available only to one who has achieved the quality of *te* which permits him to serve as a focus of meaning and value in some exemplary manner. The prerequisite of this achievement is a mastery of the tradition. The individual who achieves such mastery is the focus of *t'ien*; his is *t'ien–jen*.

5.2 *Confucian Religiousness*

Although the specific phrase denoting the unity of *t'ien* and the human being—*t'ien–jen ho-yi* (天人合一)—does not belong to the early classical period, it is a convenient formula for capturing what is generally perceived as a fundamental characteristic of Chinese religiousness.[116] The stress in this formula is upon the interdependence of focus and field rather than on the relationship obtaining

among discrete particulars. *T'ien-jen ho-yi* describes the fully integrated particular as it requires the conditions of the whole for its
explanation.

Speaking in general terms from the tradition, the classical Chinese
alternative to the dualism of creator and human creature is this
continuum: the human being in striving to realize himself becomes
deity. In the *Mencius* we read:[117]

> The admirable person is called "good." The one who has integrity is
> called "true." To be totally genuine is called "beautiful," and to ra-
> diate this total genuineness is called "greatness." Being great, to be
> transformed by it is called "sageliness." And being sage, to be un-
> fathomable is called "divinity."

Tu Wei-ming develops this theme in his interpretive study of the
Chung-yung:[118]

> The relationship between Heaven and man is not an antinomic bi-
> unity but an indivisibly single oneness. In this sense, the sage as the
> most authentic manifestation of humanity does not coexist with
> Heaven; he forms a coincidence with Heaven. . . . Despite the possi-
> bility of a conceptual separation between Heaven and man, inwardly,
> in their deepest reality, they form an unbreakable organismic contin-
> uum.

In the pre-Ch'in texts we find passages such as, "What *t'ien*
mandates is called human nature,"[119] and in the *Analects*, "*t'ien* gives
birth to the *te* in me" (7/23). As a corrective against interpreting
these texts as implying a doctrine of transcendent deity, we do well
to pay careful attention to discussions in the same texts which clearly
collapse the human/*t'ien* distinction. The *Chuang Tzu*, for example,
repeatedly describes the realizing human being as "the complement/
counterpart (*p'ei* 配) of *t'ien*."[120] This is not simply Taoist mys-
ticism. The *Mencius* in claiming that "the myriad things are fully
here in me"[121] and "one who knows his nature knows *t'ien*"[122] is
asserting the same coincidence between the human being and *t'ien*.
The *Chung-yung* moves from "the person of utmost sincerity is the
complement of *t'ien*"[123] to the more explicit description of Confucius:[124]

> So earnest, he is humanity (*jen* 仁);
> So profound, he is an abyss (*yüan* 淵);
> So pervasive, he is *t'ien* (天).

Tu Wei-ming is cautious about the implications of these *Chung-yung* passages in their application to Confucius:[125] "Of course, 'counterpart' here does not mean to suggest that Confucius is, in a sense, being deified." The fact is, however, that Confucius is deified, or rather, deifies himself: the fundamental import of "religion" common to all traditions is "to bind"—for the individual to seek integration and proper context in the whole. And in the Judaeo-Christian tradition where deity represents the order, value, and meaning of existence, religion takes the form of an individual bonding or communion with God. In the immanent cosmos of Confucius, one accomplishes this same project of bonding by achieving a quality of integration in the world which dissolves the distinction between part and whole, and makes of one a peculiar focus of meaning and value in the field of existing things.

This project of integration is captured in Confucius' definition of human realization: "to discipline oneself and practice ritual action is to become authoritative as a person" (12/1). It is in overcoming the self/other distinction and participating in the regular processes of existence through formalized actions that one becomes truly human. And in contributing to and determining the meaning and purpose of its whole—in becoming fully *t'ien-jen*—the human being becomes "deity."

In the West, "religiousness" in its most fundamental sense refers to a human being's pursuit of a fully focused comprehension and appreciation of the meaning and value of the total field of existing things. Whitehead provides a vivid illustration of this intuition:[126]

[T]ake the subtle beauty of a flower in some isolated glade of a primeval forest. No animal has ever had the subtlety of experience to enjoy its full beauty. And yet this beauty is a grand fact in the universe. When we survey nature and think however flitting and superficial has been the animal enjoyment of its wonders, and when we realize how incapable the separate cells and pulsations of each flower are of enjoying the total effect—then our sense of the value of the details for the totality dawns upon our consciousness. This is the intuition of holiness, the intuition of the sacred, which is the foundation of all religion.

Perhaps the most intense form of this religious intuition is reflexive: a human being's awakening to the awesomeness of his significance in and for the whole. This awakening comes in its intensest form when an individual sees himself as a central focus in a whole construed from his own perspective.

This relationship between part and whole, focus and field, is perceived in a contrasting manner in the dominant constructions of the Western and Chinese traditions. In the Judaeo-Christian tradition where God is the transcendent source and standard of meaning and value, religiousness is conceived fundamentally as worship. Schleiermacher suggests this in defining religion as the feeling of an absolute dependence.

Morality, in the sense of conformity with prescribed rules of conduct, becomes religious by virtue of the conviction that it derives from and coincides with Divine Law. It brings one as close to God and to the meaning of the whole as he can come on his own initiative. Even interpersonal love is achieved by participation in God-sponsored love, agapé. Because morality, like ritual actions such as communion, prayer, and confession, involves deference, it has the function of displaying the quality of one's commitment to the preeminent order.

The classical Confucian structure of religousness is fundamentally different. Religion does not impose the demand of obedience or dependence. Rather, it requires that a person constitute himself as an authoritative model. That is, meaning, value, and purpose do not exist as a given standard in the person of God, but are created in the interaction between the human being and his context, between *jen* and *t'ien*.

For Confucius, it is not only *t'ien*, but also the meaning-disclosing human being that is an object of deference and awe (16/8): "The exemplary person (*chün tzu*) has three things he holds in awe: The *ming* of *t'ien*, the great man, and the words of the sage. . . ." In the interaction between the human being and *t'ien*, a person becomes an "authority" in his deference to and embodiment of existing meaning, and beyond this, he further becomes an "author" in his creative disposition of existing meaning, and in his creation of novel meaning.

Religiousness in this tradition does require deference to inherited meaning and value as it is captured in the institutions and structures of the cultural tradition. This is apparent in the importance invested in the understanding and meaningful enactment of ritual (*li* 禮). But religiousness requires more. It requires the active evaluation, adaptation, and extension of this inherited meaning in the application of one's own moral judgment (yi 義). That is, the ritual tradition (li) is dependent upon the exercise of personal moral judgment (yi) as its ultimate origin, as its vehicle for continuance, and as its source of novelty.The human being does not pursue integration with the whole by simply deferring to and imitating a preexisting order. The capacity to act in a truly ritual way presupposes personal achievement. As Confucius states (3/3): "What does one who is not authoritative in his person have to do with ritual action or with music?" The human being has an active, participatory role. He does not just follow prescribed laws, he has a hand in legislating them. He does not simply follow a way, he has a hand in clearing it.

In classical Confucianism, meaning and value have their source in the sage as an authoritative model. This is an important contrast with traditions that define such a source in terms of a transcendent deity or principle. In the latter an antecedent standard determines the meaning of human existence; in Confucianism a model, by virtue of its achievement, invites creative emulation by others engaged in the art of becoming human. If the most profound religious intuition is in fact an appreciation of one's own significance in and for the totality, to the extent that in the classical Confucian structure the individual and his world (t'ien-jen) are interdependent and mutually determining, there would seem to be significant grounds for interpreting t'ien-jen in specifically religious terms.

It is noteworthy that for Confucius religiousness would require constant effort. The peculiarly immanent relationship of t'ien and jen demanded by the Confucian sensibility could not possibly result from a deathbed discovery. Religiousness must be the achievement and awareness of human significance cultivated through a lifetime of assiduous effort.

We can illustrate the difference between the Judaeo-Christian emphasis upon worship and the classical Confucian focus upon achieving authoritative humanity (jen* 仁) by characterizing Confucius' religiousness as it is presented in the *Analects*. If we were to understand Confucius' religiousness by interpreting it through Western categories and demanding an equal concern for worship, we would have to conclude that Confucius is religious only in a limited sense. His degree of deference is necessarily curtailed by the fact that he does not acknowledge the existence of any transcendent principle as absolute truth. He does insist on appropriate ritual observances. But the objects of such deference are those sources of meaning that have profoundly contributed to the culture, sources such as human ancestors and those various deities that represent traditional institutions. Even so, this deference is only one side of human religiousness. To be truly religious, the significance that a person has access to through acts of deference must be augmented by his own original participation and the contribution of his own excellence (6/22): "To work towards what is appropriate (*yi* 義) for the masses and to keep a distance from gods and spirits while showing them due reverence can be called wisdom." For Confucius, religiousness is not exhausted by worship; its more important component is how a person chooses to live his life (7/35):

> The Master was gravely ill. Tzu-lu asked if he might offer a prayer on his behalf. The Master queried, "Is this done?" Tzu-lu replied, "Yes, there is a eulogy which states: 'We pray for you to the gods of heaven and earth.'" The Master said, "Then I have been praying myself for a long time."

The point that Confucius is making in this passage is that the proper relationship between the human being and the gods emerges through a lifetime of self-cultivation that includes mutually reinforcing ritual observance and personal contribution. With the human being's capacity to become a meaning maker, and thus the "counterpart of *t'ien*" (*p'ei t'ien* 配天), he has an active role beyond the recognition and appreciation of the significance of an element for some objective and predetermined whole. He has his hand in the very creation of this significance. In this tradition, not only is *t'ien* personified, the human being is also deified.

6   Confucian Cosmology as *Ars Contextualis*

Our discussion of *t'ien ming, te,* and *tao* has led us to draw out some relatively novel implications of these terms. It is essential, however, that we highlight certain of the distinctive relationships among these notions if we are to have anything like a coherent picture of Confucian cosmology. One obvious criticism of such a presentation is that it suggests a greater coherence among the concepts than may have existed in the mind of Confucius or his disciples. In drawing out the cosmological implications of Confucian ideas, we have consciously run the risk of saying more on Confucius' behalf than he himself might have wished to say. It is even more risky to discuss the "systematic" relations among notions that definitely were not systematically presented by Confucius. In defense we can recall the meaning of "thinking through" discussed at some length in the first chapter of this essay. Learning (*hsüeh* 學) and reflecting (*ssu* 思) together ground realizing (*chih* 知). Our presentation of Confucius' cosmological vision, in terms of both the articulation of the principal concepts and the elaboration of the relationships that obtain among them, is a sustained attempt at realization *(chih)*.

The relationship between *te* and *t'ien* or *t'ien ming* has been elaborated in terms of the model of focus and field. *Te* focuses *t'ien*, and in the case of the exemplary person *(chün tzu)* or sage *(sheng jen)* the activity of focusing is one of integration and participation, since the more intense the particular focus, the more completely it adumbrates its whole. The ultimate form of this focus is expressed in terms of *t'ien-jen* 天人 .

The relationship of *tao* to *t'ien* and *te* is somewhat more problematic. *Tao* is emergent in the sense that it is a consequence of human action; it is the mode of being human that has accumulated as a cultural tradition. *Tao* relates directly to both *te* and *t'ien*. It is the *te* of a Confucius or a Yen Yüan which, deferred to as excellence in the tradition, is constitutive of *tao* and thus is *tao te*. Equally, *tao* may apply to the whole of things, to *t'ien*, as relevant to the social environs—that is, to the empire or the state. If Confucius, like the Taoist, had broader cosmic concerns, then the *tao* of *t'ien*, in addition to describing the achieved mode of human existence, would also have reference to the cadences of the natural environment and its achieved regularity and harmony. But because Confucius has a real preoccupation with human concerns, the field represented by *t'ien* is by and large the human world. The whole is human society. For this reason, *t'ien tao* 天道 may be but an alternative way of saying *jen* tao* 仁道, the human cultural tradition.

By "thinking through" certain of the cosmological implications of Confucius' philosophy we find further justification for some of the controversial claims we have made concerning the more explicit doctrines of the *Analects*. Throughout we have stressed the aesthetic dimension of Confucian philosophy, and of classical Chinese thought generally. The cosmological vision derived from Confucius' thinking is consistent with this emphasis. Confucius' concepts of *t'ien, te,* and *tao* are grounded in aesthetic rather than rational order. If, as has often been the case, one fails to understand this fact and gives these concepts a rational interpretation and attempts to understand them in terms of antecedent determining principles, then serious damage is done to the integrity of the Confucian vision.

Confucius is not providing the basis for a "general theory of being" or a "universal science of principles." His is an aesthetic understanding, an *ars contextualis,* in which the correlatively of "part" and "whole"—of focus and field—permits the mutual interdependence of all things to be assessed in terms of particular contexts defined by social roles and functions. *T'ien* is the source of meaningfulness, not in the sense of an eternal repository of pure possibilities; rather, *t'ien* encompasses the traditional past as the cumulated products of human activity. *Te* is the particular excellence of an individual within his or her context, not as an essential given but as a realized perspective upon things which at one and the same time centers the individual and focuses his or her context. *Tao* is emergent from the actions of persons whose self-realization is such that they are able to serve as peculiarly intense foci of meaning and value. And such persons have a determining influence on the *ming* of *t'ien*.

The cosmological doctrines of Confucius may be read as generalizations of the most basic processes associated with the activity of thinking and of becoming a person. *T'ien ming, te,* and *tao* are related as are *hsüeh, ssu* and *chih*—the appropriation of the givenness of tradition, reflective activity, and realization, or as are *li, yi,* and *jen**—the established rites, the derivation and bestowal of meaning through acts of signification, and the attainment of authoritative humanity. Confucius' cosmology is a generalized sociology, a vision of the manner in which human beings emerge from within a social context grounded in tradition, while remaining open to novel articulations insofar as these might be called for by the *ming* of present circumstances.

Of course, one might equally well claim that Confucius' understandings of thinking and of person making are specifications of the more general cosmological concepts outlined above. One ought be extremely careful in emphasizing such a claim, however. For while it is true that a cosmological vision may be employed as a means of highlighting the interpretive interplay between general and specific concepts relevant to the understanding of the whole of things, a sound appreciation of Confucius' thinking requires that we accept his reticence about speculating as a corrective to any speculative motivations of our own. Although the preceding discussion may seem to give the lie to our acceptance of this demurrer, this is not so. Our attempt to reconstitute the cosmological implications of Confucius' thought is directed against the misconstruing of those implications by Neo-Confucian thinkers of the later tradition and, as well, their potential misconstrual by contemporary Anglo-European philosophers.

Were Confucius primarily a speculative philosopher, we would be able to end our consideration of his thinking here. In fact, the unreconstructed among our Western readers might believe that the really crucial issues have now been addressed. This is, of course, definitely not so. Confucius was first and foremost an educator, a communicator. The apex of Confucius' thought is to be found in the notion of the sage, the *sheng jen* 聖人. And consideration of the *sheng jen* will involve us in a discussion of the meaning of language and the act of communication insofar as these are pertinent to the process of becoming a sage. Communication, for Confucius, is an act of attunement, of the realization of harmony between communicator and communicant. As we shall see, this attuning activity presupposes each of the important Confucian notions we have considered thus far. Therefore, consideration of the function of language in the act of communicating will permit the most fundamental expression of the Confucian sensibility.

V

". . . . at sixty my ear was attuned . . . ."

MANY THEMES have emerged in the preceding exposition of Confucius' philosophy, each of which might be taken as central to his thought and might therefore be employed as a means of organizing the alternative notions exposed. In the discussions which follow we shall be taking the most obvious (but no less important) route toward demonstrating the coherence of Confucius' sensibility. That is, we shall focus upon the concept of *sheng jen* 聖人 (sage) as the most fundamental teleological notion of the *Analects*. The primary concepts to be discussed in this chapter are *cheng ming** 正名 (the ordering of names), *shu* 恕 (deference), and *sheng jen* 聖人 (sage). In the course of our analysis we shall be entering one of the richest, most complex and subtle aspects of Confucius' thought: the meaning of language and the act of communication.

1 The Centrality of Communication

In our consideration of the principal concepts of this chapter, several crucial issues revolving about the topic of language and communication must be addressed, not the least of which is the question whether or not possible differences between the oral and written forms of classical Chinese are germane to our consideration of Confucius. This could be relevant since we are exploring the theme of Confucius as teacher, as one who made significant use of spoken discourse. The primary issues we must consider in this regard have been summarized by Henry Rosemont.[1]

According to Rosemont, the historical development of oral and of written Chinese, as well as the comparison of these two languages on other grounds, provides rather clear evidence that the written form of the classical language is significantly different from the spoken form. It follows, then, that arguments concerning the constraints of written Chinese are not necessarily applicable to the spoken language, and vice versa. Thus suggestions concerning the character of the Chinese language and its influence upon the activity of thinking, if

made by recourse to an analysis of written discourse, may not apply
directly to the spoken form of the language. Rosemont's argument
entails the consequence that the Sapir-Whorf hypothesis (the claim
that the structure of a language places constraints upon the manner
of thinking of the native users of the language) cannot easily be
applied to classical Chinese, since, presumably, the oral form of
communication provides the readiest reference to the structure of
thinking in early China and it is precisely the oral form that, for the
most part, eludes us.

Rosemont's most insightful essay develops the thesis that the
distinction between phonetic and signific elements in a Chinese
character may not be altogether helpful in determining the nature
of the written language and its relations to oral discourse, since the
variety of available phonograms permits the selection of meaning-
indicative phonograms in the construction of a character.² The consequence of this, of course, is that the function of the phonogram
is not limited to the indication of the sound of a character. The
plausibility of this claim would support the view that the written
form of classical Chinese is more than merely a transcription of the
spoken language.

Arguments such as these, although affording some corroboration
for our approach to philological analysis, do not engage our thesis
concerning the nature of classical Chinese discourse and the evidence
adduced in its favor. By looking at the development of classical
Chinese thought from the broadest of cultural perspectives throughout
this essay, we have provided support for a number of general insights
into classical Chinese culture that will undergrid our analysis of
Confucian discourse. Our arguments concerning the lack of any
significant recourse to the notion of transcendence, the relative unimportance of cosmogonic speculation, the absence of anything like
the development of a *mythos-logos* distinction, and so on, will
directly support our conclusions concerning the nature of communication. Thus, in the following pages, when we argue that Confucius
does not employ a referential language in the strictest sense and,
therefore, lacks a language of entification, we shall not draw these
conclusions merely from an analysis of the written language, or
speculations concerning the character of the oral language and its
relation to the written form; rather, our discussion will proceed by
recourse to a more general set of considerations associated with the

"uncommon assumptions" outlined at the beginning of our work and subsequently employed in a variety of contexts.

Of equal significance in our discussion of the character of language is the fact that we shall be construing Confucius' understanding of the activity of communication as encompassing ritual action and music as well as spoken and written discourse. The distinction between oral and written forms of language becomes less consequential when the mode of communication is so broadly defined as to include dance and song. In fact, given the pragmatic, performative character of Confucius' language it would hardly be an exaggeration to say that it is music—that is, musical performance—that serves as the paradigm for correctly understanding the nature of language and communication.

Listening, speaking, singing, dancing, performing the rites, all are forms of communication. Communication, so construed, is central to the understanding of Confucius. And, as we shall detail at the close of this chapter, it is the activity of "attunement," presupposed in every act of communication, that illustrates the most comprehensive form of thinking—thinking that moves toward the attainment of sagehood.

2 Sage (*sheng jen* 聖人): A Philological and Literary Analysis

Given that Chinese, classical and modern, is constituted by such a wealth of characters, there is a perception that understanding Chinese thoroughly is a function of recognizing and reading as many characters as possible. More important than the number of characters that are cognitively known, however, is the degree to which one appreciates each character as a "word-image": that is, as a repository of allusions and associations that reside in a character and its relationships, and which can be evoked for the reader as the coordinate of the author's expression and the reader's imagination. The *Analects*, for example, contain only some 1,400 characters,[3] and yet the interplay of possible meanings generated by the continued study of this text has produced a cumulative commentarial tradition that both discloses inherent philosophical insights with increasing clarity, and inspires the growth of an always "neo" Confucianism. One traditional resource for bringing to light undisclosed contours of meaning lodged in a character has been an appeal to philological analysis.

In this study, we want to assay the concept *sheng* 聖 conventionally translated "sage," first by laying bare its root meaning and examining the tangle of associations that extend out from it. With a clear understanding of this general concept in hand, we can then proceed to evaluate it in the specific context of the *Analects*. We would argue, in spite of the alternative meanings of *sheng* among the rival schools of Chinese thought, that there is a fundamental root meaning grounding the variant readings, a meaning that can serve to elucidate the important differences distinguishing school from school.

It should be noted that when we move to examine the *Analects* in search of the significance of *sheng*, "sage," it is not simply a matter of scrutinizing each instance of this particular character as it appears in the text. We must further consider that the *Analects* uses several different categories to designate various dimensions of personal growth (*jen* che* 仁-耆 for interpersonal growth, *chün tzu* 君子 for sociopolitical growth, and so on), and that these categories, once articulated, contribute significantly to the understanding of the comprehensive notion of *sheng*. That is, these other categories of self-realization represent distinct foci of the activity of realizing sagehood.[4] A second consideration is that the *Analects* refers to several paradigmatic "sage-kings" (for example, Yao, Shun, Wen, Wu, the Duke of Chou, and so forth). It is plausible to assume that their conduct as reported can be appealed to as a resource for defining sagehood.

Perhaps the most important source for understanding the sage in the *Analects* is the way in which the historical person of Confucius is himself portrayed. Although Confucius modestly disclaims the title of sage,[5] this modesty must be measured against the fact that he claims to be the embodiment of the Chou culture, and the heir to the sage-king, Wen.[6] On another occasion when a high officer suggests that Confucius is a sage, Confucius allows that this man knows him well.[7] Whether or not Confucius believed that he himself had achieved sagehood, there can be little doubt that the text seeks to portray him in that way.

As we venture into the later chapters of the *Analects* containing the sayings of several of Confucius' most mature disciples, we find the statement that "Confucius was the sun and moon which no one

can go beyond (19/24)." With Mencius and his repeated assertion
that Confucius was "the greatest sage in human history," the term
sheng gradually takes on an association with Confucius such that
throughout the tradition, "*the* sage" refers specifically to Confucius.
For this reason, Confucius as described in the *Analects* is a further
available source for the manner in which this concept ought to be
understood.

As indicated in our previous discussion of person making, a
person is a "focus of selves." This corporate conception of person
implies that "Confucius" can be construed as a project that spans
the intervening centuries since his death and continues into our own
time. Henri Maspero describes the growth of Confucius over the two
millennia since his death:[8]

> Like all the gods of the official religion, Confucius climbed all the
> steps of the hierarchy one by one: he was duke in the first year
> A.D., king in 739, reduced for a while to the rank of duke in 1075,
> emperor in 1106. He even kept his rank and title through a special
> exception made in his favor when the first Ming emperor abolished
> all the titles of kings, dukes, and so on, which had been bestowed
> upon mountains or rivers, gods of the Wall and Ditches, or officials
> of former dynasties who had been admitted into official worship. But
> this was only for a while and, on 4 December 1530, the Shih-tsung
> emperor stripped him of his status, giving him simply the title of
> Perfect Sage Ancient Master (*Chih-sheng hsien-shih* 至聖先師),
> which he has kept until our day.

As a first step in reconstructing this concept, "sage," we might
look at the *Shuo-wen* lexicon, which defines the character, *sheng,* 聖
in the following terms:

> *Sheng* 聖 means *t'ung* 通 : to communicate with, to commune with,
> to be conversant with, to penetrate, to connect. It derives semanti-
> cally from *erh,* 耳 "ear," and takes its pronunciation from the *ch'eng*
> 呈 component.

There can be no question that *sheng* 聖 is, via its *erh,* 耳 , "ear,"
component, closely related to its cognate, *t'ing* 聽 "to hear," "to
listen to." The *erh* radical further associates *sheng* with *ts'ung* 聰
"keenness of hearing." That "sage" was perceived as acutely aural
is an inescapable consequence of its etymology. As Kenneth De-

Woskin observes, this association between the sage and "hearing" is borne out in the traditional representation of the sage as having large, pendant ears.[9] Furthermore, throughout the classics, the sage is portrayed as the premier musicologist: one who can listen to music and discern in it the original details and quality of an age and its culture.[10] The *Analects* certainly does portray Confucius as developing an aural sensibility in his growth as a sage. Lau in the Introduction to his translation observes that hearing has a central role in Confucius' project of self-cultivation.[11] In support of this interpretation of sage as "audient person," commentators regularly cite the self-description of Confucius: "at sixty my ear was attuned . . . ." (2/4).

What, on the other hand, has been less noted is that the sage is also acutely oral: "one who manifests and discloses" (*ch'eng* 呈). This is suggested by the fact that *sheng* 聖 has frequently been defined in terms of its homophone, *sheng* 聲, "to sound," "sound," "voice." The *Pai-hu-t'ung*, for example, defines sage as follows:[12]

> *Sheng* (sage) means *t'ung* 通 (to communicate, to connect, to pene-
> trate through), *tao* 道 (the process of becoming and the mode in
> which it unfolds, to speak), *sheng* 聲 (to sound, sound). There is
> nothing that is not in communication by virtue of his *tao*; there is
> nothing that is not elucidated by virtue of his understanding. Hear-
> ing the sound he knows a thing's nature and conditions. He is one
> in potency *(te)* with heaven and earth, one in brilliance with the sun
> and moon, one in order with the four seasons, and one in propi-
> tiousness with the gods and spirits.

The language used to describe the sage in this passage is profoundly active. Analogous to the celestial luminaries and the cadences of the seasons, he manifests an order and communicates it broadly. This expressive dimension of the sage is illustrated by the *Erh Ya*, a late Chou lexicon with glosses on characters used in the classics, which defines sage (*sheng* 聖) as "to present, exhibit, show, to be prominent (*hsien* 獻)."

Recent research on the Ma-wang-tui *Lao Tzu* manuscripts by William G. Boltz provides a basis for challenging traditional inter-pretations of *sheng* 聖 that identify the "ear" (*erh* 耳) radical alone as semantic indicator. It is plausible to argue that the *ch'eng* 呈 portion of the character, meaning "to manifest and display," also has semantic force.[13]

In the *Analects*, the sage is described as one who transforms the world by what he says (16/8): "The exemplary person (*chün tzu*) has three things he holds in awe: the *t'ien ming*, the great person, and the words of the sage." Throughout the *Analects*, growth in the exemplary person (*chün tzu*), the "sociopolitical" dimension of sage-hood, is closely associated with the power of speech as a prompting to act.[14] Confucius is described as painfully attentive to what he says and how he says it.

With appropriate modesty, he rejects any personal claim to sagehood (7/34): "How could I dare to consider myself to be a sage or an authoritative person? It can just be said that I learn without relenting, and teach without tiring of it." In the *Mencius*, however, this same disclaimer of Confucius is revisited, and it is precisely this commitment to communication in learning and teaching that qualifies him as a sage "unsurpassed since humans have walked the earth":[15] "Tzu-kung said: 'To be unrelenting in learning is to be wise; to be untiring in teaching is to be authoritative.' Given that the Master is both authoritative and wise, he is certainly a sage."

Beyond the philological data, there is another factor that might encourage us to reinstate this creative, contributory dimension of sagehood. The notion of sage in the classics is frequently associated with *tso* 作 "to create." According to the *Yi-ching*,[16] "The Sage creates and the myriad things look on." And the *Li-chi* states:[17] "One who creates is called sagely; one who transmits is called perspicacious. A perspicacious sage means one who transmits and creates." In fact, in the *Pai-hu-t'ung* chapter on "The Sage," the citation of several classical texts is followed by the statement:[18] "In all of these passages, the character *tso* 作 'to create,' is used, and everytime means 'sage.'" It certainly can be argued that Confucius' modest reluctance to claim sagehood in the famous description of himself as "one who transmits but does not create" (7/1) reflects this same close association between the capacity to create and the attainment of sagehood.

Perhaps most significant in this revised interpretation of *sheng* is that being a sage essentially entails communication: the sage is a master communicator. In the original *Shuo-wen* definition that identifies "ear" as the signific portion of the character we found considerable emphasis on the "listening" aspect of communication. Further reflection on this etymology does suggest that a more balanced and complete explanation of *sheng* would have to highlight both the listening and expressing dimensions of communication.

The sage is one who knows the nature and conditions of some one or some thing by listening, by "attuning his ear." Speaking from that condition of attunement his words serve to further the harmonious engagement that true communication both presupposes and effects. Later, in our discussion of music as a form of communication, we shall have occasion to argue that the distinctions between hearing and expressing and between transmitting and creating are not as sharp as one might suppose.

In our previous discussion of the person as irreducibly communal we noted that the importance of an individual is a function of his or her extension into and/or integration with other selves. In this context we wish to indicate how this relationship between importance and personal extension provides grounds for the association in classical literature of "sage" and "spirituality/divinity" (*shen* 神).

Pai hu-t'ung states:[19] "The reason why the sage alone is able to foresee the future is because he shares in the concentrated essence of the spirits." The etymology of this term, *shen*, is suggestive of the extending, integrating, and enriching that the sage brings to his relationships with other aggregate selves. The character is constituted of the radicals, *shih* 示, "to display," and *shen* 申, "to stretch," "to extend," interchangeable with its archaic homophone, *yin* 引, "to draw out," "to stretch," "to guide." If we understand the sage's extension and integration as being the source of meaning in the world, it is not difficult to explain the fact that *shen* means both human spirituality and divinity, and that it is frequently associated with the rhyming *t'ien* 天, commonly rendered "Heaven." That is, as a person exercises himself as a source of meaning, he moves toward divinity. Further, this extension and integration implicates the whole: as his particular focus (*te* 德) intensifies, man and heaven become one (*t'ien-jen ho-yi* 天人合一). Maspero, in his discussion of Confucius, comments on this ascent from human spirituality to divinity:[20]

> Must one go so far as to say, as certain Europeanized modern Chinese do, that he [Confucius] is not really a god? In Chinese, which has no common general term to designate beings superior to men, the question cannot even be posed, for one cannot tell what

term to use. . . . Insofar as our term "god" can be applied to personages of Chinese mythology, it is thus clear that Confucius has been, at least until quite recently, a god (not of individuals, but of the State), to whom one prayed and from whom one expected "happiness."

3 The Sage and the Ordering of Names (*cheng ming** 正 名)

3.1 *The Aesthetic Character of Classical Chinese*

We have defined "sage" as a "master communicator" where communication is understood as the medium in which a person, as an aggregate self, transmits meaning through the orchestration and attuning of his composite dispositions. The degree of integration and diversity within this focus of selves reflects the quality and spirituality of the person. This interpretation of sage sheds some light on the importance that Confucius as described in the *Analects* invested in the performative power of language. After all, if a person is unable to communicate, he is isolated because he cannot bring other selves into the constitution of his corporate self (20/3): "One who does not understand language has no way of understanding others."

The obvious truth of this aphorism suggests that we might wish to pause at this point in order to consider the character of classical Chinese in some detail as a means of preparing ourselves for the rather complex doctrine of "ordering names" (*cheng ming** 正名). Our discussion of certain philosophically significant characteristics of classical Chinese will be further elaborated with respect to our consideration of "deference" (*shu* 恕) later in this chapter.

There is consensus that important differences exist between Western languages and classical Chinese, although there is certainly no agreement as to precisely what those differences are or on their consequences. As we stated at the beginning of this chapter, the claims we wish to make about classical Chinese are themselves consequences of the broader cultural contrasts for which we have repeatedly argued throughout this work.

Chad Hansen's recent speculations concerning classical Chinese, summarized in his book, *Language and Logic in Ancient China*, have offered some initial steps toward our understanding of the contrasting ramifications of Chinese and Indo-European languages and cultures.[21] Hansen has managed to construct an analysis of classical Chinese theoretical orientations which avoids recourse to either Platonic-realist or mentalistic understandings. Hansen's work is grounded upon a speculative model that charts the nominal function of classical Chinese discourse by employing the concept of the "mass noun" as both cause and consequence of what is most distinctively classical Chinese. Briefly, "mass nouns" (as opposed to "count nouns") may not be pluralized, are not indexed in accordance with definite articles and are understood in terms of part–whole models. "Count nouns" by contrast are based upon one–many relationships, and may therefore be pluralized and delineated by definite articles ("an," "the"). "Ship," "sail," and "king" are all count nouns (in English, of course); "earth," "air," "water" and "fire" (in its "elemental" sense) are mass nouns.[22]

The centrality of the mass noun presupposes a semantic theory rather distinct from those dominating Western thought. According to Hansen, for the ancient Chinese, "the world is a collection of overlapping and interpenetrating stuffs or substances. A name . . . denotes . . . some substance. The mind is regarded not as an internal picturing mechanism which represents the individual objects in the world, but as a faculty that discriminates the boundaries of the substances or stuffs referred to by the names."[23]

The theoretical perspective underlying this Chinese understanding of the relations of their language to the world Hansen terms "behavioral nominalism":[24]

> I use the *behavioral* because, in the place of internal mental represen-
> tations of particulars and properties, the Chinese view of mind
> (heart-mind) is dynamic; the mind is the ability to discriminate and
> distinguish "stuffs" and thereby to guide evaluation and action. I use
> *nominalism* because the Chinese philosopher is not committed to any
> entities other than names and objects.

Thus Chinese ontological understandings are "mereological"— that is, they are based upon a part–whole model and are concerned with the act of naming as the recognition or establishment of boundaries. "Identifying different members of a set of objects is the same as identifying spatio-temporally different parts of the same stuff. In learning names we learn to discriminate or divide reality into these mereological stuffs which names name."[25]

The implication of greatest interest here is that Hansen's model for understanding the classical Chinese language means that the language does not, in any important sense, employ abstract nouns. This same view is suggested by our claim about the absence of any notion of strict transcendence in classical China. A wholly immanent vision can only be expressed in a language of concreteness.

We agree with Hansen's efforts to eschew understandings of the ancient Chinese that suggest Platonism or mentalism. We further agree that the most adequate interpretation of the Chinese language depends upon an understanding of the noun function. We would also, along with Hansen, wish to highlight the relative stress of the Chinese upon pragmatic over strictly semantical considerations. That is to say, the Chinese are more concerned with the effects of language in behavioral terms than with questions of meaning as grounds for the truth or falsity of propositions.

Our disagreements with Hansen's views are, perhaps, of greater significance. It is misleading, we believe, to speak in terms of the "mass noun" insofar as this entails a "substance" or "stuff" ontology. We have given some reasons for holding that a process ontology is closer to the sort of view that Confucius, and the majority of the classical Chinese thinkers, held. Such an ontology of events precludes any literal recourse to a part–whole model as Hansen proposes for analyzing the noun function in Chinese. Again, we have provided some discussion as to why we prefer to consider the relations of putative "parts" and "wholes" in terms of the model of "focus" and "field." Chinese ontological views are closer to being "holographic" than "mereological," and this entails the idea that the activity of naming is an act of focusing or attuning in which the discriminated element at least adumbrates the whole in and through its particularity.[26]

Also, Hansen's use of the term "behavioral nominalism" is somewhat misleading. Nominalism is traditionally characterized in terms of a dialectical response to Platonic realism and, thus, has received less constructive elaboration than the doctrine might deserve. The defense of particularity and individuality too often suggests a world of extrinsically related entities in which relations are as unreal as abstract universals.[27] Finally, and this is a most significant difference: Hansen's "mass-noun hypothesis" entails a referential theory of language. Although Hansen wishes to avoid the "substratum" connotations of his substance view, it is clear that the Chinese language for him refers to a world of spatio-temporal "stuffs." We wish to argue, on the contrary, that (at least for Confucius) language does not serve primarily to refer to a world of objects, be they "things" or "stuff-kinds."

The process orientation of the Confucian sensibility and the distinctly pragmatic functioning of language as communicative activity, as well as the focus–field model for interpreting the naming function, preclude considering Confucian language as referential in the usual sense of that term. Confucius' resort to what we have termed *ars contextualis* means that words are to be understood within the context of the language system that itself is both cause and consequence of the society or community of interpretation within which Confucius lived and taught.

Language is self-referencing. The meaning of a word is a function of its use within a particular community. The "truth" of a propositional utterance is tested with respect to the sorts of effect it has upon communicants. For Confucius, the "perlocutionary" and "illocutionary" characteristics of language dominate: it is language as embodying action and as entailing practical consequences that is important.[28] The meaningfulness of a proposition (its "locutionary" character, its sense and reference) abstracted from its active and responsive (illocutionary and perlocutionary) force is broadly irrelevant. As we shall see when we consider the doctrine of the ordering of names (*cheng ming**), names "reference" functions or roles that are themselves other names. The name/thing correlation does not seem to concern Confucius. The act of ordering is not one of achieving appropriate reference to things in the world, but is an act of tuning the language, the practical consequence of which is to increase harmonious activity.

Another important characteristic of classical Chinese for our present concerns is the relative unimportance of the sorts of locutions termed "counterfactual."[29] Thus statements such as "had it not been the case that. . . ., so-and-so would have occurred" are not efficaciously present in classical Chinese philosophy. Sentences of the form, "If you had acted appropriately, you would have been praised," can certainly be expressed in the Chinese language, but the striking (for the Westerner) scarcity of conditionals such as, "If Yao had not taken *t'ien* as his model. . . .," in Confucius' reasoning does provide, we believe, a significant clue to the Confucian sensibility.

The relative absence of both a language of entification and of condition-contrary-to-fact expressions suggests that the classical Chinese would have found scientific and ethical reflections and deliberations unappealing. Both abstract nouns and conditionals are foundations of the sort of theoretical thinking which permits one's thoughts and attitudes to be detached from the manner in which one actively presents himself to the world. Theoretical thinking presupposes that one can be objective and dispassionate in the consideration of alternative modes of understanding and action. Scientific and ethical reasonings are tied together in the sense that each often requires the consideration of the differential consequences of alternative possibilities. The "either–or" sensibility underlies the dominant modes of ethical and scientific thinking.

The relative absence of scientific modes of thinking of the hypothetical-deductive and counterfactual variety has been much discussed in considering the development of classical Chinese culture.[30] What is perhaps more controversial, and certainly for our purposes more relevant, is the claim that the classical Chinese (and *a fortiori* Confucius himself) do not depend upon what we normally consider to be ethical reasoning. This sort of claim has been defended in a number of different ways in recent writing on Confucius and classical Chinese thought.

Herbert Fingarette has made this important point, but has, as was indicated at the close of the last chapter, drawn what we consider to be seriously inappropriate conclusions from this fact. Our analysis suggests that whereas Confucius presents "a way without [ethical] crossroads," his reason for doing so is embedded in the character of the language he employs.[31] Granted that this character is itself a function of the sorts of selections made with respect to the primary modes of experiencing the world which characterized the development of that language, it is clear to us that Confucius was not eliminating every sense of choice and deliberation from his model of thinking; rather, he was eliminating the sorts of choice and deliberation which required recourse to abstract forms of reasoning and to the employment of theoretical thinking as we traditionally understand it. The kinds of choices or deliberations associated with artistic activity are, we believe, definitely entailed by Confucius' views.

The key to this shift, away from ethical to aesthetic modes of deliberation and choice, is to be found in the notion of *yi* 義, "appropriateness or rightness." As we have indicated, it is distinctly aesthetic rightness that provides the fundamental meaning for the Confucian notion of *yi*. Rightness as aesthetic harmony is a function of concrete, immediate, precognitive choices made by the creator or appreciator of a given harmony. The conclusion to be drawn from the absence of ethical deliberations and, *a fortiori*, the absence of ethical alternatives is certainly not the one that Fingarette has drawn: it is not the case that there is no personal autonomy, no truly creative contribution of the individual to the ultimate choices enacted in a given context. On the contrary, the alternatives are real and the selection among those alternatives is a necessary part of any *yi* act. That the alternatives as such are not consciously entertained indicates only that these are not candidates for reflective deliberation. The ethical individual agonizes over conflicting modes of behavior presented to him, each mode of which has its own (partially) determinable consequences. The artist agonizes as well, but is usually much less conscious of the nature of that agony as involving clearly discriminated aesthetic choices aimed at the realization of the most intense form of harmony. In either case the *agon* suggests that something like alternatives are present, although in the latter case they are immanently present and not abstractable from the concrete context they serve.

In addition to the sort of analysis provided by Fingarette, there is another influential treatment of the absence of moral reasoning from Chinese thought. Rosemont has argued that the absence of terms for deliberation, obligation, duty, and so forth, indicates that there is no such enterprise as "moral theory" in classical Chinese culture.[32] Rosemont's views are not appreciably different from those of Fingarette; both borrow their concepts of ethics and moral autonomy from the Kantian model, in which the morally right course must be considered separately from immediate interest and where moral obligation is recognized through reflection upon possible alternatives for judgment and action. If ethics is to be considered always in the light of reflection, deliberation, and conscious judgment among alternatives, then one may certainly assent to the view that such ethical interests are not in any important way represented in classical Chinese philosophy.

With regard to science and morality, it may be said that Western and classical Chinese thought are predicated upon contrasting models of thinking. The distinctiveness of the classical Chinese model is a function of the concrete, immanental nature of thinking that does not depend upon abstract nouns or contrary-to-fact conditionals for its primary forms of expression. Abstract nouns are means for naming the ideas that serve as the principles to be instanced through judgments; conditions contrary to fact, as means of charting the consequences of alternative patterns of action, are indispensable to both ethical and scientific education and practice. Both ethical and scientific reasonings and practice depend upon a significantly different epistemology than that which undergirds the philosophy of Confucius.

The major concern of the present work is with the meaning of thinking in the Confucian sensibility. In our consideration of reflecting (*ssu* 思), learning (*hsüeh* 學), and realizing (*chih* 知) at the beginning of this essay, we suggested that reflecting for Confucius should not be interpreted in terms of the conscious entertainment of alternative possibilities or the analysis of the object of reflection into a complex of contrasting ideas or principles. Reflection is aesthetic articulation which, rather than involving the subsumption of particulars under generic principles in accordance with a conscious act of judging, instead involves the nonmediated appropriation of potentialities for "rightness" with respect to a given situation. *Chih* 知, as "realizing," involves the process of forecasting, but must not be thought to entail any conscious forecast in the strictest sense. The implication of the relative absence of conditionals and the language of the entities must be held firmly in mind if the implications of "reflecting" and "realizing" are to be appreciated.

To recapitulate the principal points of our argument: certain characteristics of classical Chinese, themselves effects of broad cultural conditions, provide significant clues to help us answer fundamental questions of the sort most relevant to this inquiry into Confucius' activity as a master of communication. First, the infrequent recourse to abstract nouns and counterfactuals, a consequence of the absence of notions of transcendence in the classical Chinese tradition, requires that significant communications depend neither upon the separation of the entertainment of a proposition from the act of judgment that asserts its truth or falsity nor upon the generation of conscious alternatives prerequisite to judgments or actions. Second, if knowing *(chih)* cannot be separated from judging and the act of knowing proceeds without the conscious entertainment of alternatives, then the notion of understanding is most plausibly modeled upon aesthetic rather than rational-cognitive activities. Third, in the commonest (post-Kantian) understanding of the term "moral," there is no moral theory in classical Confucian thought. Ethical actions are neither derived from, nor interpretable by, anything like moral theories. Finally, assuming the truth of these propositions, it is clear that the character of Confucius' teaching will be strikingly different from the sort of teaching that aims at the communication of significant ideas and principles that serve to structure and support conscious reflection and responsible judgments.

3.2   Cheng Ming* 正名: *The Ordering of Names*

Beyond Confucius' obvious concern about language in the *Analects*, there is the historical perception of Confucius as the editor of the *Classics* who attuned the language so as to reveal novel significances to his more astute readers. There is the association between Confucius and the "ten wings" of the *Yi-ching*—commentary that purports to explain the images of the original text and enable the wise man to integrate with and benefit from the unceasing process of change. And, significantly, there is his doctrine of *cheng ming* 正名, translated by us as "the ordering of names," but more popularly rendered as "the rectification of names." It will be instructive for us to examine the doctrine of *cheng ming* in light of our claim that the sage is a master of communication. If persons and personal relationships require a constant attuning to be meaningful, it would follow that the media or forms through which these persons are composed, related, and *performed*—mediums such as language, ritual actions, and music—also require attention.

In the immanental cosmos of Confucius, a correlative relationship obtains between idea and action, reason and experience, theory and praxis. Further, Confucian philosophy begins from an irreducibly interpersonal conception of the human being in which self, society, and state are correlates determined through communication. Under these conditions, naming for Confucius cannot simply be a process of attaching appropriately corresponding labels to an already existing reality. The performative force of language entails the consequence that to interpret the world through language is to impel it towards a certain realization, to make it known in a certain way. And the extent to which one is able to influence the world is a function of the extent to which one can articulate his meaning, value, and purpose in such manner as to evoke deferential responses from others. Given such an expectation of language, it is not really surprising to find components indicative of interpersonal communication in the etymologies of many of Confucius' major concepts. "To realize" (*chih* 知) and "to live up to one's word" (*hsin** 信) both indicate a commitment to speech. Exemplary person (*chün tzu* 君子) and "good person" (*shan jen* 善人) as levels of personal achievement, to "*ming*" 命, "to cause certain possibilities to be realized," the achievement of "aesthetic harmony" (*ho* 和) and "naming" (*ming** 名) itself all contain the mouth radical, perhaps indicating verbal articulation.

In this analysis of the doctrine of *cheng ming**, we want to begin by noting the importance Confucius invested in the appropriate use of language. In a classic passage, he describes the proper ordering of language as the immediate priority in the proper ordering of society (13/3):

> Tzu-lu asked Confucius, "If the Lord of Wei was waiting for you to bring order to his state, to what would you give first priority?"
> Confucius replied, "Without question it would be to order names properly."
> "Would you be as impractical as that?" Tzu-lu responded. "What is there to order?" . . .

Tzu-lu's surprise showed such a total lack of sympathy with Confucius' philosophical insight that the Master became uncharacteristically impatient, replying:

> How can you be so coarse! An exemplary person (*chün tzu*) remains silent about things that he does not understand! When names are not properly ordered, what is said is not attuned; when what is said is not attuned, things will not be done successfully; when things are not done successfully, the use of ritual action and music will not prevail; when the use of ritual action and music does not prevail, the application of laws and punishments will not be on the mark; and when laws and punishments are not on the mark, the people will not know what to do with themselves. Thus, when the exem-

plary person *(chün tzu)* puts a name to something, it can certainly be
spoken, and when spoken it can certainly be done. There is nothing
careless in the attitude of the exemplary person *(chün tzu)* toward
what he says.

For Confucius, then, this doctrine of "ordering names" *(cheng
ming*),* is the starting point of sociopolitical order. In so construing
this concept, however, we must be careful not to separate idea and
action. That is, we must give full account to the performative force
of naming. The prevailing interpretation of ordering names *(cheng
ming*)* as the "rectification of names" fails to do so. It tends to treat
names in terms of some theoretical schema that has been inherited
out of the tradition, and that can be hypostatized and hence rectified
by behaviors that satisfy the standing theoretical construct. This kind
of interpretation is perhaps based on a too simple reading of the
presentation of *cheng ming** in the *Analects* (6/25 and 12/11):

> Is a ritual goblet *(ku)* that is not a ritual goblet really a ritual goblet?
> Is it a ritual goblet!

> Duke Ching of Ch'i asked Confucius about effecting sociopolitical or-
> der, and Confucius replied, "The ruler ought to be ruler, the subject
> subject, the father father and son son."

The standard interpretation of *cheng ming** has it that there is
an established definition—characteristics and function—of what it
means to be a ritual goblet *(ku)* or a ruler *(chün),* and that any breach
between theoretical definition and actual performance is a source of
disorder. Hsiao Kung-chuan is a prominent representative of this
position:[33]

> The starting point of Confucius' political thought was to "follow the
> Chou," and his concrete proposal for carrying it out was the rectifi-
> cation of names. Explained in modern terms, what he called the rec-
> tification of names meant readjusting the powers and duties of ruler
> and minister, superior and inferior, according to the institutions of
> the Chou feudal world's most flourishing period. . . . The rectifica-
> tion of names demands reliance upon a concrete standard. The stan-
> dard that Confucius took as his basis was the institutional system of
> the Chou's flourishing period.

Hsiao Kung-chuan is rightly critical of Creel, who rather denies
that *cheng ming** is a Confucian concept and attributes it to later,

probably Legalist, interpolation.[34] Creel's arguments, inspired by Waley's insistence that *cheng ming** is anachronistic and has a basic
"incompatibility with the doctrines of Confucius," do not in fact
warrant his conclusions.[35] But there is merit in Creel's insight that
the sort of interpretation of this doctrine associable with Legalism
(an interpretation of *cheng ming** in fact advocated by Hsiao Kung-
chuan himself) does not square with Confucius' teachings. It would
seem more reasonable on Creel's part, however, to question an
interpretation of *cheng ming** that is inconsistent with the basic tenets
of Confucius' thought at the level of interpretation, rather than
questioning its basic legitimacy as a Confucian concept.

Hsiao Kung-chuan's interpretation fits the rational paradigm in
which definition precedes realization: a ruler must, in carrying out
his office, act according to a preestablished norm and satisfy a set
of given specifications. Such an interpretation, with its apparent
textual support, has been influential in rendering Confucius as extremely conservative. As Hsiao Kung-chuan observes, the doctrine
of *cheng ming** thus understood "clearly demonstrates that Confucius'
political attitude was that of a compliant Chou subject, and that his
political views were conservative."[36] We want to argue that this
popular interpretation of "ordering names" is partially correct, but
that it has the deleterious effect of highlighting an emphasis on
traditional continuity in Confucius' thought at the immediate expense
of overlooking a real concern for cultural diversity, originality, and
enrichment. After all, Confucius is reported to have said himself:[37]

> To be stupid yet fond of relying on oneself, to be base yet fond of
> being one's own advocate, to be born into the present age yet at
> tempt to return to the ways of the past—a person like this is disas
> ter's prey.

Unquestionably Confucius evidences a profound respect for the
institutions of the past, but this respect is by no means equatable
with a simple reconstruction of early Chou institutions and culture.
It requires selectivity and creative synthesis (15/11):

> Yen Yüan (Hui) asked how to order a state. Confucius replied, "Use
> the calendar of Hsia, ride about in the state carriage of Yin, wear the
> ceremonial cap of Chou, and as for music, there are the Shao dances
> (of Shun). Ban the sounds of Cheng. . . ."

Further, Confucius tempers his respect for antiquity with the practical consideration that inherited wisdom and institutions must be constantly revamped to accommodate the shifting circumstances of an always unique world.[38] In short, Confucius believes that human culture is cumulative and generally progressive. While his emulation of the past is much noticed, not enough has been made of his expectations for the future. To articulate a possible world and communicate it to others is an attempt to realize it. To name it is a prompting to "*actualize*" it.

The term *ming** 名 means both "to mean" and "to name." "To name" is to contribute meaning, and "to mean" is to construe names. In the *Analects*, we find that Yao, as a creator of meaning in the tradition, could not be "named" by his people, yet he himself was responsible for the patterning of culture in such manner as to accommodate his contributed meaning (8/19):

> How great indeed was Yao as a ruler! How majestic! Only *t'ien* is truly great, and only Yao took it as his model. How expansive was he—the people had no name to do him justice. How majestic was he in his accomplishments, and how brilliant was he in his cultural achievements.

Similarly, T'ai Po, whose exemplary conduct was a critical factor in the series of events leading up to the establishment of the Chou dynasty, exhibited a selfless morality that would emerge in later generations as a recognized standard. Like Yao's, his actions constituted a source of novel meaning that defied description by the people (8/1): "T'ai Po can certainly be called a person of the highest *te*. Several times he ceded his rightful claim to the empire, leaving the masses searching for language to describe him."

Of course, the most immediate and apparent "name" in which one invests meaning is his own reputation. This notion that one's name has contributed meaning explains Confucius' concern for personal reputation (15/20): "The exemplary person (*chün tzu*) hates the prospect of arriving at the end of his life without having made a name for himself."

The performative dimension of naming and its relationship to meaning is evidenced in the fact that "name" (*ming** 名) is frequently defined as "to cause certain possibilities to be realized" (*ming* 命).

In the early Chinese corpus, in fact, these two terms are frequently used interchangeably. The *Shuo-wen* defines "name" (*ming** 名) as "self-selected causal possibilities" (*tzu ming* 自命).

A full explanation of Confucius' doctrine of "ordering names", in addition to reflecting his appreciation for the way in which language conveys past realizations of the world, must provide some account of how naming can be used creatively to realize new worlds appropriate to emerging circumstances. We shall argue that Confucius' concept of "naming" (*ming**) is to be explained as a "performance" (that is, a making of form) similar to ritual action (*li*). This association between "name" (*ming**) and "ritual action" (*li*) is in fact established by Confucius himself in a passage recorded in the *Tso-chuan:*[39]

> Thereafter, the people of Wei wanted to make a present of a city to Chung-shu Yü-hsi. Chung-shu Yü-hsi declined, instead asking for suspended musical instruments, and ornamental bridles like those used by the nobility to appear at court. The Lord of Wei granted this request.
>
> On hearing of this, Confucius observed, "It is a pity. It would have been better to have given him more cities. Ritual vessels and names (titles) alone cannot be loaned to others—they are what the ruler controls. Names are used to generate credibility, credibility is used to protect the ritual vessels, ritual vessels are used to embody ritual actions, ritual actions are used to enact significance (*yi*), significance is used to produce benefit, and benefit is used to bring peace to the people. These are the important measures for effecting sociopolitical order. To loan them to others is to give them control of the sociopolitical order. And when sociopolitical order is lost, that the state will follow is an inexorable fact.

Both name and ritual action can be viewed as formal structures used to capture and transmit meaning (*yi*). To use the name or perform the ritual action meaningfully entails drawing an analogy between past and present circumstances to evoke this vested significance. An important characteristic of both name and ritual action is that they are context-specific, qualified by a unique set of circumstances. That is, their significance cannot be exhausted by a genetic analysis that only accounts for what they mean for themselves. Since meaning is not simply derived from the name or the ritual action per se, a complete accounting must also have recourse to an explanation that reveals their relationship to and meaning for their ever-particular, ever-changing context.

A given name or ritual action, although describable at an abstract level, is truly meaningful only as a particular and personal disclosure of meaning. This can be made evident in the common alternative translation of "ritual action" (li 禮) as "propriety," provided "propriety" is understood in light of its primitive sense as "to make one's own." Thus, both "appropriate" ritual actions and the "proper" use of language require a personalization and a making over fitting to one's own specific conditions. For this reason, abstract names such as "ritual goblet" (ku) and "ruler" (chün), while laden with their historically derived meanings, must remain open to particularization in their display of significance. Just as ritual actions exist only to the extent that they are considered, embodied, reformulated, and extended via the peculiar conditions of the present moment, so naming and the attuning of names is a dynamic enterprise in which the existing structure and definition is qualified by the understanding that names and their achieved harmonies are always fluid within the parameters of a context, and are in continual need of attunement.

The challenge that this fluidity of names and their patternings represents to a purely logical, referential explanation of cheng ming* is reinforced by the performative force of naming. Ritual actions are not only performed by people, but, because they actively evoke a certain kind of response, in an important sense they "perform" people. Similarly, not only do names describe, they act in that they impel a person towards a certain kind of experience. Giving a substitute vessel the name of a ku ritual goblet can, where appropriate significance is invested, effectively transform this substitute vessel into a ku. Not only are names used to name the order, they are also used for effecting order in what is to be named. The Kuan Tzu describes this function of names:[40] "Names (ming*) are the means whereby the sages organize the myriad phenomena."

Our interpretation of "ordering names" (cheng ming*) argues against the priority of formal constructions by rejecting the suggestion that Confucius simply uses names reductionistically to organize the process of human experience into some preestablished pattern that is held to define the meaning, value and purpose of life. It argues for the priority of aesthetic order by insisting that Confucius regarded the particular person in a specific context as the source of signification.

Confucius, in giving this priority to the person as a particular focus, regards the interpretive patternings constituted by the network of names to serve a sense of continuity and coherence and, at the same time, to be a malleable framework through which novelty and uniqueness are disclosed.

3.3 The Sage as Virtuoso

For Confucius, language, ritual and music are all formal media in which selves grow; they are sources of meaning as well as structures that organize and transmit it. The distinguishing characteristic of music is that it is the formative medium perhaps least dependent upon reference. Susanne Langer observes:[41]

> Music . . . is preeminently non-representative even in its classical productions, its highest attainments. It exhibits pure form not as an embellishment, but as its very essence; we can take it in its flower . . . and have practically nothing but tonal structure before us: no scene, no object, no fact.

In music, indeed, we move towards the highest level of communication insofar as meaning is lodged both in the particular tones themselves and in their structural relatedness. Music does not represent; it presents. And to the extent that it is independent of objective reference, it is receptive to and expressive of the concrete particular. For language references types of things, classes of items. Ontological particulars cannot be referenced; they must be alluded to, hinted at, suggested. Music has that allusive, suggestive power precisely to the degree that it is free of logical reference.

We have claimed, subject to further argument, that Confucius does not, strictly speaking, employ language referentially. Thus he is not concerned to articulate a "name–thing" relationship, nor is he endeavoring to formulate propositions that describe "states of affairs." His primary interest, like that of many other classical Chinese philosophers, was *cheng ming** 正 名: to order names. He wished, having attuned his ear, to tune the language in such manner as to evoke and to harmonize appropriate dispositions to act that were resident in his communicants. That Confucius deemphasized the semantic content of propositions suggests that he could well consider music the primary mode of communication, and this does, in fact, seem to be the case. At the very least, Confucius' views concerning music permit us to better understand the character of language and communicative activity.

Confucius regards music—by which he means not only instrumental music but poetry and dance as well—as an activity that provides enhanced possibilities for disclosing personal style, spirit, and consequence. In musical performances, especially those in which composition and execution are not separated, there is an emphasis on personal disclosure in a manner meaningful to one's audience. The fact that the *Yüeh-ching*, the *Classic of Music*, has been lost utterly bears some testimony to the extent to which the musical mode of expression is dependent upon concrete enactment as opposed to abstract symbol for its preservation and transmission.

For Confucius, the function of music goes beyond simply transmitting meaning from one generation to the next. Used effectively, it can give rise to a harmonious and meaningful relationship in the present moment. His understanding of music seems to be indebted to that attributed to his illustrious forebearer, Shun, as it is described in the *Book of Documents*:[42]

> Poetry gives expression to one's dispositions, song draws out one's expression in chant, the notes accord with the chanting, and the pitch pipes harmonize the notes. The eight notes sustain the harmony without overwhelming each other, and man and god alike thereby are harmonized.

That is, the process of expressing dispositions with words, augmenting words with rhythm and poetic effect, and then enhancing the poetic achievement with musical instruments is one of increasing refinement, complexity, and potential expressiveness.

Confucius himself is aware of the dangers inherent in the abuse of language. There are those eloquent dissemblers who use language to sow discord rather than create harmony (1/3 and 17/18):

> Rarely indeed is the person of clever words and pretentious appearance authoritative (*jen**).

> Detestable is the substitution of purple for vermillion; detestable is the pollution of elegant classical music with the sounds of Cheng; detestable is the subversion of family and state by glib talkers.

And, of course, there is much harmony and meaning effected in the absence of the spoken word (17/19):

> The Master said, "I think I will leave off speaking."
> Tzu-kung replied, "If you do not speak, what will we have to pass on to posterity?"
> The Master responded, "What does *t'ien* have to say? And yet the four seasons turn and the myriad things are born and grow in it. And what does *t'ien* have to say?"

In spite of these reservations and limitations, the notion of ascending levels of potential expressiveness in the direction of music is reiterated in the literature:[43]

> Confucius said: "It has it in the *Records:* 'Speech is used to give full expression to dispositions, and embellishments (*wen** 文) are used to give full expression to speech.' If one does not speak, who will know one's dispositions? And if one's speech is not embellished, it will not take one very far."

The *Yi-ching* cites Confucius as saying:[44] "The written word cannot exhaust speech, and speech cannot exhaust thought."

In these several passages, we can see that Confucius saw communication through language and, ultimately, music as a medium for achieving self-expression and its attendant enjoyment. It is interesting that the character *shuo* 説 in the classical literature which has the meaning, "to speak" and "to persuade," when pronounced *yüeh*, can mean "to enjoy."[45] Similarly, the character *yüeh* 樂, which has the meaning, "to play music," can, when pronounced *lo* or *yao*, also mean "to enjoy."[46] These two characters for "enjoyment," *yüeh* 説 and *lo/yao* 樂, with their attendant associations with speech and music, occur in the first passage of the *Analects* (1/1):

> Is it not indeed a source of enjoyment (*yüeh* 説) to practice at the appropriate time what one learns? And is it not indeed a source of enjoyment (*lo/yao* 樂) having friends come from distant quarters? . . .

Both speech and music, then, were seen as communicative modes for effecting enjoyment. For Confucius, the sage is not only the "master of ceremony," he is further a "composer" (one who makes up by putting together parts) and a "compositor" (one who composes or settles disputes: an umpire, arbiter, peacemaker). That is, the sage through the various media of communication and communion facilitates and fosters the negotiated harmony that at once achieves unity while preserving diversity, that evidences constancy while sponsoring a friendly chaos. In this symphony, the sage is the conductor who conduces to a collaboration of unique contributions.

In the *Analects*, music is frequently, sometimes explicitly and often implicitly, coupled with ritual action *(li)* to the extent that most references to ritual action should be read with music understood as an integral aspect. Music shares with ritual action the participatory, personal character of order sensitive to diversity and the insistent particularity of its constituents. In commenting upon a lengthy *Tso-chuan* passage describing a musical performance in 543 B.C., DeWoskin highlights the importance of diversity in reporting that recent archaeological discoveries have encouraged musicologists to reassess the complexity of modal resources in archaic Chinese music.[47] Apparently, prior to the movement toward establishing musical orthodoxy in late Chou and Han China, there was a considerable variation in scales and standards from area to area, reflecting what we would expect: engagement and participation at the most local level.

The *Analects* has preserved a humorous anecdote about Confucius in which he uses the very personal nature of music to serve a would-be caller an intentional slight (17/20):

> Ju Pei sought an interview with Confucius, but Confucius declined to entertain him, feigning illness. Just as the messenger carrying the summons was about to depart, Confucius got out his lute and sang, making sure that the messenger heard it.

For Confucius, the ultimate source of music, like ritual action, is the contributed significance of the person-in-context. The extent to which music is able to sustain its inherited value as well as to register the personal significance of its conveyor is always a function of the quality of the person in whom it is entrusted (3/3): "What does one who is not authoritative in his person have to do with ritual action or with music?" Ritual action and music, without the sincerity and commitment of the particular person, are bald and trivial (17/11): "In repeatedly referring to ritual action, how could we be talking about gifts of jade and silk? And in repeatedly referring to music, how could we be talking about bells and drums?" In fact, as Lau observes in his Introduction to the *Analects*, hollow form is not merely trivial—for Confucius, it is insidiously deceptive:[48]

> It should be noted that each of the things Confucius detested bore a superficial resemblance to the proper thing, and it is because of this superficial resemblance that the specious can be mistaken for the genuine. Confucius' abhorrence is directed against this spuriousness. The 'tunes of Cheng' are grouped with 'clever talkers' and 'plausible men,' since like 'clever talkers' and 'plausible men,' the 'tunes of Cheng' are capable of worming their way into our favour if we are not on our guard.

Confucius loved the *shao* music which was informed by the cultural contribution of Shun, its creator, a commoner who by virtue of his personal moral achievement was elevated as successor to Yao. And Confucius' love for this music was indeed intense (7/14):

> When the Master was staying in Ch'i he heard the *shao* music. For three months he did not even notice the taste of meat. He said, "I had no idea that the performance of music could reach these heights."

His reason for feeling so strongly about this *shao* music was because it was sedimented with the significance of Shun (3/25): "The Master said of the *shao* music that it was both utterly beautiful and utterly good. Of the *wu* music he said it was utterly beautiful but not utterly good." The *wu* music, attributed to Wu, the founder of the Chou dynasty, was laden with the martial courage of this military man, but could not be fairly described as expressing goodness.

As with ritual action, music begins as a repository through which meaning can be transmitted and from which it can be appropriated. However, as we have seen above, it further serves as a malleable apparatus for displaying one's own innovative contributions. This personal, creative side of music is captured in the *Analects* where Confucius is instructing no less than the Grand Virtuoso of Lu (3/23):

> The Master said to the Grand Virtuoso of Lu, "What can be realized in music is that one begins to play in unison, and then one goes on

to improvise with purity of tone, distinctness and flow, thereby
bringing it to its completion (ch'eng*).

This description of music reflects a need for both continuity and for
novelty. In this passage, and elsewhere, there is the repeated association between music and "completion" (ch'eng* 成) (8/8): "Be
stimulated to new levels in the songs, take your stance in the rites,
and find completion in music." Music for Confucius is an expressive
medium for the kind of aesthetic order that can be achieved by a
person in his community, a harmony consequent on a lifetime of
cultivation, the full expression of his own personhood, and his
virtuosic attunement to his world (2/4): "At fifty I realized the ming
of t'ien, at sixty my ear was attuned, and at seventy I could give
my heart-and-mind free rein without overstepping the mark."
    In appreciating the role of music in the philosophy of Confucius,
it is important to understand the pervasive idea of aesthetic harmony
in the lives of the people. DeWoskin observes:[49]

> Until the Six Dynasties, when art was identified as a particular and
> distinct undertaking, all disciplines that were geared to harmonious
> living were encompassed in the idea of what was aesthetic. Any en-
> deavor, no matter how ordinary—butchering an ox, shaving wheel
> spokes, or succumbing to a fatal illness—if properly done achieved
> an aesthetic dimension and harmonized with the prevailing order.
> No "line" separated ordinary work from the making of art, another
> point that is made manifest in the paradigmatic images of harmony
> in early Chinese texts, the well-blended musical performance and the
> well-seasoned soup.

In ancient Greek culture, "music" encompassed the arts of the
Muses, who were invoked as the sources of creative activity. Plato's
theory of education expounded in The Republic construed music as
a preparatory stage in the progress to true knowledge. It is an attempt
to recreate in one's soul the rhythm, harmony, and orderly movement
of the universe. But it produces "harmony and balance, not knowledge"[50] in that its initial object is the relation obtaining among the
embodied Forms as they are manifested in the realm of appearance,
rather than the Forms themselves.[51] Music serves an instrumental
function in that it provides one with a sensitivity to an order in the
world of becoming that mirrors the primordial order in the world

of being. Although a musical education is certainly a necessary step on the road to pure knowledge, its mimetic nature constitutes a serious limitation for Plato.

For Confucius, on the other hand, music is not imitative in the strict sense, but rather seeks to foster an attunement of the unique foci to the constitutive harmonies of the total field. The particular has a determining, enriching role in the construing of this harmony. The goal of a musical education is not pure knowledge. Rather, it is the compresent, "constatic"[52] experience of realizing a harmony in the interfusion of focus with field, and the attendant enjoyment of this achievement (6/20): "To be fond of it is better than merely to realize it; to enjoy it is better than merely to be fond of it." This relationship between "realizing" (*chih* 知) the world and "enjoying" (*yao* 樂) the world is reiterated in 6/23: "those who realize the world [that is, the wise] find enjoyment. . . ." The authoritative person *(jen* che)* not only "realizes" the world, he further enjoys it free from anxiety (9/29): "the authoritative person is never anxious. . . ."[53] Confucius in fact uses this same language to describe himself as (7/19): "one who enjoys himself such that he forgets to be anxious." Whereas anxiety is disintegrative, authoritative personhood is measured by the degree of integration achieved through the pursuit of harmony.

The fact that "music" and "enjoyment" are represented by one and the same graph would appear to be far from accidental. It is an indication of an association between the quality of achieved harmony and the consequent possibilities for enjoyment.[54] To describe the relationship between music and political administration, Mencius plays with this intersection of "music" and "enjoyment" as alternative terms for expressing harmonious order:[55]

> On another day Mencius had an audience with the King, and said, "You have said to Chuang Pao that you are fond of music. Is that so?"
>
> The King was noticeably disconcerted, and said, "Actually, it is not that I am able to appreciate the classical music of the Former Kings—I just like popular music."
>
> Mencius responded, "If Your Majesty's fondness for music is truly sincere, your state of Ch'i is almost there, regardless of whether it is contemporary or classical music that you like."

"Could you tell me how this is so?" asked the King.

"To enjoy music alone or to enjoy it with others—which brings the greater enjoyment?"

"It is better with others."

"To enjoy music with a few or to enjoy it with many—which brings the greater enjoyment?"

"It is better with many."

"Let me explain to Your Majesty about music. Now say that Your Majesty had a musical performance here. If the common people on hearing the sound of your bells and drums and the tune of your pipes and flutes, with aching hearts and furrowed brows, all said to each other, 'Since our King is fond of music, how can he push us into these dire straits? Fathers and sons do not see each other; brothers, wives, and children are separated and scattered. . . .' This is precisely because you do not find your enjoyment together with the people.

Now say again that Your Majesty had a musical performance here. If the common people on hearing the sound of your bells and drums and the tune of your pipes and flutes, with bright eyes and happy faces, all said to each other, 'Our King must be free from illness, or how could he have a musical performance? . . .' This is precisely because you find enjoyment together with the people.

Now were Your Majesty to find your enjoyment together with the people, you would be the Exemplary King."

This entire passage in *Mencius* can be construed as an elaboration on a rather succinct remark by Confucius (13/16): "The Duke of She inquired about effecting sociopolitical order. The Master replied, 'Make sure that those close at hand find enjoyment (*yüeh* 說) and attract those at a distance.' "

This idea of winning over those at a distance to participate in and enrich one's sociopolitical harmony is a recurring theme in the *Analects* (16/1):

Where the wealth is evenly distributed, there is no poverty; where harmony prevails, there is no underpopulation; where one's territory is peaceful, there is no precariousness. Having achieved this, where those from distant quarters are still not won over, one must cultivate one's virtue and refinement. And when one has attracted them, make them content.

Even where shortages of material goods might regularly be expected, if what is available is evenly distributed, there need not be a shortage of music. The harmony achievable in music and in sociopolitical ordering is a source of intense enjoyment, an enjoyment that is determined by the richness and diversity of the participating elements.

The traditional yet ultimately personal nature of music, its fundamentally intersubjective demands, its possibilities for orchestration and improvisation, and the quality of the attendant enjoyment which stands in proportion to the quality and richness of its harmony, are reflected perhaps in the attitude that Confucius himself had to his own attunement (7/32): "When the Master was singing with others and liked their song, he would invariably ask them to repeat it before harmonizing with them."

As noted above, Confucius' employment of music as a mode of self-articulation and communication is predicated upon the notion that one "begins to play in unison," then proceeds to "improvise."[56] This recalls the activity of the sage with respect to *cheng ming**: he must first listen and only then begin to speak. Speaking after listening is for the sage the same activity as harmonizing or improvising after playing or singing in unison with others. Attunement occurs when one first listens and places oneself into a position of potential harmony, then brings what is given to completion (*ch'eng** 成) by adding those elements to the situation which maximize harmony. The method of realizing harmony by first entertaining the given circumstances and only then addressing oneself to that given in such way as to communicate order is the method of *shu* 恕, deference.

4 *Shu* 恕 : The Unifying Thread

4.1 Shu 恕 as "Deference"

We have suggested elsewhere that there is an important distinction to be made between the project of philosophy grounded in the presumption of transcendence and its counterpart in the immanental cosmos of Confucius. In the transcendent paradigm, knowing is the consequence of cognizing an objective order that structures the cosmos, and understanding involves the apprehension of general relations that obtain among particulars. The sciences of metaphysics and epistemology become the main business of philosophy. By contrast, we have urged that for Confucius, given the emergent nature of cosmic and social order, the project of philosophy requires an active participation in realizing the world. Further, the extent to which one's interpretation of the world is realized is very much a consequence of one's effectiveness in leading others to construe their own importance along sympathetic lines.

This orchestration of the importance of one's community requires from both self and others harmony rather than uniformity, creative enrichment rather than mere amplification. Against the ecstatic and hence self-effacing sense that knowledge of transcendent, unifying truth generates in the beholder is the self-disclosing enjoyment of realization that integrates pleasurable intensity with the richness that difference guarantees.

The realization of interpersonal and social harmony is the effect of yielding to appropriate models of aesthetic orderedness as constituted by rituals, language, and music. These communicative media provide the primary tools of the sage in his role as master of communication. The functions of rituals, language, and music are all of a kind. Each serves to promote aesthetic order. We shall have more to say on the precise way in which music and language serve this purpose, and in the concept of *shu* 恕 we shall discover the clue to the specific manner in which Confucius achieves his status as a master of communication. *Shu* is, in fact, the unifying theme in Confucius' thinking (15/3):

> The Master said, "Ssu (Tzu-kung), do you consider me to be a person who learns a great deal and remembers it all?"
> "Indeed, I do. Is it not so?"
> "No, it is not." Confucius replied, "I pull it all together on one unifying thread."

Not only does Confucius on several occasions allude to a methodology that brings coherence and meaning to his philosophical reflections, there is one passage in which Tseng Tzu, one of Confucius' closest disciples, defines this methodology for us in conceptual terms (4/15):

> The Master said, "Ts'an (Tseng Tzu), my *tao* is bound together with one unifying thread."

Tseng Tzu replied, "Indeed."

After the Master had left, the disciples asked, "What was he referring to?"

Tseng Tzu said, "The *tao* of the Master is *chung* and *shu*, nothing
more."

But what do *chung* 忠 and *shu* 恕 mean?

Lau provides us with a significant corrective for the popular
understanding of *chung* as simply "loyalty" by reconstructing its more
primitive meaning: "doing one's best":[57]

> Translators tend to use "loyal" as the sole equivalent for *chung* even
> when translating early texts. This mistake is due to a failure to ap-
> preciate that the meaning of the word changed in the course of time.
> . . . *Chung* is the doing of one's best and it is through *chung* that
> one puts into effect what one had found out by the method of *shu*.

Lau's interpretation of *chung* is reinforced by the *Shuo-wen* lexicon
which defines *chung* as *ching* 敬, "reverence." Commentary on the
Shuo-wen further clarifies this concept: "It is because exhausting
oneself (*chin chi* 盡己) means *chung* 忠 that *chung* has the import
of 'having integrity' (*yu ch'eng* 有誠)." That is, *chung* 忠 means
"doing one's best" or "giving of oneself fully" to the task at hand.
Taking Lau's clarification one step further, the "oneself" in this
definition of *chung* is one's unique particularity. Thus *chung* means
"doing one's best as one's authentic self."

Understanding the full implications of the second concept, *shu*
恕, is somewhat more problematic. The range and variety of prevailing translations of this concept is perhaps a fair indication of the
problem: "altruism" (Chan), "reciprocity" (Tu Wei-ming), "consideration" (Waley), "do not do to others what you do not want them
to do to you" (Fingarette), "using oneself as a measure in gauging
the wishes of others" (Lau). Whatever *shu* might mean, there can
be no doubt that Confucius saw it as his methodology, his "unifying
thread." In fact, he defines it for us in precisely these terms (15/
24): "Tzu-kung asked, 'Is there one expression that one can act on
to the end of his days?' The Master replied, 'There is *shu*: do not
impose on others what you yourself do not desire.'" This formula,
"do not impose on others what you yourself do not desire," is

repeated on several other occasions in the *Analects*,[58] and reformulated in both the *Chung-yung* and *Ta-hsüeh*. The *Chung-yung* passage is particularly important in that it describes the method of *shu* specifically as evoking analogy between oneself and other people, or perhaps stated in more appropriately Confucian terms, within the field of the relationship constituted by self and other:[59]

> The Master said, "The *tao* is not far from man. Where someone takes as *tao* something distant from man, it cannot be the *tao*. The *Book of Songs*[60] states: 'In hewing an axe-handle, in hewing an axe-handle, the pattern is not far off.' We grasp an axe-handle to hew an axe-handle, but when we look from one to the other with a critical eye, they still seem far apart. Thus, the exemplary person *(chün tzu)* brings proper order to man with man, and having effected the change, stops. *Chung* and *shu* are not far from the *tao*: what you do not want done to yourself, do not do to others."

This passage makes several points that are central in the philosophy of Confucius. To begin with, the *tao* of man, that is, the order or mode of man, always emerges out of what is close at hand—out of the particular, concrete person. The *Book of Songs* passage cited and the *Chung-yung* commentary on it describe this emergence analogically. Although the pattern is close, there always remains a critical difference between the template and the product, between the established pattern and the one that is presently being fashioned. The new and unique axe-handle is not only hewn against the pattern of the existing one, the existing axe-handle itself actually participates actively in bringing the new axe-handle into proper form. Similarly in the human world, man is used to bring order to man.

Perhaps the most telling phrase in this passage is "and having effected the change, he stops" That is, just as the fashioning of the new axe-handle results in something similar yet discernibly different, so the fashioning of one man in relation to another is directed at harmony, not sameness. The dynamics of this analogizing between the existing pattern and the newly fashioned article, when applied to the proper ordering of man, is captured conceptually in *chung* and *shu*.

This *Chung-yung* passage has further significance in disclosing the appropriate relationship in the interaction between one man and another. The concept *shu* is defined frequently in the classical texts in terms of *jen** 仁, "authoritative person." The *Shuo-wen* is a case in point. In our extended discussion of *jen** above in Chapter II, we indicated that *jen** 仁 etymologically reduces to "person" and "two," a combination of ideas indicating that achieved person as *jen** is irreducibly relational. This association between *jen** and *shu* helps us understand the analogical nature of this relationship. *Jen** is not a relationship between two identical persons; it is a harmony existing between persons that is constituted by both similarity and difference, and by both excellence and deference. The methodology of *shu* requires the projection or recognition of excellence as a means of eliciting or of expressing deference. *Shu* as a methodology requires that in any given situation one either display excellence in oneself (and thus anticipate deference from others) or defer to excellence in another. Again, *shu* is always personal in that it entails *chung:* "doing one's best as one's authentic self."

The personal starting point and the interpersonal implications of this process of *shu* are made apparent when Confucius turns to define *jen** in the *Analects* (6/30).

> The authoritative person (*jen** 仁) establishes others in seeking to establish himself, and promotes others in seeking to get there himself. To be able to take the analogy from what is closest to oneself can be called the methodology of becoming an authoritative person.

Herbert Fingarette, in his reflections on this passage from the *Analects*, rejects a strictly Kantian interpretation of *shu* because of the difficulty faced in arriving at universal maxims that are not themselves thwarted by the problem of "relevantly similar circumstances." That is, the application of the categorical imperative would require the moral equivalent of a legislator to formulate an inexhaustible code that would cover all possible situations. As an alternative explanation of *shu*, he, like us, suggests that it functions as analogy in Confucius:[61]

> One key word here is *p'i* 譬, a word used with some frequency in the *Analects*. Although it is rendered in bi-lingual dictionaries by the English "to compare," the important features of its use in the *Analects* to which I would direct attention are these: First, *p'i* in the *Analects* is always a "comparison" of likenesses, not differences. Hence "analogy" is an appropriate term. Second, the comparison is

expressed in terms of imagery, of persons, situations or activities, not in terms of abstract traits. Hence, *p'i* is in the *Analects* typically metaphorical . . . . The use of *p'i* is characteristic of Confucius' way of teaching. . . . It contrasts sharply with the method of abstract analysis, theory building, universalizing. *Shu*, in turn, is a specific kind of *p'i*. To be able from what is close—i.e., oneself—to grasp analogy with the other person, and in that light to treat him as you would be treated—that is *shu*.

Fingarette's definition of *shu* in terms of analogy is certainly borne out by the etymology of the character 恕, composed of its cognate *ju* 如, which means "like, as if, to resemble," and *hsin* 心, "heart-and-mind." Proceeding one step further, there are two important questions that are still unresolved. First, if *shu* is "extending oneself to other things" (*t'ui chi chi wu* 推己及物) and "weighing others with oneself" (*yi chi liang jen* 以己量人) as explained in the traditional commentaries on the *Analects*, it would seem (as Fingarette indeed suggests) that one's own judgment is the starting point of *shu*. If this is the case, it would seem that *shu* is one-directional. This personal judgment on how to act with respect to another is then going to be qualified by one's own achievement as a person, one's own excellence. Under these circumstances, it is difficult to understand how deference enters into it. In what way is *shu* to be understood as "deference"? The second question is: why is the definition of *shu* as, "do not extend to others what you yourself do not desire," persistently framed in negative rather than positive terms?

We can respond to the first question by examining the only occurrence of *shu* to be found in the *Mencius*:[62]

Mencius said, "Everything is complete here in me. There is no greater source of enjoyment than, upon introspection, to find that one is true to oneself. And there is no method of pursuing authoritative humanity more immediate than carrying *shu* into practice with earnestness.

This passage suggests several points. First, one's own self is defined in terms of one's relations with all other things. It is for this reason that "everything is complete here in me." In exercising the methodology of *shu*, one must first move from other to self in order to clarify self. To say that "there is no greater source of enjoyment than, upon introspection, to find that one is true to oneself" is to say that one must have a clear awareness of one's own self and act in such a way as to be true to that self. Being "appropriate" (*yi* 義) begins with being true to oneself, and, on that basis, negotiating harmony with one's context. This is a source of enjoyment because enjoyment involves attuning the dispositions represented by the constituent particulars.

It is only once one has moved from other to self in order to clarify oneself that one can move in the opposite direction and extend oneself to the other in order to determine appropriate conduct. This same point is made in stating: "to discipline oneself and to practice ritual action is to become authoritative as a person" (12/1). To discipline oneself is the movement inward to clarify self in terms of other, and "to practice ritual action" is the extension of self outward in the direction of other. Thus, it is because *shu* is bi-directional that it can be defined as reciprocity and described in terms of excellence and deference. *Shu* is not simply taking oneself as the model and projecting it onto others; rather, it is first clarifying oneself in terms of others, and then either displaying excellence oneself or deferring to the excellence of others in personal relations. *Shu*, then, is both the act of deferring and the demand for deference. It is the sense of deference we are employing that grounds the approach in a specific sort of analogical procedure which we shall seek to articulate in the following pages.

Why is *shu* always expressed negatively? *Shu* as an analogy involves both continuity and novelty. The existing structures, such as ritual action, take care of the continuity. To the extent that one can positively specify what ought to be done, one must "do ritual action." But not all meaningful actions are covered by existing ritual and, because any performance of ritual action is necessarily personal, it does in some measure introduce novelty. What are the constraints upon this novelty? Since one cannot be fully aware of the possibilities represented by another, *shu*, in covering this novelty, can only be expressed negatively. This novelty cannot be specified. The only bounds that can be drawn on it emerge out of the limitations of one's own possibilities: what one would find discordant for himself.

What, for example, is the responsibility of a voice coach to a singer? He must discipline the voice through existing forms while at the same time giving the voice room for creative expression. What limits can the voice coach place upon the creative side? Only what the coach, plumbing his own experience and focusing it with respect to the idiosyncrasies of the singer, finds creatively unproductive. He must leave the opportunity for novelty open by advising in "negative" terms in those situations in which technical advice is not pertinent.

In asserting that *shu* is to be understood in terms of giving and receiving deference, we are making a rather far-reaching claim. For if it is true that Confucius believed *shu* to be the single thread that served as the unifying theme of his thinking, and if *shu* may appropriately be understood in terms of deferential relations, then the notion of deference must be employed interpretively in a variety of ways as a means of understanding Confucius' philosophy. One of the most significant implications of our discussion of *shu* as deference is, as we shall now begin to argue, that the activity of thinking itself must be understood in terms of *shu*. To make sense of this claim we must consider, in somewhat greater detail, the sort of language that both presupposes and is presupposed by thinking as a deferential, analogical activity.

4.2 The Language of Deference

In the Western tradition, dominated by cosmogonic myth and speculation, in the beginning, at the origin, there is chaos. The transition from religious to philosophic and scientific speculation occurs in terms of the transition from *mythos* to *logos*. In our tradition, because of the dominance of scientific thinking in the last four or five centuries, it is forgotten that, before there was a *logos* of *mythos*, there had to be a *mythos* of *chaos*; before scientific thinking could rationalize the myths, the myths had to organize chaos. In this view, reasoning is twice removed from the sources of individual and social experience in the primordial chaos at the time of the beginnings. Thus the *logos* of *mythos* is discovered when principles are extracted from their mythical substratum and posited as the grounds for reasonings and practice. Henceforth what is grasped by reason is not primordial chaos or the myths that have organized it, but the principles extracted from these mythical accounts. In place of participation through myth and ritual, we have recourse to reflection, speculation, and theoretical construction.

The relative unimportance of distinctly cosmogonic speculation in classical Chinese entails the consequence that mythico-poetic language cannot serve as the paradigm for figurative language. China, however, is certainly not without imagery drawn from poetry, folklore, and so forth. That Chinese imagery is not contained primarily within explanatory myths means that it functions less discursively within its cultural context. This suggests that the movement from *mythos* to *logos* as it occurred in the Anglo-European tradition did not take place in any important way in ancient China. Images were permitted to serve an evocative instead of an explanatory function and were not, therefore, rationalized through a transition from myth to scientific rationality. The consequence of this has been that the coexistence of imagery and conceptual discourse creatively interplaying in Chinese culture was a primary inhibitor of the development of science as an autonomous cultural interest. On the other hand, this same interplay helped to insure the richness of the Chinese aesthetic tradition.[63]

The imagistic and metaphorical characteristics of the *Analects* are present alongside its more discursive, conceptual elements. Such language is actually constitutive of classical Chinese discourse, not merely a substratum or imaginative extension of it. "Metaphor" and "concept" interplay without the presumption of a hierarchical relationship. Meaning is a function of the allusive character of this interplay. Philosophic discourse conditioned by the presupposition of a necessary transition from *mythos* to *logos*, by contrast, must consider mythico-poetic language either as the ground or the aim of philosophic discourse. That is to say, figurative language emerges either within the context of a transition from *mythos* to *logos* or by an appeal to *mythos* beyond *logos*.

The speculative tradition of the West permits two contrasting uses of language insofar as verbal communication is concerned: the language of rationalization, which certain deconstructionists (particularly Jacques Derrida) have come to call the "language of presence";[64] and secondly, the sort of language that consists of the appeal to *mythos* or mythico-poetic significances as existing beyond *logos*, what may be called the "language of absence." The former use of language is associated with the tradition of *scientia universalis*, the latter with that of *ontologia generalis*. As was suggested in our discussion of Confucian cosmology, the context of linguistic usage associated with the *logos-mythos* relationship is not relevant to the characterization of Confucian thought. Neither the rational-literal employment of language associated with the language of presence, nor the mystical-ineffable language associated with the language of absence captures the sense of the Confucian discourse. Confucian language is a language of *difference*.

By "language of difference" we mean to allude, of course, to the understanding of language derived from the work of Ferdinand Saussure.[65] Saussure's principal theses regarding language are the following: language is a system of signs; signs have their origin in sounds; signs are constituted and function by virtue of the differences that exist among them in the linguistic system, and signs are arbitrary and conventional.

These theses have a number of interesting consequences, the more important of which for our purposes are: first, meaning is not a function of reference, but is discovered by noting the differences of the signs within the system. Second, signs have no positive status but exist merely by virtue of these differences. Third, an implication of the first two, language does not re-present (make present) objects or ideas, but rather aims to constitute meaning through the usually implicit articulation of the differences among linguistic units. The consequence of greatest relevance for our discussion of Confucius' use of language is that which denies primary importance to reference as determining the functions of language.

We can demonstrate the relevance of this notion of language as a "play of differences" to Confucian thought more easily if we articulate Derrida's extension of this insight.[66] This will lead us into a discussion of Derrida's concept of *différance*. The use of the neologism *différance* ("*ance*" substituted for "*ence*") is meant to introduce the consequences of accepting language as a play of differences. *Différance* suggests that difference has both an active and a passive dimension. As a linguistic system permitting speech, the difference among signs is "passive"—and thus is simply a function of the system as presently constituted. As constituted by speech acts, and with regard to the specific speech acts themselves, difference is active. The chicken–egg character of the relationship between the first sense of language and the second is what grounds the primary meaning of *différance*. But the implication of the unresolvable alternation between structure and act or event is that meaning is always deferred. In being deferred, meaning is never present either in language as structure (when that is the focus) or as event (when speech acts are the focus). The concept of *différance*, then, is determined by the nuances of the notions of differing and deferring.

To this elaboration of Saussure's concept of difference we would ourselves like to add a supplementary note. The sense of *différance*, we believe, ought to include not only that of "defer" as "postpone," but should include the sense of the homonymic meaning of "defer," "to yield," "to give deference to." With this emendation we have a complex notion that can provide a means of articulating Confucius' use of language.

Classical Chinese is a system of differences, and the notion of difference must include the standard sense of "being distinct or distinguishable from," in the sense of constituting acts of differing, as well as the allied notion of deferring as "postponing." Finally, the meaning of the homonym, "defer," must be added to the above. The meaning of a given sign is then determined by its active and passive difference, and that meaning is never altogether present but deferred ("postponed"). This postponement is a function of the fact that meaning is not established through reference but through deference ("yielding"). Deference is the means whereby one defers meaning. Just as difference has both an active and passive meaning, so deference means both "postponement" and "yielding."

It is the addition of the notion of deference in its "yielding" sense that renders the interpretation of language as a play of differences peculiarly relevant to the interpretation of Confucius' thinking. To understand the precise manner in which this rather complicated analysis applies to Confucius' use of language, it will be necessary to draw upon the sort of speculative model outlined in our discussions of the cosmological character of Confucius' thought. As we have said, Confucianism represents neither *ontologia generalis* nor *scientia universalis* but is rather an *ars contextualis*, employing a language of particularity and concreteness, and as such is to be contrasted readily with the language of abstract generalizations which ground Western references to objects.

Both the languages of presence and absence are referential; the former language presents items purportedly known through the medium of names, which are generally abstract nouns that identify the thing that is known: "pot," "chrysanthemum," "whistle," and so on. Particular reference is achieved by further description or identification associated with pronominal referencing—that is, *"this* pot;" *"these* chrysanthemums," "*his* whistle." Proper names ("King Henry IV," "Maurice," "Teresa") aim at the identification of particulars. But in most referential contexts these are actually descriptive or require further description if they are to serve. Such further description employs the abstract language of generalizations associated with class terms and concepts.

The relationship between class names and proper names insofar as it might apply to classical Chinese must be something like this: the proper name denotes ostensively and descriptively, but only the latter sense is philosophically significant. The referential character of naming is not nearly as significant as the descriptive function; thus no ontological referencing serves to discipline the acts of naming. That is, there is no object language in the strict sense. Language is, in this sense, nonreferential. For if we understand the term "refer" in the strict linguistic sense to mean "denote" or "to stand for," then the denotation of a term is the class of particulars referenced by that term.

The relative absence of abstract nouns in classical Chinese militates against the denotative or referential employment of language (in any but ostensive manners) to the degree that such employment requires the class name as ground for the referencing of an item. For example, the denotation of a concept such as "courageousness" would be all of the instances of courageous activity, past, present and future, to which the term would appropriately refer. The strict connotation of the term is all of the characteristics that permit a formal definition of the concept. The ability of a linguistic expression to be referenced seems to depend upon the existence of a formally definable concept which permits the identification of an item as a member of a class of such items. In a language that does not explicitly depend upon abstract nouns, there can be neither connotative nor denotative definitions in the strict sense.

The language of presence attempts to present or re-present an otherwise absent subject. The language of absence notes, through indirect discourse, the absence of a nonpresentable subject. In either case there is a referent—real or putative—beyond the act of referencing itself.

By contrast, the language of deference, which we are claiming to be the language of Confucius, is one in which meaning is disclosed and/or created by virtue of a recognition of mutual resonances among instances of communicative activity. Language is the bearer of tradition, and tradition, available through linguistic expression and ritualistic evocation, is the context of all linguistic behavior. The language user appeals to present praxis and to the repository of significances realized in the traditional past, and he does so in such a manner as to set up deferential relations between himself, his communicants, and the authoritative models invoked.

The understanding of language as both deferential and self-referential can lead to the closing of discourse upon itself in a potentially dangerous fashion. Authoritarian political systems are often associated with this closing of the context of viable communication which leads of necessity to the operationalizing of linguistic activity. In a totalitarian regime, the univocal concept is demoted to a station beneath that of images and slogans, and language is functionalized. In such a situation names are the indicators of roles and functions defined in advance by the administrative system that forms the political structure. In languages possessing abstract nouns, concepts transcend in meaning the propositions within which they are housed. Operational accounts, on the other hand, identify the meaning of nouns with their expression and/or with the activities or functions described within the locutions that house the nouns.

The importance of tradition for Confucius is to be seen precisely here. To avoid positivistic, totalitarian, or authoritarian implications of a language without strict transcendence, there must be a repository of significances which provide an excess of meaning beyond that characterized in the statement which houses the idea or image. In the Confucian tradition, imagination is not tied to present praxis as long as there is deferential access to the appropriate traditional models. This access is maintained provided the expression of traditional significances and the appropriation of models from the past are not monopolized by a centralized political or administrative power.

The language of deference is the language of *shu*. The act of giving and receiving deference involves comparison and, therefore, analogy. The recognition of excellence in tradition or in interpersonal relations occasions a yielding to that excellence which, when communicated appropriately, serves as a model to which others will also yield. This yielding begins with "listening." Confucius first "listens" to the excellences of tradition and of present praxis and through this deferential act thereby attunes himself. Only in so doing does he constitute himself as a model calling forth deference from others. Having attuned himself to the tradition, he can channel and transmit it. And in the act of transmission he becomes the focus of the tradition, its completion (ch'eng* 成). In this manner Confucius becomes a sage.

The language of deference depends upon both continuity with the traditional past and the novel appropriation of that past in such way as to render it relevant to particular circumstances in the present. Shu, as deference, depends upon the modeling relationship which permits the recognition of similarities among individuals, activities or circumstances that could occasion appropriate personal, interpersonal, and social harmony. Such similarities, however, always presuppose novelty and difference as background. As our discussion of the musical mode of communication evidences, harmony presupposes similarity as the ground of improvisation. Social harmony, like musical harmony, emerges from the balanced complexity of similarity and difference.

The language of shu is analogical, to be sure. But to say as much without indicating precisely what we mean by "analogy" is to invite confusion. Elucidating the connection between the notions of shu, "deference," and "analogy" will provide significant understanding of the meaning of sagely activity.

5 The Sage as Master of Communication

5.1 Allusive Analogy

We have had occasion to describe the sage as master communicator and virtuoso, both characterizations reflecting the central role played by communication in Confucius' conception of cultivation and growth. In our discussion of the several modes of formal expression through which communication is effected—ritual action, language, and music—we have tried to elucidate the dynamics of the creative use of analogies both drawn from the authority of past personal and cultural achievement and authored in a novel present. A specific terminology used in the immediate context establishes an analogy that immediately reveals similarity and continuity between past and present and, at the same time, serves as a structure for disclosing differences. In a comparable manner, a ritual action performed in the context of the present establishes an analogy that draws the cultural tradition forward and brings it into the present moment, while at the same time, providing a formal apparatus through which to define and record personal uniqueness. This pervasive application of analogy in ancient Chinese philosophy is evident in the constant appeal to historical incidents and models as concrete instances of conduct that can serve as a resource for organizing and articulating present experience. In the broadest terms, an immanental view of reality that does not subscribe to absolute and objective principles must employ models rather than norms as the means of evoking appropriate behavioral responses. The establishment and cultivation of modeling relationships is effected through analogy.

Since, for Confucius, cultivation at all levels is accomplished in the various media of communication, it would not be an exaggeration to describe analogical communication as the central methodology that prevades his teachings. After all, it is not the transmission of past achievements alone that concerns the sage. Rather, it is the dynamics of making the present cultivated by selecting the most appropriate of these cultural resources and communicating them through analogy to refine the present. *Shu*, then, as deference is performed by recourse to a specific sort of analogical activity.

There are two fundamental goals of communication: to say what something is or is not, and to suggest, allude to, hint at, or mention. The first activity is that of literal or metaphorical expression; the second, allusion.[67] So-called referential languages have a literal ground permitting the expression of presence or absence. In referential languages, concepts have priority over images, and the inability to say precisely what something is or is not is considered a limitation of the language. Allusive languages do not employ reference in the traditional sense and do not, therefore, have a literal ground. The function of the language is primarily evocative. Metaphor and imagery are primary tools of communication in no sense to be subordinated to literal concepts.

As one no doubt has noticed, the contrast of "expressive" and "allusive" uses of language suggests a contrast between rational and aesthetic understandings of order. Rational order can only be characterized by a language that names or describes objects, concepts, or words, or their patterns and relationships. Universals, conceived as either real or conventional, form the basis of this sort of language. By contrast, the language permitting characterization of aesthetic order is not based upon general patterns or logical forms expressible as nouns.

Allusive language is metaphorical. But allusive metaphors are not to be contrasted with literal expressions; they constitute an autonomous medium of discourse. Metaphors when construed as the extensions of literal locutions are "expressive" metaphors, whereas allusive metaphors permit language to be used to "hint at," "suggest," or "mention" particularities. The suggestive character of the language of allusion serves the sort of communicative activity that evokes the particular feelings in communicants which constitute the "meanings" of the language.

Allusive language is indirect. The reason for the indirectness is that whereas expressive language permits the channeling of meaning through the medium of generalizations associated with abstract nouns, allusion suggests particular events which cannot appropriately be generalized or classified. In a world characterized by allusive language, general statements cannot be true, for generalizations apply to "no one in particular." Natural laws as general statements of relationship, universal ethical principles, and so forth, are functions of the expressive language that undergirds the languages of presence and absence. Allusive language is the language of the parable, the teaching story. The truth of allusive statements is realized in the communicant: "He who has ears to hear let him hear." It is the evocation and inner articulation that guarantees the truth, or more appropriately, the efficacy of a statement.

5.2 Thinking as Attunement

Classical Chinese is not, as are most Western languages, grounded in the propositional utterance. The dominance of the noun function precludes limiting meaningful statements to those possessing the sentential, subject-predicate form. The tendency of classical Chinese philosophers to be concerned with the ordering of names is a consequence of the dominance of the noun function. The striking claim that classical Chinese doesn't depend upon sentences and propositions for the expression of semantic content entails the consequence that all Chinese words are names, and that compound terms, phrases, and sentences are strings of names.[68] This consequence, in turn, requires that one appreciate the lack of interest on the part of the early Chinese in questions of "truth" and "falsity." Words, as names, may be judged appropriate or inappropriate; only propositons may, in the strict sense, be true or false. The importance of this fact for our present argument can be grasped by noting the precise sense in which classical Chinese is a "pragmatic" language:[69]

> Where Western philosophy of mind dealt with the input, procession, and storage of content (data, information), Chinese philosophers portrayed heart-mind as consisting of dispositional attitudes to make distinctions in guiding action.

A word in classical Chinese, certainly in Confucius, functions as a name. Acceptance of a name as appropriate involves a disposition to act. Language is dispositonal, and the ordering of names is per se an ordering of dispositions. The semantic content of propositions cannot be conditioned by objective or logical reference. The activity of thinking in language is a dispositional activity; it entails the disposition to make distinctions that result in appropriate names and to act in accordance with the disposition engendered by those names.

Chinese language is pragmatic in a way that even the strictest of the pragmatists in the Western tradition would applaud. As Hansen indicates, Western forms of pragmatism have always had to move upstream against the traditional belief in propositions as primarily carriers of semantic content:[70]

> Western philosophy . . . has a modern pragmatic tradition of regarding beliefs as "habits of action." Critics of pragmatism insist that the pragmatic analysis fails precisely because it cannot capture the "content" component of belief. That component figures centrally in inference—especially conditional inference.

Chinese philosophers are not inclined to depend upon inference or inference-like statements since, as we have said, they deemphasize propositional utterance. Chinese pragmatic theories, therefore, would not be threatened by claims that they failed to express the importance of "content." Ironically, perhaps, the Chinese could more easily defend the slogan of the American pragmatist, "Knowing is a kind of doing."

Of course, Western thinkers inherit a tradition in which not only are knowledge and action separated but both are distinguished from "feeling." Heart-and-mind (*hsin* 心) must synthesize the functional equivalents of "knowing," "acting," *and* "feeling." So, to speak of an "idea" or "concept" (a name as entertained) is to speak of a name-as-disposition-to-act.

Confucius claimed that at sixty his ear was attuned. By this he meant that he could grasp the dispositions communicated through language and music. The acuity of Confucius with respect to the meaning deposited in music, for example, is part of his legend:[71]

> It is said: with music, if one hears its sound, one will know what kind of customs there were, and if one sees the customs, one will know how the people were transformed.

> That Confucius, studying the lute under Master Hsiang, understood the purposes of King Wen was because on seeing the faintest outline he could fill in the rest clearly.

The sage first listens, then he speaks or sings in harmony. Listening is of little value to one who lacks "ears to hear." The attunement of one's ear constitutes a mastery of the modes of communication—language, ritual action, and music.

The analogy between language and music suggested by the concept of attunement is a felicitous one. A long-standing truism celebrates the "musical" quality of the Chinese language.[72] The tonal character of Chinese permits a more immediate and perhaps richer interaction between music and discursive language than would be the case in nontonal languages.

Chinese language is dominated by the name and Chinese music by "the note." And notes, like names, are dispositional. The "Great Preface" to the *Book of Songs*, traditionally attributed to Confucius, contains the following:[73]

> Song (poetry) is the consequence of dispositions. It resides in the heart as dispositions and is articulated in language as song. One's feelings stir within his breast, and take form in words. When words are inadequate, they are voiced in sighs. When sighs are inadequate,

they are chanted. When chants are inadequate, unconsciously, the hands and feet begin to dance them. One's feelings are expressed in sound, and when these sounds are refined, they are called musical notes.

This account of the origin of words and notes indicates that the syntactical elements of language and music are not given the emphasis one might expect. The dominance of names and notes suggests that communication is grounded in the particularity of the elements in the communicative act. Harmony is a function of the particularity of names and notes and of their mutual resonances emerging from their deferential relationships.

Such emphasis upon the particularity of names and notes would, of course, be an implication of the notion of aesthetic order discussed throughout this work. Further, given the analogous relationship of the Chinese language and Chinese music, and given the nonpropositional character of the language, one might infer that musical syntax would be less important in composition and performance than has been the case in the West insofar as Western music has depended upon the logical or rational understanding of order. Certainly the importance of percussive instruments such as bells and drums would suggest that melody—the formal, patterned succession of musical notes—would not be as highly valued in classical China as is the case in those cultures that have treated percussive instruments mainly as rhythmic reinforcement for other instruments.

Both the ordering of names and the ordering of notes are presupposed by the act of communication per se. And each requires that one's ear be properly attuned. Communication, of the form illustrated by Confucius in the *Analects*, involves the act of attunement as both cause and consequence. Confucius, as master of communication, is also the most appropriate model for the thinker. Thinking and communicating cannot be separate activities since the modes of communication—language, ritual action, and music—are, in fact, the modes of thinking itself. The performative character of each of these modes insures that the act of thinking and the act of communicating are mutually entailing.

The allusive, deferential character of communication and of thinking is best illustrated by Confucius in his role as teacher. The key to understanding Confucius as a teacher is to be found in the character of the specific analogical method he employs. This method principally involves resort to the sort of allusive analogies discussed above. A language of deference is an allusive language. Analogies of the sort employed by Confucius must be understood as forms of allusion.

Allusive analogies are attempts to set up resonances between poles of a modeling relationship. The model evokes activity that is conditioned by the circumstances of the modeler. The ideal situation of two tuning forks resonating one with the other is *not* the primary example of the modeling activity. The goal of emulation is harmony, not simply resonance. The imitative activity is not to be construed as strictly conformative in nature. Such would be the rational interpretation. Rather one strives to harmonize with the model by attuning one's behavior by recourse to the model. The educating function of the model is defined not in terms of imitation but evocation.

The distinction between imitation and evocation is rooted in the English meaning of the word "education." The roots of that word are the Latin *ēdūcere*, "to evoke", and *ēdūcare*, "to bring up". It is the latter sense that has dominated our understandings of education, although the sense of "educing," "leading forth," "drawing out" has at times been appreciated in our considerations of education.

Education as evocation cannot be merely an exercise in drawing out from an individual the same feelings and ideas already housed in the teacher. Evocation means the stimulation of novel responses in the individual to be educated. One may recall that the so-called Socratic method employs evocation in both the stong and weak senses. The weaker sense involves the evocation of the remembrance of truths already known by the teacher but not yet grasped by the student. In the *Meno*, Socrates teaches the slave-boy a mathematical truth that Socrates was perfectly aware of, but does so through the elicitation of knowledge by question and answer which causes the slave-boy to uncover that truth. The level of joint inquiry is reached when Socrates and Meno address a question neither has yet come to answer—"Can virtue be taught?" The stronger sense of evocation is operative here. The dialogue permits mutual evocation which leads, presumably, to increased understanding of complex issues.

But even this strong sense of evocation does not quite suit the Confucian sensibility. Confucius employs something like the first sense of teaching when basic questions associated with the ritual action (*li* 禮) are to be addressed. His use of the second sense of evocation, however, is much stonger than that of Socrates. Platonic philosophy assumes the preexistence of the truths sought through the dialectical method. Such cannot be the case with Confucius. The *yi* 義 acts of the sage-kings were not performed in accordance with an already existing standard, but were themselves creative acts which established models of appropriate activities. In Confucius' appeals to the ingenuity of his disciples as well as to the models of rightness in the tradition, he is involved in a joint inquiry without a specific *telos*, without, that is to say, an idea or set of ideas that, when encountered, would serve as the truth of the matter under investigation.

Let's look more closely at the teaching situation in which Confucius functions. In the *Analects*, for the most part, the words of Confucius are addressed to listeners. In the act of communication two sorts of appeal are in evidence: there is the implicit or explicit appeal to the ingenuity of his hearers, and there is, more often than not, the appeal to the models of received tradition or present praxis— be they the appropriate ritual actions (*li*), or persons as models of rightness, or music and poetry as expressions of the *li*.

There is simply no reason to claim that Confucius has "in mind" what he wishes to teach. However specific he might wish to be concerning the appeal to tradition, his appeal to the ingenuity of his disciples involves the recognition that appropriating the tradition will depend upon the novel circumstances of his disciples' context. The aim is not, as is the case in Platonic philosophy, to discover in the teaching situation principles of the sort that may then be subsequently applied to various alternative situations. The aim for Confucius is the transmission of a tradition that contains the appropriate models of behavior (including, of course, the communication of his own behavior as such a model). The difference between the two forms of teaching is primarily one characterizable in terms of the presence or absence of rational deliberation.

For Confucius, the act of communication is somewhat more direct and immediate, at least as regards the contrast between the transmission of models and the communication of principles. The communication of a principle requires analytic and/or dialectical procedures leading to definitions. Once defined, concepts can be employed, singly or in combination, to construct propositions that serve as guides for thought and action. For example, the principle:

"It is wrong to lie" requires that, beyond some reasonably explicit account of the meanings of "right and wrong," we have a definition of "lying" that can permit us to understand the range of applicability of the propositions. In any given situation one might have to deliberate concerning the rightness or wrongness of an action by asking oneself, "Would I be lying if . . .?" Also, if confronted with a situation from which it seemed that there could be no escape without recourse to lying, one would surely deliberate among a number of possible alternative lies to discover one that would entail a lesser degree of moral wrongdoing.

Compared with this procedure, Confucius' form of communication is more direct. Like Jesus and the Buddha, Confucius employs the "he who has ears to hear let him hear" mode of discourse. By pointing to the behavior of traditional figures acting in situations similar to the one forming the immediate occasion of his remarks, Confucius is holding up an analogical model. There is no attempt to define concepts or to construct or discover principles; there is rather the effort to mark similarities by allusive referencing. Such allusive acts depend not only upon what is articulated with reference to the specific models, but predominantly upon the welter of causally efficacious feelings associated with the affective appropriation of the traditional past. The past for Confucius is, then, the causally efficacious past replete with the feelings by which, and in accordance with which, the past is appreciated.

The primary method of teaching for Confucius is that associated with acts of evocation in the strongest sense of that term. His orientation to tradition entails the consequence that in the act of communication he is attempting to re-present some past or present excellence through deferential acts. This re-presentation does not involve recourse to doctrine or dogma, but to the more primitive sources of experiencing—namely, actions and affective tones.

The direct connection between language, ritual action, and music is realized through the evocative character each possesses. Modes of communication are not forms through which feelings are channeled; they are, rather, performative activities that directly constitute such feelings and their relationships through the process of attunement. And thinking is performed through each of these modalities. To think is to communicate; to communicate is to think.

VI

". . . and at seventy I could give my heart-and-mind free rein without overstepping the mark."

1 The Failings of Confucius

In this work, we have begun from Confucius the fifteen-year-old cultural neophyte, disposed to defer to the tradition, and progressed to the fully personal Confucius who, at seventy, simply does as he pleases (2/4): " . . . and at seventy I could give my heart-and-mind free rein without overstepping the mark."

We have begun from the abstract "uncommon assumptions" that vein Chinese culture as an implicit aesthetic order, and progressed toward an interpretation of Confucius, not as a remote ideal, but as a warm-bodied, profoundly concrete example of a sage, personally disclosing himself for that harmony called Chinese culture.

We have defined Confucius as an historical person who, through achieved excellence has had a protracted career in the Chinese tradition as a corporate personality. Consistent with the pattern of China's most influential philosophers, the incipient Confucius is himself irrepressibly syncretic (tsa chia 雜家), literally making the most of his cultural legacy. He assumes the "body" of the tradition, both in his selective compilation of a curriculum out of the existing corpus of cultural documents, and in his creative embodiment of meaning-invested ritual actions (li 禮). From this organic beginning, his influence then expands through dynamic patterns of deference, recruiting into his corporate self at first a small number of immediate disciples, and later, over the centuries, the authors of a massive commentarial tradition. In Confucius, we can witness the growth of a sage from a single historical person into a corporate person with a truly cultural character.

Regardless of Confucius' description of himself as a "transmitter rather than an innovator" (7/1), it is only too clear from the preceding discussions of his thought that there was a very real element of personal creativity involved in his mode of transmission. Both in his teachings and in his personal life, Confucius devoted himself to fostering the order and harmony of his cultural context. And his was a most practical ambition. Despairing of his vain attempts to secure political office, he complained (17/7): "Am I some kind of gourd? How can I allow myself to be strung up on the wall and not be eaten." In an effort to bring harmony to a world writhing in internecine warfare, he embarked on a thirteen-year tour of the central states at the end of his life. And quite in keeping with Confucius' penchant for music, it was predicted that he would be used as a bell-clapper to rouse the empire to the *tao*.[1]

In our discussion so far, we have presented the philosophy of Confucius as a sophisticated complex of ideas which, once clarified in their own historical context, might serve us in the extension of our own tradition. We have, we believe, presented Confucius to the reader not as the stereotypical moralist so characteristic of other Western understandings, but as the maker of a tradition whose thinking might provide an alternative model of what it means to do philosophy. In trying to give Confucius his best argument, we have discovered good philosophical reasons to take him seriously. And it is precisely because of our desire to appropriate relevant aspects of this Confucian philosophy for addressing issues of contemporary Western concern that we hasten to sharpen the portrait by making clear the limitations of this newly quarried resource.

Put bluntly, taken on its own terms, the extent to which the philosophy of Confucius has failed historically is a devastating criticism of its worth. By "taken on its own terms," we refer to the fact that the pragmatism of Confucian philosophy places no stock in impracticable theories, regardless of their intrinsic appeal. Further, since Confucianism is so dependent upon the Chinese cultural tradition as its storehouse of rational and evaluative structures, the quality of the achieved culture is a very real gauge of the potential that it affords for the future. With these concerns in mind, we must look critically at the tradition, impressed so deeply as it is with the signature of Confucius, and must make an accounting.

The most serious failings of Confucius' philosophy are due to the provincialism and parochialism that seem inevitably to result from the institutionalization of his thinking. In Confucius' reliance upon traditional culture we find the principal cause of what we might call "the Chinatown phenomenon." The Chinatown phenomenon is a parochialism built into the Confucian structure that retards cross-cultural communication. This parochialism is a function of the fact that all of the various dimensions of human order emerge out of personal participation in particular circumstances. Its signals are many: graduated love and responsibility, intense family loyalties, identity with a specific village even after generations as emigrants, enduring cultural identity as "Chinese," as captured for example in the concept of "overseas Chinese" (*hua-ch'iao* 華僑), and so on. Under these conditions, there is a natural tension between legitimate concern for what is most immediate in one's social environment, and the far less legitimate pursuit of personal advantage (*li** 利). As would be expected, the Chinese culture has traditionally been plagued with abuses that arise because of the fine line that keeps social order beginning at home separate from nepotism, personal loyalties from special privilege, deference to excellence from elitism, appropriate respect from graft.

The Great Wall is an interesting symbol of this Chinatown phenomenon. There is a real sense in which China itself can be fairly described as the Chinatown of the world. The Wall is a composite structure linking up the numerous smaller walls of the China of the Warring States, joining these together initially, of course, with specifically Ch'in dynastic interests in mind. As enduring a monument to unity as it is, it has been built and rebuilt over the centuries in response to expanding and contracting lines of communication, bounding within it a society of such enormous diversity that it bears closer comparison to a whole Europe than to any one European country. Even with this diversity, historically the Wall has served to separate off the culturally non-Chinese with whom communication is not possible, and to bound the heterogeneous Chinese community. Even today, the cost of a ticket to visit the present Wall, itself a reconstruction from Ming remnants, varies with your cultural identity: local tourists (*nei pin* 內賓) pay only a fraction of the cost for foreigners (*wai pin* 外賓). In a classless society, this anomaly is explicable by the simple fact that foreigners are not an integral part of the social fabric.

In our contemporary world, the doors of "Chinatown" China have opened just a crack after centuries of isolationism that have been interrupted only by the unwelcome incursions of the military, of profiteers, and of ineffectual missionaries. Even Marxism, a formal ideology with aspirations to be a social science, has been parochialized in its Chinese form to the extent that in the community of Communist countries, China is viewed with incredulity and concern.

Of course, the Confucian position fairly understood requires that the prevailing cultural norms remain ever open to negotiating novel circumstances. At least theoretically, the patternings of these norms are in fact enhanced by an increasing degree of difference. This, then, has been another failing of the Confucian tradition. Confucianism historically has been prone to ossify and become an ideology. There is a fine line between appropriate deference to the tradition and a cultural dogmatism that has too frequently been in the interests of particular groups. The patterns of deference defining this culture have been expressed in the attitudes of respect and of expectation. And where one, by whatever means, assumes the authority of the tradition, he has a basis for asserting expectations of deference.

We have represented Confucian culture and the society that embodies it as a dynamic calculus of interrelating patterns of deference. While this aesthetic model has its appeal, we must be aware of its inherent dangers. We have seen that Confucius' foremost concern was with dissemblers: persons who were not what they purported to be. And so it should have been. Where the excellent person rather than abstract principle is the final arbiter of rightness and value, the most fundamental problem shifts from judging correspondence with an existing standard or compliance with a set of defining criteria to an appreciation of personal excellence. This excellence can only be evaluated on the basis of analogies drawn from the cultural tradition in concert with an openness to creative discontinuity. Ultimately, excellence must be self-evident. It must earn others' appreciation by the disclosure of its own intrinsic worth.

Excellence so defined is the only appropriate basis for privilege and responsibility. This being the case, with the ever-present danger of dissemblers, there is a thin line between informed taste and ad hominem argument, between righteous moral indignation and self-righteousness. And where social and political status are necessary conditions for the cultivation of excellence, it is only a short step to construe such position as a guarantee of superiority.

Enculturation through education is an inescapable premise of Confucius' philosophy. Without broad-based access to a cultural tradition, the masses remain an amorphous body of subhumanity largely excluded from the possibilities of personal fulfillment. Today, one in four of China's population is still functionally illiterate. In the prerevolutionary days of this century, it was at least three in four. This is an uncomfortable fact in a community that demands education as a condition for meaningful participation. There is a great irony in the Confucian failure to provide the opportunity for widespread education. The dilemma is that opportunities for education are dependent upon economic strength and the facilities of communication and transportation that it provides. And yet the technology that has been needed to achieve these goals has been precluded in China historically by the low prestige accorded instrumental reasoning.

There is, perhaps, some wisdom in the aphorism which states: "The only problem with messiahs is that they must have disciples." This lament applies as well to sages as to messiahs, and Confucius has suffered from its truth. Adverting to Confucius' own metaphors, one might be tempted to say that the Chinese have treated their principal sage as a gourd to be hung on the wall rather than as a source of nourishment. Doubtless, that would be going too far. It would, however, be true to say that Confucius' disciples have been unable to give the same "free rein" to their hearts-and-minds as could Confucius toward the end of his life. Which is but to say that disciples seldom reach the heights of their masters. But, of course, that should not be a source of consolation or of discouragement, but of stimulation to renewed effort on the part of those who would employ Confucius as model.

The failings of Confucius' philosophy as we have described them have, in large measure, been failings of imagination. As we have interpreted Confucius, the given is the historical culture; the variable is the degree of creativity and imagination the successors have been able to muster in making the cultural tradition their own. The philosophy of Confucius as reported in the *Analects* is far from cultural dogmatism. But it has become a cultural dogmatism when those who appropriate from it do so uncreatively, failing in this enterprise to personalize it for their community by an investment of their own sense of value and importance. Where Confucianism fails, it is a failure of Confucianists to give sufficiently free rein to their creative spirit. In Confucian society where the norms are emergent from the bottom up, this responsibility has rested heavily on the higher cultural echelons of the society who have not always been of the quality to sustain these norms against the possible tyranny of imposed rulership.

Historically, creativity has been most in evidence under two prevailing conditions. There is a creativity that is sponsored by a sense of strength and authority in the state where the country feels that it can extend itself into parallel traditions and entertain external influences without threatening its cultural stability. There is also a creativity in periods such as that of the Warring States where conditions are in such turmoil that there is no cultural edifice to resist foreign influences. These influences infiltrate the society to be grafted onto the culture as the tradition again rises and reasserts itself. Contemporary China appears to have emerged from the second condition. The tradition, raising its head after a period of considerable turmoil, seems to be gradually recovering its influence on the future.

Recently, largely in the person of Tu Wei-ming, there has been talk of "third-wave Confucianism." The first wave was Confucius as a man of Lu whose teaching spread throughout the central states to become the acknowledged state ideology in the Western Han. The second wave was the gradual spread of Confucian teachings to Korea and Japan and to Southeast Asia. And the third wave, then, is the imminent impact of Confucianism as it becomes a significant factor in the evolution of Western philosophy. These extending phases of Confucian influence have always entailed an important bi-directional influence, digging deep furrows in the influenced culture, while itself being qualitatively enriched and transformed.

Our analysis of Confucius is an argument that supports this thesis, but with qualifications. The starting point is bleak. There is a perception that, up to the present, the impression of Western thought on Chinese culture has been relatively superficial. Christianity is an appropriate example. After much effort on the part of foreign missionaries, there is a Christian presence in China, perhaps, but not a cultural penetration. And the converse is true. The West is aware of Chinese culture, but there is much that is stereotyped and superficial in the quality of this understanding. Popular Western understanding of Chinese philosophy is a clear illustration, where complex ideas are so often reduced to platitudes with zither accompaniment.

But there are good cultural reasons to alter the present state of affairs. The Confucian position, as we have understood it, defines enjoyment in terms of the richness of differences. The harmony that would emerge out of the communication of Confucian philosophical ideas to the West would, from the perspective of corporate Confucius, be a desirable source of enrichment. If the failure of Confucius in the Chinese tradition has been a failure of imagination, perhaps the speculative and creative spirit of contemporary Western philosophy can go some distance to activate and enliven it.

2 Opportunities for Engagement

Third-wave Confucianism represents a phenomenon of real importance to the philosopher interested in the mutual engagement of China and the West. There is, of course, nothing inherent in the movement as it is presently constituted to require that such engagement take place. It is, after all, not necessarily the case that the most significant activities associated with the resurgence of Confucianism are taking place in China alone. There is a clear irony in the fact that the recent renewed interest in Confucius is so little a Chinese and so much a Western concern. Interpreters of Confucius such as Herbert Fingarette, Tu Wei-ming, and the authors of this work are based in American universities. Most important, neither in the People's Republic nor in the Republic of China is there widespread evidence of the desire to engage the Anglo-European philosophic scene by appeal to the Confucian sensibility. Those who are advocates of Confucianism seem to have little or no interest in Western philosophy and frequently regard Confucianism as a bulwark serving to protect Chinese culture from unwanted foreign influences.

One of the principal concerns of this essay has been to provide the basis for comparative philosophical discussions of the Confucian sensibility, with regard to both a selection of classical Western thinkers and certain contemporary Western philosophers as well. In this manner we have sought to promote the possibilities of exporting third-wave Confucianism back into the culture out of which it emerged. But our interest in comparative philosophy is motivated by a great deal more than simply the desire to provide a hearing for Confucius' thinking. There are two sides to the conversation that we hope will emerge from the present opportunities for philosophic engagement.

It is our responsibility, therefore, to indicate the bases for philosophic dialogue not only from the perspective of the Confucian sensibility, but from that of Anglo-European thought as well.

The two principal alternatives for engagement offered by Anglo-European philosophy are those of the "deconstructionist" and of the "reconstructionist" varieties. The crisis in Western philosophy has been met, as might have been expected, by two radically distinctive approaches. Not the least interesting fact about the contemporary Western philosophical scene is that, though these two types of philosopher have little if anything to say to one another, each provides important strategies for engagement with the Chinese cultural sensibility. This has much to do with the fact that the alterations in the grounds for philosophic activity in the West are such as to challenge the fundamental assumptions that have undergirded philosophic culture almost from its beginnings. Both the deconstructionists and the reconstructionists have begun to reconsider the consequences for the philosophic enterprise of the resort to notions of transcendence, dualism, and strictly historical interpretation.

Jacques Derrida[2] is responsible for the term, "deconstruction," which we shall use to designate certain of the representative thinkers of the West. Drawing the substance, if not the style, of his critique of the Western metaphysical tradition from Hegel, Nietzsche, and Heidegger, Derrida exposes the self-referential inconsistency of the mode of thinking determining that tradition. Thinking is undermined, says Derrida, by its grounding in the claim of referentiality. Referential language, the language of presence, seeks to make present the object of referral. But language only serves to mediate and cannot, therefore, make objects present. If it is the case, as Derrida claims, that the language of philosophy is a language of presence which contradicts its primary intentions by placing itself outside that which is to be made present, then the act of thinking, insofar as it employs this language, is continually unable to make good its referential claims. Thinking about "the World" in its most general character is futile because the meaning and activity of thinking is never directly characterizable; every attempt to say what we mean actually defers the meaning beyond the present moment of thinking to the contexts of mediation, temporal and textual, that constitute the matrix of interpretation sustaining thought.

There is something quite reminiscent here of the dialectical and Sophistic critiques of speculative philosophy at the end of the pre-Socratic period of Greek philosophy. Parmenides' claim, "Only Being is," defended dialectically by Zeno by recourse to a series of arguments *reductio ad absurdum* which demonstrated the rational indefensibility of motion and change, produced a variety of responses from defenders of the claims of concrete experience. Among these were the Sophists, who sought to counter the severity of the Parmenidean conclusions by making the distinction between rhetoric and reference the basis for a defense of language and thought. Thinking does not have to comport itself in accordance with the demands of reference. The persuasive, performative character of language is that which best models the activity of thinking.

In spite of a number of possible demurrers that might suggest otherwise, the consequences of Derrida's deconstruction of the Western metaphysical tradition involve a capitulation to the demands of language construed as rhetoric. And these demands shape thinking along the lines of praxis in such a manner as to make the Derridean position fall within the family of philosophic perspectives encompassed by linguistic philosophy and illustrated, as well, by Rorty's form of pragmatism considered briefly in Chapter I.

Rorty does not call himself a deconstructionist, and the resources of his critique of the tradition, although they significantly overlap those of Derrida, are drawn more from the tradition of American pragmatism, specifically that of Dewey. Nonetheless, there is a striking convergence of Rorty's programmatic aims and those of the deconstructionists. If Derrida has named deconstruction as a method, Rorty has provided a felicitous term for the immanent aim of this activity. The term is "edification." We recall from our initial discussion of his thought that edification is an activity consequent upon the rejection of the traditional aim of philosophic thinking as establishing general theories which ground cultural experience and expression. We do not seek to understand "the World," but to articulate our relations to our different intellectual and social contexts and the relations of these contexts to one another.[3]

> The attempt to edify (ourselves and others) may consist in the hermeneutical activity of making connections between our own culture and some exotic culture, or between our own discipline and another

discipline which seems to pursue incommensurable aims in an incommensurable vocabulary. But it may consist in the "poetic" activity of thinking up new aims, new words, or new disciplines, followed by, so to speak, the inverse of hermeneutics: the attempt to reinterpret our familiar surroundings in the unfamiliar terms of our new inventions.

Rorty's proposal is an interesting one, certainly. With specific reference to the aims of this work, which involve making connections between our culture and that of the "exotic culture" of the Chinese, the role of mutual edification is certainly to be desired. Indeed, in Rorty's terms it does appear that such connections should be given priority as an endeavor. Discourse of the edifying variety is always dialectically related to "normal discourse," the traditional language of one's culture. To be truly "edifying," one's language must be sufficiently alternative to count as in fact novel. Otherwise, edifying discourse is an altogether polite form of "on the contrary" or "on the other hand" thinking that merely perpetuates in a tediously interminable manner the inventory of alternative notions displayed by the traditional culture.

Dialectical engagement, even of the conversational variety endorsed by Rorty, entails the obvious fact that the antithesis of any given thesis is shaped by the character of the engagement itself. The dialectic of such philosophic alternatives as idealism, materialism, and existentialism, which patterns Anglo-European history does not seem to provide real hope that thinking proceeds to anything novel, but rather suggests that there can only be the substitution of one style of thinking for another. And, as the history of Western philosophy seems to illustrate so well, any given style of thinking may be expected to come into its own again and again.

Thinking, at the level of philosophical ideas (as opposed to technical applications) merely perpetuates our historical culture through the dialectical exchange of one complex of ideas for another. This *agon*, this contest, which purports to substitute edifying thinking for systematic thinking, may in fact be nothing more than an alternative manner of describing what in fact the history of philosophy amounts to when viewed from a dispassionate perspective. That is to say, the actual interchange between one system and another, which leads to alterations in the character of an epoch, constitutes a "conversation" of sorts. After all, progress in philosophy is difficult to defend. The clearer, more cogent understanding of philosophy seems to be that it is a complex, nonprogressive interchange of theories, the primary expressions of which have derived from the classical period and which are found to be alternatively relevant as history moves from one epoch to another.

Rorty's philosophic program shares with the Derridean form of deconstruction the view that the function of the "philosopher," if such a term survives, is to provide polemical deconstructions of the tradition aimed at demonstrating the consequences of taking up one theoretical stance as opposed to another. To the deconstructionist activity Rorty allows the addition of the constructive endeavor of engagement with alternative cultures and "thinking up" new aims or ideas. In this latter sense, Rorty's philosophic program is consistent with the one implicit in this essay. For, on the one hand, the search for active interchange with Chinese philosophic culture is motivated by the disconstitution of the Western philosophic tradition which has been the intended product of the deconstructionists and the unintended by-product of the frustrated purpose of the systematic philosophers. And, on the other hand, this interchange, we recognize, requires "thinking up" what from the perspective of our traditional culture may be new ideas in order to establish a common language. Effectively, then, the attempt to engage Chinese and Western philosophic sensibilities can lead to edification in the strictest sense, for there is true novelty to be found in the mutual articulation of Chinese and Anglo-European cultures.

Rorty's rather polite notion of thinking as edification provides, if not a cultural ground, at least a cultural reference for thinking. There is another thinker of the "deconstructive" variety who promotes a decidedly more serious-minded approach to philosophic activity. Michel Foucault[4] holds thinking to be inexorably politicized, culture itself being but a complex of practices which, at any given moment, determine the nature of a particular cultural epoch. Neither Rorty nor Foucault suggests that thinking must be characterized in terms of a general theory; each focuses upon the practical constitution of thinking in the process of reacting to and critiquing current forms of thought and practice. Foucault, however, is much more inclined than is Rorty to discover the roots of knowledge in the particular activities that characterize the manner in which power is distributed in any given society.

The direct link between knowledge and power for Foucault entails the consequence that there are always ideological commitments which define the character and limits of knowledge, and that knowing, therefore, is never anything other than political. The discovery, organization, and dissemination of knowledge in society is a function of disciplines, professions, and institutions that qualify some and disqualify others to perform authoritatively with respect to these enterprises. Authoritative activities of the physicians, psychiatrists, philosophers, and so forth, determine the nature of the objects investigated by these functionaries, as well as the distinctive character of the functionaries themselves. Disciplinary, professional, and institutional practices are discursive in the sense that they are constituted by the sort of language employed to originate the intentions, decisions, and actions associated with these practices. Such practices cannot be said to exist naturally; they are, on the contrary, ideologically based, grounded in the arbitrary and partisan activities associated with the attainment and maintenance of power in a society.

Under conditions such as these, thinking in its purest form is (and this is, ironically enough, consonant with Rorty's less radical view) an ad hoc, reactive response that challenges the ideological character of a specific act of disciplinary, professional, or institutional practice. This is a rather subtle form of the Sophistic view that "man is the measure," but no less Sophistic for that. Knowing is a kind of doing; more specifically, it is a kind of making. But, except in the rarest of circumstances, no one makes himself or herself; one is the product of societal practices that come into being in a piecemeal fashion.

It is possible to see lurking behind Derrida, Rorty, and Foucault, and a host of other contemporary thinkers, the figure of Friedrich Nietzsche, whose claim "God is Dead!" was meant to sound the death knell of all philosophic programs grounded in the notion of transcendence—which is to say, effectively all classical philosophic programs in the West. It is the ideological ground of philosophic culture that the deconstructionists wish to consider. The distinction between the types of deconstruction is, in fact, a distinction between the specific sense each gives to the notion of philosophy as a rhetorical activity. Whereas Rorty and Derrida consider the rhetoric of texts per se in terms of the styles of thinking and the consequences of employing certain narrative principles, Foucault conceives thinking to be contextualized by quasi-political ideologies. Thus, thinking, except in rare instances, is always an apology for present social, political, and economic praxis.

The variant forms of the "deconstructing" mentality eschew theoretical formulations. The trouble with the sort of thinking that rejects theoretical constructions is that it tends to be reductive. The capacities of deconstructionist alternatives to generate creative modes of thought are limited to the parasitical operations of undoing theoretical constructions in order to celebrate the incoherent, uncentered, unprincipled character of texts and traditions (Derrida, Rorty) or the dissolution of belief in the objectivity of professions and institutions as means of guiding the acquisition of knowledge (Foucault). The realization of an essential unity of theory and practice cannot be achieved simply by reducing theory to practice—either in Derrida's manner of deconstructing the texts in order to demonstrate their dependence upon narrative principles that are arbitrary and ad hoc nor in Rorty's manner of finding in thinking an expression of edifying discourse that challenges normal discourse nor in Foucault's way of characterizing thinking as an ideological response to ideological discourse that has come to have an institutional ground.

Perhaps the principal value of deconstructive thought, from the perspective of this present work, is that it provides a critique of transcendence. And, in so doing, it brings an interpretation of the character of philosophic activity that suggests strong commonalities with the Confucian sensibility expressed in this essay. In Derrida's critique of the "language of presence," in Rorty's rejection of the vision of philosophy as a foundational discipline, as well as in Foucault's claim that knowledge is a function of the power relations expressed in social practices, there is a consistent challenge to any notion of transcendence, whether theological or rational. And without such transcendence there can be no appeal to standards or ideals, principles or methodologies that serve to guide historical process. Viewed historically, there is discontinuity and incommensurability. The context of interpretation in which the philosopher operates is one of culture as the presented repository of received significances. History becomes tradition, and tradition serves as an immanent matrix of intrinsically related significances that constitute the resource for all meaning-disclosing and meaning-creating activities.

Do reconstructive programs, those that demand the activity of theory construction, provide grounds for engagement with Chinese culture and philosophy? Jürgen Habermas is one of the most significant of the reconstructive thinkers. Like Foucault, Habermas notes the intrinsic relationship between knowledge and the specific character of effective discourse employed within a given social context. For Habermas, the character of discursive communication is determined by those human interests that guide the construction of conventions and institutions, and that serve as the basis of interpretation by providing the standards of "objectivity." The difference between Foucault and Habermas is considerable, however. For Habermas, interests have a certain universality with respect to the condition of being human. In particular, the "emancipatory interest" defines the central human motivation that permits the construction of a theory of communication having the power to free individuals from bondage to narrow, dehumanizing interests. Foucault is, of course, much less sanguine about the possibility of thinking oneself out of such bondage.

Habermas, in his earlier work, attempted to develop a theory of knowledge that accedes to the practical character of knowing by noting the connection between knowledge and human interests but which conjoins theory and practice by discovering in the notion of emancipation the focal point of both interest and knowledge.[5]

> In self-reflection knowledge for the sake of knowledge attains congruence with the interest in autonomy and responsibility. The emancipatory cognitive interest aims at the pursuit of reflection as such. . . . [I]n the power of self-reflection, knowledge and interest are one.

Lately, Habermas has sought to provide a theory of "communicative competence" which promotes universal structures for social discourse. He seeks a theory which is ideologically free of the sorts of partisan interests which Foucault deems ineradicable from our language. The chief defect of this theory is not found within the theory itself but is, rather, a function of the fact that there are no grounds for expecting that it will have any significant sort of influence. To have the sort of impact on the notion of "thinking" that would be required to meet the perceived ambiguity which that concept has acquired for the past generation, Habermas' theory would have to be extensively applied. But as yet there are few programmatic suggestions concerning the manner in which the theory may be implemented. And the inherent pluralism of the contemporary Anglo-European philosophic scene argues against the extensive implementation of any single theory.

From the perspective of the Chinese, Habermas' thinking may be found interesting for two closely related reasons. First, Habermas has been influenced by Marx and is in the broad sense interpretable as a Marxist thinker. Second, Habermas has assessed the interrelations of science and technology with the humanistic elements of contemporary culture more insightfully than most contemporary thinkers. The desire to understand Western thought and culture must lead one to an understanding of the social consequences of science and technology. In fact, the brand of Marxism that one finds in Habermas is shaped in large measure by his understanding of the technological phenomenon. His thinking, therefore, provides a unique opportunity for the Chinese to understand the manner in which Marxist thinking has been adjusted by a recognition of the consequences of technology.

Unfortunately, Habermas has himself paid little attention to Chinese thought. There is another important reconstructive thinker, however, who has taken some notice of Chinese philosophic thinking in the development and explication of his systematic philosophy. Robert Neville has in fact made an attempt to assess the value of the Neo-Confucian tradition, particularly as expressed through Wang Yang-ming, for his philosophic thinking.

Neville's project is nothing short of an attempt to reconstruct the meaning of thinking in the Western tradition. He hopes to supply a systematic philosophy that can again give philosophy a metaphysical grounding. Directly challenging Heidegger's claim that philosophic thinking can be "neither metaphysics nor science" and Rorty's assertion that foundational thinking is no longer productive, Neville has provided a subtle and sophisticated reconstruction of philosophic thought.

Neville notes the limitations of Dewey's similar reconstructive endeavor in *The Reconstruction of Philosophy*. He criticizes Dewey because he "did not carry out the reform of the categories necessary for his proposed reconstruction."[6] Neville's work is a self-conscious attempt to reinstate philosophy as metaphysics and to position it once again in a normative relationship with the special sciences.

For Neville, philosophic thinking involves or presupposes the construction of a theory. The concepts or categories of the theory are offered as relatively undetermined constructs, the meanings of which may be stipulated within the various specialized disciplines, or with respect to a general cosmological scheme. Thinking moves "upward" toward increased generality and "downward" toward increasing specificity. The thinker is an articulator, an interpreter. And this function of interpretation presupposes, in addition to theory construction, the full expression of the imagination, and a commitment to a responsible appropriation of the consequences of one's thinking.

Neville has directly challenged the deconstructionist thinkers at the level at which the latter claim philosophic thinking in our age must be neither metaphysics nor science. On the contrary, Neville responds, thinking ranges between the abstract generality of metaphysics and the concrete specificity of the various sciences, as well as the pre- and post-theoretical spheres of imagination and responsibility. But there is a fundamental agreement between Neville and the deconstructionists, and Habermas as well. All these philosophers agree that thinking is a fundamentally valuative enterprise.[7]

> Thinking is founded in valuation . . . [which] supplies and justifies
> the norms that guide thinking to be rational when it is; therefore,
> valuation, in several related senses, is the foundation of reason.

Thinking is broader than reasoning. The activity of the thinker involves a number of dimensions that expand its role far beyond that of mere "cognition."

Neville's style of philosophizing may in fact be found altogether too rationalistic from the perspective of proponents of classical Chinese philosophy. And Chinese Marxists may find it insufficiently oriented toward praxis. Given Neville's systematic intent, however, he cannot ignore the tradition of Chinese philosophy. His project is to say something relevant about the nature of thinking per se, and to do so he must apprise himself of the major philosophic traditions which have given some meaning to that activity. His interest in the Chinese tradition is, therefore, a necessary implication of his philosophic perspective.

The selected thinkers presented here in but the sketchiest of outline do not by any means exhaust the alternative expressions of the philosophic spirit in contemporary Anglo-European culture; they do, however, represent significant options for engagement in the enterprise of comparative philosophy. Derrida and Rorty provide models of philosophic activity that concentrate upon its conversational function. Each deemphasizes dogmatic content in favor of the form of the engagement itself. Parties to the activity of "edification" are not forced into a defensive stance. Habermas and Foucault promote alternative styles of thinking that have some important relationship to Marxian philosophy. Even though their forms of Marxism might be unpalatable, they could well permit productive engagement by providing a philosophic resource and vocabulary relatively familiar to an important segment of the Chinese intellectual community. Finally, Neville's desire to create a philosophic system adequate to the task of grounding general cultural understanding motivates him to engage Chinese philosophic resources as a means of avoiding provincialism.

3   Invitation to a Future

In the process of thinking through Confucius we have highlighted his commitment to a pattern of interrelating structures that emerge out of concrete situations to reflexively organize and regulate human life in the world. This "patterning" is culture (*wen**文*). Significantly, culture is not simply *wen**文*, but *wen* hua 文化: patterning as a dynamic, emergent process. Having examined Confucius from the vantage point of our own Western philosophical tradition, we can focus on the nature of these norms as a major point of contrast with our own tradition's persistent appeal to universal principles. The appeal to abstract reason, categorical imperatives, scientific laws, ethical principles, and historical "facts" has served us well, and provided our tradition with a stabilizing foundation. In fact, an argument can be made that idealizations grounded in these universal principles are a necessary condition for respectable science, both natural and moral.

This commitment to objective principles has provided us with more than natural science and philosophical rigor. In our own time, at the broader level of social and political science, it has inspired internationalism and provided us with a basis for talking across cultures. Practically, it gave birth to the concept of a United Nations, arms us against racism, and supports our democratic ideals. But it has not been an entirely unmixed blessing. The kind of objective certainty derived from our commitment to universal principles has convinced us of the unassailable worth of scientific knowledge, encouraging us at times to equate scientific progress with civilization itself.

There has been a tendency to exaggerate the rational aspect of the human being in the definition of humanity. This rational prejudice has fostered an unwarranted confidence in the quality of our own cultural achievements and social institutions. In comparing the "progress" of our tradition with that of the Chinese, we, from the brink of nuclear holocaust, ask condescendingly, "Why didn't the Chinese develop science?" Rather than apologetically invoking their "gunpowder, compass, and moveable type" rejoinder, a more Confucian response, that would in fact account for how the Chinese used these specific inventions, is that scientific knowledge has served cultural norms. Put another way, we are preoccupied with science; China, with culture.

If we look at ourselves critically, our principled beliefs have at times given rise to cultural chauvinism. They help to justify our economic tyranny over the Third World, propel us confidently into our Vietnams, and are our warrant for pronouncing judgment on the cultural standards of other nations. These negative consequences, as we all know, go some way toward subverting our erstwhile ideals.

The problem for our tradition has been simple yet enduring, taking us back in one form or another to the birth of Western philosophy: how do we translate abstract principles into the concrete world? The Chinese experience, both in terms of successes and failures, in many ways has been the mirror opposite. With norms and structures that emerge out of particular circumstances, the perennial problem in that tradition has not been to bring abstract principles into the world, but rather to extend concrete norms outward and broaden their jurisdiction to the widest possible community.

The Confucian model of negotiating analogy from particular instances of reasonableness imbedded in the past or certain remembered examples of goodness to serve as appropriate models for present circumstances means that in order for one to be persuaded, one must have a shared cultural heritage, and must acknowledge its historical authority. In this way of thinking, culture as the repository of those historical instances that have evoked deference serves to some significant extent as the functional equivalent of our abstract reason. This reasoning by analogy is most immediately compelling where situations are more similar than different. In fact, the applicability of the available norms would seem to decrease in inverse proportion to the degree of difference. In this case, the person who is not persuaded by such appeal is not pronounced "unreasonable" or "unethical," but "uncultured" or "a barbarian." To "prehend" the incomprehensible or "scrute" the inscrutable, as it were, one must in some real sense become culturally Chinese.

Where rationality is determined by immanent cultural norms, a wholesale repudiation of culture is a repudiation of normality. Under these conditions, the recent Great Cultural Revolution and its constitutive "Criticism of Confucius (p'i K'ung 批孔) Campaign," as a patent rejection of the worth of traditional culture, must be construed, like the Ch'in "Burning of the Books," as a period of national madness mitigated only by the obvious extent of its failure. Ironically, the insanity of the Cultural Revolution has added needed impetus to the positive reevaluation of traditional culture that is occurring in contemporary China.

Were we to attempt a realistic assessment of the likelihood of future dialogue between China and the West, we might initially find little about which to be encouraged. It is quite likely that the majority of Western philosophers would refuse Confucius a membership in the official canon of Anglo-European philosophy, since he did not consider the "real philosophic problems." And how would Western philosophic discussions be digestable by the Chinese whose sense of the philosophic enterprise has always been predicated upon a rather provincial attitude toward other cultures? Common sense would tell one that both of these types of exclusiveness surely ought to undermine themselves due to the fact that, in each case, they are predicated upon a rather narrow selection of philosophic evidences. The reverse is true, however: narrow methodologies promote the most pernicious forms of obscurantism. The dogmatic character of both Anglo-European and Chinese philosophies would seem to be no exception.

Allied to these considerations there are the linguistic and conceptual barriers to be considered, although these have become less serious recently due to the gradual yet promising maturation of the linguistic and philosophic skills of the interpreters of Chinese thought. Vigilance is essential, nevertheless, for the temptation to construe an alien culture in the more comfortable terms of one's own interpretive constructs is altogether too powerful to ignore. The dogmatism of some analytic philosopher is no less detrimental to an understanding of Chinese philosophy and culture than was the theological dogmatism of previous generations of translators and interpreters who introduced China to the West. And the provincialism of the Chinese can easily motivate the attempted sinicization of all things Western, including Western philosophy.

There are, perhaps, more specific ideological barriers standing between China and the West. One would certainly want to take seriously the importance of Marxist ideology in China. Is there now, as seemed to be the case but a few years ago, a "party line" in China which permits neither contradiction nor critique? The fact that a translation of this book is being published in China would seem to argue the contrary, for we can hardly be said to have presented a Marxist Confucius. China is opening its doors to other cultures and forms of thinking in a most dramatic manner. Marxism is no longer the only perspective from which to interpret the Chinese or from which the Chinese themselves view the world. This is but to say that Marxism may be fading as an ideology and may soon exist in the form of a philosophy, a form in which its principal contentions may be discussed and debated. Moreover, the existence of vital strains of Marxism in the West, in thinkers as divergent as Michel Foucault and Jürgen Habermas, ensures that such discussions, fruitful to both parties, may in fact take place.

Even if Marxist criticisms of Confucius are no longer determinative of the Chinese intellectual scene, just how important is Confucius and Confucianism in contemporary China? Are the Chinese again open to explicit utilization of Confucian categories in their cultural analyses? Is "third-wave Confucianism" a movement which can only be nurtured outside of China? It is our hope, indeed our expectation, that this will not be the case. We must assume that the underlying importance of traditional continuities in China will reassert themselves in a manner that will promote a resurgence of interest in Confucian studies.

Of course, a renewal of interest in Confucius may itself be ideologically shaped. For it may express itself in terms of that special form of Neo-Confucianism against which the communist revolution was ostensibly directed. Such an eventuality would certainly suggest the resurgence of the familiar pattern of Chinese provincialism that has traditionally been assumed essential to protect the cultural homogeneity and autonomy of the Chinese people.

This is a legitimate concern. It certainly is the case that China has prized its continuity with its past as one of the principal guarantors of its social stability. The genius of Confucius was directed precisely toward understanding and articulating the value of tradition as the source and foundation of society and culture. Chinese continuity with its past has been realized only by recourse to the exercise of a cultural provincialism that rejects uncontrolled interactions at the political, economic, intellectual, and artistic levels. The least attractive form of this provincialism is the Chinatown phenomenon to which we have alluded.

The threat to productive communication inherent in this provincial perspective raises a question that readers of this work may have already asked themselves: "Is Chinese philosophy importable?" Confucian thought grounds itself in a continuous tradition, eschews dialectical forms of argumentation, rejects the value of abstract hypotheses, shows little interest in questions of a scientific and technological nature, and approaches ethical and social concerns along distinctively aesthetic lines which challenge the traditional Western belief in the value of ethical reasoning and ethical theories. The problematic of Chinese thinking is sufficiently different from that of traditional Western thought to raise serious questions in some philosophic minds about the possibility of translating it into a Western idiom. And even if our attempt to provide grounds for believing Confucian thought relevant to contemporary philosophic discussions were successful, it is unlikely that any serious comparative endeavor could proceed without the serious commitment of the Chinese. There is as yet little indication that such a commitment is to be forthcoming.

There is certainly nothing wrong with claiming that we ought learn about Chinese thinking simply in order that we may better communicate with our Chinese neighbors. There is a problem, however. The West believes the ideology undergirding its technological societies to be eminently exportable. Inherent in the technological state of mind is the belief that scientific and technological progress is essential to the attainment and maintenance of an acceptable standard of human life on the surface of this planet. We have a true missionary zeal for exporting our ideology to our neighbors. Such zeal is a consequence of our essentially quantitative mode of thinking in economics and science, which leads us to be perhaps overly impressed by our *measurable* successes. China may not be disposed to engage the West, preferring to maintain its traditional isolationist stance. But the Western world is eager to engage the Chinese. Indeed, the small concessions of the Chinese to capitalist motivations and to the importation of technologies have many Western entrepreneurs believing that it is only a matter of time before China accepts the capitalism and technicism of the West.

The fact that Western cultural commentators have now begun to raise serious questions about the consequences of scientific and technological interests is significant. At the very least the putative value-neutrality of the scientific and technical enterprises has been called into question. Questioning the objectivity and value-neutrality of scientific and technical interests is both cause and consequence of various philosophic debates in contemporary Anglo-European culture. As noted in our discussion of the conditions of thinking in Western philosophy, there is an emerging consensus that thinking is intrinsically valuational, a view that directly challenges the objectivity of scientific reasoning and its applications. But as we have also suggested, the attempt to reconstruct philosophy in such a manner as to employ an interpretation of thinking as valuational flies in the face of four centuries of the dominance in the West of the mathematical-physical model of thinking as primarily calculative and logistic in nature.

We are faced with a most interesting dilemma. This present essay is written in the belief that Anglo-European culture is in need precisely of the sort of philosophic enterprise which Confucius' valuational thinking represents. Moreover, recourse to Confucian thought could conceivably inspire the creation of new models for the activity of thinking by Western philosophers. But the provincialism of the Chinese militates against the sort of engagement that would render this a real possibility. And certainly it is the case that the theoretical pluralism of Western culture would not permit the easy development of a style of thinking that requires continuity with the past in the manner of Confucian thought.

On the other hand, there is suspicion that the eminently exportable method of scientific and technical reasoning and practice may be much less culture-neutral than has heretofore been claimed. That is, Chinese intellectuals may not be far off the mark in their concern for damaging effects that Western science and technology may have upon Chinese culture and values.

One may recall the impact on China of pragmatism and various forms of scientism in the early decades of this century. When Dewey lectured in China in 1919–1920, he was perceived primarily as a champion of scientific reasoning and practice.[8] The later reaction against the West and specifically the character and consequences of Western technology came to be a reaction against Dewey himself, inappropriately. Recognition that the importation of science and its attendant technology, fueled by the capitalist impulse, would require a social reconstruction of vast and far-reaching consequences made the cultural Chinese extremely suspicious. It is not a question of right and wrong sytems, but of the need to preserve a way of life that by virtue of its stability and continuity has insured the persistence of important values. Will Chinese react once more against what they perceive to be a too rapid incursion by the West? One way such a reaction can be avoided is if Westerners learn something of the culture of China so as to be sensitive to the manner in which a limited and value-shaped exportation of technological and economic accomplishments can insure the long-term success of the mutual engagement.

But China really has no choice. Isolation is increasingly less feasible, and becoming a member of the world community involves a nation in the technological matrix that sustains its economic and political activities at the international level. And although it would be an exaggeration to say that the West likewise has no choice but to seek out the intellectual and cultural resources of the Chinese, it is clear that failure to do so carries with it great risk. This is so if for no other reason than that we are too likely to make serious and humiliating diplomatic blunders if we attempt communication at economic and political levels without a better understanding of the Chinese cultural sensibility.

Paradoxically, it is more essential that the technicians, politicians, and businessmen who are courting the Chinese appreciate the Chinese culture at the level of art and philosophy than that they understand their own. The rift between theory and practice is a given of Anglo-European culture. There is little expectation that a politician, technician, or business executive need know much about the art or philosophy of his own culture, and were he to have such knowledge it would be of little use to him in his professional life. There is the claim of greater continuity in China, however, between the ideas and values of the culture and its economic and political activity. Some understanding of the lineaments of Chinese high culture would render one more effective in dealing with the Chinese sociopolitical establishment.

But there are more subtle risks. Failure to engage the Chinese intellectual scene at this crucial period of our contrasting histories could lead us to miss a singular opportunity to discover something momentous about ourselves. It is at least possible that we could learn to appreciate that the cluster of philosophic orientations that have dominated our intellectual history is in fact incomplete. Such an understanding would motivate us to recognize that the failure of our philosophic program so often mourned and celebrated in contemporary Western philosophy does not mean the end of philosophy per se nor of the culture that sustains it. Also, the recognition of our intellectual limitations could seriously qualify the chauvinism implicit in our all-too-smug appraisal of the efficacy of our science and technology.

The increased possibilities for dialogue are partly a result of the transformation of the Western philosophic scene, away from the forms of thinking that define philosophic thinking narrowly in accordance with quantitative criteria of the sort that ground science and technology, in the direction of activities that constitute critiques of just those modalities. In style and substance Anglo-European philosophies are less technical, less dogmatic, and more open to a significant plurality of perspectives than was formerly the case. As we indicated in our introductory discussions of the problem of philosophic thinking in Chapter I, the primary sorts of philosophic activity in the contemporary West are predicated upon the recognition of a crisis in the nature of philosophy itself. There has been a turn toward praxis in its pragmatic, existential, phenomenological, and speculative dimensions. This turn toward praxis has been experienced as a demand for the reconceptualization of the task of philosophy per se. Thus, one of the principal areas of engagement with Chinese thought and culture could well be that which leads to discussions about the role and function of the philosophic enterprise.

The philosophic vision underlying this interpretation of Confucius has a reconstructive intent, although its conclusions may in fact seem to share much with the deconstructionist position. Much of our analysis of Confucius is decidedly sympathetic, and both within this work and beyond it we have sought to develop insights into the philosophy of culture and comparative philosophy that offer possibilities for productive engagement with Chinese philosophy and culture. In our attempt to employ the classical Chinese sensibility as a means of understanding the crisis of Western philosophy, as well as in our endeavor to bring Western notions of pluralism and process to bear upon Confucius' sensibility as a means of articulating his position with greater clarity and relevance, we have attempted to model the activity of comparative thinking that has served as the subject matter of this essay.

The reconstructive project underlying this work is bound by a method of philosophical construction that has been employed often in the past. This culturalogical method might be outlined as follows:[9] turning away from the apparently impoverished sources for speculation in our philosophic present, the philosopher moves to the more esoteric elements of his cultural milieu, in order to find novel evidence. But if he is to find such novelty, he needs to discover a place from which to view it. The dominant modes of his cultural present offer no such vantage point, since these are seen to be consequences of the historical past as construed from that dominant present. For this reason, it becomes necessary to seek out other cultures as well. What from our perspective might appear radically novel may be found within an alternative cultural mainstream.

The culturalogical method we have employed ultimately justifies the cross-cultural anachronism that characterizes our resort to Confucius' thinking as a means of addressing philosophic issues of contemporary concern in Anglo-European culture. Comparative philosophy has as one of its most significant aims the uncovering of neglected elements of one's own culture by recourse to the stimulation that comes from investigation of alternative cultural sensibilities. In fact anachronism is a false issue unless one is enamored of the strictest forms of progressivism. We are always involved in mining the resources of the past in order to meet the presumed needs of a particular historical present. We would certainly be naive were we to think that we had avoided imputing to an earlier thinker some of the senses of his notions that have accrued over time. Likewise, would it really be possible to articulate the thinking of the past in a meaningful manner if we did not risk reshaping the present, to however slight a degree, in terms of our (one hopes responsible) assessment of historically prior reflections?

It would be impossible to appreciate the thinking of an archaic Chinese sage were we to permit our matrix of interpretation to be patterned only historically. For even if we agreed, as most philosophers surely would, that the history of philosophy must be considered as both a story of "how we got this way" and a collection of accounts that should be examined *in situ*, it is most unlikely that a particular philosopher, abstracted from his place in the received interpretations of developmental history, would be found altogether interesting except insofar as his thinking provided an eccentric vantage point from which a contemporary philosopher might eye the present with respect to his own particular past, or served as a model of abstract or speculative thinking. And each of these motivations for looking at a particular philosopher outside of the historical timeline is but a thinly disguised form of provincialism.

The creative use of anachronism can involve resort to a past view that might serve as a resource for the development of such an alternative to a present doctrine. Or it can facilitate the correction of explicit or implicit interpretations of a thinker in order to present the original source in a purer way, permitting it to serve as a repository of insights for future constructions. We have yielded to both motivations in this work. In the first sense, we have sought to demonstrate the value of Confucius' sensibility for certain conceptual reconstructions already begun in contemporary Anglo-European philosophy. In the second sense we have attempted to correct in some measure the traditional interpretations of Confucius' philosophy in order, first, to provide a novel perspective upon his thinking within his own cultural milieu and, of equal importance, to preclude the misconstrual of Confucian insights by those for whom classical Chinese thinking is not only exoteric but unfamiliar. All this is but to say that we are not only offering Confucius as a supplement and corrective to thinking in the West, but we are, as well, offering Confucius to the Chinese Marxists and Neo-Confucians within contemporary China.

It is simply not possible, nor would it be productive, to accept historicist assumptions as the basis for comparative considerations when the two cultures being compared do not agree on the validity of these assumptions. Our discussion of the distinctive attitudes toward "history" and "tradition" in Chinese and Western cultures should have called attention to the necessity to bracket any historicist impulse we might wish to exercise in cross-cultural comparisons of the sort contained in this work. And, fortunately for our approach, it is no longer the case that historicism dominates the Western sensibility nearly to the degree that it once did.

By claiming that contemporary Western culture is increasingly less dominated by historicist and progressivist assumptions, we are assenting to the sort of claim made by those who find that the character of intellectual culture in the West is "postmodern." Postmodernism, admittedly a rather faddish movement in recent cultural analysis, does have the virtue of summing up in its most popular expressions the same kind of criticisms as those forwarded by the deconstructive thinkers considered above. The term "postmodernism" suggests that we are in a period of transition in which we no longer consider ourselves defined by the elements of modern culture whose primary expressions were rationalism, industrial capitalism, and belief in scientific and technological progress, but not yet in a position to delineate in any positive sense any emergent cultural self-consciousness.

Three intertwined beliefs help to articulate the concept of modernism. The first and most pervasive by far is that which affirmed the importance of "quantitative thinking." When Descartes mapped geometry onto algebra and then mapped nature onto the resulting analytic geometry, he provided a most powerful impetus to quantitative thinking. This procedure, anticipated by Francis Bacon and Thomas Hobbes with respect to somewhat simpler arithmetical models, and ramified by Leibniz and Newton with regard to the differential calculus, found its way into the major streams of Western thought after the seventeenth century.

The second belief was that which asserted the possibility of developing complete systems of thought that would be finally true of the world. This presumption was both cause and consequence of the quantification of the speculative imagination. The quantification of thinking and the attendant "quest for certainty" together gave powerful support to the third belief: the belief in scientific and technological progress.

The presumption that the present and the future transcend the past along some desirable line of development is fundamental to the historicist assumptions of modern Western culture. Claims to programmatic certainty provide present knowledge with some privileged position vis-à-vis the past. And quantitative thinking is the primary support for such a claim at both the theoretical and practical levels, since the sorts of things that may be measured, quantified, are the sorts of things about which we can become "certain." Postmodernism has emerged out of the conflict occasioned by the challenge to these three beliefs.

It might seem difficult to discover any changes away from the quantitative character of contemporary Western culture given the pervasive spread of computer technology. What could be more indicative of the persistence of quantitative thinking than the "bits and chips" patois so prevalent among computer literati? But the ad hoc character of computer processes gives an alternative rendering to the notion of quantitative activity. For without the interpretive schemes that make sense of stored data, there is simply an accumulation of information passive to numerous interpretations. History, insofar as it is conditioned by the computer as a "retrieval device," becomes the blind process of mere accretion open to as many distinctive accounts as there are individuals to provide them. Choices concerning what sorts of interpretive schemes may be employed are qualitative choices to the extent that they eschew the acceptance of a single overarching systematic matrix of meaningfulness and move toward the exercise of a plurality of tactical principles of interpretation. The mere existence of retrieval devices which guarantee that uncoordinated data will not be lost makes it unnecessary to resort to theoretical narratives in advance as a means of saving the events of history and rendering them meaningful.

The sharpening debate among the sciences and humanities is a consequence of a series of critiques of quantitative thinking which began most dramatically with Nietzsche in the late nineteenth century, but which have realized their greatest strengths only very recently with contemporary philosophic critics of the sort we have previously discussed. Postmodernism's flight from certainty, its capitulation to theoretical relativity and incommensurability, its reintroduction of the qualitative dimension into both its humanistic and scientific understandings, have challenged contemporary intellectuals' continued belief in the unilateral transcendence of the past. In fact, postmodernism renders the very notion of linear history suspect.

There is no reason for us to be concerned, therefore, about the unsynchronized comparisons of classical Chinese and contemporary Western culture. We do not have to fit Confucius into some dominant interpretive scheme that defines our historical movement. For at the level of historical consciousness, there is no clear path laid out for us, no Manifest Destiny. Our resources for cultural self-understanding contain a congeries of methods, principles, and interpretations that have shown a most insistent ability to remain intact and available—"our name is legion."

The vision of contemporary Western culture emerging from the postmodernist critiques is, we believe, neither desperate nor cynical. There is no longer history, there are "histories." These histories constitute ways of conceiving a (selected) present in relation to its effective past. In the West the search for a single thread connecting present and past can only be motivated by political ideologies upholding the rapidly disintegrating myth of consensus or by romanticized rationalists propounding the equally anemic myth of progress.

No longer viewed in terms of epochs, or ages, or unfolding absolutes, history need not be distinguished from culture. Historicist reductions of cultural experience become increasingly difficult the greater is our sense of cultural self-consciousness. For if culture, as the presented immediacy of communal experience and expression, is thought to contain the meaningful past in its entirety and show it forth in a conceptually exhaustive manner, the sense of novel historical genesis may be lost. The Hegelian claim that history, construed as the unfolding of cultural self-consciousness, has come to an end seems increasingly to be a given of those persuaded by the postmodernist analysis of Western society and culture. Culture and history are now jointly constituted. Together they form a diachronous web, the strands of which lead backward into multifarious pasts and forward toward a presently unintegratable plurality of presents. History, thus, becomes tradition; not, to be sure, a contin-

uous tradition, for the postmodernist finds the notion of such continuity neither desirable nor possible. Nevertheless, taking its pluralistic assumptions into account, the possibility of the West freeing
itself from-the notion of linear, progressive history suggests an
interesting convergence between traditionalist China and the West.

On balance, the final pages of this essay might appear less
optimistic than one might wish. Western culture, we have said,
through the theoretical activities of its principal philosophers, ad-
vertises its need for the resources of Confucian thinking. But the
significant gap between philosophic activity and the technological,
political and economic activities which will most directly shape any
encounter with the Chinese, suggests that, even if philosophic discussions took place, they might not touch the concrete issues addressed by Anglo-European practical culture. And we have argued
that, willy-nilly, the Chinese will be compelled to seek interaction
with the West because of practical motives associated with the need
to forego isolationism. They will certainly not be inclined to interact
at a level they feel will not serve their most immediate needs. Hardly
the best conditions for dialogue.

To the charge of overly cautious optimism, we plead guilty, but
with extenuating circumstances. We cannot, by literary fiat, undo
conditions shaped by the inertia of centuries. The specific issues
fundamental to any possible cultural interactions, as well as the
character of these interactions, will be determined beyond these pages.
Whether such engagements will be experienced as a clash of ideologies, receding into the grudging sidewise glances of two mutually
suspicious cultures, or as an enriching and productive sharing of
intellectual and aesthetic sensibilities with informative, even transformative, potential, no one of us is, at present, in any position to
say.

Notes

Apologia

1 Northrop. When we discuss the distinction between types of order and harmony dominant in Western and classical Chinese cultures we will introduce a contrast not unlike that of Northrop. We believe our distinction between "rational" and "aesthetic" order, however, to be capable of more detailed explication and more relevant and subtle application than Northrop's notions of "postulation" and "intuition."

2 Fingarette (1). Fingarette has elaborated his distinctive interpretation of the Confucian sensibility in several important articles. See the bibliography of works cited.

3 The Chinese language edition of this work will be published by Shanghai People's Press.

Some Uncommon Assumptions

1 See, for example, Hall (1), pp. 169–228 for a discussion of some of the relations between classical Chinese thought and Anglo-European process philosophy.

2 The distinction we are insisting upon between "logical" and "aesthetic" order will be discussed in some detail at the beginning of Chapter III, below.

3 Indeed, one may question the appropriateness of dualistic categories in Western thought, as well. See Hall (1), Chapter 3, "What 'God' Hath Wrought," for a consideration of some of the cultural consequences of conceptual dualism.

4 Loewe, p. 63.

5 *Chuang Tzu*, 5/2/49.

6 Loewe, pp. 63–64.

7 Relative to this observation, it is significant that the notions of "birth" and the process of "growth" (or "life") are not clearly differentiated in Chinese; both are denoted by the character, *sheng* 生 . Since reality in the early Chinese tradition is conceived in terms of cyclical process,

the absence of cosmogony is compensated for by an elaborate cosmological tradition, to which the *Yi-ching* and the Taoist, *Yin-yang* and *Wu-hsing* (Five Phases) schools bear witness.

8   Loewe, p. 68.

9   Schwartz, pp. 50–62.

10 We should again stress that our employment of contrasting terms such as "transcendence and immanence," "polarity and dualism," and, in this section, "tradition and history" is not to be construed as descriptive of contrasts existing within the Confucian culture itself. On the contrary, these contrasts are couched in terms more congenial to the Anglo-European intellectual tradition and, as such, have the sort of dualistic associations supported by that context. Freed from these dualistic associations, the concepts of immanence, polarity, and tradition as stipulated here, are the most pertinent we have been able to discover in order to illumine the Confucian world view from a comparative perspective. The proof of their value, however, must be realized pragmatically as one attempts to use these uncommon assumptions in order to understand the discussions in the body of this work.

11 See de Bary, (1) vol. II, pp. 188–91. Even the term *ju** 儒, typically rendered "Confucian" and taken as the emblem of Confucian thinkers, has the etymological association with *ju*** 柔 (weakness, servility).

12 See Chapter II, pp. 118–25 and Chapter V, passim.

Chapter I

"At fifteen my heart-and-mind were set upon learning. . . ."

1   Wittgenstein (1).

2   Wittgenstein (2).

3   Austin (1), (2).

4   Quine, Goodman, Sellars.

5   Heidegger, pp. 376–77.

6   Rorty, p. 356.

7   Rorty, p. 360.

8   Rorty, pp. 365–66.

9   Austin (1), p. 149.

10 Boodberg (1).

11 See Rosemont (1), who has made this argument with considerable persuasion. Rosemont's claims relevant to the relations of phonetic and

signific elements of classical Chinese are briefly discussed in Chapter V below, pp. 253–54.

12 That this original character, *hsiao* 敩 , meaning "to teach, to become aware," discloses the basic meaning of *hsüeh* is borne out by the definition of *hsüeh* found in the classical literature and lexicons. The *Pai-hu-t'ung* (4/15/16b), for example, states that "the meaning of *hsüeh* is to become aware (*chüeh* 覺), "to comprehend what one does not know." The *Shuo-wen*, our earliest lexicon, also defines *hsüeh* with its cognate, "to awaken, to become aware" (*chüeh* 覺), and with "to comprehend" (*wu* 悟). It further suggests in its etymological analysis that *hsüeh* is constituted by "to teach" (*chiao* 教) and "border prairie" (*chiung* 冂) meaning here, "still ignorant,"—thus, "to teach those still ignorant." The *Kuang-ya* glosses define *hsüeh* as "to teach," and there are numerous examples in the early corpus where *hsüeh* has this meaning. The *Tuan Yü-ts'ai* commentary on the *Shuo-wen* highlights the fact that *hsüeh* is not exclusively either "studying" or "teaching"; rather, it is "learning"—an activity which involves both studying and teaching.

> In studying one becomes aware of his own inadequacies, and it is only in so doing that he is able to introspect. This is why becoming aware of one's inadequacies is called "awakening." In teaching, one becomes aware of difficulties, and it is only in so doing that he is able to strengthen himself. Thus it is said that teaching and studying reinforce each other.

The sense of "mutuality" in this character, *hsüeh*, is apparent from its component, *chiu* 臼 , which has the meaning of the two hands interlocked in mutual support. For an enlightening discussion of *hsüeh*, see Lau, (1), pp. xxxviii–xl.

13 This is underscored by its definition in the *Kuang-ya* glosses, "*hsüeh* is to imitate (*hsiao* 效)."

14 It is interesting that according to Karlgren's (1) reconstructions of archaic Chinese, "culture" (*wen* 文) is homophonous with the character *wen* 聞, which has a core meaning of "to hear," but which is used frequently in the early literature with its extended meaning, "to be told/to hear = to learn." For example, in the *Analects* 5/9: "On learning (*wen* 聞) one thing, Hui understands ten."

15 *Analects*, 9/5.

16 See *Shih-chi*, 47 (biography of Confucius).

17 *Analects*, 5/28, 7/2, 7/3, and 7/34.

18 *Analects*, 6/3 and 11/7.

19 *Analects,* 8/17.

20 *Analects,* 17/2.

21 *Analects,* 6/11.

22 *Analects,* 7/8.

23 *Analects,* 2/12, 9/2, and 15/1.

24 *Analects,* 2/18, 8/12, and 14/24.

25 The central place of ritual action (*li* 禮) in learning *(hsüeh)* is suggested by the similarity between this passage and 8/2.

26 *Analects,* 7/1.

27 *Analects,* 17/8.

28 The character for "reflecting," *ssu,* is a corrupted form of the character with "the top of the head" *(hsin*** 囟) and "the physical and psychical heart-and-mind" *(hsin* 心) as its constituent elements. The *Shuo-wen* commentary explains the graph: "since the heart-and-mind and the spirit *(shen* 神) commune at the brain, the character derives from 'the top of the head' *(hsin*** 囟)." The *Shuo-wen* lexicon defines *ssu* as "a deep river gorge" *(hsün* 容). The Tuan Yü-ts'ai commentary elaborates: "Deep passageways are generally called *hsün* 容. That it defines 'reflecting' as *hsün* 容 here is because one can thereby pass through things deeply." In the commentarial tradition, there is some debate as to whether *hsün* is a graphic corruption of *jung* 容 (to contain = to tolerate). This speculation is reinforced by the *Ch'un-ch'iu fan-lu* 14/2b–3a which contains the passage:

> "Reflecting" *(ssu)* means tolerance *(jung* 容), and tolerance
> means having nothing that one does not tolerate. Toleration can
> be considered sagacity *(sheng* 聖), and sagacity means to estab-
> lish things. Where the king's mind is broad and impassive and
> there is nothing that it does not tolerate, sages will be able to
> establish things and disseminate them abroad, and all affairs will
> achieve what is appropriate to them.

Consistent with the sense of "capacity" and "tolerance," the *Shuo-wen* goes on to define "reflecting" *(ssu)* as a generic term which covers the various modes of thinking: considering, pondering, calculating, meditating, and so on. The *Erh Ya* 3/1B/22 also characterizes *ssu* in this way: "To brood, to grieve, to fret is *ssu.* To harbor, to think, to reflect, to wish, to entertain, to crave is *ssu.*" This notion of "tolerance" associates further with "reflecting" in the repeated insistence of Confucius that learning encourages tolerance (1/8. See also 9/4 and 14/32): "The exemplary person *(chün tzu)* . . . who learns will not be inflexible." In fact, this same expression, *jung* 容, is used to express this concern for tolerance in the *Analects* (19/3):

> The exemplary person *(chün tzu)* honors those of superior character and is tolerant *(jung* 容*)* of the multitude. . . . If I am indeed a person of superior parts, what is it that I should be intolerant of in others?

Ssu, in addition to denoting the entertainment of things learned, seems purposeful and directional in that it pursues a clear apprehension of the conditions and implications of this learning (16/10):

> The exemplary person *(chün tzu)* has nine things in mind (literally nine *ssu*): in looking he intends clarity; in hearing he intends acuity; in countenance he intends cordiality; in bearing he intends respectfulness; in speech he intends conscientiousness; in carrying out affairs he intends due reverence; in entertaining doubts he intends questions; in his anger he intends his reluctance; in sight of gain he intends appropriateness.

29 See Ames (1).
30 This same point can be made with respect to the inapplicability of the dualistic categories of "individual" and "society" to the Chinese context. Tu Wei-ming (1) p. 53, comments upon the absence of strictly psychological and sociological language in Confucian philosophy and argues that such language is undesirable and empirically unsound even in the Western world. We shall have occasion to revisit and elaborate upon Tu's insight below by reference to the work of George Herbert Mead, the social psychologist, and others who in more recent times have benefited from his interpretation of person as irreducibly social.
31 See Ames (2), pp. 1–6.
32 *Hsün Tzu*, 1/1/6.
33 *Chung-yung*, 20. Cf. *Analects*, 19/6. *Chung-yung* is commonly translated *The Doctrine of the Mean*. The perhaps unfortunate association of this translation with Aristotelian philosophy is avoided in Tu Wei-ming's happier rendering, *Centrality and Commonality*. Later, when we discuss the "focus-field" model of social relationships as a means of interpreting Confucian thought, the greater appropriateness of Tu's rendering may be appreciated.
34 See also *Analects*, 2/22, 5/10, 5/14, 13/3, and 17/14.
35 *Mencius*, 58/7B/37.
36 Lau (1), p. xiii.

37 The *Shuo-wen* analyzes *chih* 知 as deriving from "mouth" (*k'ou* 口) and "arrow" (*shih* 矢), and defines it as "verbal expression" (*ts'u* 詞]). Several commentaries on the *Shuo-wen* speculate that the character "to understand" (*shih* 識) should precede *ts'u* in this definition, thus expressing "understanding expressed orally." That the character *chih* is constituted with the "mouth" (*k'ou*) radical and is defined in terms of "verbal expression" (*ts'u*) and possibly "to understand," all having strong verbal associations, is significant.

Commentators generally understand the "arrow" (*shih*) element as the phonetic, even though, according to Karlgren (1), the archaic pronunciation of *shih* 矢 , *síər/sí:/shï, is significantly different from *chih* 知 : *tieg/tie/chï. We might want to consider the semantic associations of "arrow": a missile meant to be cast in a given direction towards some specific target. This association is challenged by Karlgren's suggestion that lexicographers misunderstood the original graph constituted of "man" (*jen* 人) and "mouth" (*k'ou*), and turned the "man" into the graphically similar "arrow."

Commentary on the *Shuo-wen* introduces an important implicit sense of *chih*:

> [The Ch'ing commentator] Wang Nien-sun 王念孫 observes: "Some gloss *chih* as 'come in contact with' (*chieh* 接). The 'Yüeh-chi' 樂記 (of the *Li-chi* 禮記) contains the phrase '*wu chih chih chih*' 物至知知 , which means that when phenomena occur *chih* makes contact with them." Since the ancients called making mutual contact *chih*, mutual contact with others was also called *chih*. Hence, there is the expression, *chih-chiao* (知交), "intimate acquaintance." Because of this, to constitute a match (*p'i* 匹) is also called *chih* . . . Wang Nien-sun says that *chih* can also be glossed as "to manifest" (*hsien* 見), that is, to manifest in one's countenance.

Chih would seem to denote participation in the realization of a relationship wherein the realizer and that realized are two integral aspects of a given event.

One final connotation of *chih* that should be noted is the sense of "to do," "to administer," "to determine," as in the expression "one who administers and determines the government = governor" (*chih-kuo* 知國 or *chih chou* 知州 , etc.) This usage is important in disclosing the active and creative dimensions of *chih*.

38 *Ch'un-ch'iu fan-lu*, 8/10b.

39 *Pai-hu-t'ung*, 8/30/1b.

40 *Chung-yung*, 24.
41 Waley, p. 200, n. 1.
42 Waley, p. 200, n. 2.
43 *Analects*, 2/1.
44 Ch'en Ta-ch'i, pp. 78ff.
45 We follow Lau in rendering as "two minds" the expression *huo* 惑 (most frequently translated as "doubts" or "delusion"), benefiting from his insight that *huo* 惑 refers to that kind of doubt which arises from confusion over alternative directions. *Huo* 惑 is cognate with if not derived from *huo** 或 , meaning "either/or."
46 See Chapter V below.
47 Deutsch argues that truth is a quality of anything to be what is right for itself according to its own specific intentionality. "The nature of truth is thus seen as a qualitative achievement. It is not given; it is attained" (p. 98).
48 Huston Smith, p. 430. It may certainly be argued that classical Chinese has no word or phrase that translates as "truth." Our concern here is to deal with the concept of truth as it might be analogized in Chinese culture. For further discussion of the reasons why the classical Chinese had so little regard for stricter notions of "truth" and "falsity," see below Chapter V, pp. 298–300.
49 Huston Smith, p. 432.
50 *Chung-yung*, 25.
51 Tu Wei-ming (4), p. 107.
52 *Chung-yung*, 24. The language of "signs," "portents," and "divination" in this text may not be taken to suggest a Confucian belief in magical powers. The authority of Confucius and the Confucian tradition weighs against interest in supernatural doctrines. The point of this passage is carried in the assertion of the importance of "anticipating the good and the bad" and forecasting with regard to such anticipations.
53 *Mencius*, 51/7A/4.
54 *Mencius*, 28/4A/13.
55 *Chung-yung*, 20.
56 For a full discussion of this point, see Chapter IV below.
57 *Analects*, 19/6.
58 *Analects*, 7/25.
59 *Analects*, 1/6.
60 *Analects*, 1/4, 1/8, 5/28, 7/25, 9/25, 12/10, and 15/6.
61 *Analects*, 15/18.
62 *Mencius*, 57/7B/25.
63 Waley, p. 108.
64 *Analects*, 1/4, 1/6, 1/7, 1/8, and 5/26.

65 *Analects*, 12/7, 17/6, and 19/10.

66 See also *Analects*, 17/9.

67 *Analects*, 5/28.

68 *Analects*, 15/18.

69 See Lau (3).

70 *Shih-chi (Historical Records)*, 47. Confucius' free-wheeling use of the *Shih-ching*—the open interpretive use of cultural scripture—demonstrates in a dramatic way the extent to which creativity must be accounted for in any appreciation of his thought.

71 For an introduction to the *Book of Songs*, see Watson, pp. 202ff. While the *Songs* is one of our most valuable windows to the world of the early Chou, it is not entirely unclouded. There are many difficulties with the language of the text. As poetry, it has a tendency toward elliptical, symbolic, and evocative expression which was perhaps never intended to receive complete articulation. Also, the frequent use of archaic and provincial language renders the *Songs* extremely difficult to interpret. Many of the allusions to customs and the subtle significances of cultural institutions are meaningless due to the paucity of our resources for understanding the Chou period.

72 See also *Analects*, 7/18 and 16/13.

73 *Analects*, 8/8.

74 See also *Analects*, 15/13.

75 *Shih-ching*, 79/297/4.

76 There is an alternative interpretation of Confucius' creative use of the *Book of Songs* that bears notice, especially given its wide advocacy among contemporary scholars in China. Ts'ai Shang-ssu 蔡尚思 (ed. Chu Wei-cheng 朱維錚) is a fair representative of what is regarded as an "objective" evaluation of Confucius' motives. That Confucius uses the *Songs* creatively is not in dispute. The question is why? Ts'ai, in his *K'ung Tzu ssu-hsiang t'i-hsi* 孔子思想體系 (*The System of Confucius' Thought*), esp. pp. 124–31, begins from the position that "Confucius' thinking on the arts has one clear characteristic, that is, art is a tool of politics" (p. 125). Working with basically the same passages we have cited, Ts'ai interprets Confucius' creative use of the *Songs* as politically motivated:

> In summary, then, Confucius in editing the *Book of Songs* did something good, and it was reasonable to discuss the relationship between these songs and political life. But making these songs the handmaiden of politics and encouraging the interpretation of the original verses out of context, reading into them whatever was needed, and using them as a necessary device for

satisfying the promotion of the powers-that-be to "not swerve from the right path"—this then had a very deleterious effect on later ages. (p. 131)

Ts'ai's argument is based on the assumption that Confucius was a spokesman for the feudal powers-that-be, and that he philosophized in service to the rigid continuance of an established political system. Our entire book, step by step, is an argument against collapsing the distinction between the teachings of Confucius and the political order that interpreted it, and against casting Confucius as a conservative advocate of Chou feudalism.

Chapter II
". . . at thirty I took my stance. . . ."

1 Gadamer, pp. 5–39.
2 Rorty, p. 359.
3 Rorty, p. 360.
4 A caution is in order here, directed particularly toward our Chinese readers whose understanding of Western philosophy, particularly of pragmatism, is still predominantly influenced by John Dewey's China lectures of 1919–1920. The scientific chauvinism that one may all too easily find in those lectures may lead to a misconstrual of the fundamental significance of Dewey's philosophic project. Read in terms of the distinctly aesthetic character of his thought, Dewey provides an interesting point of comparison between Confucian and Western philosophies. Something of the same might be said of existentialism. For despite the intensely individualistic strain in the latter (which would, of course, be quite unacceptable to the Chinese), existentialism and pragmatism share an immanental, aesthetic perspective which permits them to serve as grounds of comparison with Confucius' thinking.

It may also be necessary to warn Westerners possessed of the rather popular misunderstandings of Dewey's pragmatism that we are not simply rehearsing the vague claim that Dewey and Confucius are compatible because of the "concrete" and "practical" character of both thinkers. The very meaning of *praxis*, as we shall attempt to show, is altered due to the aesthetic sensibility underlying both Confucian and pragmatic philosophies. One of the burdens of this work is to demonstrate that it is the aesthetic dimension of Confucius which is most prominent and most important and that it is precisely this element that connects him with Dewey, Mead and, of course, with the American thinker by adoption, Alfred North Whitehead. For an interpretation of the tradition of American philosophy which stresses this aesthetic dimension, see Hall (2), pp. 93–110.

5 See Lévi-Strauss, p. 99.
6 Sartre, p. 433.
7 Sartre, p. 24.
8 Sartre, p. 24.
9 Dewey (1), pp. 222–23.
10 Dewey (1), p. 233.
11 Dewey (1), p. 233.
12 Dewey (1), p. 280.
13 Dewey (1), p. 78.
14 Dewey (1), p. 162.
15 For example, Mead attempted to show that physical relativity may be explained in terms of the activity of role taking in society, thus construing the special theory of relativity in social-psychological terms.
16 Mead, pp. 154–55.
17 Mead, pp. 175, 177–78.
18 Mead, p. 178.
19 Mead, p. 182.
20 See also *Analects*, 8/8 and 20/3.
21 See Gimello's discussion of *li*, passim.
22 This radical is possibly derived from the pattern formed by divining stalks. See Karlgren (1).
23 For example, *Pai-hu-t'ung*, 2/6/6b–7a:

> Therefore, Confucius said, "What is there to see in a person who is not reverent in the performance of ritual actions?" [from *Analects* 3/26] Now, ritual actions are the boundary between *yin* and *yang*, the confluence of all phenomena, whereby one exalts heaven and earth, welcomes the ghosts and spirits, orders that above and below, and regulates the way of being human.

24 Gimello rightly cautions against using a Western religious/humanist distinction.
25 Gimello, p. 204.
26 In fact, in *Pai-hu-t'ung* 8/30/1b, ritual action is defined in precisely these terms: "Ritual action (*li* 禮) means 'to tread a path' (*li** 履); to tread the proper way and actualize culture."

27 The only other two cognates that Karlgren (1) lists are 醴 and 鱧 , "newly fermented spirits" and a "mullet-like fish" respectively.

28 Boodberg (1), p. 326–27.

29 This association between *yi* 義 and "raw stuff" (*chih*** 質) also occurs in *Analects* 12/20: "Extending (*ta* 達) describes a person who is straight in his raw stuff and who is fond of *yi*."

30 See in particular *Mencius*, 42/6A/1 and 43/6A/4.

31 *Mencius*, 52/7A/21 and 51/7A/15.

32 *Mencius*, 44/6A/7.

33 *Hsün Tzu*, 28/9/69.

34 *Ch'un-ch'iu fan-lu*, 8/7a.

35 *Ch'un-ch'iu fan-lu*, 8/8b.

36 For example, see an extended discussion of *tzu-te* 自得 in *Huai Nan Tzu*, 1/15a. See also *Chuang Tzu*, 22/8/31 and 77/28/7 and 54; *Hsün Tzu*, 2/1/18. See de Bary's (2) work on this concept, from which we have adapted our translation.

37 *Mencius*, 57/7B/31: "People all have things that they are not willing to do. To manifest this in what one is willing to do is *yi*."

38 In the reconstructions of Archaic Chinese in his *Grammata Serica Recensa*, Karlgren has determined that the structure of the character "signification" (*yi* 義) contains *yang* 羊 ("sheep") as radical or classifier, and the first person personal pronoun *wo* 我 ("I, we, me, us") as its phonetic. Its radical associates *yi* with characters such as *shan* 善 ("good"), *mei* 美 ("beautiful"), and *ch'ün* 群 ("herd, group, sociable") where *yang* 羊 seems to contribute the positive element of "auspiciousness" (*hsiang* 祥). There are several characteristics of the so-called "phonetic" *wo*, which might extend semantically to *yi* and have some bearing on its meaning. Initially, in Early Archaic Chinese (11th–7th centuries B.C.), *wo* in contrast to *yü* 予 denotes high status and, in contrast to the self-deprecatory *chen* 朕, is the "exalted" form of first person. Secondly, whereas *wo* in Early Archaic Chinese has both a determinative and nominative usage, in Middle and Late Archaic texts (7th–3rd centuries B.C.), there seems to be an observable tendency for it to be replaced by *wu* 吾 in the nominative position and for it to assume the objectified "me, us" function.

Lexical tradition has classified *yi* with *yang* 羊 as signifier and *wo* 我 as phonetic. We shall argue *yi* is more properly understood as a *hui-yi* 會意 character—that is, a character in which both radicals contribute to the meaning. Thus, we shall argue that "significating" must be understood as both originating in, and originative of, personal identity.

39 For example, *Analects*, 4/16, 14/12; *Mencius*, 44/6A/10.

40   A similar passage also occurs in *Tso-chuan*, 379/ 昭 12/9 左.

41   *Mencius*, 50/7A/4.

42   *Mencius*, 11/2A/2.

43   *Mencius*, 13/2A/6.

44   Wilhelm, p. 176, makes the point that "the word *meaning* (*yi* 義) here refers to the given meaning (signification), and not the grasped meaning (significance); to the meaning one ascribes to a time situation and not the meaning one analyzes out of a time situation. One's own judgment gives meaning to time in this case, and meaning is not something recognized in the situation as such."

45   There is a passage which seems to contradict this relationship between "courage" (*yung*) and *yi* (17/23): "An exemplary person who has courage but lacks *yi* is a source of disorder. . . ." "Courage" is used in this passage as "name without substance" in a way similar to ritual action (*li*) in 17/11: "In repeatedly referring to ritual action (*li*), how could we be talking about gifts of jade and silk! . . . ."

46   *Mencius*, 31/4B/11.

47   Ch'en Ta-ch'i, pp. 125 ff., discusses Confucius' notion of *yi* in terms of flexibility.

48   See also *Analects*, 1/8, 9/4, and 14/32.

49   For example, see *Li-chi*, 24/35 and 31/14. The homophonous and semantic relationship between these two characters might suggest that they can be tracked back to one original root concept which, in the evolution and refinement of its meaning, gave rise to a distinction significant enough to warrant two different characters. At a very basic level, these two characters are congruent in their meaning of "appropriateness, rightness, propriety." The contrast between *yi* 義 and *yi** 宜 illuminates the meaning of *yi* as both deriving and bestowing meaning. *Yi* is "divided" into itself and *yi** in much the same fashion as Aristotle divides *praxis* (πρᾶξις) into *praxis* and *techne* (τέχνη).

50   As we have seen, Tung Chung-shu defines *yi* explicitly as "appropriateness to one's own person."

51   This sense of *yi** 宜 is exemplified in the classical literature. The *Book of Songs* (*Shih-ching*, 2/6/1,2,3), for example, contains a passage in which a bride is going into her new home and must accommodate herself to the family, the household, and the individual members of her husband's family. In such a situation, she must be yielding and deferential, and so must appropriate meaning from her new environment. As the *Shuo-wen* defines *yi** 宜, she must do or be "that which pacifies or placates" (*so an* 所安), making herself over to be appropriate to her situation. This same lexicon defines the cognate *yi** 宜

as "that which others deem appropriate," making the focus of this appropriateness on context rather than oneself.

52 As we shall see below, this is an important reason for Confucius' persistence in defining *shu* 恕 in negative terms.
53 *Mencius*, 39/5B/1.
54 *Tso-chuan* 26/ 桓2/左附
55 Compare this with *Mencius*, in which only 6 out of 110 occurrences of *yi* are juxtaposed with *li*.
56 *Mo Tzu*, 14/11/1.
57 *Tso-chuan*, 130/ 僖 27/5 左 .
58 See *Analects*, 7/3 and 12/10.
59 See *Mencius,*, 20/3A/4.
60 For example, *Mencius*, 28/4A/11, 41/5B/7, and 45/6A/11.
61 *Mencius*, 31/4B/19.
62 *Analects*, 12/1.
63 Cheng Chung-ying, p. 270.
64 Lau (1), p. xxiii.
65 See above, "Some Uncommon Assumptions," pp. 16–17.
66 Fingarette (1), pp. 69, 63.
67 Fingarette (1), p. 63.
68 Chan, pp. 10ff.
69 Takeuchi, pp. 5ff.
70 Fingarette (1), p. 37.
71 Tu Wei-ming (1), p. 48.
72 Tu Wei-ming (1), p. 28.
73 Chan, passim.
74 Tu Wei-ming (2), pp. 33–34.
75 Tu Wei-ming (1), p. 51.
76 Fingarette (1), pp. 35, 47.
77 Fingarette (1), pp. 43, 45.
78 Fingarette (1), p. 47.
79 Fingarette (1), p. 42.
80 Boodberg (1), p. 328.
81 *Mencius*, 9/1B/15; *Chung-yung*, 20.
82 Boodberg (1), p. 328.
83 *Chung-yung*, 25.
84 Later Confucians saw the project of person making as beginning with human exchange, but, perhaps influenced by the more cosmologically minded Taoists, extended the integrating efficacy of *jen** to the world at large (*Ch'un-ch'iu fan-lu*, 8/7b): "While the basis lies in loving the people, everything from them down to the birds, beasts, and insects will be loved."

85 Lau (1), xiii.
86 The sense of "analogy" is readily identifiable in the etymology of *shu*, which derives from *ju* 如 , meaning "such as," "as if." It is not surprising that *ju* 如 is also used as the second person pronoun: "you." The Han Confucian, Chia Yi (*Hsin-shu*, 8), defines *shu* as "using oneself to assess others." See further discussion of this term, *shu*, in Chapter V.
87 Fingarette (2).
88 *Analects*, 12/1.
89 *Analects*, 4/12 and 14/12.
90 *Mencius*, 13/2A/7.
91 *Ch'un-ch'iu fan-lu*, 8/8b.
92 Mead, pp. 201, 214–15.
93 Booth, pp. 114, 132, 134. This association was first suggested in an article by Tu Wei-ming (1).
94 Fingarette (1), p. 45, states: "The metaphor of an inner psychic life, in all of its ramifications so familiar to us, simply isn't present in the *Analects*, not even as a rejected possibility."
95 *Analects*, 12/22.
96 We might speculate that it is because this love (*ai* 愛) entails an encompassing of another's interests that it also denotes the seemingly unrelated sense of "to grudge" or "to be sparing with." That is, a ruler who loves his people by making their interests his own expresses this concern by being circumspect in his expenditure of their energies. A person who loves another and assumes that person's concerns as his own is reluctant to make unreasonable demands.
97 *Hsün Tzu*, 105/29/29ff.
98 A similar passage occurs in *Tso-chuan* 379/ 昭 12/9 左.
99 Lau, Ma Jung, Chan, Fingarette, and Waley, respectively.
100 Tu Wei-ming (3), p. 6.
101 Fingarette (1), p. 43.
102 Fingarette (1), pp. 46 and 42.
103 Tu Wei-ming (2), pp. 33–34.
104 See pp. 237–41.
105 See *Analects*, 5/9, 5/19, 6/7, and 8/7.
106 *Analects*, 7/32. See also *Mencius*, 10/2A/2.
107 The following version of this story is based on the *Historical Records* (*Shih-chi*, 61) biography and its Suo Yin commentary.
108 *Analects*, 5/23 and 7/15.
109 *Analects*, 19/22 and 8/20.
110 *Analects*, 7/15.

Chapter III

". . . at forty I was no longer of two minds . . ."

1 For a more complete discussion of this concept of praxis see Hall (1), pp. 238ff.

2 Ruskin, Part III, Sect. I, Ch. 2:1.

3 We use the terms "logical" or "rational" order, since the Greek *logistikos* (λογιστικός) and the Latin *rationalis*, the etymological roots of "logical" and "rational," express the sense of order as *measure*, and as possessed of pattern- and rule-regularity. Our reasons for selecting the term "aesthetic" to name the sort of order comprised by particulars construed precisely in terms of their particularity require a more extended explanation. It is the connotations of "immediacy" and "preoccupation" suggested by the Greek *aisthetikos* (αἰσθετικός) that we wish to exploit by the use of the term "aesthetic order." The direct entertainment of one's environs entails no conceptual or ideational mediation. The environing world as in some sense "felt" rather than cognitively entertained consists in ungeneralized particulars. The various orders presented by such particulars are such as to be constituted by the uniqueness of each particular rather than by sets of formal relationships that may be abstracted from these particulars.

The primary inspiration for this contrast between logical and aesthetic order may be found in Whitehead (3), Ch. 3. Significant differences in our philosophic commitments and those of Whitehead, however, do not permit us to endorse his discussion in an unqualified manner. For a more detailed consideration of our logical–aesthetic contrast, see Hall (2), pp. 131ff, and Hall (4).

4 Louie, in his *Critiques of Confucius in Contemporary China*, outlines the recent history of this debate. A representative discussion of the Marxian version of this distinction is Chao Chi-pin's "Shih jen min 释人民 (An Explanation of *jen* and *min*)" in his *Lun-yü hsin-t'an (A New Exploration of the Analects)*.

5 See *Analects*, 4/5, 12/5, 18/6, and 19/21.

6 See the *Shuo-wen* definition of *jen*.

7 *Li-chi*, 9/26.

8 It was only much later in the tradition—perhaps in the Sung—that *jen** 仁 came into use.

9 See *Analects*, 1/2 and 14/9.

10 See, for example, *Analects*, 15/21.

11 See *Hsün Tzu*, 105/30/7.

12 *Ch'un-ch'iu fan-lu,* 10/1a.
13 See Karlgren (1).
14 See also *Analects,* 5/16, 13/4, and 19/19.
15 *Analects,* 2/19.
16 *Analects,* 2/20 and 6/2.
17 *Analects,* 5/16.
18 *Analects,* 6/22.
19 *Analects,* 13/3.
20 *Analects,* 8/2, 12/19, 13/4, and 15/33.
21 Yang Po-chün, p. 69.
22 *Analects,* 1/5.
23 For example, *Analects,* 13/25.
24 For example, *Analects,* 8/9.
25 See Chapter IV for an extended discussion of *te* 德 as "particular focus."
26 See *Analects,* 1/9 and 6/29.
27 See also *Analects,* 8/7, in which authoritative humanity (*jen** 仁) is described as a heavy burden. See also Lau (1), p. xviii.
28 *Analects,* 8/9.
29 Legge, Vol. III, p. 158.
30 See *Mencius,* 2/1A/4; 7/1B/7, 12/2A/5 and 19/3A/3.
31 See *Analects,* 6/30, 13/29 and 13/30.
32 Chia Yi, 9/a-b.
33 *Analects,* 20/1.
34 *Analects,* 12/2.
35 *Analects,* 11/26, 13/4, and 13/9.
36 Legge, Vol. III, p. 288.
37 Legge, Vol. III, p. 292. Cf. *Mencius,* 36/5A/5.
38 *Analects,* 7/23.
39 *Analects,* 17/19.
40 *Analects,* 6/11. See also 7/7.
41 *Chung-yung,* 20.
42 Hobbes, pp. 25–26.
43 Hobbes, p. 26.
44 Hobbes, p. 24.
45 Hegel, par. 258.
46 For a fuller discussion of the role of technology in challenging the viability of the public sphere see Hall (1), pp. 157–65, 346–66.
47 Whitehead (3), 54–55.
48 See below, pp. 237–41.
49 See, for example, Horkheimer and Habermas (1).
50 See Ortega.

51 Boodberg (1), p. 323.
52 Boodberg (1), p. 323.
53 See also *Analects*, 13/3 and 13/6.
54 There is a development in classical Chinese thought which bears notice at this point. The distinction that we are drawing between two fundamentally different senses of order, the rational or logical and the aesthetic, can be used to describe a paradigmatic shift in the evolution of classical Chinese philosophy. With the death of Confucius, the interpretation of his teachings went in several directions. Perhaps most important among these rival positions are those represented by *Mencius* and *Chung-yung* on the one hand, and *Hsün Tzu* on the other. An argument can be made that, whereas the emphasis in the *Mencius* and especially the *Chung-yung* is on the primacy of the aesthetic order, in the *Hsün Tzu*, influenced strongly by the movement toward political unification and its attendant standardization of language, measures, laws, and so forth, there is a development of Confucianism in the direction of the logical order. This shift in Confucianism is particularly evident, for example, in Hsün Tzu's appeal to reason, and in the narrowing distinction between ritual action *(li)* and law *(fa)*, which helps to explain the relationship between Hsün Tzu, as teacher, and his Legalist students, Li Ssu and Han Fei. The intellectual impact of this shift from aesthetic to logical order was considerable if we bear in mind that Hsün Tzu, celebrated by leading Han Confucians such as Tung Chung-shu, dominated the emergence of a state Confucianism in this period that was largely elaborated through Legalist institutions inherited from the Ch'in.

   On the Taoist side, we can witness a similar shift if we track the movement from the immanental cosmos of the *Lao Tzu* and *Chuang Tzu* "Inner Chapters" in the direction of the two-world orientation of religious Taoism. An interesting illustration of this shifting orientation can be found in the *Huai Nan Tzu's* reiteration and reinterpretation of the *Chuang Tzu* passage cited above. While the intention of the *Chuang Tzu* passage is to challenge the principle of an absolute beginning, the *Huai Nan Tzu*, Ch. 2, assumes precisely the opposite position and uses it to describe a series of increasingly abstruse stages in a cosmogonic evolution of existence. Significantly, it was during this late Ch'in and early Han period that various cosmogonic theories appear and are developed in the early Chinese corpus, for cosmogonic theories are primary signals of the conception of logical order.
55 Hsiao Kung-chuan, p. 103.
56 See also *Analects*, 12/19, 13/4, and 13/13.
57 See Dilthey and Gadamer.

58 Taylor, p. 179.
59 See also *Analects*, 8/14.
60 Hsiao Kung-chuan, pp. 140ff.
61 See *Analects*, 13/5.
62 Yang Po-chün.
63 *Tso-chuan*, 402/ 昭 20/ 左 .
64 See *Analects*, 14/32.
65 Commentators generally read *chen* 貞 as *cheng* 正.
66 See *Analects*, 17/5 and 20/1.
67 For a fuller discussion of the importance of *wu-wei* in Confucius' political theory, see Ames (2), pp. 29ff.
68 See also *Analects*, 13/11.
69 See *Analects*, 20/2 and 13/3. For a fuller discussion see Ames (2), pp. 115ff.
70 See above, p. 23.
71 Needham, pp. 519–20.
72 Needham, p. 519.
73 The former is captured in the understanding of *cheng** as "administrative policies" in the first phrase of the passage, and the latter is described in the contrasting implications of the last character of the passage: *ko* 格. There are alternative interpretations of *ko* offered by the commentaries, the most prominent among these being "to order" (*cheng* 正), but here clearly with a noncoercive connotation. The sense of personal involvement is strong in the Kuo Hsiang commentary's suggestion that this "ordering" is reflexive—that is, it is "self-ordering" (*tzu cheng* 自正). Chu Hsi's gloss on *ko* as "to reach to, arrive at" (*chih* 至) and Cheng Hsüan's "to come, to be attracted to" (*lai* 來) both indicate the same notion of immediate particular engagement in the achieved order.
74 See Hall (1), pp. 249–50, and Hall (2), pp. 244–50, for discussions of this distinction between power and creativity.
75 See, for example, Hsiao Kung-chuan, pp. 118–19.
76 Hsiao Kung-chuan, pp. 118–19.
77 Creel, p. 335, n. 62.
78 Tu Wei-ming (4), pp. 70–71.
79 Lau (1), Appendix I.
80 *Huai Nan Tzu*, 9/20b. See Ames (2), p. 205.
81 Lau (1), Appendix I.
82 Ch'en Ta-ch'i, pp. 247–51.
83 See also *Analects*, 16/8.
84 *Analects*, 7/34.
85 *Analects*, 7/33.

86   *Analects*, 3/24, 7/31, 9/6, 9/14, and 10/6.

87   *Analects*, 6/7.

88   *Analects*, 5/3 and 14/5. Beyond the frequently used and relatively clear categories of *sheng jen*, *jen* che*, and *chün tzu*, there are several other alternatives which, because they rarely occur, are more problematic. Confucius has never met a *sheng jen* 聖人 (7/26), but allows that Yen Hui is a *hsien jen* 賢人 (6/11). Yen Hui is also described as a *jen* che* 仁者 (6/7), a characteristic he shared with the *hsien jen* 賢人 of old (7/15). Hence, the *hsien jen* 賢人 does not rank with the *sheng jen* 聖人, but is at least as high as the *jen* che* 仁者. Although *shan jen* 善人 on occasion is associated with *sheng jen* 聖人 (7/26), this category is described explicitly as being lower (11/20). *Ch'eng* jen* 成人 occurs only once (14/12), the content of and qualifications for this category seem to be a function of the times, standards being higher in the past. Becoming a scholar-official (*shih* 士), although seeming to refer specifically to a junior official, is an achieved status. It does not, however, seem to be on a par with these other terms. And, finally, the *ta jen* 大人 also occurs only once as one of three things a *chün tzu* 君子 holds in awe (16/8). This being the case, *ta jen* 大人 is at least higher than *chün tzu* 君子, and since Yao, the revered sage-king, is described as "*ta* 大." (8/19) *ta* 大 has direct association with *sheng jen* 聖人.

89   *Analects*,

(1)   14/28, 9/29: . . . the *jen* che* is not anxious. . . .

        12/4: . . . the *chün tzu* is not anxious or fearful. . . .

(2)   12/22: Fan Ch'ih asked about *jen**, and the Master replied, "Love others."

        17/4: . . . the *chün tzu* in learning the *tao* comes to love others.

(3)   4/3: Only the *jen* che* is able to like and dislike others.

        17/24: Tzu-kung asked, "Does the *chün tzu* have his dislikes?" The Master replied, "He does indeed. . . ."

(4)   6/30: The *jen* che* establishes others in seeking to establish himself, and promotes others in seeking to get there himself. To be able to take the analogy from what is closest to oneself can be called the methodology of *jen**.

        14/42: Tzu-lu asked about becoming a *chün tzu*. The Master said, "In cultivating himself he inspires reverence. . . . In cultivating himself he brings peace and stability to others. . . . In cultivating himself he brings peace and security to the common people."

(5) 12/1: Becoming *jen** emerges out of oneself—how could it emerge out of others?

15/21: The *chün tzu* seeks for it in himself; the small person seeks for it in others.

(6) 12/3: Ssu-ma Niu asked about *jen**. The Master replied, "Being *jen** is being circumspect in what one says."

1/14: The *chün tzu* . . . is careful in speaking. . . .

4/24: The *chün tzu* wants to be slow in speaking. . . .

13/3: When it comes to speaking, the *chün tzu* takes nothing lightly.

19/25: Since the exemplary person *(chün tzu)* will be deemed wise or not because of one word, how could he be but careful about what he has to say.

(7) 13/19: Fan Ch'ih asked about *jen**. The Master said, "Be respectful wherein one dwells, be reverent in the handling of official duties, and do one's best in dealing with others."

17/6: Confucius said, "The person who is able to promote the five attitudes in the world can be considered *jen:** . . . [displaying] respect, tolerance, living up to one's word, diligence, and generosity. . . ."

5/16: There are four ways in which he is consonant with the *tao* of the *chün tzu:* he conducts himself with respect; he serves his superiors with reverence; he nurtures the people with generosity; he employs the masses with appropriateness.

90 For example, both can be described in terms of their dispositions and the quality of their deportment. See *Analects* 1/8, 6/7, 16/10, and 19/7.

91 See Ames (4).

92 See also *Analects*, 9/6 and 15/34.

93 *Analects*, 2/14, 4/11, 4/16, 6/13, 7/37, 12/16, 12/19, 13/25, 13/26, 14/23, 15/2, 15/21, 15/34, and 17/4.

94 *Analects*, 13/23.

95 *Analects*, 1/14, 2/13, 4/24, 13/3, 14/27, 15/23, 16/1, 16/6, 16/8, 19/9, and 19/25.

96 See above, p. 127.

97 See also *Analects*, 2/18 and 7/28. For further discussion, see Munro (2), Ch. 6, "The Use of Models."

98 See also *Analects*, 1/8 and 9/25.

Chapter IV

" . . . *at fifty I realized the* ming *of* t'ien. . . ."

1 Whitehead (1), p. 71.
2 Waley, p. 138, comments: "He did not discuss whether Heaven determines all human actions. . . . He refused to define Goodness. . . ."
3 There is an interesting similarity between Confucius' and Socrates' attitudes toward "rationalized" thinking. Toward the beginning of the dialogue which bears his name, Phaedrus asks Socrates his opinion of the truth of a particular myth which had been subjected to rationalization by the Sophists. Socrates disdains to speculate, saying:

> I must first know myself, as the Delphian inscription says; to be curious about that which is not my concern, while I am still in ignorance of my own self, would be ridiculous. (Plato (1), 229e-30a)

There is no claim here by Socrates, nor does there seem to be in Confucius' *Analects*, that such speculations are impossible, only that they lack priority. And this for two reasons: the injunction "know thyself" is altogether more significant than speculation associated with abstract philosophizing; and such philosophizing, if it is done, must presuppose ethical intuitions as its appropriate ground.

4 See Martin.
5 Aristotle combined both *ontologia generalis* and *scientia universalis* in his philosophic work. Yet the priority of his classificatory impulses as illustrated in his organizing the disciplines along theoretical, practical, and productive principles, and his discussion of the methodology of *episteme* (ἐπιστήμη) or scientific knowledge in the *Posterior Analytics*, shapes his thought manifestly in the direction of *scientia universalis*. In terms of modern examples, it is clear that the late Heidegger engaged the traditional questions of *scientia universalis* in his critique of technological society and its "calculative thinking." Whitehead likewise did not wholly avoid the ontological question. His doctrine of "Creativity," "Many," and "One" as constituting the Category of the Ultimate and his characterization of the actual entities of this world in terms of the "ontological principle" (all conditions constituting real and possible existents must be found within the actual entities comprising that which is) suggest tendencies toward a general ontology. But clearly Whitehead's emphasis upon *scientia universalis* shapes the manner in which he deals with ontological questions.

6 See below Chapter V, pp. 254; 290–92.

7 The term *ars contextualis* is used here to capture the meaning of Confucius' form of "aesthetic" cosmology. In contrast to investigating the general character of the being of things *(ontologia generalis)* or to articulating the principles of a universal science *(scientia universalis)*, the Confucian sensibility may be said to presuppose the activity of contextualization in which any element in a context is assessed by the contribution it makes to construing the context, and alternatively the contribution made by the context to the constitution of that element. The specific connotations of the term as a description of Confucian cosmology will become clearer with the analysis of the relations of *t'ien ming, te,* and *tao,* which is the main purpose of this chapter.

8 Karlgren (1).

9 *Tao Te Ching,* 25.

10 *Tao Te Ching,* 14, 22, 39.

11 Tu Wei-ming (3), pp. 94 and 101, for example, dismisses the obvious anthropomorphic characterization of *t'ien* in *Mencius,* 54/7A/38. Citing Lau's translation, "Our body and complexion are given to us by Heaven," Tu Wei-ming comments: "I believe if Heaven is not misunderstood as anthropomorphic, it conveys the meaning of the Chinese word *t'ien* quite well."

12 See, for example, Legge, III, p. 74.

13 Wilhelm, p. 40.

14 For example, Tu Wei-ming (4), pp. 104, 116, 127, and 129.

15 Mou Tsung-san, p. 20.

16 Mou Tsung-san, p. 16.

17 Mou Tsung-san, p. 16.

18 *Analects,* 9/6.

19 *Analects,* 12/5.

20 *Analects,* 14/35.

21 *Analects,* 9/12.

22 *Analects,* 16/8.

23 Tu Wei-ming (4), p. 116.

24 *Mencius,* 50/7A/1.

25 T'ang Chün-i, p. 195.

26 *Tso-chuan,* 234/ 成 13/2 左 .

27 *Mencius,* 50/7A/2.

28 *Mencius,* 37/5A/6.

29 *Chung-yung,* 26.

30 T'ang Chün-i, p. 195.

31 Yates, p. 560.

32 Lau (1), p. xxv.

33 *Mo Tzu*, 62/39/10.
34 Lau (1), p. xxv.
35 See also *Analects*, 14/38.
36 See also *Analects*, 19/1.
37 See *Tso-chuan*, 489/ 哀 14/10 左 .
38 See *Analects*, 7/23.
39 *Analects*, 15/4.
40 Lau (2), p. xxiv.
41 Lau (2), p. xxiv.
42 Neither the *Tao Te Ching* nor the "Inner Chapters" of the *Chuang Tzu* use the term *hsing** 性.
43 See Hsiao Kung-chuan, passim.
44 See, for example, Munro (1), p. 147.
45 See Ames (3).
46 Their argument is that *sheng* 升 also means "to climb," as does *teng* 登, and that idiomatically in the Ch'i dialect *teng* 登 can mean "to get" (*te*** 得). Therefore *sheng* here really means "to get."
47 Karlgren, (2), p. 120.
48 The *Shuo-wen* gives the graph with "tree" (*mu* 木) as a constituent element, as an archaic form of *chih*, the small seal script.
49 Ch'ing commentators such as Tuan Yü-ts'ai have tried to twist the second portion of this explanation, "to get from others without," to account for the "to bestow bounty" meaning of *te*, but grammar is the victim in this kind of speculation.
50 *Tao Te Ching*, 34.
51 *Analects*, 1/9.
52 *Analects*, 14/33.
53 *Analects*, 8/20.
54 *Tao Te Ching*, 54.
55 *Tao Te Ching*, 54.
56 *Tao Te Ching*, 54.
57 For example, *Li-chi*, 19/15 states, "*Te* is the germ of natural tendency (*hsing**)." We use "natural tendency" rather than "nature" as an equivalent for *hsing** to underscore its process and growth connotations, and to avoid the notion of essentialistic self-nature.
58 *Chung-yung*, 1.
59 *Tao Te Ching*, 28.
60 *Yi-ching*, 3/1 言 .
61 *Tao Te Ching*, 55.
62 *Han Fei Tzu*, 95:8, and *Tao Te Ching*, 38.
63 *Chuang Tzu*, 2/1/32 and 12/5/8.
64 *Analects*, 12/19.

65 *Analects*, 2/1.
66 *Analects*, 7/1.
67 *Chuang Tzu*, 19/6/89ff.
68 *Analects*, 12/10 and 12/21.
69 *Analects*, 12/21, for example.
70 *Tao Te Ching*, 79.
71 *Chuang Tzu*, 7/3/4ff.
72 *Chuang Tzu*, 19 passim.
73 See Boodberg (2). He also argues for the primacy of the verbal meaning.
74 This explains why *tao* is always "heard" (*wen* 聞), rather than "seen" as one might expect with the road metaphor.
75 *Analects*, 1/12 and 19/22. In *Mencius*, the list is extended to include the Duke of Chou (21/3A/4), Yao and Shun (16/4A/1), Yü and Chi (33/4B/29), Confucius himself (25/3B/9) and even his disciple, Yen Hui (33/4B/29).
76 *Analects*, 15/25 and 3/16.
77 *Analects*, 14/28, 19/12, and 11/20.
78 *Analects*, 1/14, 6/12, 1/11, and 4/20.
79 *Analects*, 4/15 and 6/12.
80 *Ta* 達 means "to break through," as for example growing grain.
81 *Yu* 由 , as the character suggests, means "to go out from a field." See Karlgren (1).
82 *Analects*, 11/20. See also the notion of *hsiang yüan* 鄉原 , the "village worthy" in *Analects*, 17/13, elaborated in *Mencius*, 58/7B/37.
83 This passage is often considered among the most problematic in the *Analects*. Yang Po-chün states:

> All we can do is translate the words literally. It is difficult to understand what Confucius means, and to make any sense of "it is not the *tao* which broadens the human being." Since Chu Hsi has already forced an interpretation from it, and Cheng Hao 鄭皓 in his 論語集註述要 then asserts "this passage has been explained without enough consideration and is dubious," we do well not to add our speculations.

Ch'en Ta-ch'i (p. 107) also struggles to make sense of it, and provides only an uncharacteristically inadequate explanation.
84 See also *Analects*, 4/5, 14/28, and 17/4.
85 *Mencius*, 33/4B/29.
86 *Analects*, 5/2, 5/7, 8/13, 11/24, 14/1, 14/36, 15/7, 18/7, and 19/19.
87 *Analects*, 19/4.

88 *Analects,* 15/40.
89 *Analects,* 4/9 and 7/6.
90 *Analects,* 11/20 and 19/12.
91 *Analects,* 15/42.
92 *Analects,* 3/16.
93 *Analects,* 11/24.
94 *Analects,* 5/13.
95 See, for example, *Analects,* 3/24, 5/2, 6/24, 16/2, and 18/7.
96 Waley, p. 30.
97 Waley, pp. 30–31.
98 Lau (1), p. ix.
99 Lau (1), p. ix.
100 Lau (1), p. ix.
101 Fingarette (1), Ch. 2, passim.
102 Fingarette (1), p. 20.
103 Fingarette (3), p. 135. Fingarette is not interested in claiming transcendence in any metaphysical sense for the Confucian *tao.* He seems only to intend that *tao* transcend any given individual. However, the interpretation we have given of the relation of individual to context in terms of focus and field must exclude this sense of transcendence, as well as the putatively stronger meaning.
104 Fingarette (1), p. 22.
105 Fingarette (1), p. 21.
106 Fingarette (1), p. 34.
107 Fingarette (1), p. 35.
108 Fingarette (3), p. 136.
109 Fingarette (3), p. 135.
110 Fingarette (4), p. 346.
111 Fingarette (4), p. 345.
112 Fingarette (4), p. 345.
113 *Chung-yung,* 30.
114 *Chung-yung,* 27.
115 One is reminded of Albert Camus' well-known rendering of the myth of the unfortunate Sisyphus who responded defiantly to the judgment of the gods that he be condemned to the meaningless task of repeatedly rolling a stone up a hill. Sisyphus' defiance gave meaning to the act and established his dignity.
116 As Lin Yi-cheng, p. 197, states:

> The Confucians of later ages have especially elaborated this level of learning, describing it as that level of learning from man penetrating *t'ien* to "the unity of *t'ien* and man *(t'ien-jen ho-yi)."*

This level, although not specifically designated as such by Confucius, was popular with later Confucians and developed as "t'ien-jen ho-yi" on the basis of the transmission of those *Analects* passages cited above.

117 *Mencius*, 57/7B/25.
118 Tu Wei-ming (4), p. 129.
119 *Chung-yung*, 1.
120 *Chuang Tzu*, 16/6/20, for example.
121 *Mencius*, 51/7A/4.
122 *Mencius*, 50/7A/1.
123 *Chung-yung*, 26.
124 *Chung-yung*, 32.
125 Tu Wei-ming (4), p. 135.
126 Whitehead (2), p. 120.
127 "Religion is (subjectively considered) the recognition of all duties as divine commands." Kant, p. 142.

Chapter V
" . . . at sixty my ear was attuned. . . ."

1 Rosemont (1).
2 Rosemont attributes this thesis to Erwin Reifler of the University of Washington.
3 See Chow Tse-chung, p. 152. Richard J. Smith, p. 84, calculates that there are 2,200 lexical items.
4 See Ames (3).
5 *Analects*, 7/34.
6 *Analects*, 9/5.
7 *Analects*, 9/6.
8 Maspero, p. 136.
9 DeWoskin, pp. 32ff.
10 See for example, *Tso-chuan* 327/ 襄 29/8 左 .
11 See Lau (1), p. xl.
12 *Pai-hu-t'ung*, 6/23/5b.
13 See Boltz, 101–2, n. 17. From the fact that *sheng* 聖 is regularly written as *sheng* 聲, ("sound," "voice") on Ma-wang-tui *Lao Tzu* A and as an abbreviated *sheng* 耵 on Ma-wang-tui *Lao Tzu* B, Boltz argues that *erh* 耳 , "ear," must have had a second reading, "*lhan(s)*,"

with a meaning associated with "hearing" such that it could contribute phonetically as well as semantically to *sheng* 聖 and the set of aural characters of which it is a part: *t'ing* 聽 "to hear" [*lhan(s)*] and *sheng* 聲 "to sound" (*lhan*). Applying this insight specifically to *sheng* 聖, "sage," Boltz speculates that *erh*/**lhan(s)*, "ear"/"to hear"

> is also functioning *semantically* in 耶/聖 (where it is "pho-
> netic" in the reading **lhans* as we noted above), and that the
> primary meaning of 聖 is related to the set 耳 聲 聽, and
> should be understood as something like "one who is adept at
> 'hearing'." . . . This is what we think the *sheng jen* 聖人 or
> *sheng wang* 聖王 was: someone who heard (and understood).

Building on Boltz's suggestion that 耳 *erh*/**lhan(s)* seems to have both semantic and phonetic consequences, we might turn the argument the other way and suggest that if 耳 *erh*/**lhan(s)* is in fact phonetic, then *ch'eng* 呈, the previously identified phonetic element in *sheng* 聖, might make a semantic contribution to this character, especially given that *ch'eng* is reduced to *k'ou* 口 on the *Lao Tzu* Ma-wang-tui B manuscript. *Ch'eng* 呈, cognate with *sheng* 聖, means basically "to manifest (orally)," "to disclose," "to express." It would seem plausible that *sheng* 聖 is a *hui-yi* character, which would mean that both components collaborate in its meaning.

14 See, for example, *Analects*, 1/14, 2/13, 4/24, 14/27, 15/23, 16/6, 16/8, 19/9, and 19/25.

15 *Mencius*, 10/2A/2.

16 *Yi-ching*, 2/1 言.

17 *Li-chi*, 19/3.

18 *Pai-hu-t'ung*, 6/23/5b-7b. In personal communication, Kenneth De-Woskin has suggested to us that in most cases where *tso* 作 is associated with the sages, the meaning is "when the sages arose." As such, it implies a point of innovation.

19 *Pai-hu-t'ung*, 6/23/7b.

20 Maspero, pp. 136–37. *Mencius* 57/7B/25, cited above, p. 242, also describes this extension of a person in his process of self-cultivation.

21 See also Hansen (2).

22 The distinction is a bit overdrawn, perhaps, since most mass nouns can be typified and then pluralized. Even if clumsy, it would be proper in English to distinguish kinds of earth ("earths"), kinds of water ("waters"), and so on. Hansen's point, however, is that words functioning as mass nouns serve as the paradigm for understanding the Chinese language.

23 Hansen (1), p. 30.

24 Hansen (1), p. 31.

25 Hansen (1), p. 31.

26 Recall our previous discussion of the focus-field and holographic concepts in our considerations of the *tao-te* relationship in Chapter IV.

27 For a more constructive alternative nominalism, see Hall (2).

28 Austin (2).

29 See Bloom's discussion of the putative absence of counterfactuals in the Chinese language. Wu Kuang-ming argues persuasively for the presence of certain counterfactual locutions in classical Chinese philosophy. Doubtless, Wu is correct and Bloom has overstated his case. Our argument, however, does not depend upon the absence of counterfactual locutions in classical Chinese, only upon the infrequent resort to such locutions in Chinese philosophic argument.

30 Our argument, to the effect that the deemphasis upon scientific and ethical reasoning of the sort most closely associated with Western philosophy is intrinsically related to the relative absence of counterfactuals in the classical Chinese philosophy, may not receive support from Joseph Needham. See Needham, pp. 578–80 for the claim that the theories of *Yin* and *Yang* and of the Five Elements possessed the status of proto-scientific hypotheses. From the perspective of this work, however, much depends upon when one dates the formal construction of these proposed "hypotheses." As we have argued above (See Chapter III, note 54), there was a shift in the direction of logical or rational order on the part of some thinkers after Hsün Tzu that might account for interest in what Needham has called proto-scientific hypotheses. In any case, we would argue that the failure to develop such putative hypotheses into full-fledged scientific theories had much to do with the relative absence of any disposition to frame thought in hypothetical or counterfactual terms.

31 Fingarette (1), Ch. 2.

32 Rosemont (3).

33 Hsiao Kung-chuan, p. 519.

34 Hsiao Kung-chuan, p. 98, n. 43.

35 Waley, p. 22.

36 Hsiao Kung-chuan, p. 98.

37 *Chung-yung*, 28.

38 See, for example, *Analects*, 2/11, 2/15 and 13/5.

39 *Tso-chuan*, 211/ 成 2/2 左.

40 *Kuan Tzu*, 2:65–9.

41 Langer, p. 209. Langer interestingly points out the tension between music as pure form and any attempt to rationalize it in citing Kant's lack of regard for music (p. 210):

> In Kant's day it hinged on the conception of the arts as cultural agencies, and concerned the place of music among these contributions to intellectual progress. On this basis the great worshipper of reason naturally ranked it lowest of all art-forms (in his *Kritik der Urteilskraft*).

Langer departs radically from Confucius, however, in her unwillingness to acknowledge the performative if not transformative power of music. She states unequivocally (p. 212):

> Music does not ordinarily influence behavior. . . . On the whole, the behavior of concert audiences after even the most thrilling performances makes the traditional magical influence of music on human actions very dubious. Its somatic effects are transient, and its moral hangovers or uplifts seem to be negligible.

42 Legge, Vol. III, p. 48.
43 *Tso-chuan*, 307/ 襄 25/ 附 2.
44 *Yi-ching*, 44/ 繫上 /12.
45 The character *yüeh* 悅, which establishes this distinction, apparently was not introduced until the post-classical period.
46 DeWoskin, pp. 58–59, summarizes recent research on the etymology of the character 樂, and provides us with insights useful to our argument.

According to DeWoskin, the *Shuo-wen* commentary which has taken the character 樂 to refer to a stand with bells suspended from it has been challenged by an alternative interpretation:

> A consensus has emerged that it was a pictograph of an instrument with strings drawn over a wooden sounding board. The additional center component might be another string, slightly reshaped, or the element *pai* 白, which in this context would mean to "strum" or "press" the strings. . . . The character *yüeh* pictured a zither or, with the addition of the central *pai*, possibly meant the playing of the zither.

Important in this analysis is 樂 as a stringed instrument which produces music as a function of the tension of the stretched strings.

Music is a stretching or extending to achieve concordant relationships. Also, the interpretation of 樂 as *"playing* music" rather than just as "music" reinforces the personal, performative implications of this concept.

47 DeWoskin, pp. 21ff.
48 Lau (1), p. xxxvi.
49 DeWoskin, p. 178.
50 Plato (2), 522a.
51 See Plato (2), 398c-403c.
52 See Hall (1), p. 247, for a discussion of the notion of "constasy."
53 See also *Analects*, 14/28.
54 That music can actively contribute to the quality of harmony is further evidenced by the use of this same character in the classical language to denote medicinal therapy.
55 *Mencius*, 5/1B/1.
56 *Analects*, 3/23. See p. 279–80 above. This passage is most irregular and can only be translated in the most tentative terms.
57 Lau (1), pp. xiii-xiv.
58 *Analects*, 5/12 and 12/2.
59 *Chung-yung*, 13.
60 Karlgren (3), no. 158.
61 Fingarette (2), pp. 382–83. We should note that our notion of *shu* highlights the function of "difference" in a manner that Fingarette might not find wholly congenial.
62 *Mencius*, 51/7A/4.
63 Hall (4).
64 Derrida (1), Ch. 4.
65 See Saussure.
66 Derrida (1), pp. 129–60.
67 See Hall (2), pp. 180–82 for a discussion of this distinction between "expressive" and "allusive" metaphors.
68 Hansen (2), p. 500.
69 Hansen (2), p. 501.
70 Hansen (2), p. 502.
71 *Huai Nan Tzu*, 9/4a; Ames (2), p. 173. See also *Lieh Tzu*, 1/4b; *K'ung Tzu chia-yü*, 4/7a-b; *Shih-chi* 47, p. 1925.
72 DeWoskin, Ch. 1 passim; Levi; Hartner.
73 Legge, Vol. IV, pp. 34–35.

Chapter VI

". . . and at seventy I could give my heart-and-mind free rein without overstepping the mark."

1 *Analects,* 3/24.
2 One can best approach Derrida's thinking by reading, first, one of his earlier books of essays, *Writing and Difference,* then undertaking one of the more ambitious of his mature works, *Margins of Philosophy.* Derrida is a subtle thinker, although much less difficult than he is reputed to be by those who have not read him seriously. Moreover, Chinese readers possessed of French or English will find him a great deal more comprehensible than Anglo-European readers, since the dominant Chinese understanding of the character and function of language is similar to that to which Derrida subscribes.
3 Rorty, p. 360.
4 Michel Foucault's extensive writings, which evolved in a rather complex manner throughout his relatively brief career, are difficult to classify. A book of interviews entitled *Power/Knowledge* provides a clear introduction to the major themes of his work and some comment on its development. One of the best of his mature works is *Discipline and Punish.*
5 Habermas (1), p. 314. Habermas' later work has moved beyond the speculations of *Knowlege and Human Interests,* though that work is perhaps still the best introduction to his thought. A balanced appraisal of his later thinking, with a lengthy response by Habermas, may be found in Habermas (2).
6 Neville, p. xi.
7 Neville, p. 12.
8 If one reads the published text of an apparently representative selection of Dewey's lectures in China, such an interpretation of Dewey is not, in fact, borne out. But the assessment of Dewey as a Western rationalist is hardly surprising if one reflects upon the fact that he has been at least as misunderstood by the majority of his American and European readers as by the Chinese. See Dewey (2).
9 Hall (1) is a work of comparative philosophy that explicitly employs this culturalogical method.

Bibliography of Works Cited

A LL OF THE translations from the *Analects* and other Chinese sources
are original except when alternative translations have been specified
in the Endnotes. Multiple listings by a single author are placed in the order
of their citation in the text.

Ames, Roger T. (1) "The meaning of body in classical Chinese philosophy."
International Philosophical Quarterly 24 (1984): 39–54.

Ames, Roger T. (2) *The Art of Rulership: A Study in Ancient Chinese Political
Thought.* Honolulu: University of Hawaii Press, 1983.

Ames, Roger T. (3) "The common ground of self-cultivation in classical
Confucianism and Taoism." *Tsing-hua hsüeh-pao,* 1985.

Ames, Roger T. (4) "Religiousness in classical Confucianism: A comparative
analysis." *Asian Culture Quarterly* 12:2 (1984): 7–23.

Aristotle. *Politics.* Trans. Benjamin Jowett. In *The Basic Works of Aristotle,* ed.
Richard McKeon. Chicago: The University of Chicago Press, 1941.

Augustine, Saint. *The City of God (Civitas Dei).* Trans. Marcus Dods. New
York: Modern Library, 1950.

Austin, J. L. (1) "A plea for excuses." *Philosophical Papers.* Oxford: Clarendon
Press, 1961.

Austin, J. L. (2) *How to Do Things with Words.* 2nd ed. Cambridge, Mass.:
Harvard University Press, 1975.

Bloom, Alfred H. *The Linguistic Shaping of Thought: A Study in the Impact
of Language and Thinking in China and the West.* Hillsdale, N.J.: Law-
rence Erlbaum, 1981.

Boltz, William G. "The religious and philosophical significance of the 'hsiang
erh' Lao Tzu in the light of the Ma-wang-tui silk manuscripts." *Bulletin
of the School of Oriental and African Studies* 45 (1982): 101–2.

Boodberg, Peter. (1) "The semasiology of some primary Confucian concepts."
Philosophy East and West 2 (1953): 317–32.

Boodberg, Peter. (2) "Philological notes on chapter one of the *Lao Tzu.*"
Harvard Journal of Asiatic Studies 20 (1957): 598–618.

Book of Songs. See *Shih-ching.*

Booth, Wayne C. *Modern Dogma and the Rhetoric of Assent.* Notre Dame,
Ind.: University of Notre Dame Press, 1974.

Chan, W. T. "Chinese and Western interpretations of *jen* (humanity)." *Journal
of Chinese Philosophy* 2 (1975): pp. 107–129.

Chao Chi-pin 趙紀彬 . *Lun-yü hsin-t'an* 論語新探 . Peking: Jen-min ch'u-pan-she, 1962.

Ch'en Ta-ch'i 陳大齊 . *K'ung Tzu hsüeh-shuo* 孔子學說 . Taipei: Cheng-chung shu-chü, 1964.

Cheng Chung-ying. "On *yi* as a universal principle of specific application in Confucian morality." *Philosophy East and West* 22 (1972): 269–80.

Chia Yi 賈誼 . Hsin-shu 新書 . SPTK.

Chow Tse-chung. "The early history of the Chinese word *shih* (poetry)." *Wen-lin*, ed. Chow Tse-chung. Madison: University of Wisconsin Press, 1968.

Chuang Tzu 莊子 . Harvard-Yenching Institute Sinological Index Series, Supp. 20. Peking: Harvard-Yenching Institute, 1947.

Ch'un-ch'iu fan-lu 春秋繁露 . Ssu-pu pei-yao. 四部備要 . Shanghai: Chung-hua, 1936.

Chung-yung 中庸 . In *Ssu-shu chang-chü chi-chu* 四書章句集註 . Shanghai: Commercial Press, 1935.

Creel, H. G. *Origins of Statecraft* v. 1. Chicago: University of Chicago Press, 1970.

de Bary, Wm. Theodore. (1) *Sources of Chinese Civilization*. New York: Columbia University Press, 1960.

de Bary, Wm. Theodore. (2) *Ch'ien Mu Lectures: The Liberal Tradition in China*. Hong Kong: Chinese University Press, 1983.

Derrida, Jacques. (1) *Speech and Phenomena*. Trans. David B. Allison. Northwestern University Press, 1973.

Derrida, Jacques. (2) *Writing and Difference*. Trans. Alan Bass. Chicago: University of Chicago Press, 1978.

Derrida, Jacques. (3) *Margins of Philosophy*. Trans. Alan Bass. Chicago: University of Chicago Press, 1983.

Deutsch, Eliot. *On Truth: An Ontological Theory*. Honolulu: University of Hawaii Press, 1979.

Dewey, John. (1) *Experience and Nature*. New York: Dover, 1958 reprint.

Dewey, John. (2) *Lectures in China, 1919–1920*. Trans. and ed. Robert Clopton/ Tsuin-chen Ou. Honolulu: University of Hawaii Press, 1973.

DeWoskin, Kenneth. *A Song for One or Two: Music and the Concept of Art in Early China*. Ann Arbor: Center for Chinese, University of Michigan, 1982.

Dilthey, Wilhelm. *Gesammelte Schriften*. Stuttgart: Teubner, 1959–1968. Vols. I and VII.

Erh Ya 爾雅 . Harvard-Yenching Institute Sinological Index Series, Supp. 18. Taipei: Chinese Materials and Research Aids Service Center, 1966 reprint.

Fingarette, Herbert. (1) *Confucius: The Secular as Sacred.* New York: Harper Torchbooks, 1972.

Fingarette, Herbert (2) "Following the 'One Thread' of the *Analects.*" *Journal of the American Academy of Religion,* Thematic Issue 47, no. 3S (1979): 373–406.

Fingarette, Herbert (3) "The problem of self in the *Analects.*" *Philosophy East and West* 29 (1979): 129–40.

Fingarette, Herbert (4) "The music of humanity in the *Conversations* of Confucius." *Journal of Chinese Philosophy* 10 (1983): 331–56.

Foucault, Michel. (1) *Power/Knowledge: Selected Interviews and Other Writings by Michel Foucault, 1972–1977,* ed. Colin Gordon. New York: Pantheon Books, 1980.

Foucault, Michel (2) *Discipline and Punish: The Birth of the Prison.* Trans. Alan Sheridan. New York: Vintage/Random House, 1979.

Gadamer, Hans-Georg. *Truth and Method.* New York: Seabury Press, 1975.

Gimello, Robert M. "The civil status of *li* in classical Confucianism." *Philosophy East and West* 22 (1972): 203–11.

Goodman, Nelson. *Ways of Worldmaking.* Indianapolis: Hackett, 1978.

Graham, A. C. "Chuang Tzu's Essay on Seeing Things as Equal." *Journal of the History of Religion* 9 (1969): 137–59.

Habermas, Jürgen. (1) *Knowledge and Human Interests.* Trans. Jeremy J. Shapiro. Boston: Beacon Press, 1971.

Habermas, Jürgen. (2) *Habermas: Critical Debates,* ed. John B. Thompson, et al. Cambridge, Mass.: The MIT Press, 1982.

Hall, David L. (1) *The Uncertain Phoenix.* New York: Fordham University Press, 1982.

Hall, David L. (2) *Eros and Irony.* Albany: State University of New York Press, 1982.

Hall, David L. (3) "The width of civilized experience: comparative philosophy and the search for evidence." In *Buddhism and American Thought,* ed. Kenneth K. Inada and Nolan P. Jacobson. Albany: State University of New York Press, 1981.

Hall, David L. (4) "Logos, mythos, chaos: Metaphysics as the quest for diversity." In *New Essays in Metaphysics,* ed. Robert C. Neville, Albany: State University of New York Press, 1986 pp. 1–24.

Han Fei Tzu 韓非子 . *Chu-tzu yin-te* 諸子引得 . Taipei: Nan-yü Press, no date.

Hansen, Chad. (1) *Language and Logic in Ancient China.* Ann Arbor: University of Michigan Press, 1983.

Hansen, Chad. (2) "Chinese language, Chinese philosophy and 'Truth.'" *Journal of Asian Studies* 44 (1985): pp. 491–517.

Hartner, Willy. "Some notes on Chinese musical art" (review of J. H. Levi, *Foundations of Chinese Musical Art*). In *Science and Technology in East Asia*, ed. Nathan Sivin, pp. 32–54. New York: Science History Publications, 1977.

Hegel, G. W. F. *Hegel's Philosophy of Right*. Trans. T. M. Knox. New York: Oxford University Press, 1962.

Heidegger, Martin. *Basic Writings*, ed. David Krell. New York: Harper and Row, 1977.

Historical Records. See *Shih-chi*.

Hobbes, Thomas. *De Cive or The Citizen*. Ed. Sterling Lamprecht. New York: Appleton-Century-Crofts, 1949.

Horkheimer, Max. *Critical Theory: Selected Essays*. Trans. Matthew J. Connell, et al. New York: Herder and Herder, 1968, 1972.

Hsiao Kung-chuan. *A History of Chinese Political Thought*. Trans. Frederick W. Mote. Princeton, N.J.: Princeton University Press, 1979.

Hsün Tzu 荀子. Harvard-Yenching Institute Sinological Index Series, Supp. 22. Peking: Harvard-Yenching Institute, 1950.

Huai Nan Tzu 淮南子. Ssu-pu ts'ung-k'an 四部叢刊. Shanghai: Commercial Press, 1935–1936.

Kant, Immanuel. *Religion Within the Limits of Reason Alone*. Trans. T. M. Greene and H. H. Hudson. New York: Harper Torchbooks, 1960.

Karlgren, Bernard. (1) *Grammata Serica Recensa*. Stockholm: Museum of Far Eastern Antiquities, 1950.

Karlgren, Bernard. (2) "Glosses on the *Book of Documents*." *Bulletin of the Museum of Far Eastern Antiquities* 20–21 (1948–1949).

Karlgren, Bernard. (3) *The Book of Odes*. Stockholm: Museum of Far Eastern Antiquities, 1950.

Kuang-ya shu-cheng 廣雅疏證, ed. D. C. Lau and H. K. Chan. Hong Kong: Chinese University Press, 1978.

K'ung Tzu chia-yü 孔子家語. Ssu-pu ts'ung-k'an 四部叢刊. Shanghai: Commercial Press, 1935–1936.

Langer, Susanne. *Philosophy in a New Key*. Cambridge, Mass.: Harvard University Press, 1951.

Lao Tzu 老子. See *Tao Te Ching*.

Lau, D. C. (1) *Confucius: The Analects*. Chinese Classics: Chinese-English Series. Hong Kong: The Chinese University Press, 1983.

Lau, D. C. (2) *Tao Te Ching*. Chinese Classics: Chinese-English Series. Hong Kong: The Chinese University Press, 1982.

Lau, D. C. (3) "On the expression *fu yen*." *Bulletin of the School of Oriental and African Studies* 36 (1973): 424–33.

Legge, James. *The Chinese Classics*, 5 vols. Hong Kong: London Missionary Society, 1861–1873.

Levi, J. H. *Foundations of Chinese Musical Art*. Peking: French Bookstore, 1936.

Lévi-Strauss, Claude. *Totemism*. Trans. Rodney Needham. Boston: Beacon Press, 1963.

Li-chi 禮記 . Harvard-Yenching Institute Sinological Index Series, Index 27. Taipei: Chinese Materials and Research Aids Service Center, 1966 reprint.

Lieh Tzu 列子. Ssu-pu ts'ung-k'an 四部叢刊 . Shanghai: Commercial Press, 1935–36.

Lin Yi-cheng 林義正 . "Lun K'ung Tzu ssu-hsiang te chi-pen ko-shih" 論孔子思想的基本格式. *Che-hsüeh lun-p'ing* 哲學論評 6 (1983) pp. 181–200.

Loewe, Michael. *Chinese Ideas of Life and Death*. London: Allen and Unwin, 1982.

Louie, Kam. *Critiques of Confucius in Contemporary China*. Hong Kong: The Chinese University Press, 1980.

McKnight, Brian E. *The Quality of Mercy*. Honolulu: University of Hawaii Press, 1981.

Martin, Gottfried. "Metaphysics as *scientia universalis* and as *ontologia generalis*." In *The Relevance of Whitehead*, ed. Ivor Leclerc, pp. 219–31. New York: Macmillan, 1961.

Maspero, Henri. *Taoism and Chinese Religion*. Trans. Frank A. Kierman, Jr. Amherst: University of Massachusetts Press, 1981.

Mead, George Herbert. *Mind, Self and Society*, ed. Charles Morris. Chicago: University of Chicago Press, 1934.

Mencius (Meng Tzu 孟子). Harvard-Yenching Institute Sinological Index Series, Supp. 17. Peking: Harvard-Yenching Institute, 1941.

Mo Tzu 墨子 . Harvard-Yenching Institute Sinological Index Series, Supp. 21. Peking: Harvard-Yenching Institute, 1948.

Mou Tsung-san 牟宗三. *Chung-kuo che-hsüeh te t'e chih* 中國哲學的特質 . Hong Kong: Jen-sheng ch'u-pan-she, 1963.

Munro, D. J. (1) *The Concept of Man in Early China*. Stanford, Calif.: Stanford University Press, 1967.

Munro, D. J. (2) *The Concept of Man in Contemporary China*. Ann Arbor: University of Michigan Press, 1977.

Needham, Joseph. *Science and Civilisation in China*, Vol. 2. Cambridge: Cambridge University Press, 1954.

Neville, Robert C. *Reconstruction of Thinking*. Albany: State University of New York Press, 1981.

Northrop, F. S. C. "The possible concepts by intuition and the concepts by postulation as a basic terminology in comparative philosophy." In *The*

Logic of the Sciences and the Humanities, pp. 77–101. New York: World, 1959.

Ortega y Gasset, José. *The Revolt of the Masses*. New York: Norton, 1957.

Pai-hu-t'ung 白虎通 . Harvard-Yenching Institute Sinological Index Series, Index 2. Taipei: Chinese Materials and Research Aids Service Center, 1966 reprint.

Plato. (1) *Phaedrus*. In *The Dialogues of Plato*, Vol. I, trans. and ed. Benjamin Jowett. New York: Random House, 1920.

Plato. (2) *The Republic of Plato*. Trans. F.M. Cornford. New York and London: Oxford University Press, 1941.

Quine, W. V. O. *From a Logical Point of View*. New York: Harper and Row, 1976.

Rorty, Richard. *Philosophy and the Mirror of Nature*. Princeton, N.J.: Princeton University Press, 1979.

Rosemont, Henry, Jr. (1) "On representing abstractions in archaic Chinese." *Philosophy East and West* 24 (1974): 71–88.

Rosemont, Henry, Jr. (ed.) (2) *Explorations in Chinese Cosmology. Journal of the American Academy of Religion*. Thematic Studies 50, no. 2. Chico, Calif.: Scholars Press, 1984.

Rosemont, Henry, Jr. (3) "Against relativism." In *Interpreting across Boundaries*, ed. Eliot Deutsch and Gerald James Larson. Forthcoming.

Sartre, Jean-Paul. *Being and Nothingness*. Trans. Hazel Barnes. New York: Philosophical Library, 1956.

Saussure, Ferdinand. *A Course in General Linguistics*. London: Peter Owen, 1960.

Schwartz, Benjamin I. "Some polarities in Confucian thought." In *Confucianism in Action*, ed. David S. Nivison and Arthur F. Wright. Stanford: Stanford University Press, 1959.

Sellars, Wilfred. *Science, Perception and Reality*. New York: Humanities Press, 1963.

Shih-chi 史記 . *(Historical Records)*. Shanghai: Chung-hua shu-chü, 1959.

Shih-ching 詩經 . *(Book of Songs)*. Harvard-Yenching Institute Sinological Index Series, Supp. 9. Peking: Harvard-Yenching Institute, 1934.

Smith, Huston. "Western and comparative perspectives on truth." *Philosophy East and West* 30 (1980): 425–37.

Smith, Richard J. *China's Cultural Heritage*. Boulder, Colorado: Westview Press, 1983.

Takeuchi Teruo. "A study of the meaning of *jen* advocated by Confucius." *Acta Asiatic* 9 (1965): pp. 57–77.

T'ang Chün-i. "The t'ien ming (heavenly ordinance) in pre-Ch'in China." *Philosophy East and West* 11 (1962): 195–218.

Tao Te Ching 道德經 . *Chu-tzu yin-te* 諸子引得 . Taipei: Nan-yü Press, no date.

Taylor, Charles. "Interpretation and the Sciences of Man." Excerpted in *Critical Sociology,* ed. Paul Connerton. New York: Penguin, 1976.

Ts'ai Shang-ssu 蔡尚思 . *K'ung Tzu ssu-hsiang t'i-hsi* 孔子思想體系 . Shanghai: Shanghai Peoples' Press, 1982.

Tso-chuan 左傳 . In *Ch'un ch'iu* 春秋 . Harvard-Yenching Institute Sinological Index Series, Supp. 11. Peking: Harvard-Yenching Institute, 1937.

Tu Wei-ming. (1) *"Jen* as a living metaphor in the Confucian *Analects."* *Philosophy East and West* 31 (1981):45–54.

Tu Wei-ming. (2) "The creative tension between *jen* and *li."* *Philosophy East and West* 18 (1968): 29–39.

Tu Wei-ming. (3) *Humanity and Self-Cultivation: Essays in Confucian Thought.* Berkeley, Calif.: Asian Humanities Press, 1979.

Tu Wei-ming. (4) *Centrality and Commonality: An Essay on Chung-Yung.* Honolulu: University of Hawaii Press, 1976.

Tung Chung-shu 董仲舒 . See *Ch'un-ch'iu fan-lu* 春秋繁露 .

Waley, Arthur. *The Analects of Confucius.* New York: Random House, 1938.

Watson, Burton. *Early Chinese Literature.* New York: Columbia University Press, 1962.

Whitehead, Alfred North. (1) *Science and the Modern World.* New York: Macmillan, 1925.

Whitehead, Alfred North. (2) *Modes of Thought.* New York: Free Press, 1968 reprint.

Whitehead, Alfred North. (3) *Adventures of Ideas.* New York: Macmillan, 1933.

Wilhelm, Helmut. *Heaven, Earth and Man in the Book of Changes.* Seattle: University of Washington Press, 1977.

Wittgenstein, Ludwig. (1) *Tractatus Logico-Philosophicus.* New York: Humanities Press, 1961.

Wittgenstein, Ludwig. (2) *Philosophical Investigations.* New York: Macmillan, 1953.

Wu Kuang-ming. "On Chinese Counterfactuals." *Philosophy East and West* 37 (1987) forthcoming.

Yang Po-chün 楊伯峻 . *Lun-yü yi-chu* 論語譯註 . Taipei: Yüan-liu Press, 1982.

Yates, Robin R. E. "The Mohists on warfare: Technology, technique, and justification." *Studies in Classical Chinese Thought,* ed. Henry Rosemont, Jr., and Benjamin I. Schwartz. *Journal of the American Academy of Religion* Thematic Studies 47, no. 3S, 1979.

Finding List for Passages from the *Analects*

Subscribing to the principle that any translation requires an act of interpretation, we have worked from the original *Analects (Lun-yü)* and provided our own renderings. For the sake of easy reference to our commentary on the passages from the *Analects* as they occur in our discussion, we have listed them with their page location. For purposes of comparison, all citations of the *Analects* have been keyed to the D.C. Lau translation cited in the *Bibliography*.

1/1	277	2/21	157	5/6	61
1/2	120	2/21	185	5/9	339
1/2	229	2/22	60	5/13	196
1/3	276	2/24	95	6/2	142
1/8	340–41	3/3	245	6/10	213
1/13	62	3/3	278	6/14	140
1/13	174	3/8	65	6/17	229
1/15	65–66	3/13	206	6/18	145
2/1	168	3/14	45	6/20	53
2/2	66	3/23	279–80	6/20	281
2/3	175	3/24	230	6/22	142
2/4	85	3/25	279	6/22	196
2/4	258	3/26	167	6/22	246
2/4	280	4/5	187	6/23	53
2/4	307	4/10	96	6/23	114
2/11	48	4/15	199	6/23	281
2/12	188	4/15	284–85	6/25	270
2/12	191	4/17	190–91	6/26	187
2/13	49	4/25	222	6/29	141
2/14	166	4/26	222	6/30	119
2/15	47	5/1	174	6/30	123

6/30	186	12/1	243	15/22	166
6/30	287	12/1	289	15/23	114
7/1	259	12/2	122–23	15/24	285
7/1	307	12/3	123	15/29	99
7/8	146	12/5	214	15/29	115
7/14	279	12/7	144	15/29	229
7/19	281	12/10	223	15/31	47
7/21	197	12/11	270	15/33	52
7/22	190–91	12/13	169	15/34	52
7/23	242	12/17	158	15/35	143
7/24	197	12/19	169	15/36	48
7/25	186	12/20	347	15/37	167
7/30	120	12/22	55	15/39	146
7/32	283	12/24	187	16/1	282
7/34	259	13/3	173	16/2	143
7/35	246	13/3	269	16/2	163–64
8/2	143	13/5	48	16/8	244
8/7	229	13/6	160	16/8	259
8/8	280	13/9	145	16/9	46
8/9	227	13/13	158	16/9	54
8/13	185	13/15	167	16/9	142
8/16	60–61	13/16	282	16/10	341
8/19	201	13/19	122	16/11	127
8/19	240	13/20	61	16/11	228
8/19	272	13/23	165	16/13	85
9/1	196	13/24	190	17/2	220
9/4	196	14/6	186	17/3	54
9/5	54	14/6	187	17/6	122
9/5	206	14/12	214	17/7	308
9/6	191	14/26	164	17/8	48
9/11	230	14/27	49	17/10	66
9/17	201	14/36	230	17/11	279
9/18	66	14/41	141	17/11	348
9/23	281	14/42	160	17/13	49
9/29	55	15/3	50	17/18	276
9/30	165	15/3	284	17/19	63
11/12	196–97	15/4	52	17/19	206
11/19	213–14	15/5	168	17/19	207
12/1	91	15/7	231	17/19	277
12/1	93	15/11	271	17/20	278
12/1	120	15/16	96	17/23	95
12/1	123–24	15/18	90	17/23	348

Index

Accommodating will, 24–25
Accountability. See *hsing ming**
Aesthetic order, xiv, 16, 131–38;
Chinese culture as, 307. *See also*
Order; Rational order
Agapé, 244
Aggressive will, 24–25
Ai 愛 (love), 121. *See also*
Graduated love
Aisthesis, 132–34
Alienation, 181–82
Allusive language, 296–98, 302. *See
also* Chinese Language; Language
Altruism. See *shu* (deference)
Anachronism, 7, 12, 195–96, 271,
332
Analects. See Finding List for
Passages from the *Analects*
Analogy: as allusive, 288–90,
296–98, 298–304; Fingarette on,
287–88; reasoning by, 325
Analytic philosophy, 35, 38–39
Ancestral worship, 202
Aristotelianism, 18
Aristotle, 13; and Confucius on
family, 147; on imitation, 178–79;
man as *zoon politikon*, 149;
naturalistic cosmology, 18; on
polis, 163; self-reflexivity in, 31;
on *theoria*, 147
Ars contextualis: 246–49; as
aesthetic cosmology, 200; and the
Chinese language, 264; as
generalized sociology, 247–48;
and language, 293
Assumptions. *See* Uncommon
assumptions
Atomism, 31–32
Attunement. *See* Thinking
Augustine, St., 33, 151

Austin, J.L., 35, 41, 43
Authoritative person. See *jen** and
jen che*
Authority, 84, 180–82

Bacon, Francis, 333
Benevolence. See *jen**
Bergson, Henri, 16
Body. See *t'i*
Bohr, Niels, 31
Boltz, William G., 259
Boodberg, Peter: on *cheng**
(effecting sociopolitical order),
156–57; on *jen** (authoritative
person), 113–14; methodology of,
41
Book of Change(s). See Yi-ching
Book of Documents. See Shu-ching
Book of Songs. See Shih-ching
Booth, Wayne C., 118–19
Buddha: metaphysical agnosticism
of, 198; statue of, 239; as
teacher, 304
Buddhism, 16. *See also* Hua Yen
Bureaucratic rationalization, 162
Burning of the books, 325

Chan, Wing-tsit: 2; on *jen**
(authoritative person), 111; *shu* as
"altruism," 285
Charisma, 178
Chen jen 真人 (authentic
person), 58, 225
Ch'en Ta-ch'i: attitude toward
Confucian cosmology, 198; on
categories of personal
achievement, 185–88; on *chih*
(realizing) and *yi* (significating),
55; on flexibility, 95

Waley, Arthur: 52–53, 61; *cheng ming** (ordering names) as anachronistic, 271; on *tao,* 232–33; on *te,* 217; translation of *shu* as "consideration," 285
Wang Fu-chih, 182
Wang Yang-ming, 321
Weber, Max, 162–63
Wen 聞 (to hear), 44
Wen (founder of the Chou dynasty): 125, 206, 233, 241, 300; excellence of, 189; as sage, 256; *tao* of, 227
Wen* 文 (culture); 323; embellishments, 277; and the learning process, 44–45
Wen T'ien-hsiang, 182
Whitehead, A.N.: 15, 16, 195; on individual absoluteness and individual relativity, 152; and *scientia universalis,* 199; on sense of the holy, 243
Wilhelm, Helmut, 203
Wisdom. See *chih**
Wittgenstein, Ludwig, 34–35
Wu (founder of the Chou dynasty): 51, 125–27, 233, 241; excellence of, 189; music of, 279; as sage, 256; *tao* of, 227
Wu hua 物化 (transformation of things), 225
Wu-wei 無為 (non-action/acting naturally), 168, 223

Yang and yin. See *yin* and *yang*
Yang Po-chün, 141, 165
Yao (sage-emperor): 160, 240, 241, 264–65, 279; as creator of meaning, 272; excellence of, 189; as model of *yi* acts, 106; as sage, 256
Yates, Robin, 210–11

Yen Hui, 45–46, 121, 146, 189, 223, 230, 271
Yen Yüan. See Yen Hui
Yi 義 (significating/appropriate/meaningful): and aesthetic choice, 266; as aesthetic rightness, 105; alternative interpretations of, 101–04; and *chih* (realizing), 55; and the *chün tzu* (exemplary person), 95–96; as dispositional, 105; and ego-self, 93; and exalted self, 93–94; immanence of, 101–03, 108; and *jen** (authoritative person), 110–125; as meaning-bestowing, 95–96, 105–06; as meaning-deriving, 95–97, 105–06; in *Mencius,* 90–91; metaphors for, 99; and *min* (masses), 141–42; and modeling, 178–79; as moral judgment, 244–45; and music, 278–79; mutuality of agency and act in, 102–04, 106; normative force of, 102; as origin of *li* (ritual action), 108–10; and person-in-context, 95; and political office, 184; as primitive source of *tao,* 228; and *shu* (deference), 289; as source of *li* (ritual action), 89–110, 273–74; and *wo* (personal self), 90–94
Yi-ching (Book of Change(s)): and Confucius, 268; on *sheng* (sage), 259; on speech and thought, 277; on *te,* 220–21; on *ti* and *t'ien,* 203
Yin and yang, 17
Yu 友 (friendship), 61
Yüeh-ching (Classic of Music), 276

Zeno, 32, 315
Zoon politikon, 149